Leisure & Pleasure

Leisure & Pleasure Reshaping & Revealing the New Zealand Body 1900–1960 Caroline Daley

AUCKLAND UNIVERSITY PRESS

First published 2003

Auckland University Press
University of Auckland
Private Bag 92019
Auckland
New Zealand
www.auckland.ac.nz/aup

ISBN 1 86940 291 X

National Library of New Zealand Cataloguing-in-Publication Data
Daley, Caroline.
Leisure & pleasure : reshaping & revealing the New Zealand
body / Caroline Daley.
Includes bibliographical references and index.
ISBN 1-86940-291-X
1. Body image—New Zealand—History. 2. Physical fitness—
New Zealand—History. I. Title.
306.4—dc 21

Publication is assisted by the History Group, Ministry for Culture and Heritage

Cover design: Sarah Maxey
Printed by Astra Print Ltd, Wellington

For my sister, Sarah, with love

COVER AND FULL-PAGE PHOTOGRAPHS

Contents

Acknowledgements

In the late 1990s, when I began this project, I expected to write a journal article on strongman Eugen Sandow's tour of New Zealand. But as I researched that tour, and found out more about the father of modern body building, my interest grew. In large part this was due to the work of Sandow's biographer, David Chapman. David has been incredibly generous in sharing his knowledge about Sandow and the wider physical culture movement of the early twentieth century with me, and in opening up his archive to me. I thank him for all of his support and help, and hope he enjoys *Leisure & Pleasure*.

Doing the research for this book has been very pleasurable indeed, in no small part because of the expert assistance I have received from librarians and archivists. At the University of Auckland I would like to give particular thanks to the incredibly helpful and efficient team in the interloans section, and Giles Margetts in the microtext room. Down town, David Verran, Kirstie Ross and the staff of Special Collections at Auckland City Libraries were wonderful. Patrick Jackson, at the Auckland City Council Archives, aided my research in many ways. In Wellington I enjoyed the usual high standards of assistance and advice at the National Library and the Alexander Turnbull Library, and although my time at Archives New Zealand was sometimes frustrating, it was ultimately rewarding. Jo-Anne Smith at Canterbury Museum, the New Zealand room staff at Christchurch City Libraries and the librarians at the Macmillan Brown Library at the University of Canterbury were always helpful, as were the staff at the Hocken Library in Dunedin. In Sydney I would like to thank the librarians at the State Library of New South Wales and the Mitchell and Dixson libraries. I would also like to acknowledge the warm welcome and assistance I received at the American Nudist Research Library in Kissimmee, Florida.

The picture research for this project was most enjoyable, and I am grateful to all of the libraries which provided me with images. I would especially like to thank Auckland City Libraries, the Alexander Turnbull Library, and the Hocken for waiving reproduction fees.

Needless to say, I could not have undertaken these research trips, nor ordered the many photographs illustrating this book, without financial assistance. I am most grateful to the University of Auckland for providing me with two Research Grants and awarding me short leave with a grant-in-aid, as I worked on this book.

Alongside the help of librarians, archivists and my university, researching this book was pleasurable thanks to the support and help of friends and family. For putting up with me, and putting me up, I thank Angela Pearce in Wellington, Doreen and John Endacott and Philippa Mein Smith and Richard Tremewan in Christchurch, and Pauline and the late Joe Ryland in Florida. For listening to me talk about the book and offering me advice and references, I thank Judith Binney, Peter Boston, Barbara Brookes, Malcolm Campbell, Tim Frank, Helen Laurenson, Charlotte Macdonald, Malcolm MacLean, Dot Page, Bobby Petersen, Kim Phillips, Barry Reay, Grant Rodwell, Greg Ryan, Terry Ward, and Matt Wilcox. In the course of this project I have given conference papers throughout New Zealand and Australia on various aspects of the modern body at play. I would like to thank the conference organisers and participants for listening and responding to my work. I would also like to take this opportunity to thank my immediate family for the interest they have shown in this project, and the support and love they always give me and my work. I've dedicated this book to my sister, Sarah, with whom I spend much of my leisure time. Thank you for always being there.

If researching the book was pleasure, writing it was pure hard work. The task was lightened by the wise counsel of Elizabeth Caffin, the Director of Auckland University Press. As always, Elizabeth has been incredibly supportive of this project and of me, and I am most grateful. Working with the award-winning team at AUP is always pleasurable. I would like to thank Katrina Duncan for making my words look good, Annie Irving for keeping the administration under control, and Christine O'Brien for her marketing expertise. I would also like to acknowledge AUP's anonymous reader, for being so favourably disposed towards the book, Sarah Maxey for her beautiful cover design, and the History Group at the Ministry for Culture and Heritage for awarding the book a publication subsidy.

Three other people deserve special mention (and medals) for the support they offered me as I wrote up my research. Two of my colleagues read my entire manuscript and offered careful, helpful suggestions. I can only apologise to Deborah Montgomerie and Joe Zizek for not following through on more of their recommendations. They are wonderful friends and very dear to me. Finally, I want to thank my partner and best friend, David Braddon-Mitchell, for listening to me, reading my work, offering a non-historian's perspective on the text, and making me dinner. Your love and support mean the world to me.

August 2003

Introduction

In 1955 Daisy Martin, a farmer's wife in Nelson, received an interesting Christmas present: a bronze statue of a naked strongman, holding a barbell. The sculpture had belonged to her father, Harold Robinson. As a young Lancashire lad Harold had been 'a seemingly hopeless cripple', but at the age of 21, walking with the aid of a stick, he sought help from the famed physical culturist, Eugen Sandow. Despite having one shortened leg, under Sandow's expert guidance Harold became 'well-known' as a cyclist and swimmer. Indeed, it was claimed that he was Sandow's 'star pupil', and was given the statue in recognition of his success.[1]

By the beginning of the twentieth century Sandow was an international superstar. His well-developed body and his system of exercises had gained him attention throughout the British Empire and the United States. He was famous enough to have his own magazine, and to hold 'The Great Competition', a search for the most perfectly developed man. To reward those who followed his system, gold, silver and bronze statuettes of Sandow were given to the first, second and third place-getters in the contest.[2] The third prize may have been what Daisy Martin received in the post half a century later, though her father did not win the bronze.[3] But regardless of how he came to own it, Harold Robinson clearly treasured his little bronze Sandow, and made sure that this family heirloom was passed on to the next generation. And Daisy was an appropriate recipient. In 1937 she had been judged the most 'perfect girl' in Britain and her twin, Rose, was runner-up.[4] Harold had raised his daughters as Sandow girls, physical culturists who reshaped their bodies and were proud to reveal the results for all to see.

The headline on the newspaper story about Daisy's gift – 'Sandow Statue In Nelson Home: Gift to Star Pupil' – indicates that even in 1955 Eugen Sandow remained sufficiently famous to warrant column inches in

1

New Zealand dailies. Despite the fact that he had been dead for 30 years, his name still had resonance. The father of modern body building had not been forgotten.

Why was a German-born, London-based strongman, who spent only a few weeks in New Zealand, so well known here years after his death? The answer to that question lies at the heart of this book.

In 1889 Eugen Sandow made an impressive entrance onto the London stage.[5] At that time a French-born strongman known as Samson was performing at the Alhambra Music Hall in Westminster. He and his assistant Cyclops issued a challenge to the audience: if anyone could repeat the feats of Cyclops they would be rewarded with £100; if anyone could copy Samson's feats of strength they would receive £500. On 29 October 1889 Sandow accepted the challenge. With a party of supporters he approached the stage, and literally burst onto it. Dressed in an evening suit, Sandow looked no match for the thickset Cyclops but the challenger was already well versed in the art of theatrical showmanship. Once on stage he ripped off his specially made evening suit to reveal a superb, muscled body in an athletic costume. Cyclops began to lift dumb-bells above his head. Sandow matched and bettered each feat, sometimes using only one hand where Cyclops had relied on two. Despite Samson's protestations, the audience rallied behind the newcomer and eventually even Samson had to concede that Sandow had outperformed Cyclops. The prize money was handed over. Sandow's first stage performance in London had been a triumph. Next he had to prove himself against Samson, who billed himself as the 'Strongest Man on Earth'.

Three nights later the second challenge took place. Samson stood on the stage and offered £500 to anyone who could match his performance. He waited for Sandow to come forward, but no one stirred. Such a large crowd had gathered to watch the showdown that the doorman was refusing to open the stage door – and Sandow was on the wrong side of it. He had to break the door down to get into the theatre so that the contest could begin.

Samson was a wilier opponent than Cyclops and Sandow found it harder to replicate his tricks but with perseverance and crowd support Sandow triumphed. To rub salt in Samson's wounds, one wit in the audience offered Samson £50 if the so-called strongman could replicate any of Sandow's feats of strength. Samson left the stage and, shortly after, left town. Sandow, meanwhile, went to bed that night assured of a career on the London stage. He signed a £150 a week contract with the Alhambra Music Hall, replacing Samson as its star attraction and taking on the title of the 'Strongest Man on Earth'. [6]

But Sandow was not content just to be a local music hall performer, albeit a very well-paid one. Over the next decade or so he built an empire based on his body. His stage performances continued to be important, but in addition to performing feats of strength to amazed crowds in Britain and the United States he also opened several Institutes of Physical Culture (refusing to use the more working-class term 'gymnasium'), launched his first pieces of patented exercise equipment, appeared in a series of short films made by Thomas Edison's company, wrote his first two books and began to publish a monthly physical culture magazine generously illustrated with photographs of his own semi-clad body. In 1901 the British Museum made a plaster cast of Sandow's naked body to represent Caucasians in an exhibition featuring the major races of the world. He personified the ideal modern man.

It is no wonder that by the time Sandow toured Australia and New Zealand in 1902–03 newspapers could claim that even in Australasia his name was a household word. [7] But Sandow was not just a spokesman for his generation. As the Daisy Martin story indicates, his legacy lived on into the mid-twentieth century. Both his presence and his legacy are the subjects of this book.

It may seem odd to use an international strongman's tour as a catalyst for and a refrain throughout a work on New Zealand – and to use a photograph of him on the book's cover. Sandow was in the country for less than two months. Apart from a dispute with the tax authorities (they claimed he owed tax; he claimed that he had never had to pay tax when touring anywhere else) there was nothing about his New Zealand tour to distinguish it from his recent visit to Australia, or to other parts of the world. [8] He performed the same show in Masterton and Stratford as he did in Manchester and San Francisco, and his New Zealand audiences responded in the same ways as their English and American counterparts. We have become so accustomed to history books telling national stories that we often forget to place those tales in their international contexts.

For example, much of the academic writing we have on the history of leisure in New Zealand is about the 'national game', rugby. Many of those studies make large claims about rugby being uniquely suited to the particular characteristics of New Zealand and New Zealanders. It is said to suit the rough and ready conditions of the landscape, cope with the wet winter weather better than other ball games and epitomise the egalitarian, matey ethos of the pioneers. With the success of the 1905 All Blacks in Britain New Zealand proved itself to the mother country. A nation was born and with it a unique national story.[9] This is all well and good, except that rugby was also adopted in Queensland, with its very different landscape and climate, and in parts of Great Britain where there was no pretence to egalitarianism. If New Zealand historians were less intent on trying to crack the code of New Zealand's uniqueness, and not so obsessed with quests for national identity, they might notice that many of the supposedly particular characteristics of this society are really not so particular after all. They might also come up with some more robust explanations as to why New Zealand has such a proud history when it comes to playing rugby.[10]

In the same way, so we misunderstand our history of leisure and pleasure if we ignore its international context. Sandow's sole visit to New Zealand and the long history of how New Zealanders reshaped and revealed their modern bodies can help us to break out of our geographic boundaries and think about New Zealand's history in a larger framework.[11]

When historians started to think about the history of leisure and what it could tell us about the past many looked to the nineteenth century as the time when industrialisation transformed leisure and made it modern. Changes in workplace practices meant that the 'human motor' (the worker) had to be efficient and productive. Streamlined production techniques were devised to maximise outputs. Control and discipline were to the fore. It was the era of Henry Ford's mass production line and Taylorism.[12]

Leisure time became more clearly demarcated than it had been in pre-industrial societies. Work and play were now clearly defined, by time and space. This development, the historians noted, concerned middle-class reformers. What would the workers do with their free hours? Worried that they would waste their time in idle and dissolute pursuits, the reformers set about providing 'rational recreation', sanctioned leisure activities that mimicked the control workers faced on the factory floor. Leisure became an opportunity for improvement, a time when the mind and body could be regulated and disciplined, rather than an excuse for inertia or immodesty. The workers might enjoy rational recreation, but these leisure activities were not designed to be pleasurable. Leisure and pleasure were two very different things.

Although the workers' minds came in for a fair amount of attention in this rational recreation moment (with lectures at Mechanics' Institutes, public reading rooms and libraries), much of the reformers' attention was directed at corporeal control. The modern body had to be as streamlined and efficient as a factory production line. It needed regulation, discipline and categorisation. To fit the modern era, bodies had to be reshaped.[13]

At a time when the emphasis was on the body rather than the mind, when activity and rationality were celebrated and passivity and irrationality decried, Sandow stepped onto the stage and discovered he had a worldwide audience. He brought the 'modernist preoccupation with physicality' to New Zealand, and found a very responsive audience for his leisure message.[14] New Zealanders were awed by his body, the like of which they had never seen before. But, more than that, they were converted by his message. Sandow claimed that as a young man he had been 'weak chested', so ill that his father took him to the more 'genial climate' of Italy to recover. This decision saved him, not because the sun shone and the air was warm, but because in Italy he first saw the bronze and marble statues of David and Hercules. It was a road to Damascus conversion for the young Sandow. The beauty and majesty of these classical bodies inspired him. How, he asked himself, had such bodily perfection been achieved? He set about answering the question, studying anatomy to better understand his body. By the time he burst onto the Alhambra's stage he believed that he had unlocked the ancients' secret. The perfect body required a systematic, rational, scientific exercise programme. The Sandow System was born.[15]

Although it was a very modern response to contemporary concerns, Sandow always stressed the classical dimension of his system. To properly exercise your body you had to concentrate your mind. He shared Aristotle's belief that people could be genuine citizens only when they controlled their minds *and* their bodies. Simply going through the motions would not achieve bodily perfection. Sandowites had to think about what they were doing. A sound mind in a sound body was the goal, and Sandow's body was living proof that anyone could achieve it. He had rebuilt himself: now others, too, had to shape up.

Whether Sandow actually went to Italy as a young man, or studied anatomy, is debatable. Also questionable is the claim that he took the stage name Eugen (he was born Friedrich Wilhelm Müller) in 'admiration for

Francis Galton's new science of Eugenics'.[16] Many stories about Sandow – especially ones he told about himself – may be more grounded in fiction than fact, but beyond dispute is the impact he had on early twentieth-century leisure.

The Sandow System suited the rational recreation desires of middle-class reformers. Like the recently devised Alexander technique of posture reform, the new obsession with dieting and the general infatuation with achieving physical fitness, Sandow offered contemporaries a fresh way to achieve bodily control.[17] If devotees spent 15 to 20 minutes a day focusing their mind on the 400 muscles he had identified in the human body, and following his exercises, they could reshape themselves for the modern era. This could happen at an individual level, as readers of his books and subscribers to his magazine picked up a pair of Sandow's patented dumb-bells and followed an exercise programme, but he was also keen to spread his physical culture gospel among society at large. At every opportunity he preached the benefits of the Sandow System to education boards, police forces, armed services and firefighters. He sought the backing of doctors and civic leaders, and was often rewarded with endorsements and speaking engagements.

In order to garner such support Sandow had first to attract attention to himself. He realised that in the slick, commercial world of modern leisure he needed a gimmick to draw the public's eyes away from the lure of the barmaid or the boxing match. The *Sandow Season*, his phenomenally successful stage show, did just that. By the time he visited New Zealand his stage routine was as finely honed as his body.

Sandow's claim that he played the part of the showman 'not because he likes [to], but as the best available method of extending a knowledge of his system of obtaining health and strength' seems a little disingenuous.[18] He was an entertainer as well as an athlete, and he never let a business opportunity pass him by. But his desire to distance himself from the crasser aspects of show business makes sense when the concerns of rational recreation are taken into account. Posing on the stage in a leopard skin loincloth assured him of a large working-class audience: the same people who went to the music hall and boxing matches would buy tickets to see a strongman perform. But to widen his appeal, and gain both respectability and revenue, he had to attract the middle classes. The Sandow System explained and justified their presence at the *Sandow Season*.

In many ways the stage show looks like irrational rather than rational leisure, unsanctioned pleasure rather than sanctioned leisure. Audiences sat and watched as Sandow performed for them, relishing the spectacle in much the same way as they enjoyed watching films. Image and desire, not work and production, had become their markers of modernity.[19] But as Sandow explained it, the rational and irrational could not be separated in such a calculated way: the boundaries between them were blurred. His tour and his system were about both leisure and pleasure. It is an argument that some historians of leisure are beginning to embrace.

In the 1970s Peter Bailey pioneered the debate about the rise of rational recreation. By the late 1990s, however, he was less sure that the social control arguments he had once advocated held sway and suggested that historians should think about the history of leisure in other ways. Two of those suggestions are picked up in this book: a need to focus on the body at leisure, and a recognition that 'The gospel of fun dissolved the strict prescriptions of rational recreation'.[20]

Bailey's caution about the 'ideological presumptions' that have clouded the debate over rational recreation and social control does not mean that control was not a feature of leisure.[21] Bodily control and constraint were key aspects of modern leisure, but we should not assume that they were always imposed from above. Many of Sandow's followers were individuals who welcomed the bodily discipline offered by the Sandow System. This was as true in Johannesburg and Calcutta as it was in Napier and Oamaru. Sandow enthusiasts lived in a world where social barriers were breaking down: music hall and vaudeville constantly pushed the boundaries of what was sexually appropriate; the new technologies of photography and film meant pornography was widely available; women were demanding greater rights and freedoms as citizens. The New Woman challenged ideas about everything from posture and dress to language and sexuality. In such a society taking control of one's self and one's body made sense.

New Zealand was a long way from many of the problems of urban, industrial England and the United States, yet New Zealanders shared the concerns of their northern hemisphere counterparts. They worried that the sturdy pioneers of old had given way to sickly city types as factories and offices replaced the rural frontier. Men were now pushing pens rather than ploughs. Children lurked on street corners instead of running though fields. Young women seemed to prefer clerical work to their proper role as wives and mothers. Fears of 'race suicide' were aired as women shunned the joys of marriage and motherhood in order to pursue their own, selfish interests.[22] And on top of all of this, there was war to contend with. The

South African War saw some 6000 men (and 3000 horses) sail from New Zealand to South Africa to fight for the empire. The troops were joined by doctors, nurses, veterinary surgeons and teachers. As news of casualties and deaths reached New Zealand shores, leaders further worried about the well-being of their citizens.

Sandow arrived just in time. Well aware of contemporary fears that the modern body was degenerating, he offered New Zealanders the perfect way to strengthen their society. In the eugenic language of the day, citizens had a duty to lift themselves from C3 to A1 status. Through the Sandow System they could perform their duty every day.

This personal adoption of the rational recreation message sits well with our understanding of early twentieth-century New Zealand society. As James Belich has recently written, the period from the 1880s to the 1930s was a time of 'moral harmony',[23] an age when cleanliness became a national obsession, at least in the abstract, and when sexual repression was preached if not practised. It was a time when laws were passed to suppress juvenile smoking and abolish barmaids. Whether such legislation achieved its ends, or whether anyone listened to the clergy who denounced sex for the sake of pleasure rather than procreation, is beside the point. These public pronouncements were all about control and accepting personal responsibility – the cultures of constraint. Exercise programmes offered individuals the ultimate in self-control: the ability to govern their bodies.

The Sandow System, in its pure form, was short-lived. By the outbreak of the Great War Sandow was no longer a major figure in the world of physical culture, but men and women who had trained with him and had been trained by his followers continued to espouse his approach. The war generated new concerns about the health of the New Zealand nation, as many of the country's supposedly fine young men were deemed medically unfit and unable to serve. Over 100,000 of the fittest were sent off; many did not return. After 1918, the need to rebuild and physically re-equip the nation became a renewed priority.

Throughout the 1920s and 1930s bodily perfection received further attention. Hollywood film stars replaced vaudeville strongmen as the ideal types: instead of gazing at Sandow on stage, the public now went to watch Elmo Lincoln in the first screen adaptation of Edgar Rice Burroughs' *Tarzan of the Apes*.[24] Girls raised doing Sandow exercises entered 'perfect girl' competitions. Sandow's influence lurked in the wings rather than taking centre stage, but he had definitely not been forgotten.

The outbreak of the Second World War, like the Great War and the South African War before it, revived fears about the poor physical state of the nation. Although proportionally fewer were killed and wounded between 1939 and 1945 than in the First World War, bodies still needed to be rebuilt and strengthened after years of fighting. Pre-war physical improvement programmes continued in the post-war era.

By the time Daisy Martin received her father's Sandow statue in 1955, the idea and ideal of the modern body as disciplined and controlled, ordered and orderly, was well established. Around New Zealand men and women had bought the message of physical culture, and reshaped their bodies accordingly. This was mainly a voluntary effort: self-control rather than imposed, governmental control, propelled this culture of constraint. But the state shared individuals' concerns about the instability of modern society. Although it was not until the election of the first Labour government in 1935 that the state explicitly stepped in and tried to reshape adults' bodies through leisure (and even then they followed in the footsteps of volunteers rather than creating their own path), when it came to children's bodies, parents were far happier to step aside and allow local and central government to take the lead. This meant imposing policies and programmes designed to improve young bodies and save them from the flux of modern society. It also meant measuring bodies and gathering statistics. As James C. Scott argues, the modern state shared in 'a strong (one might even say muscle-bound) . . . belief in scientific and technical progress'. Young bodies had to be described and then they could be prescribed.[25] There may be some truth to Michel Foucault's idea that schooling and more general adult control of young people's lives was an attempt to impose order on the bodies of children, and thus produce bodies for an orderly society.[26] But though the state and local government may have thought that introducing a new physical education programme into schools, measuring young bodies, or supervising children in council parks would allow them to control the young, the boys and girls did not always respond to their PE lessons and playground sessions as their teachers and supervisors expected or wanted. Similarly, the adults who reshaped their bodies may not have been motivated by a desire to lift the nation's racial classification to A1 status. As Mike Huggins has pointed out, the gap between 'public rhetoric and private life' was often very large when it came to leisure.[27]

Leisure and pleasure are not synonymous. Leisure has been defined as 'what is *licensed* . . . as legitimate pleasure'.[28] The *Sandow Season* was leisure for some of its audience, an opportunity to see their master in action, a lesson in the benefits of taking bodily control. For others it was pure pleasure, an opportunity to sit back and feast their eyes upon a semi-clad body posing for their entertainment. James Belich has described New Zealand as a 'Tight society', full of restrictions and restraints, but the only tight thing some New Zealanders wanted to see was Sandow's clenched buttocks. They were not disappointed.[29]

In this book leisure and pleasure stand side by side, just as the *Sandow Season* and the Sandow System did. Cultures of constraint cannot be ignored, but reshaping and revealing the modern body was not just about racial fitness and good health, or about order and decency. New Zealand social historians have tended to focus on the wowsers of our past, the prescribers who preached a message of personal temperance if not prohibition. In this book actions speak louder than the words of clerics, doctors and politicians. The prescribers' voices can still be heard, but alongside their messages of constraint we also need to consider the enjoyment modern bodies offered, and take into account Bailey's idea of 'The gospel of fun'. We need to explore the potential of bodily pleasure to upset the cultures of constraint treasured by so many. Gyms and pools, beaches and playgrounds could reinforce messages about control and discipline, but they could also be places of abandon and instability.[30] Classical references could cloak the modern body in the civility of the ancient world, or they could be an excuse to reveal more flesh than the censors allowed.[31] One man's leisure was often another man's pleasure.

All this may come as a bit of a shock to some readers of New Zealand history. It is rare for our historians to study the 'pleasures of the flesh'. Rather than write about people enjoying sex, for example, they have tended to focus on venereal diseases and abortions.[32] Their stories of alcohol revolve around violence and the long campaign to suppress drinking, rather than enjoyable nights spent at the local hotel and the conviviality bar rooms offered.[33] Historians seem to have bought the message of bodily constraint and shaped our history books accordingly.[34]

Leisure and Pleasure may strike readers as a very idiosyncratic book. It is about the body at leisure, but ignores sport;[35] it is about New Zealand, but does not purport to tell a national story; and it does not pretend to be comprehensive.[36] It is about bodies but, though they are explored along the way, gender and sexual desire are not a focus. This is a history of the modern body at play, a study of how and why New Zealand bodies were reshaped and revealed between 1900 and 1960. It begins with Sandow's only tour of New Zealand and ends with the demise of the government's Physical Welfare and Recreation Branch. In between I explore Sandow's legacy on New Zealand bodies, which took the form of physical culture classes and gyms (Chapter Two), beauty contests (Chapter Three), swimming and sunbathing (Chapter Four), nudism (Chapter Five), physical education programmes and supervised play (Chapter Six) and state interventions in leisure (Chapter Seven). I am not trying to suggest that we would not have had beauty contests or nudist clubs if Sandow had not spent a few weeks in New Zealand. His legacy was less direct than that. Sandow was a catalyst who helped to make the reshaped and revealed body respectable and non-sexual for some, while providing others with a voyeuristic feast. He was one of many who made the focus on the body possible in modern society. What society then chose to do with these bodies was beyond his control.

Many other aspects of the modern body at leisure could be fruitfully explored in this book: the history of dieting to achieve the body beautiful; dancing for health and beauty; waka races and haka; tramping, mountain climbing and skiing. None is covered here. Some have already been written about;[37] others, though interesting, were not part of Sandow's legacy, so fall outside my framework.

Sandow's main concern was to spread his physical culture message as far and wide as possible. Books and magazines helped, but there was nothing like seeing the high priest of physical culture in the flesh.[38] In the summer of 1902–03 the strongest man on earth blessed thousands of New Zealanders with a visit, described at the time as 'an event of unusual interest'. The moment has come to sit back and enjoy the *Sandow Season*.

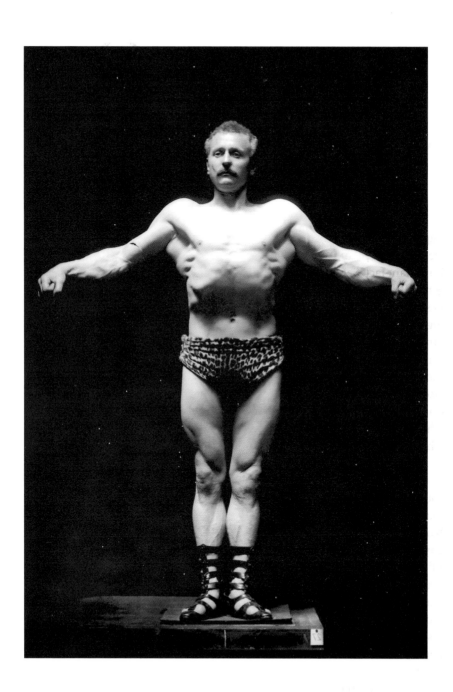

One **The Strongman Cometh**

Eugen Sandow's sense of timing was usually superb. He read his era well. But the planning of his only tour of New Zealand overlooked one important fact: Sandow arrived in Auckland on 17 November 1902, and a general election was to be held on the 25th. So while the dailies and weeklies noted that Sandow had arrived in the country, politicians and local dignitaries did not go down to the port to greet him as they had throughout his triumphant tour of Australia. Politics, rather than physical culture, was grabbing the headlines. Moreover, survivors from the shipwreck of the steamer *Elingamite* were landing in Auckland as Sandow disembarked. Used to well-wishers fêting him as he arrived in town, Sandow had to look on as the crowds flocked instead around the men, women and children who had survived the *Elingamite* disaster. It was an inauspicious start to what would nevertheless soon become a spectacularly successful season.

The *Sandow Season* opened at Auckland's City Hall on Tuesday 18 November 1902. After five evening performances and a matinée, he moved south. Two nights in New Plymouth were followed by a single performance in Stratford. From there Sandow took in Wanganui, Palmerston North and Masterton, before heading to Hawke's Bay. He spent two days in Hastings and two in Napier, then caught the train to Wellington. Alighting in the capital, he was delighted to be greeted by converts and curious onlookers, and was amused to hear one 'young lady' exclaim to her companion, 'Why, he's just a MAN!'[1] In his street clothes Sandow looked much like other men, but as the crowds at the Alhambra had discovered in 1889, it was a different matter once the suit was off. Sandow performed in Wellington's Opera House for a week and then headed across Cook Strait for his South Island season. He entertained and edified packed houses in Christchurch and Ashburton before Christmas, and on

Sandow as he appeared in
street clothes, every inch
the respectable citizen and
'just a man'. *Weekly Press*,
31 December 1902.

Boxing Day was back on stage, this time in Timaru. Next was a one-night
stand in Oamaru, before Sandow graced the stage at His Majesty's Theatre,
Dunedin. He played for a week, then, after a single performance in Gore,
he closed with a two-night stint in Invercargill.

Total attendance figures for the matinées and evening shows are not
available, but reports indicated that Sandow played in theatres 'crowded
to excess'[2] and before 'large and appreciative audiences'.[3] Never one to
undersell himself, Sandow claimed in his own account of the tour that
'huge' venues in New Zealand were 'packed to suffocation'.[4] His promoter,
Harry Rickards, was certainly happy with the door-take. Several years later
he still ranked Sandow's tour as one of his best-ever engagements.[5] Given
what took place on and off stage during Sandow's time in New Zealand,

it is no wonder that Sandow, his promoter and the public all judged the *Sandow Season* a huge success.

When the curtain rose at Wanganui's Opera House or Masterton's Town Hall the first sight to greet the audience was not the mighty man of muscles but his support acts. Sandow travelled with a vaudeville troupe who provided the first half of the night's entertainment. Audiences were amused by Mark Anthony's 'clever, breezy monologue entertainment', the singing and mimicking of 'Little Fanny Powers', Professor Maccan's concertina solos and the Drews, a husband and wife sketch team. Although a 'first-class programme' this was not what most people had paid 5 shillings for.[6] In Christchurch a reporter noted that while the audience 'sat through the first part of the entertainment patiently enough and not without an appreciation of the items produced for their benefit . . . they were obviously waiting for the "star" turn'.[7] The New Plymouth audience 'denied itself the pleasure of insisting upon a repetition of the duet' by two of the singers, 'in order that the curtain might be raised upon the "corrugated muscles" of the famous Sandow'.[8] In Dunedin they grew 'a little impatient' with the vaudeville company,[9] while in the Manawatu 'a raucous voice from the pit' demanded 'We want to see Sandow'.[10] Throughout New Zealand, though, audiences had to wait until the second half of the show before they could feast their eyes on the figure Harvard Professor Dudley Sargent had pronounced to be 'The best-developed man who ever lived'.[11]

As the curtain rose after the interval audiences gasped. There, bathed in limelight, was Sandow, standing 'in statuesque attitude' upon a slowly revolving pedestal.[12] A plum-coloured velvet curtain hung behind him, throwing his semi-clad body into stark relief. Wearing a leopard skin, Roman sandals and a smile, Sandow posed for his public. It was a carefully orchestrated performance, one he had given thousands of times over the previous decade. Designed to show off the development of all of his muscles, it caught the eye of reporters the length and breadth of New Zealand:

> Anyone who saw the magnificent display given by Mr Sandow in the opening part, in which he illustrated his unrivaled muscular development could not but feel a thrill of admiration. The graceful poses into which Sandow falls naturally and easily, bringing into view the great rows of muscles which stand out like coils of cordage, are certainly wonderful. There is no exertion, no

straining whatever. Sandow closes his hand lightly and straightway a mass of
muscle tense and firm as steel springs out. He places his hands lightly locked
together above his head, and as the pedestal revolves great bands of muscles
stand out in bold relief on the broad surface of his back. In the inflation of his
chest Mr Sandow seemed to grow into gigantic proportions, so immense was
the extension.[13]

Sandow began each performance standing still, allowing his audience
to take in the perfect symmetry of his physique. Then, as the pedestal began
to revolve, Sandow turned his body into the statues of ancient Greece: he
became Apollo and Discobolus.[14] As a Wellington reporter noted, 'There
he stood, like a beautifully-chiselled statue of an Olympic giant'.[15] Sandow
was both 'a veritable statue' and the sculptor – a masterpiece for his audience to gaze upon.[16] His poses brought 'into full relief bunches of muscles
which are undreamt of in the ordinary individual'.[17] His was a body so well
developed 'That [it] would not be considered possible had not the living
reality been present to convince beyond a doubt'.[18]

In some towns Sandow stepped off his pedestal at the end of the
show's first half and went to the front of the stage where he 'literally made
his muscles dance to the music of the orchestra'.[19] Muscles that a moment
before had been pumped as hard as steel now quivered in time to fast
music and much applause.[20] In other places, Sandow's posing culminated
with inflating 'his massive chest', increasing it by 14 inches, from 48 to 62
inches.[21] The curtain fell to thunderous applause.

The men and women in Sandow's audience had seen with their own
eyes an extraordinary body, and they had seen far more of it than was
normally permissible. By the standards of the day, Sandow's costume
was risqué. Men who swam at the pool or beach had to wear neck-to-
knee bathing suits, but here was a man showing off his chest and back,
requiring his audience to look closely at all parts of his body, so that
they could admire his muscular development. For over a decade before
his New Zealand tour, Sandow had deliberately turned his body into a
marketable commodity. With the aid of business managers such as the
legendary Florenz Ziegfeld Junior, of Ziegfeld's Follies fame, Sandow
had prepared his body for public consumption. In order to have mass
appeal, and so reap greater profits, Sandow had to attract the attention
of respectable society as well as those who ordinarily frequented music
halls. Vaudeville devotees were used to leg shows and performances that
'bordered so closely upon what is called in "Trilby" the "altogether" as to

Sandow as he appeared to his startled audiences. The photograph above was taken in Melbourne, just before the New Zealand tour, and was later used in Sandow's book *Body-Building, or Man in the Making*.

shock the sensibilities of the nervous'.[22] Trilby, the eponymous heroine of George Du Maurier's novel, was a stage sensation at the time. She smoked, dressed like a man, danced, was promiscuous and posed in the nude without shame.[23] Trilby had her followers, but her audience was limited to those who were not made anxious by such behaviour. Sandow wanted more than Trilby could ever achieve, so he needed to stretch the boundaries of permissible behaviour while at the same time convincing the public that he was a paragon of respectable manhood.

Sandow poses like the statues of the ancient world. On the left, he stands
contrapposto on a pedestal. This photograph is claimed to be by Schmidt
(F-59774-1/2, Alexander Turnbull Library, Wellington). The illustration on the
right appeared in his book, *Body-Building, or Man in the Making.*

First, Sandow had to justify semi-nudity on stage. Why did he need
to reveal more flesh than other strongmen? The answer was simple: stage
strongmen were mere circus performers, masters of tricks and sleights of
hand. Sandow was an athlete, an exponent of physical culture. He had
more in common with the great Olympic athletes of Greece and Rome
than with fraudsters such as Samson and Cyclops. Indeed, he held up the
figures of Apollo and Michelangelo's 'David', immortalised in stone and
bronze, as his role models. Such heroes, as visitors to art galleries and
museums knew, were displayed in their natural state. A judicious fig leaf
might be required, but nothing else should interrupt the viewer's gaze and
admiration of the bodily perfection before them. These bodies were not
undressed, they were *natural*. As nudists were soon to argue, a naked body
titillated viewers, but a nude body was above such prurient longings.[24]

On stage, Sandow became a figure from antiquity. He wore more than
a fig leaf – although many photographs were taken of him posing in the

Many photographs of Sandow appeared with a judicious fig leaf. This 'rare photo. of Sandow' appeared after his death in the Australian magazine *Health and Physical Culture*, 1 September 1932. Mitchell Library, Sydney.

nude or with just a leaf to cover his modesty – but in other respects he imitated his role models. Like the statues of Italy, he stood on a pedestal. He dusted his shaved body with powder before each performance to stress the resemblance to classical marble statues.[25] Like Michelangelo's famous sculptures, he stood contraposto, twisting his body on its axis so that his arms and shoulders contrasted as strongly as possible with his legs and hips. As a living statue he cast himself in the world of classical art and highbrow culture. It was a long way from the iconography of circus strongmen.[26] Though simply looking at his body might give his audience pleasure, they could, if they chose, persuade themselves that the classical references gave them a licence to gaze intently.

Sandow's body was clothed in respectability even as he shed his evening suit and took to the stage. His public knew this before they bought tickets to his shows. Several years before he toured, a film of a semi-clad Sandow was screened in New Zealand theatres.[27] By the time of his tour,

Two of the Swiss Studio shots of Sandow taken during his Melbourne stay, and
reproduced in the *New Zealand Graphic*. The photographs also appeared in *Sandow's
Magazine* and in his book, *Body-Building, or Man in the Making*.

photographs of him in classical poses were freely available. If his New
Zealand audiences had not purchased these through his magazine, or
feasted their eyes on them in his lavishly illustrated first book, they could
enjoy a series of shots taken in Melbourne, and reproduced in the *New
Zealand Graphic* just as box offices were beginning to sell tickets for his
New Zealand season.[28] They could also admire a plaster replica of the
statue the British Museum had cast of Sandow's naked body. This toured
New Zealand, arriving in towns just ahead of Sandow himself, to whet
local appetites. Standing in the windows of stores selling Sandow's exercise equipment, it attracted much attention. As one reporter commented,
'it is well worth a visit of inspection'.[29] Sandow's name may have been a
household word in New Zealand, but images of his clenched buttocks
and rippling abdomen were also becoming increasingly familiar.

Sandow's management was not, however, content to let the matter rest
there. They knew that the classical references would not persuade every-

one that the *Sandow Season* was indeed leisure rather than just pleasure. It became commonplace for press releases advertising the show to stress how 'above board' Sandow's performance was; there was 'nothing coarse or re-pulsive in his entertainment'.[30] Suspicions that Sandow's exhibition would shock right-minded people were dismissed as 'Totally ungrounded'.[31] 'The whole performance was clean and accurate, and wholly free from the slightest offensiveness.'[32] Sandow worked hard to make stage semi-nudity respectable, although the number of press releases he issued stressing his respectability may have smacked of protesting too much.

Nevertheless, emphasising classical allusions and using press releases to reassure the public helped Sandow and his managers to convince women that the *Sandow Season* was not for men only. Getting women into the dress circle and stalls as well as the pit was no mean feat. Again, Sandow's management team employed a variety of tactics to encourage the 'right sort' of women to feel comfortable in the crowd. Wherever pos-sible, Sandow was booked to perform in a 'better class' of theatre than other vaudeville acts.[33] Much was also made of the fact that the wives of local luminaries were in the audience. This strategy was put to good use in New Zealand. The weekly press helped to reassure women that ladies in other centres had enjoyed Sandow's show. For example, 'Phyllis', who wrote 'A Lady's Letter from Napier' for the *Weekly Press*, informed her readers that:

> The Theatre Royal has been engaged for two nights by Mr H. Rickards's Vaudeville Company. The greatest attraction was Mr Eugen Sandow. Amongst the audience were Mrs Ronald, Mrs Donnelly, Misses Hoadley, Mrs Humphrey, Mrs Perry, Mrs Kettle, Mrs Wilson, Miss Spencer, Misses Margoliouth, Mrs Wenely, Mrs Logan, Miss Shaw, Mrs and Miss Coleman, Mrs Fairlea, and Mrs Bernan.[34]

In other words, the wives of prominent merchants, landholders and professionals had sat in the dress circle and marvelled at Sandow's perfor-mance. Even Bessie Spencer, headmistress of the local girls' high school, had attended; in fact, she was a Sandow devotee. So, before Sandow had opened his South Island season, respectable women were reassured that seeing Sandow was safe, but enjoyable. And women in New Zealand clearly took pleasure in the *Sandow Season*. 'Priscilla', who wrote the 'Girls' Gossip' column for Wellington's *Evening Post*, reported that Sandow was 'positively marvellous'.[35] 'Childa', the author of 'A Lady's Letter from

A cheeky shot. Sandow's briefs became briefer in his
desire to show off his tight buttocks. G-1838-1/1,
Alexander Turnbull Library, Wellington.

Oamaru' noted that Sandow 'was the great attraction, and what a man he
is!'[36]

'Childa' and other women in New Zealand relished looking at this
'splendid specimen of manhood', the like of which they had never seen
before.[37] Sandow was all man, a potent sexual symbol on show for their
enjoyment.[38] 'Priscilla' wrote about women 'longing' to look at him.[39]
Unfortunately for them, after Sandow married in 1894 he stopped allowing women to caress his muscles, a publicity ploy Ziegfeld had intro-

duced the previous year.[40] The women of Wellington had to be content with gazing upon his body instead. His muscles delighted them, as did his Teutonic good looks: 'What appeals to Hebe about the champion athlete are his curls, aggressively tight little twists that seem to indicate his strength almost as plainly as his muscles'.[41]

Men were also gazing, and enjoying what they saw. Most of the journalists writing about the show were men, and they lavished praise on Sandow's body. They commented on his perfect skin,[42] called him 'beautiful'[43] and described him as 'a superb picture of manhood'.[44] Such praise may seem almost homoerotic today, but at the turn of the twentieth century boundaries between homosexual and heterosexual cultures were far less fixed and certain than they were to become 50 years later. Unlike women, men could admire the man of muscles without anyone questioning whether this was 'proper' behaviour.[45]

When the curtain rose again, for the second half of Sandow's performance, the stage was set as a Roman amphitheatre, with Sandow centre stage as 'The modern Hercules'.[46] Surrounded by attendants dressed as slaves, Sandow began to perform feats of strength. As one Wanganui journalist noted, the first half 'was merely the exhibition of unexpended power'.[47] 'What', the scribe from Wanganui asked, 'could Sandow achieve with those magnificent muscles?'[48]

Sandow's achievements in the show's second half were as stunning as his posing had been. This came as no surprise to his audiences. Press releases from Sandow's manager, describing the feats of strength the star would perform, had made their way into local newspapers before Sandow took to the stage. His public already knew that his 'Roman Column and Tomb of Hercules feats are said to be almost superhuman, and have been astounding vast audiences in all parts of the world'.[49] But seeing was believing, and for many Sandow's reputation was so incredible that he had to be seen to be believed.

The 'modern Samson',[50] as several newspapers called him, began by playing with his barbells and dumb-bells: 'He lifted the bar-bells as though they were walking-sticks, raised them above his head with but little apparent effort, and toyed with the dumb-bells as if they were nothing in particular'.[51] Before a thrilled crowd, he did the same with various of his attendants, lifting them above his head as though they were made of cardboard. But three of his feats in particular were singled out for praise.

In the first, to display his finger strength, he attacked full packs of playing cards:

> He tore one pack in half as an ordinary mortal might tear a piece of tissue paper; he placed two whole packs together and tore them similarly asunder; and then he made a solid pile of three packs and, with a sudden vigorous wrench, split it in twain and threw the surrendered pieces to the delighted patrons in front.[52]

Fans all over the country went home clutching pieces of playing cards that the mighty Sandow had not only touched, but torn.

His Roman Column Feat did not provide keepsakes but, as promised, it astounded audiences. 'Suspended by his knees from a pillar he lifts a 212lb barbell from the ground, over his head, and rising with it places it on his thighs, and in this position supports its weight and that of two men who hang by either end.'[53] This mid-air stomach crunch with weights was less impressive, though, than Sandow's grand finale, the Tomb of Hercules. Sandow reclined backwards, using his hands and feet as support. A platform was then placed on his upturned chest, and on that platform was placed the entire collection of dumb-bells and barbells used throughout the show. As if this was not enough, six of his assistants then also climbed onto the platform. Reporters had some difficulty in assessing how much all of this weighed. Some believed it to be half a ton, others three-quarters of a ton, while one decided it was 'not far short of a ton'.[54] Regardless, all agreed that Sandow's ability to stay in that position for over a minute, never wincing when more weight was added, was a fitting finale to what had been an extraordinary demonstration of human strength and control.

Sandow's posing had entertained the crowd, but his feats of strength astonished them. The strongman's muscles were not just for show; he could and did use them. Sandow embodied the ideal citizen, someone who was healthy, strong *and* hardworking. This was what modern man must strive to become. Ironically, in order to be modern, Sandow had to allude both to ancient civilisation and to primitive societies.

In the first half of his performance Sandow had posed like an ancient statue. In the second half he performed the Roman Column and the Tomb of Hercules. Even the most classically illiterate members of his audience could not fail to pick up on the references, and most people sitting in the stalls and crowded in the pit were better educated in such matters than

audiences 100 years later would be.[55] Safe in the knowledge that he would
be understood by his readers, a reporter in New Plymouth wrote: 'The
warm applause showed that there is a healthy admiration in the community for physical strength, and that the old Roman idea of true "virtue"
(manliness) is as strong to-day as it was among the ancients from whom
Mr. Sandow took his models'.[56] A Wellington reporter similarly picked
up on classical themes in his report. 'Mr. Sandow,' he wrote, 'The apostle
of physical culture, illustrates in his own person that perfection of muscular development which the modern world knows only from ancient
statues of a Hercules, or paintings of a Niebelungen hero.'[57] Sandow may
have spelled out the classical references, but his audience understood the
allusions and applauded a modern man of muscles who turned to the
ancients for his role models.

The abundance of classical references in reports by and about Sandow
helped to distance his performances from any hint of the savage or the
primitive. Despite his stage costume, Sandow was grounded in the civilised world of Europe. He was well aware, too, of the power of modern
science. People may have understood and applauded references to ancient
Greece, but they were also enthralled by rational, scientific discourse. Press
releases detailed Sandow's measurements, and the endorsement he had
received from Professor Dudley Sargent,[59] but it was away from the stage
that Sandow most effectively preached a message of scientific exercise.
When he was on stage the strongman never spoke – his body said it all
– but off stage Sandow never missed an opportunity to declare the merits
of his system.

There were two main reasons why the Sandow System enjoyed widespread support around the world in the late nineteenth and early twentieth centuries. First, unlike other strongmen, Sandow did not hold up
his strength as something innate. Instead, he always stressed that his

extraordinary body had been achieved only through persistent exercise and using his mind to control his muscles. His teachings offered others the same opportunity. Anyone could become strong and healthy if they adopted the Sandow System. This message was not lost on local reporters. Before he arrived in the country, readers of the *Graphic* were told:

> The ordinary strong man glories in his strength as if it were a special gift from heaven vouchsafed only to him. His whole attitude seems to say to his lesser fellows: 'You poor weaklings, you couldn't be strong like me even if you tried your very hardest.' But that's not Sandow's attitude. 'I am a marvel,' he says modestly, 'but there is nothing hindering you, my brother, to be the same. I lift mountains, metaphorically speaking, but if you have only faith in me you can go and do likewise.'[60]

As the tour progressed, the message was reinforced. In Christchurch readers were reminded that 'It is the man as he stands, not the man as he was created, who is of interest in the public eye.'[61] This was a very popular and appealing message in an era full of concerns about the nation's physical health.

The second key ingredient of the Sandow System, which again marked it off from other physical culture programmes of the day, was its scientific nature. In an age when doctors and scientists were held in high esteem, systematic, rational approaches to the problems of life were seen as the modern response. Statistics meant certainty. Sandow played to all these beliefs. He ensured that his system was endorsed by leading doctors, scientists and professors, and made sure this information was freely available to the press. While in New Zealand he continued his habit of performing special 'expositions' for medical men, and stressed that his system offered its practitioners a new, rational way to exercise. There was nothing random about the Sandow System, nothing left to chance.

Many New Zealand journalists were clearly enamoured with this idea that exercise could have a scientific basis. One thought that the knowledge Sandow provided would allow 'The bony skeleton that is our physical base' to be 'gloved in living steel'. He liked the fact that this was a 'scientific conception' rather than a circus trick, and hoped that, once exercised, 'The average civilised man' would be 'able to throw the strongest savage' in a wrestling match.[62] Properly trained, nothing could thwart modern man.

In part, Sandow built up his system by denigrating other exercise programmes. These, he claimed, not only failed to realise that the mind con-

trolled the muscles, but were also incomplete. Whereas Sandow had identified all the muscles in the body, and devised exercises for each and every
one of them, most other schemes merely targeted a few muscle groups,
leaving most to waste away. Some local journalists were astonished and
impressed that 'even those [muscles] scarcely known outside medical
circles or the art schools devoted to antique statuary' were not 'allowed
to atrophy' under the Sandow System.[63] Sandow made it clear that this
was in stark contrast to the training offered by other sports. Athletics, for
example, was often 'unintelligently administered', and therefore became a
'harmful craze', developing one set of muscles at the expense of another.[64]
Despite the contemporary popularity of athletics, no one rose to defend
the sport against Sandow's challenge.[65] Even when he criticised the physical fitness of rugby football players, his statements were allowed to stand.
He did, after all, have science on his side.

He also had statistics close at hand, ready to back up some of his more
extreme pronouncements. When discussing the limitations of football as
a form of exercise, for example, he claimed that it exercised only 64 of the
400 muscles in the body, and treated those 64 in a violent and harmful
way.[66] Gymnastics was little better. According to Sandow, the gymnast
had a 'development of 75 per cent of the pulling muscles, and only 25 per
cent of the stretching muscles', and had not developed the muscles used in
everyday life at all.[67] In the face of such evidence, how could locals do anything but take to their Sandow developers and spring-grip dumb-bells?

In many cases, though, Sandow was preaching to the converted. He
already had many devotees in New Zealand before he arrived. Some had
written to his London-based magazine, sending in articles and photographs showing the beneficial effects of the Sandow System.[68] Sandow
exercises were being performed in the privacy of bedrooms around New
Zealand, and also in classes held in local halls and gymnasia. So when
newspapers announced that the *Sandow Season* was coming to town, they
often noted that the show would have special appeal to his followers. The
first part of his performance, when he posed on the pedestal, would be
'particularly interest[ing]' to 'pupils of the Sandow classes . . . as they will
be able to see what can be accomplished by gradually developing the body
by judicious and scientific exercises'.[69] These exact words appeared in so
many different newspapers that it seems likely this was yet another press
release, printed verbatim in the local press. But it illustrates again how well
Sandow knew his audience and how keen they were 'To see the originator
and to observe what in his own person is the result of his teaching'.[70]

Sandow cruises the Wanganui River with some of his 'legions' of followers. Sandow
(front, left) stands with the women members of the Wanganui School of Physical
Culture. *Sandow's Magazine*, April 1903. David Chapman Collection.

The nationwide spread of the Sandow System was also reflected
in other reports announcing his visit. In Wanganui his followers were
claimed to already be 'legion',[71] in Palmerston North 'nearly everyone
you meet is engaged in exercising his muscles in a well-directed manner',[72]
in Hastings 'his pupils' were preparing to 'gaze upon the original himself',[73] while in Napier, 'Sandow perhaps needs little introduction to the
public, for his methods of training have been adopted in many homes,
and this fact alone will be sufficient to create a desire to see the originator
and to observe in his own person what is the result of his teaching.'[74] The
South Island was the same. In Dunedin it was thought that 'The already-
awakened interest locally in physical culture is likely to receive no small
fillip by this visit of the strong man'.[75] Wherever Sandow went in New
Zealand he was met by fans and followers. Familiar with his system, they
wished to look at and learn from their master.

If Sandow had been just another circus strongman, his tour of New
Zealand would have entertained the crowds, perhaps encouraged a few

young boys to dream about running away to join a circus, but no more than that. After a week or two, another travelling entertainment troupe would have come to town and Sandow's feats of strength would have been forgotten. That they were not indicates not just the power of his stage presence, but the strength of his off-stage message. Sandow not only recognised the widespread concern in the Western world about the effects of modern living on the bodies of men, women and children, but also offered a solution. And this ensured that his name lived on long after he left town.

New Zealand in the summer of 1902–03 seems an unlikely place to worry about the effects of the modern age on the body. The colony still relied economically on farming and extractive industries such as coal mining for its income. Its people mainly lived in rural communities and small towns rather than in congested cities. By the standards of the day, this was not a heavily industrialised or urbanised country. It seemed more traditional than modern. Yet people were anxious. They worried about high rates of infant mortality, which peaked during the summer months.[76] They worried that children and young people were out of control. Young boys were turning into larrikins, slouching on street corners rather than standing upright as the young soldier-citizens of tomorrow. Larrikinism concerned the honest burghers of Auckland's Mount Roskill to such an extent that they considered appealing to the Minister of Defence, in the hope that he could solve the problem.[77] Young girls were also causing concern. They were more interested in having a good time than learning the essentials of mothercraft. How could they become worthy mothers of the future when they preferred to stroll the streets and use rowdy language rather than stay at home under the watchful eyes of their parents? Adults, too, were often seen as a problem. Parents were accused of neglecting their duty. They were not imposing the necessary discipline on their offspring. Too many fathers were deserting their families, or seeking solace in the whisky bottle instead of the loving embrace of their wives and children. Mothers were either too concerned with making ends meet to worry about the whereabouts of their children, or too busy exercising their newly gained political rights to concern themselves with mundane domestic matters. Even worse were those young and not-so-young men and women who had not married. These were bodies out of control, people so intent on pleasure that they had forgotten that being a citizen involved responsibilities as well as rights.

The very nature of colonial society also came in for a fair amount of attention. Domestic architecture meant that young people could easily leave the home without their parents noticing – if their parents were at home in the first place. The warmer weather in the colony, especially in the north, was also said to be leading to the wrack and ruin of society. Juvenile immorality was often put down to the mild climate, which allowed young people to get up to mischief outside all year round. Even the diet in the colony encouraged poor behaviour. The vast amount of meat eaten in New Zealand was said to heat the blood and encourage sensuality. [78]

Many of these fears were, of course, ungrounded or wildly exaggerated, but enough people believed and perpetuated these ideas to give them some currency. The nation was ill and, in part, a physical remedy was needed to restore it to good health. As one contemporary put it:

> We are sick because we have done physical wrong to ourselves, and when
> we are sick we are commonly cross and ill-tempered, and we like to pose as
> victims when by rights we ought to be tried before a special jury and heavily
> fined unless we prove that we couldn't help it. For health and strength are not
> only the highest physical state but the natural state. [79]

Sandow had come to heal the nation. He had identified these modern woes, and offered a system to cure them. Locals recognised this:

> He has done something – a great deal, indeed – to check the physical
> deterioration of the race that has resulted from the concentration of men and
> women in great cities, and he has given to the weary brain-worker, to the city
> clerk and shop assistant a simple and effective means of obtaining the healthy
> body that is necessary as the dwelling-place of a healthy mind. [80]

The Sandow System was his gift to the twentieth century.

Bearing such a gift, it is not surprising that Sandow was given many opportunities to espouse his faith in his exercise programme. And it was a faith. Sandow appropriated the language of religion. While in Melbourne, just before his New Zealand tour, he agreed to the publication of the talks – the sermons – he gave on strengthening the body. The book appeared until the title *The Gospel of Strength According to Sandow*. In New Zealand, he was happy to announce that the Sandow System was his 'gospel' and that he was here to preach it. [81] Sandow positioned himself as the saviour of the race, and plenty of people were prepared to accept that salvation. Throughout his tour a religious fervour surrounded him, his teachings,

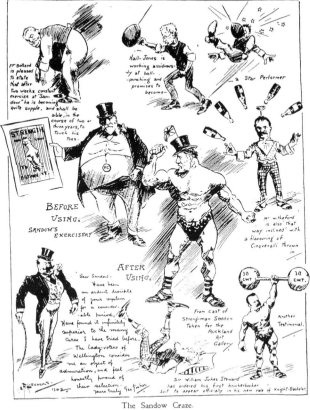

The Sandow Craze.

A FEW OPINIONS AND TESTIMONIALS WE EXPECT TO BE FORTHCOMING IN THE NEAR FUTURE.

After the Wellington welcome, the *Graphic*'s cartoonist went to town,
suggesting that many politicians, including Premier Richard Seddon, were
adopting the Sandow System. The classic 'before' and 'after' shots indicate the
benefits of the programme. Seddon has clearly followed the Sandow System,
as set out in *Strength and How to Obtain It*, the book he clasps in his right hand
in his 'before' pose. *New Zealand Graphic*, 13 December 1902.

and his followers. Sandow was frequently referred to as 'The high priest',
here to spread his 'gospel of physical culture'.[82] He was 'The apostle of
physical development' and his followers were his 'disciples'.[83] Sandow
was on a 'mission'.[84]

The man with the mission was also the man who called on statistics
and scientists to help him sell his exercise system. For Sandow there was
no tension or contradiction between the rational, systematic exercise pro-

gramme he had devised, and the language of Christianity. Just as he could wear a leopard-skin loincloth and claim to be the embodiment of civilised man, so he could preach a gospel of secular health and strength. All that mattered was reaching his disciples and converting non-believers.

During his tour he used four main avenues to spread the Sandow System, each as managed and as practised as his stage show. What he told his congregations in New Zealand echoed what he had said in Australia, the United States and England; the positive response also echoed those that he received elsewhere.

Wherever possible, Sandow liked to begin his stay in a new town with an official welcome. By 1902 it was becoming difficult for touring acts to gain mayoral welcomes as mayors ran shy of being seen to endorse money-making acts.[85] This proved to be the case in Christchurch,[86] but not in the capital, where Sandow was received at the council chambers by the mayor and members of the council. Sir Joseph Ward and two members of parliament were also on hand, representing the government. Mayor Aitken was the vice-president of the Wellington School of Physical Culture, so he needed no persuading about the benefits of Sandow's presence in the city: 'without a healthy body, one could not have a healthy mind, and if young people were to be developed on right lines it was absolutely necessary that their physical culture should be looked after'. Ward, who later became prime minister, assured Sandow that he intended to take up the Sandow System, and extended an invitation for the strongman to migrate to New Zealand. While such occasions allowed men like Aitken and Ward to associate themselves with a popular performer, they also provided Sandow with the right of reply. He could praise local physique, claiming that he had 'never seen such material, such a fine race of men, as he had seen in this colony'. He could play to local prejudices, noting that the locals 'were ahead of Australia in this respect (Applause.)' He could paint himself as a humble teacher of the Sandow System: 'He was always pleased to give instruction on the subject, and was ready at any time to give away what he knew. (Applause.)' And he could remind listeners (and readers) of his larger goal: 'To see men as strong, and if possible, stronger than himself'.[87] Official welcomes provided Sandow with a perfect opportunity to sell himself, his show and his system.

Mr Marcus, Sandow's touring manager, did not always manage to arrange mayoral welcomes but he was very successful at setting up 'expositions' for local doctors, journalists and gentlemen. These were invitation-only events, often held in the same venue where Sandow performed in the

Taken from Sandow's book, *Life is Movement: The Physical Reconstruction and Regeneration of the People (A Diseaseless World)*, this photograph shows Sandow and his living model, James Young, during one of their New Zealand 'expositions'. Several of the men in the audience are in uniform. Sandow was always keen to spread his gospel among police, firefighters and the armed services. David Chapman Collection.

evening. Four of these were held during the New Zealand tour, one in each of the main centres, and each was reported extensively in the local press.[88]

All these events followed the same format. Like his stage show, they began with Sandow posing, showing to best advantage his muscular development. This was show and tell, with Sandow explaining the system behind his physique. It was also show and touch: Sandow always insisted that some of his audience, usually those seated on the stage with him, feel his muscles. They got to touch various parts of Sandow's body as he contracted and relaxed his muscles. Several doctors were also called upon to listen to Sandow's chest. They always announced him to be in perfect condition, his mighty body placing no detectable strain on his heart.[89]

Next came a demonstration of the exercises at the heart of the Sandow System. This time Sandow's body was not the centre of attention. He stood to one side, explaining the principle underlying each of the exercises which his pupil, James Young, performed for the invited audience. During the tour Young also gave public demonstrations of the right ways to carry out Sandow's exercise system and use his exercise equipment.

Standing in the windows of stores that sold the Sandow range, Young used the Sandow combined developer and spring-grip dumb-bells to best advantage. Such demonstrations, which usually coincided with workers' lunch breaks and school boys returning home, were generally trouble free.[90] In Christchurch, though, Young's performance in the window of Strange & Co. in High Street, led to a court appearance. His demonstration was so popular that crowds blocked the footpath; passers-by had to walk on the road to get past but the street was obstructed by the large number of cabs parked by the shop. The police were unable to keep the way clear, so charged Young and one of the store's proprietors with obstruction. The magistrate agreed that an obstruction had taken place. Although he 'fully recognised the advantages which had resulted from Mr Sandow's exposition of physical culture' and 'Thought everybody should go and see the system explained for themselves', he convicted Young. No penalty or costs were attached to the conviction, however.[91] Perhaps in light of this unfortunate incident Young decided to give his Dunedin demonstration at the Choral Hall rather than in the window of a department store.[92]

Young's demonstrations at the 'expositions' were not as dramatic. Once he had shown the assembled men how to exercise the Sandow way he stepped aside and let the master resume his position, centre stage. Now it was time for questions and answers, and the assembled men usually had quite a number of queries about the Sandow System. Sometimes these were quite flippant, allowing Sandow to show his lighter side: 'Asked if he had devoted any time to developing some of the minor organs, such as moving the ears, Sandow replied that he had not this accomplishment, adding further that he did not see its value, unless one desired to become a professional listener'.[93] Generally, though, they wanted further information on the virtues of the system and how it could benefit anyone who took it up.

Each 'exposition' concluded with a hearty vote of thanks that often heaped further praise on Sandow. In Auckland the president of the medical association 'spoke in frankly eulogistic terms of the great athlete and his system'.[94] In Christchurch Dr Henry Thacker, a leading light in the local physical culture movement, used the opportunity to make a political point. 'He felt certain that if the system they had seen illustrated spread and flourished throughout the colony they would have no need of prohibition, or legislation of any kind to improve the morals of the people.'[95] Thacker's comments came not long after the country had been to the polls to decide whether local electoral areas would go dry. Two new South

Instructing and inspecting young Sandowites during his visit to Wanganui. As with all such visits, Sandow was accompanied by a photographer, and used the resulting shot to illustrate his magazine. *Sandow's Magazine*, April 1903. David Chapman Collection.

Island districts had voted to impose prohibition. If Thacker was right, the widespread adoption of the Sandow System would see the emergence of a new breed of self-controlled, disciplined citizens. Bodily constraint would have social benefits.

School visits were the third avenue Sandow pursued to spread his gospel. He seemed to share with the Jesuits the belief that if you could train the boy you could shape the man. Although many of his pupils were adults, Sandow focused on his school-boy pupils during his tour, offering them cheap tickets to his matinées and visiting their exercise classes. In Wanganui he went to the Collegiate school twice. On his first visit he inspected the pupils while they did their Sandow exercises, offering their instructors some 'very valuable hints' on how the boys could gain even more through his exercise programme.[96] The next day he returned with James Young, and while Young performed Sandow talked the group of school boys, doctors and others through the correct and incorrect ways to follow the Sandow System. Ever one to remind his audience that they too might be able to achieve a body like his, he complimented the Wanganui boys 'upon their fine physique, and assured them that if they kept up the drill many of them would probably arrive at his own standard of excellence before very long'.[97]

After Christmas Sandow visited another school, Fred Hornibrook's Timaru Sandow Class. Hornibrook was the most prominent Sandow teacher in the greater Christchurch area, and his work seems to have impressed Sandow more than what he saw in Wanganui. Once again, Sandow

examined the boys, complimented them and their teacher on their fine
work, and then held a personal audience with the 'young "Sandows"': each
young boy was introduced to his 'father' who showed off his wrist strength
with a hearty handshake. The visit concluded, as it had in Wanganui, with
a photograph. Sandow, of course, was the centrepiece.[98]

School visits provided Sandow with further photo opportunities and
press coverage, but he knew that if he wanted more column inches in the
dailies and weeklies he had to give interviews. This he did whenever it
could be arranged. He could spell out the Sandow System for those who
had managed to stay unfamiliar with it, and explain how it held the key to
solving the problems of the day. If Sandow were to be believed, his exercise
programme would ensure that children would grow into fine, upstanding
(and well-muscled) citizens of tomorrow, men would gain inner strength
to complement their outer strength, women would become fit wives and
mothers. 'Problem' citizens – the drunk, the lunatic, the consumptive
– would no longer exist. Less than half an hour a day doing Sandow exercises would truly turn New Zealand into God's own country.

Sandow insisted that his system offered the best possible way to
improve the health of children, hence his support of local Sandow classes.
He worried that at home and at school children were not being trained in
the appropriate way. Parents, he felt, were so insistent that their children
develop their minds 'only with the idea of making money' that they overlooked the very important role physical culture could play in strengthening the 'self-control' of the young.[99] As a father, he understood the parents'
concern that a child be well educated 'in order that he may be great in
medicine, great in art, a commanding figure in the business world'. But,
Sandow insisted, all this was 'useless . . . if he has not the physical equipment. It is the robust men – the men whose physical and mental development are attuned on a high scale – who "make their mark," who present
an unflinching front to destiny and who see the race through from first to
last.'[100] Parents had a duty to develop their children's minds and bodies
– too many were failing in their responsibilities.

Schools were little better. They encouraged children to exercise, but
expected all pupils to do the same drill, regardless of their individual
bodily needs. Sandow claimed that the drill routines used in New Zealand
schools were attractive for spectators, but had little else to recommend
them. This was as provocative as suggesting that rugby was not a good way
to exercise, but Sandow managed to get away with it. He made his criticism
palatable by first directing it at the Australians. As his speech in Wellington

had made clear, he was well aware that New Zealanders were fiercely com-
petitive when it came to their neighbours, so his first criticism of the education system drew attention to the uniform drill exercises carried out across
the Tasman: 'He rather laughs at the methods of physical culture which are
in vogue in Australia'.[101] New Zealanders laughed with him, despite the
fact that, as with so many aspects of their leisure history, they shared the
same practices. Next Sandow criticised the American system, again noting
that uniform exercises were as good as useless. Young people's potential
could be realised only if their individual weaknesses were recognised and
addressed through his system.[102] Having softened his audience, he could
then attack the New Zealand system, reiterating that the exercises being
done here were 'simply a farce' since they lumped all the children together.
Nor was he happy with the amount of time spent exercising, and with the
training of those administering the system.[103] But then, Sandow was on a
'mission' to persuade governments to adopt his system.[104]

In childhood, boys were encouraged to play sport and exercise, but as
they grew older they became more sedentary, and were 'only saved from
annihilation by the violent exercises of [their] youth'.[105] The Sandow
System promised to remedy this sad state of affairs. 'Tohunga', a regular
columnist in an Auckland paper, asked his readers:

> Did it never occur to you that the great suffering of civilised men is due to the
> cessation of that dire necessity which once kept every muscle trained and every
> digestion sound? Even manual labourers in civilisation only ordinarily use
> certain muscles and allow the rest of their bodies to fall into decrepitude. . .[106]

Sandow's system promised to restore men to peak physical condition, not
by resorting to the hard labour of the past, but through intelligent, modern
training. Sandow claimed that his system was more efficacious than physical work, since 'Work was the mere automatic use of the muscles, [while]
exercise was their use with the mind concentrated on them. The first produced improper action and development, the latter way could only develop them properly.'[107] As one journalist wrote, Sandow understood that,
in the contemporary era, brute physical strength was often not required:

> The mere possession of physical strength by individuals, though extremely
> useful, is not a prime necessity for the welfare of the race; a lever, a screw, a
> steam crane, or a few more hands can be got to help with heavy work. But
> good health, vigour to use the strength one had with ease and pleasure, the

beauty which accompanies full health and strength, toughness to withstand
accidental shocks, and a will cultivated by exercise upon the outward frame
itself until it is master of inner cravings and injurious emotions – these are
among the conditions for the improvement of the race on its physical side;
and from these, he argues, are also the conditions for the existence and
manifestation of strength and activity of mind.[108]

Sandow was always keen to point out that his system improved 'The
race'. He did not need to elaborate what he meant by this, since local audiences always understood it in their own terms. While in New Zealand he
seems to have only associated with Pakeha, but he published positive articles on Maori in his magazine.[109] He was proud of sending men to fight for
the empire in the South African War,[110] and happy to include photographs
and testimonials from non-white men in his publications. The ambiguity
suited Sandow, since his aim was to make his system of training compulsory in every country, regardless of which 'race' it contained.

'Racial fitness' and 'race suicide' were topical issues. It was a eugenic
era, but what contemporaries like Sandow meant by eugenics should not
be confused with the Nazis' understanding of the concept in the 1930s
and 1940s. Eugenics has come to be widely understood as a belief in the
power of nature over nurture. In the early twentieth century, though, it
was not necessarily a language of genetic determinism. Sandow was a
eugenicist, but he did not believe that heredity defined the man. Like
many of his contemporaries, Sandow was an environmental eugenicist.
He insisted that the racial stock had to be improved, but he believed in
the power of nurture to overcome any natural defects. The Sandow System
was his contribution to the nurturing of modern man.

Hard-core eugenicists, such as the New Zealand-born surgeon and politician, W. A. Chapple, advocated far more radical solutions to the problems of the day. Around the time of Sandow's visit, Chapple published a
eugenic treatise called *The Fertility of the Unfit*.[111] In it, he outlined the three
tenets of radical eugenic thought: that the 'fit' and the 'unfit' should be seg-
regated, so that the 'good' genes of the fit could not be tainted by the 'bad'
genes of the unfit; that 'unfit' women and women married to 'unfit' men
should be sterilised (unfit men thus did not need to have vasectomies, a
procedure Chapple thought had too many negative side effects); and that
couples should be required to obtain a medical certificate indicating their
genetic compatibility before marriage.[112] If one of the partners was found
to be 'unfit', then the woman should be sterilised before they could marry.

On the other hand, Chapple thought it should be a criminal offence for the 'fit' to seek sterilisation: they had a responsibility to propagate their good genes. Chapple's definition of 'unfit' was broad. It included 'all those mental and moral and physical defectives who are unable or unwilling to support themselves according to the recognized laws of human society. They include the criminal, the pauper, the idiot and the imbecile, the lunatic, the drunkard, the deformed and the diseased.'[113]

Sandow disagreed with Chapple and his ilk. He saw that it was not desirable for the 'unfit' and the 'fit' to mate, but believed that physical culture was a more effective solution than legal measures prohibiting the marriage of the unfit. As he explained to a journalist:

> What are we doing to-day with regard to the improvement of the human race? We take a consumptive man off the street and mate him with a healthy woman, or vice versa. Of course that is wrong, and no law can prevent it directly. But it can be prevented indirectly by physical culture all over the world. That is my ambition: that is what I am striving for. When men breed animals to-day they put the best they can find together, and so it should be with the human race.[114]

Any individual could be made better by regular, systematic exercise. This was especially important for women, who had a duty to give birth to healthy children. They must exercise for the sake of the nation. Any enjoyment they got out of this was secondary; the primary reason was to become better wives and mothers.

Sandow's belief in nurture over nature knew no bounds. The Sandow System could take the 'unfit' and make them well again. The drunkard, for example, would not exist if Sandow's system was adopted. Dr Thacker had mentioned that prohibition would not be necessary if men enrolled in a Sandow class, and it was a line Sandow was fond of pushing. Men who were 'physically cultured' knew when to stop drinking because they had learned self-control and bodily respect.[115] As he headed further south, into the strongholds of prohibition, he suggested that:

> if you had compulsory physical culture in New Zealand you would never have any need of prohibition in this country. Men who study physical culture take care of their bodies, and when they have a drink or two have the will power to say, "No, old man, I have had enough. This stuff does not do me any good if I take any more."[116]

Never a wowser, he believed that physical culture encouraged its disciples to embrace a culture of self-discipline and moderation in all things.

The chronically ill and those with mental illnesses could also be cured through the Sandow System. Indeed, Sandow was said to be 'much prouder of having been the means of restoring consumptives to physical and lunatics to mental health, than of having taught young men to train themselves to lift great weights, break chains, or perform other feats to make the ordinary strong man envious'.[117] He told his New Zealand audience of his successes with the 'lunatics' at Coney Island, and praised Fred Hornibrook for having cured 30 consumptives in Christchurch through a judicious use of the Sandow System.[118]

Even the old and feeble could have their 'vitality and power' restored if they picked up a pair of his dumb-bells. The system allowed the young to 'lay the foundation of their health in life', but it was never too late to join a class.[119] If Sandow were to be believed, it seemed that no one, old or young, male or female, strong or weak, would not benefit from adopting his exercise programme. No wonder the public, press and politicians embraced him and his message.

The *Sandow Season* and the Sandow System were a formidable duo – leisure and pleasure combined in a slick, commercial production that took considerable risks but at the same time had a larger purpose. Sandow's magnificent body had been reshaped and revealed in a way that encouraged attention, and once he was the centre of attention, he preached a message of salvation through physical culture. In a society that longed for bodily constraint as much as it enjoyed the pleasures of the flesh, his message was well received.

In the ensuing years Sandow's legacy became apparent in many forms of leisure and pleasure but in the immediate aftermath of his tour the air was almost as full of Sandow as it had been during his brief stay in New Zealand. The strongman may have departed these shores, but he left behind many followers who picked up his dumb-bells and posed in annual physique competitions.

Two **Sandow's Legacy**

While Sandow was still touring the country, a newspaper columnist suggested that all over New Zealand men and women had bought pieces of Sandow's exercise equipment only to realise that 'They invested in haste to repent at leisure'. They were the first of many generations who bought the promise of tight buttocks and flat abdomens, only to relegate their unused spring-grip dumb-bells and combined developers to the dusty depths under their beds. For 'Eire' this made perfect sense, especially when it came to women:

> Few women in our busy life have either the time or the strength to give up to [a] 'Sandow's course.' Already there are a number of fagged-out girls, and the sofas of many houses are fully occupied. Of course, they have over-done the exercises, but it is the sad experience of many that a very little of that sort of thing goes a long way.[1]

'Eire' might have discarded his Sandow Developer after a couple of sessions, but many of his readers were not so hasty. They had invested a considerable amount of money, purchasing tickets to see Sandow's stage show, buying his books and magazines and acquiring his patented exercise equipment. At 12s 6d for a pair of dumb-bells and 21s for a developer, this was serious expenditure for many people.[2] A young man could have bought a gallon of rum for the price of Sandow's Combined Developer, while the dumb-bells cost the same as a fashionable gold and pearl brooch at Stewart Dawson's the jewellers.[3] Having made the investment, many were determined to get a return.

The *Sandow Season* was an important vehicle for spreading the physical culture message and movement in New Zealand. Existing Sandow

devotees, such as Napier school principal Bessie Spencer, saw their master
at work, and understood the full potential of following Sandow's system.[4]
Other members of the audience, who had not yet enjoyed the delights of
systematic exercise, were soon investing in their future. J. Cullington saw
Sandow perform at New Plymouth's Theatre Royal and was spurred into
action. He bought Sandow's books, purchased the patented grip dumb-
bells and the developer, 'and have a go at them every day. I think a few
minutes a day with them is the finest thing a man can have.' Cullington
went on to convert others, including several female friends. It was not
always easy:

> With one young lady it took me over six months to get her to start. She
> believed in physical culture herself, only she was frightened her sisters would
> laugh at her. However, she started at last, and got a bit of chaffing at first, but
> she stuck to it all the same, and it has improved her in every way. She used to
> suffer a lot with colds, and now she does not know what it is to have a cold,
> and now one of her sisters is taking it up and getting along finely.[5]

Cullington's friend was not 'fagged' by her daily dose of exercise.
Like many in the early twentieth century, she enjoyed better health as a
result of regular exercise. And alongside the individual benefits, she knew
– because Sandow and his acolytes told her, again and again – that by
exercising she was helping to 'raise the average standard of the race as a
whole'. That, Sandow claimed in the inaugural editorial of his magazine,
was the ultimate goal of his system.[6]

The New Zealand men and women who embraced systematic exercise
were not alone. As Lois Banner has noted in the American context, physical fitness was as much an obsession in the early twentieth century as it
became at century's end.[7] New Zealanders were part of an international
trend. And like their counterparts in North America, Australia, Great
Britain and Europe, local adherents of the Sandow System offered various
reasons for their desire to reshape their bodies.

Early twentieth-century New Zealanders moved around a lot, traveling the
length and breadth of the country in search of work and better opportunities.[8] But wherever they went, they could probably join a gym or a physical
culture class. All over New Zealand men who had trained under Sandow
in London, or who had 'graduated' from one of his mail-order courses,

A full gymnastics class at Ponsonby's recently opened Leys Institute.
The gymnasium's motto, 'mens sana in corpore sano' (a sound mind in a sound
body), was very familiar to Sandow's followers. *Auckland Star* Collection,
G-2943-1/1, Alexander Turnbull Library, Wellington.

were setting themselves up as directors of Sandow schools. Some women
climbed onto the bandwagon, offering classes in dancing and deportment alongside Sandow exercise programmes. A major leisure revolution
was taking place.

Retracing Sandow's touring route reveals the pervasiveness of this
exercise culture. In Auckland, for example, Carrollo's Gymnasium at the
Young Men's Christian Association (YMCA) had been offering classes for
men, boys and young ladies before Sandow came to town.[9] After Sandow
left, Professor Potter began his gym club for men and women, and was
soon using the new gymnasium at the Leys Institute to good effect.[10] Mrs
Malcolmson Boult offered classes in physical culture, deportment and
dancing,[11] while Mrs Thornton Lees ran health classes alongside her physical culture sessions.[12] G. Wilson Corbridge, who claimed to be a Sandow
pupil, also offered Aucklanders a chance to learn the Sandow System.[13]
It is not known if Edward Roskruge or H. S. Innes-Jones junior went to
these classes, but both wrote to Sandow's magazine, telling him that after

his Auckland performances they went out and bought his equipment and had enjoyed good health ever since. Both also mentioned that they did not exercise alone: like so many Sandow followers around the world, they had encouraged friends to join them in their quest for A1 health.[14]

Sandow's next stop was New Plymouth, where Cullington and his friends were soon gripping their dumb-bells and running their own, informal, Sandow school. Dr Francis Hutchinson was also living in New Plymouth by this time. As we will see, he took a particular interest in the reshaped and revealed bodies of young men who had adopted Sandow's exercise programme.[15]

In Wanganui, where Sandow spent a couple of days, the physical culture movement was thriving, thanks in large part to the efforts of Dick Jarrett, a classic Sandow System success story. As a young man he had worked in a bakery but suffered from lung trouble. Doctors could offer no cure, and claimed he did not have long to live. Jarrett's response was to take himself into the countryside and rebuild his body.[16] He wrote to Sandow for a course of instruction, and within months had become 'The New Zealand Sandow'.[17] In the years that followed, Jarrett instructed hundreds of Wanganui school children (among then the boys Sandow visited), and taught Sandow's system to their teachers. He is also reputed to have introduced New Zealand sprinters to the crouch start.[18] He also found time to conduct classes for adults. His pupil, G. H. Marshall, won a gold medal in one of Sandow's competitions and in turn became an instructor at the Wanganui Young Men's Institute. From May to September Marshall led classes, as well as helping his male and female friends who strove for bodily perfection.[19] Wanganui's Young Men's Institute had been holding physical culture classes since its establishment in 1896. Marshall helped to make it 'one of the best-known social organisations' in the town.[20]

Although he spent a lot of time teaching the Sandow system in Wanganui, Jarrett also ran classes in Palmerston North and held the occasional public demonstration. E. N. Boddington was such a keen attender of Jarrett's Tuesday night classes that he began to subscribe to *Sandow's Magazine*.[21]

After his performances in the Manawatu, Sandow visited Hawke's Bay. His time there left a lasting impression on many young men. Some attended classes at Napier's St Paul's Gymnastic Club, where D. S. Laing was the instructor.[22] There were even plans to set up a Sandow school in the township of Dannevirke.[23] Many others sought instruction and guidance from Sandow himself, writing to his magazine, buying his books

Dick Jarrett's Sandow class on display. Their Wanganui gymnasium was decorated with Sandow's pictures and charts, as were the bedroom walls of many young New Zealanders. *Sandow's Magazine*, April 1903. David Chapman Collection.

and practising at home. Horace E. Bourgeois turned his Napier bedroom into a shrine to Sandow, with a 'mass of charts and photos., all round the walls, and every night I have some different chaps in, showing them and teaching them how to make themselves strong'. He was adamant that before he took up the Sandow system 'I would often break down for want of strength and sticking power. My occupation is a clerk in a merchant's office.'[24] Hastings man J. Cullen had improved his body so much that Sandow published his photograph.[25] Other Hawke's Bay men went one further, winning Sandow's monthly prizes for best physique. Robert Meechan won in June 1905, P. Culliford in February 1906. Both were from Napier.[26]

From Hawke's Bay Sandow travelled to Wellington, home of the Wellington Physical Training School and Gymnasium which had featured in the magazine before his New Zealand visit, and continued to be popular for many years.[27] J. W. M. Harrison also ran a school of physical culture along Sandow lines. Harrison was the former director of the St Peter's and Polytechnic Gymnasia in London; such credentials always helped when it came to membership drives.[28] Royd Garlick, who was later appointed

Charles Ward in front of his stall at the Canterbury Jubilee Exhibition. Sandow's patented
spring-grip dumb-bells are well displayed, as are his combined developers. Ward's
devotion to the Sandow System led him to name his Christchurch business premises
Sandow House. *Sandow's Magazine*, June 1901. David Chapman Collection.

by the government to run its physical education programme, was another
prominent Sandow instructor in the capital. A regular correspondent to
Sandow's Magazine, Garlick sent in 'before and after' photographs of some
of his pupils, showing how Sandow's system had cured their lateral cur-
vature.[29] His own photograph was also published.[30] By 1907 Garlick was
the director of the Wellington School of Physical Culture.[31] Sandow's
Wellington followers wrote in to his magazine asking for advice on how
to remove body hair (Sandow's reply: 'There is no lasting cure for what is a
constitutional peculiarity') and offering opinions on the state of amateur
athletics.[32] Some contributed articles, others had their photographs reproduced.[33] All were devoted to the Sandow System.

The pattern was repeated in the South Island, where Sandow's first
venue was Christchurch. Before the star's visit, Charles J. Ward had been

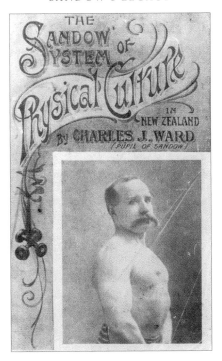

The cover of Charles Ward's booklet advertising his Christchurch Sandow School,
c.1899–1900. Ward claimed that the Sandow System had added 3 inches to his chest
and taken 7 inches off his waist. After two years of training his abdominal muscles
could support 17 stone. Terry Ward Collection.

busy introducing locals to systematic exercise. He trained young men
like T. Cook, winner of the silver medal at the 'Sandow Rules' weight-
lifting contest, organised in association with the Canterbury Jubilee
Exhibition.[34] Ward operated a 'Sandow Specialities' stall at the exhibition, selling Sandow's exercise equipment and generating interest in his
Sandow school.[35] Thomas Tankard also alerted locals to the importance
of physical culture. He ran the Christchurch Physical Training School and
Gymnasium, and from 1898 members of his gym entertained the public
with annual physical culture displays.[36] Like Harrison in Wellington, the
fact that he had been the director of the City Gymnasium in Sheffield
helped him to attract pupils.[37] For those who preferred a woman instructor, in 1900 physical culture instruction was available from Miss
Madeline Nunneley and Miss Lowe.[38] But from the turn of the century on,

This picture, by cartoonist David Low, appeared in the Christchurch International
Exhibition's magazine in June 1907 as the monthly competition. Readers had
to guess who the club-swinger was. The first four who guessed it was Thomas
Tankard, 'The Renowned Muscle Maker', received half-a-crown each.
Exhibition Sketcher, June 1907. Canterbury Museum, Christchurch.

the most popular Sandow instructor in town was an Irishman called Fred
Hornibrook.

Hornibrook had trained at Sandow's London Institute, and on his
arrival in Christchurch began to spread the good word. Although his
claim to have inaugurated the Sandow System in New Zealand when he
began classes at his Christchurch Sandow School of Physical Culture in
April 1900 is uncertain,[39] it is certain that he soon became the best-known
Sandow instructor in the country. Within six months he had instructed
157 men, including racing cyclist G. C. Body, who increased his chest
measurement by a whopping 4½ inches after only three months' training.[40] Like Garlick in Wellington, Hornibrook sent Sandow 'before and
after' photographs of his pupils, and was rewarded when some of them
were reproduced in *Sandow's Magazine*.[41] And like Jarrett in Wanganui,

Hornibrook also offered classes in neighbouring towns. By the time of Sandow's visit he provided instruction in Temuka, Geraldine, Timaru, Waimate, Oamaru and Leeston.[42] But whereas Jarrett attracted a lot of attention from his work with school children, Hornibrook's claim to fame was a little more sensational. In 1900 he began to hold annual physical development competitions, public displays of reshaped male, and later also female, bodies.

Hornibrook's first contest was held within seven months of establishing his school. On a spring night, 37 Christchurch men braved the cold and the critical eye of the judge to parade their improved bodies. Wearing as little clothing as possible – Sandow recommended that contestants strip down to either bathing or running drawers – they flexed and posed and vied for the title 'best-developed man'.[43] There could be only one winner, and that night it was W. H. Trengrove.[44] Physique contests had come to New Zealand. Before Sandow had held his 'Great Competition' in London, and before there was even a whisper of a similar contest for women, local men's bodies were being scrutinised and judged by physical culture experts.

The following year 40 men competed for the title. The private self-control and bodily improvement they had achieved through physical culture was not enough: they were weighed and measured in public, their gains recorded and praised. Given that Hornibrook measured his own chest every week, noting his improvements, it is hardly surprising that this was how he gauged the success of his pupils.[45] The judge in City Hall was local boy made good Dr Henry Thomas Joynt Thacker. He had played inter-provincial rugby and been a football Blue at Edinburgh.[46] He was also involved in swimming and physical culture, especially the Sandow system.[47] Later the Mayor of Christchurch and the MP for Christchurch East, in 1901 he was merely a supporter of healthy exercise. Thacker awarded F. Wright the gold medal, and W. Clarke, the best-developed man under 20, the silver.[48]

By 1903 Hornibrook was holding his contest in the Art Gallery, a fitting place for the Greek gods of Christchurch to pose before an admiring audience.[49] When Hornibrook gave public lectures on physical culture, as he often did, he illustrated them with limelight views of world-famous statues.[50] His students knew what they were up against. Despite the high expectations, in 1903 almost 100 men put themselves forward to be judged by Thacker. To manage so many entrants, Hornibrook divided them into categories: under 18 years, under 21, over 21, under 9 stone,

Fred Hornibrook lounges in front of the winners of his 1904 Physical Development competition. Seated behind him are judges Dr Cecil Greenwood (on left) and W. A. Bowring. In the back row, on the left, is C. C. Jennings, who was awarded the gold medal, open championship. Standing at the back on the right is W. Wood, who won the gold medal for the best-developed man among the 1904 pupils. In the front on the left are L. W. Walshaw (best-developed youth under 21) and R. H. Bennetts (best-developed man under 9 stone). Seated on the right are C. H. Schmidt (best-developed man under 10 stone) and L. W. D. Jelfs (best-developed youth under 18). *Canterbury Times*, 14 December 1904. Christchurch City Libraries.

under 10 stone, best newcomer, best developed with an expanded chest under 35 inches. Although the men were being judged in terms of their physique, Hornibrook made it clear that he had a greater goal in mind. Sounding just like Sandow, he informed his invited guests, and the journalists present, that 'The great object of the system was the acquirement of a sound, healthy development'. Worried about the deterioration in men's bodies, Hornibrook pleaded for a compulsory physical culture system: 'when the lawmakers of the colony placed physical culture upon the same basis as mental culture in elementary schools, they would provide the only real remedy to secure a better and healthier race'.[51]

The following year so many men entered the contest that it had to be held in heats.[52] The judges in 1904 were W. A. Bowring and Dr Cecil Greenwood. Bowring was an artist: aesthetic appeal was clearly important. These revealed bodies had to be symmetrical and pleasing to the eye. In recognition of this, the following year a new prize was awarded to

This 'snap-shot' of
Dr Greenwood was drawn by
well-known cartoonist David
Low who, in later life, was one
of Fred Hornibrook's London
patients. *Exhibition Sketcher*,
26 January 1907. Canterbury
Museum, Christchurch.

the 'Man with best skin'. J. McKinley, the inaugural winner, also won first
prize for best development in a man under 21 years, and came second to
G. Gaul in the contest for best new pupil.[53] Although the word 'beauty'
was not bandied around, Hornibrook's competitions could be seen as
male beauty contests. The other judge, Greenwood, was a medical man.
A well-known advocate of living a natural, outdoors life, he warned men
to avoid drugs and tight-fitting clothes.[54] He later ran a gymnasium in the
Canterbury settlement of Oxford.[55]

Hornibrook's contests continued along similar lines for several more
years. In 1907 he was able to present the 'open champion' of his school, W.
J. Caldicotte, with a gold medal donated by Sandow. With typical under-
statement, the half-ounce medal had a laurel wreath on one side, and an
image of Sandow's head on the other.[56] And then in 1911, having decided
that 'The majority of the people have formed the physical culture habit',
Hornibrook was instrumental in establishing the New Zealand Physical

Flanked by judges Dr Greenwood and C. R. Woledge, Hornibrook sits centre
stage, surrounded by the men he trained to bodily perfection. Behind Hornibrook
is G. E. Sollitt, who won the open championship in 1906. *Canterbury Times*,
31 October 1906. Christchurch City Libraries.

Culture Association, the first national body devoted to the physical culture movement.[57] Dick Jarrett and Robert Meechan joined Hornibrook on
the managing committee.[58] With the organisation in place, New Zealand's
first national physical development competition could be held. Judging
was based on 'anatomical measurements, points also being given for symmetry, grace of carriage and ideality of proportions'.[59] Norman Kerr from
Auckland, who had recently won the All-Ireland physical development
competition, was expected to be a strong contender for the overall title,
but C. Clifford Jennings took first prize. Having toured the world with
Sandow, he knew a thing or two about physique contests.[60]

In the years before the Great War Hornibrook's annual 'best-developed' man contests helped to raise the profile of physical culture, and
were a good advertisement for his school. Large crowds gathered to watch
the men flex and pose, and regardless of what motivated them to gaze at

Having won the open championship at Hornibrook's 1904 contest, C. Clifford Jennings
was offered the chance to tour the world with Sandow. Six years after these photographs were
taken he won the inaugural national physical culture competition, becoming, in effect, the
first Mr New Zealand. *Canterbury Times*, 22 March 1905. Christchurch City Libraries.

semi-clad male bodies, Hornibrook hoped that some would be inspired
to sign up for a course of systematic exercise. Like Sandow, he was prepared to put on an entertaining show for the greater good of physical
culture. And also like Sandow, Hornibrook believed that women, too,
belonged in the gym.

At his Sandow classes for women and girls, Hornibrook encouraged
young women – including his future wife, Ettie Rout – to discard their corsets and embrace their dumb-bells. He also held annual physical development competitions for his female pupils, though these were lower key
affairs held in his school's rooms, rather than in more public spaces.[61] As
with the men's contests, the women were judged according to age, weight
and who had the best skin. The women's events were never as heavily subscribed as the men's contests: in a good year there were 40 or 50 entrants.[62]
By 1910, though, only two women vied for the title of 'Best skin', and

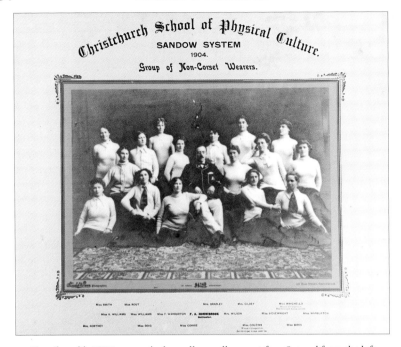

Hornibrook's 1904 women's class, all proudly corset-free. Second from the left
in the back row is Ettie Rout, his future wife. Also in the back row, on the right, is
Miss B. Whichello, winner of the competition for best-developed woman over 9 stone.
Whichello ran a Sandow class for women in Kaiapoi. Standish & Preece Photograph,
Mavis Simmonds Collection, 5107, Canterbury Museum, Christchurch.

Hornibrook's enthusiasm for such competitions seems to have passed.[63]
Young women were still keen on showing off their physical development
and having their complexions admired, they simply switched the venue.
Hornibrook's contests were superseded by competitions run by local
movie theatres.

When Sandow visited Christchurch he singled out Fred Hornibrook
for attention. He inspected his classes, praised his work and during one of
his performances invited Hornibrook on stage to receive a gift in recognition of his sterling work.[64] Sandow's instinct was correct. Although men
like Ward, Thacker and Greenwood were important in supporting the
local Sandow movement, Hornibrook was the mainstay. His hold on the
Christchurch physical culture movement was broken only when he left
the country to serve in the Great War.[65]

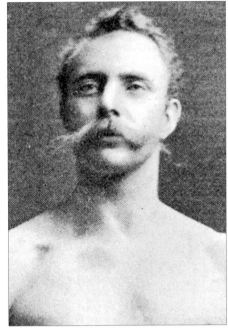

" The weak things of the world. . . . . confound the things which are mighty."

LEFT Often referred to in the press as 'Brawnibrook', Hornibrook's reshaped body sometimes became a figure of fun. Here he is drawn by Andrew Kennaway with a Bovril medal around his neck. His hero, Sandow, endorsed Plasmon cocoa powder. *Kennaway's Fun*, October 1903. Canterbury Museum, Christchurch. RIGHT Before he moved to Dunedin, J. P. Guy won a bronze medal in one of Sandow's 1899 photographic competitions. *Sandow's Magazine*, October 1899. David Chapman Collection.

From Christchurch, Sandow moved down the east coast of the South Island, making brief stops in several small towns where Hornibrook held classes.[66] Then he arrived in Dunedin for a week of performances. J. P. Guy, a bronze medallist in one of Sandow's many physique competitions, was already teaching the Sandow System in the Edinburgh of the south.[67] Between Guy's school, the high school classes led by John Hanna and the work of the Otago Gymnastic Association, physical culture was a force to be reckoned with.[68] The movement was strengthened when one of Hornibrook's pupils, A. Cracroft Wilson, opened the Otago School of Physical Culture. Its motto was 'Health is the Key of Happiness, Physical Culture the Key of Health'.[69] Guy, Hanna and Cracroft Wilson encouraged the likes of Charles Kouffe, Thomas Fogarty and Albert Zwicker to pick up their dumb-bells and improve their bodies.[70] Down in Invercargill, the final town on Sandow's itinerary, the Invercargill Physical Culture Club performed the same function.[71]

Of course, there were physical culture clubs and Sandow devotees in towns and communities not blessed with a visit from the apostle of physical culture. The gymnasium at the Feilding Young Men and Boys' Club had 150 members.[72] In the township of Martinborough 40 men attended the Gymnastic Club each week.[73] Down in Blenheim, the Sandow school boasted 30–40 members at each session.[74] The success of such leading sportsmen as runners S. Pentecost and W. Anderson, cyclist H. Amos and swimmer R. C. Murphy was often put down to their devotion to the Sandow system.[75] Parliamentarians who sailed to New Zealand's colonial possessions in the Pacific in 1903 did Sandow exercises on deck each morning, as did the All Blacks on their 1905 voyage to Great Britain.[76] Local pig hunters limbered up by doing Sandow exercises.[77] Policemen stayed fit by attending Sandow classes. In Auckland, Constable Arthur Skinner led a Sandow class for his fellow officers. He gained more notoriety in years to come, when he was involved in breaking up the Waihi strike and invading Rua Kenana's stronghold at Maungapohatu, but early on in his career he engaged in less controversial and more beneficial pursuits.[78] Those who could not attend a class could subscribe to the *New Zealand Health Journal* along with Sandow's own magazine and learn about the importance of natural health and moderate exercise, or contact a bookseller like A. Schlesinger in Christchurch, who would send physical culture books and magazines all over the country.[79]

By the time of the Great War, Sandow no longer enjoyed the same sort of international profile – in 1918 *Truth* erroneously reported that in the early days of the war he had been executed in the Tower of London for espionage – but his exercise programme and the wider physical culture movement showed no signs of abating.[80] Those who lived in an area without a gym could subscribe to a physical culture magazine and exercise at home. For those who could not afford the equipment, Kiwi ingenuity and the pioneering do-it-yourself approach came to the fore. While working in a back-country school, G. H. Marshall used two bits of rounded wood in place of dumb-bells.[81] John Flynn suggested that men make exercise mats out of chaff bags filled with straw, and build their own barbell by tying bags of sand or bricks to a bar. He even suggested that flat-irons could be substituted for dumb-bells.[82] In this he was echoing years of advice about how to turn the kitchen into a gymnasium. Women had long been told

Although this illustration, specially drawn for *Sandow's Magazine*, encouraged women to exercise with whatever they could find in the kitchen (provided the window was open, to allow fresh air in), Fred Hornibrook was not so sure. He worried that there was too much dust and dirt in the home to make it an appropriate place to exercise, and that cleaning and sweeping only used certain muscles. *Sandow's Magazine*, January 1902.

that potato-mashers were a good substitute for Indian clubs, and that rolling-pins, coal-scuttles, pokers and dishpans could all be employed in the pursuit of health and bodily control. If you were in the know, the humble kitchen broom could become 'a gymnastic gem of the purest ray serene'.[83] With their equipment at hand, all that was needed was a magazine full of exercise programmes. *Sandow's Magazine* ceased publication in 1907, but by 1910 the *Journal of Physical Culture & Health* had taken its place. Published in Sydney, and 'delivered to any address in Australia or New Zealand, post free', within a year this local take on physical culture boasted a circulation of more than 50,000 copies a month.[84] The journal owed much to North American and British publications. It reproduced articles from *Health and Strength* (London) and Bernarr Macfadden's New York-based *Physical Culture*.[85] New Zealanders were part of a regional sub-group of physical culturists, who were in turn part of a much larger Western world movement.

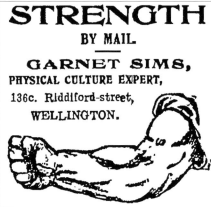

STRENGTH

BY MAIL

—

GARNET SIMS,
PHYSICAL CULTURE EXPERT,
136c. Riddiford-street,
WELLINGTON.

If you want the greatest muscle and strength possible, you must lift weights. My advanced Course consists of scientific and progressive weight-lifting exercises, and will give you the utmost development and strength in the shortest possible space of time. I give you with the course a splendid set of disc loading bar-bells and dumb-bells. After three months training on my Advanced Course you may easily tear in halves a pack of playing cards, and after twelve months training you may lift your own weight overhead, using one arm only. Write NOW for my terms, they are Free.

Promising 'Strength By Mail', Garnet Sims assured his followers that within three months they would be able to tear a pack of playing cards in half. He did not say how long it would take before they were able to match Sandow's feat of ripping three packs in half. *Truth*, 15 October 1910.

This Australasian dimension was also apparent when mail-order physique courses began to be advertised. As early as 1907 Royd Garlick was offering a six-week postal course for those wanting to improve their health and development.[86] Hornibrook began offering postal instruction in 1910,[87] as did George Sims Marley, better known at Garnet Sims, who promised subscribers 'Strength By Mail', and recommended his 'Vigorous Health Course' for those with physical defects.[88] Christchurch teacher Robert Veitch was not satisfied with just reaching New Zealanders through his mail-order service;[89] by 1912 he was offering courses 'To pupils throughout Australasia'.[90] Given that Sydneysider Reg 'Snowy' Baker had already infiltrated the New Zealand market, with the 'Baker Postal Course of Physical Culture', it was not surprising that Veitch struck back.[91] Despite Veitch's best efforts, by the 1920s Australians like Hastings Woolley were advertising in New Zealand newspapers, claiming that their mail-order

Muscular

Development, combined with perfect health, is obtainable by means of the VEITCH SYSTEM OF PHYSICAL TRAINING. Every successful pupil receives a solid silver medal at conclusion of course. No high fees. Costs only a few shillings. Write for particulars to

PROF. VEITCH.
F.D.,H.A.,S.D.
115 CASHEL-STREET, CHRISTCHURCH.

The headline says it all. 'Professor' Veitch offered men the chance to improve their bodies and health. The illustration was typical, as was the claim that the Veitch system was value for money. Like Sandow, Veitch rewarded his pupils with medals. *Truth*, 11 February 1911.

courses could cure everything from flat chests to torpid livers. Woolley offered men 'Dynamic Development', a programme that 'builds muscles. It makes strong men out of weaklings. It trains the mind as well as the body. It'll put inches of muscles on your arms, deepen your chest, broaden your back, build out your shoulders, and wonderfully improve your whole body.'[92] From that it was only a short step to Alfred J. Briton's 1928 campaign, 'Be a Man She'll Admire', a mail-order physical culture course designed to turn weaklings into 'he-men'.[93] At the same time, on the other side of the Pacific, Charles Atlas was launching a comic-strip advertising campaign for his Dynamic Tension course. The strip featured 'Mac', a 97-pound weakling who had sand kicked in his face until he invested in an Atlas course and turned into a 'he-man'. By the time Atlas began advertising in the local press, others had already adopted his comic-strip approach,

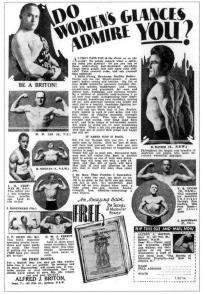

LEFT In 1931 Alfred Briton began his 'Do Women's Glances Admire You?'
campaign. Advertising his book *The Secrets of Muscular Strength – And How to
Acquire It*, Briton played on his surname, inviting readers to 'Be a Briton!' The
empire — and the empire's women — needed Australasian men to take better
care of their bodies. *Health and Physical Culture*, 1 June 1934. Mitchell Library,
Sydney. RIGHT Briton's 'Men are Amazed at their Strength!' advertisement was
very similar to his 'Do Women's Glances Admire You?' campaign. Illustrated with
photographs of his pupils, letters from satisfied customers were quoted to prove
that Briton was Australasia's leading physical director. Here the endorsements
came from an Australian, a New Zealander, a South African, a Fijian, an American
and a Scotsman. J. M. Craig of New Zealand was clearly part of an international
community. *Health and Physical Culture*, 1 August 1934. Mitchell Library, Sydney.

showing men that they would keep their girls only if they muscled up to
beat the bullies.[94]

Alongside the mail-order instruction, gyms and organisations like the
YMCA and the Young Women's Christian Association (YWCA) continued to play an important part in spreading the physical culture message
and training the next generation of New Zealanders. Images of Sandow's
toned body became less common, only to be replaced with photographs
of his American equivalent, Bernarr Macfadden.[95] Macfadden's books and
his magazine could be mail-ordered from suppliers like H. I. Jones & Sons

PADDLE YOUR OWN CANOE.
Stand feet apart, swing arms
in a big circle down by right knee,
then up in the air, twisting body
vigorously. Swing over and repeat
on left side. Do about 12-18
paddles. Count 1, 2, 3, 4.

Rather than hitching a ride in
someone else's boat, Briton
encouraged Australasians
to paddle their own canoes.
Individual responsibility was
at the heart of the physical
culture message. Alfred J.
Briton, *The Book of Life: A Work
for Everyman, His Wife and His
Family*, Sydney, 1933. Mitchell
Library, Sydney.

in Wanganui, the shop James Young had performed in years before, when
Sandow toured.[96] New regional magazines replaced the *Journal of Physical
Culture & Health*. During the 1920s there was *Withrow's Physical Culture
Annual* and then *Withrow's Physical Culture Magazine*, another Sydney-
based, Australasian production. And then in 1929 Alfred Briton, the man
who offered mail-order courses designed to turn seven stone weaklings
into 'he-men', began a magazine called *Health and Physical Culture* (*HPC*).
It ran through to the end of the Second World War, and each month
reminded men and women that it was their duty 'To maintain a healthy
mind in a healthy body'.[97]

HPC was full of illustrated articles on the exercises Australasians
needed to do in order to retain their position as the most physically perfect people in the 'civilised world'.[98] Like the articles that appeared in the
daily and weekly press, the message was simple: physical culture should
be regarded as a necessity, rather than a luxury.[99] Everyone had a duty to
reshape his or her body. Books authored by Hornibrook and his wife,
Ettie Rout, also provided locals with instruction in the 'culture of the abdomen' and 'bedroom gymnastics'.[100] By the time they wrote their books,
they were living in London, but their New Zealand connections remained. Hornibrook held up Maori dances as having the three necessary

components of physical culture: vibration (to loosen and relax the body), breathing exercises and body movements centred on the abdomen.[101] Rout also maintained that the dances of 'native races' offered ideal physical training. Conceding that many critics viewed the sexually explicit nature of such dances as obscene, she reminded readers that although 'Some of the postures and gestures may be "unbecoming[,]" [c]onstipation and obesity are still more "unbecoming"'.[102] Rout and Hornibrook were very keen on exercising to keep one's self 'regular'. Just as Frederic Truby King instructed Plunket mothers that their baby's bowels should be made to move at the same time every day, so Rout and Hornibrook offered adults the ultimate in bodily self-control.

In the first few decades of the twentieth century thousands of New Zealanders were playing sport, going to gyms and exercise classes and working out at home. Even those who had never lifted a dumb-bell or pulled on a chest developer understood the appeal of the cult of exercise. They may not have joined a gym, but they often joined in the rhetoric, urging others to reform their deformed bodies. Politicians were drawn into the culture, puffing and panting and preparing their bodies for their public.

As Sandow well knew, physical culture was a perfect fit with the public culture of the early twentieth century. If bodies were not strong enough to withstand the rigours of modern life, they could be built up. If bodies were corpulent, exercise helped with weight reduction. Peter Stearns has pointed out that by the 1900s fat had become a moral concern in the Western world. Being overweight indicated that you had a bad character.[103] Percival R. Waddy understood this. In his 1909 lecture to the YMCA Literary and Debating Society on 'The Cultivation of Character', he reminded his listeners that 'True bodily culture implies discipline, chastity, temperance, self-control, for one unbridled passion is enough to destroy the beauty of life'.[104] Systematic exercise was a 'blessing' that could be bestowed on every citizen.[105] Although they could not always live up to the rhetoric, New Zealanders were well aware that they had a moral responsibility, to themselves and to their nation, to seek and maintain bodily perfection.[106]

When individuals like Horace E. Bourgeois explained their attachment to physical culture they usually noted the health benefits they derived from regular exercise. Like Sandow, they were concerned that modern life did not offer them physical challenges. The sedentary existence of the office worker, the lack of fresh air in factories, the cramped living condi-

CAN JOE COME BACK?

In 1902 MP Joseph Ward had greeted Sandow, and encouraged everyone to adopt the Sandow System. By 1912 he was fighting for his parliamentary life. In this illustration, entitled '"The Hope" of the Liberal Party', Sir Joseph tries to skip on, despite his party losing public support. The Liberal era was over; the reign of Reform was about to begin. *Truth*, 15 June 1912.

tions so many endured – all were taking their toll on the bodies of the nation.[107] Hornibrook warned city men that 'Thousands of brain workers wreck their nervous systems, become dyspeptics, even go insane.'[108] Office girls, too, were said to suffer from 'dull, aching pain in the shoulders, arms, and small of the back', thanks to their work in front of typewriters. Exercises could relieve their discomfort and restore them to perfect health.[109] Gardening, too, offered relief from the 'worry and hurry of city life'; it was claimed to be 'physical culture in its most effective form'. Out in the fresh air, digging the soil, women could reduce their 'nerve tension' and exercise muscles that otherwise went unused in their modern lives.[110]

Reducing Instructor: "Now, boys. The first lesson—lie flat on the floor—let's go!"

Too rotund to lie flat, these men were aware that being obese was, as Ettie Rout put it, 'unbecoming'. They had a moral duty as well as a physical responsibility to pay attention to their 'Reducing Instructor'. *Auckland Star*, 19 February 1927.

Health concerns continued to be aired in magazines and newspapers between the wars.[111] Technology and other changes in the economy might mean city workers no longer had much say about their workplaces and practices, but a systematic exercise regime could give them control over their bodies. With a stronger body, and a more disciplined attitude to life, thanks to their exercise programme, physical culturists believed they were better able to meet the challenges of modern life.

Physical culture was presented as a panacea, a cure for all the problems the nation faced. In 1907 one writer claimed that:

In the future, thanks to more generally practised, more scientific, more sensible, more interesting, more truly educational exercise, we shall find a people with stronger lungs, and therefore with more endurance and power; with stronger hearts, and therefore with more courage and energy; with stronger digestion; with better eliminations of poisons, with more beauty and gracefulness, more manual skill and success, more happiness, more all-round prosperity, more capacity to inspire each other. We shall find people a step nearer the ideal of manhood and womanhood, and improving in every way from generation to generation. We shall find such scourges as heart disease, consumption, and insanity being swept away from our land.[112]

Those who taught and practised physical culture often spoke and wrote about the national benefits of regular exercise. Physical culture was seen as being especially important for children but among adults, too, there was a strong sense that the dutiful citizen was the exercising citizen. Fred Hornibrook liked to remind others that Rome and Greece had been great as long as citizens

> looked upon physical training as a duty they owed to themselves and to the State; but when the Greek games fell into disrepute and were handed over to the professional athletes, and when the Greeks became a nation of lookers-on, then Greece declined as a nation. So with every nation that has placed amusement first.[113]

Exercise was not about having fun; it was a personal and patriotic duty, especially for those who had lost control of their bodies and suffered from problems such as consumption and alcoholism.

Hornibrook was the most famous Sandowite healer of consumptives in New Zealand, praised by Sandow for this work. In the years that followed, Hornibrook continued to preach the need for tuberculosis sufferers to exercise the Sandow way. At the Avon Pine Sanatorium in Christchurch he set up a Sandow Room, fitted with dumb-bells and Sandow developers, where all the patients exercised under the strict supervision of their doctor.[114] In his many lectures on physical culture he discussed cases of men cured of consumption and asthma, thanks to the Sandow System.[115] He also wrote about the evil of consumption and the toll that it took on the nation.[116]

Hornibrook was equally adamant that alcoholism could be cured by systematic exercise. He shared Sandow's belief that if a man had already taken up physical culture, then the bodily control and respect he had gained would prevent alcohol abuse. But for those already afflicted, exercise was the cure.[117] To escape from the hold alcohol had over him, Fred Atkins took up the Sandow System. He was soon rewarded with a Sandow gold medal and the knowledge that his healthy, strong body made him a credit to his country.[118]

There was a definite eugenic flavour to many of the utterances and writings of these local physical culture advocates. Alongside groups like the Plunket Society and the Eugenics Education Society, local physical culturists worried about environmental factors leading to racial decay, and that the genetic stock was being weakened as the 'wrong sort' had more and more children. The fear of miscegenation – in particular of non-white men and women marrying into the population – was a central feature of this debate. '[T]he shadow of China' worried Premier Richard Seddon and Fred Hornibrook.[119] As Hornibrook wrote, 'if a nation is not fit to inter-marry with our people, then the presence of such aliens becomes a national menace'.[120] New Zealanders must be strong enough to fight against the numerous and fatalistic Chinese or else, Hornibrook argued, it would be a case of 'God help New Zealand'.[121] Systematic exercise, of course, could provide that strength, and thus preserve the White New Zealand policy.

This eugenic discourse was not unique to New Zealand. Nor was the belief that regular exercise offered an important antidote to racial degeneration. Sandow's books and other writings made much of the idea that his system promoted racial improvement.[122] Two of the other benefits he suggested were also welcomed in New Zealand. The first had to do with the military defence of the nation, the second with populating it.

The South African War had been a 'striking object-lesson' for many. To Fred Hornibrook, it revealed how unfit the nation's men were, and therefore how ill-prepared to fight for their country. He noted that, in ancient Greece, 'one of the greatest disgraces that could befall' a man was if he was 'physically unable to bear arms and fight for his country if needed'.[123] Hornibrook was concerned that even among the young, fewer than 40% were fighting fit. He shared with Sandow a belief that men needed to adopt physical culture so that they were ready for war.[124] The MP F. M. B. Fisher also spoke publicly on the subject. Like Hornibrook, he maintained that the solution to this woeful state of affairs was for young people to accept their 'physical responsibilities to the State', and exercise.[125]

Concerns about the poor physiques of New Zealand men continued to be aired in the years leading up the Great War. In 1909, when news got out that half the New Zealand men who applied to serve in the British navy were rejected as medically unfit, there was a public outcry.[126] Fred Hornibrook responded by holding a public meeting at his gym. 'The crux of the whole matter,' according to Hornibrook, 'lay in the fact that there was no adequate system of national physical and military training.' If men joined his gym, New Zealand would not have to endure this shame.[127]

REJECTED FOR THE FRONT !

HAVE YOU BEEN REJECTED FOR THE N.Z.
EXPEDITIONARY FORCES ?

If so, join

F. A. HORNIBROOK'S

CORRESPONDENCE CLASSES

OF

PHYSICAL CULTURE

**You can gain One Inch in Chest
Measurement in a Month.**

Many "rejects" have taken a course of training from
me and then been successful in passing the tests.

**OVER EIGHTY OF F. A HORNIBROOK'S PUPILS
ARE NOW SERVING AT THE FRONT.**

During the last 14 years hundreds of men have been
passed by means of my training for Police, Railway,
Tramway, &c., &c., who were first rejected as under
the height standard or chest-girth measurement.

F. A. HORNIBROOK,
Physical Culture Institute,
CHRISTCHURCH.

No matter where you lived, Fred Hornibrook was only a postal course away. Appearing just after the disaster at Gallipoli, this advertisement played heavily on the idea of rejection, reassuring men that even if they were too short to serve, Hornibrook could help them. *Auckland Truth*, 15 May 1915.

As Paul Baker has pointed out, medical examinations at the beginning of the Great War were 'a haphazard business'. Most volunteers, regardless of their physical fitness, passed.[128] Those who failed could turn to physical culturists like Hornibrook for a special course of instruction. Besides the claims in his own advertisements, the press reported on his success with men who had been declared medically unfit. A few weeks of instruction with Hornibrook, and one group of 70 men had successfully retaken the medical test. Thanks to the Sandow System, they would now serve their country at the front.[129]

Although it is impossible to say how many other men exercised so that they could best serve their nation as soldier-citizens, it is clear that the rhetoric of national duty was pervasive in the first 20 years of the century. The link between physical culture and military obligations was often made and it seems likely that many young men understood the connection and acted on it. Similarly, we do not know if young women took off their corsets and took up physical culture because instructors like Fred Hornibrook told them this was the best possible preparation for marriage and motherhood. But we do know that year after year, young women were told that they, too, had a duty to take control of their bodies. Men had an obligation to become fighting fit; women had a responsibility to give birth to the citizens of tomorrow.

The low birth rate was a major concern in the early twentieth century. Couples who had once had four or five children were now settling for two or three, and some were deciding not to have any children at all. As contraceptive devices became more reliable and knowledge about birth control improved, family limitation became feasible. Many contemporaries were particularly disturbed that the middle classes, those deemed to be the most suitable parents, were the very people who were limiting their families. The poor and those considered eugenically 'unfit' were not taking similar precautions. Unless something was done racial degeneration was only a generation or two away.[130]

In this climate, Hornibrook claimed that 'The subject of physical culture for women is of far greater importance than that of men, for, as the mothers and future mothers of the race, it is absolutely essential that their physical well-being should be considered'.[131] He was, no doubt, aware of the criticism claiming that the current exercise fad was 'unfitting the modern girl' for her natural role in life. Such critics worried that young women were taking exercise too far, and instead of achieving health, grace and beauty, were turning into 'loud-voiced, short-skirted, flat-heeled' young women with no interest in feminine pursuits, let alone in marriage and motherhood.[132] Like Sandow, Hornibrook rebutted such views, arguing instead that if young middle-class women exercised, they would be better prepared to fulfil their natural role in life, which was, of course, giving birth.[133] The logic behind their pro-natalist claim was simple. At present, the 'right sort' of young woman was rejecting childbirth, fearing she would not be able to withstand the pain of labour. But if she joined a gym, took off her corset and built up her muscles, she would see that there was nothing to fear. With her body no longer deformed by tight lacing, she would find it easier to breathe and exercise. Her corset and the dictates of fashion would no longer rule her life. Instead, she would be in control of her body, and thus be able to fulfil her destiny, as a wife and mother. As Dr William Henry Symes, one of the judges at a 1906 women's development competition declared, women's adoption of physical culture would 'mean the regeneration of the race'.[134]

Corsets, which could be seen as the ultimate garment of constraint, and thus particularly well suited to the era, were regarded by physical culturists as the antithesis of bodily self-control. They rejected the artificial support of bone and tight lacing in favour of women enjoying the natural support of their own muscles.[135] These muscles had to be developed, slowly, but women were reassured that this could be achieved without turning them into muscular maidens.[136] The aim was a graceful, symmetrical form, attractive to men and easily able to withstand the discomfort of childbirth, several times over.

As tight lacing was loosened, so concerns about the harmful effects of corsets faded from public debates. But the eugenic, pro-natalist agenda remained through the 1920s and 1930s. Women continued to be reminded that the nation's very survival was in their hands, and that they had to be fit for the task. Magazines and newspapers offered women exercise programmes and healthful hints, and advertisers tried to sell them products like breakfast cereal in the name of national well-being.[137] The rhetoric of bodily responsibility was ever-present.

Perhaps J. Cullington's lady friends were thinking of the future and preparing their bodies for the national service of childbirth when they joined his Sandow class. Or perhaps their goals were a little more short-term and a little less altruistic. For while physical culture fits the idea of a puritanical, 'Tight' society, marked by constraint and repression, it is also at home in a far less controlled world, where bodies are enjoyed, and where looking and being looked at is desired. Many local physical culturists seem to have revelled in reshaping and then revealing their new physiques in public. The pleasure they derived from the cult of exercise was often at odds with the idea that physical culture was a national good, a licensed leisure activity. Alongside self-denial and moral responsibility, physical culture allowed for the celebration of the body beautiful.

Like Sandow, locals knew that they could not simply flaunt their semi-clad bodies and expect to get away with it. But if they joined a gym and entered a physical development competition, then they, too, could preen and pose and enjoy the admiring looks of others. Under the guise

From the moustache to the leopard skin, this unidentified man appears to have modelled himself on Sandow. Perhaps he hoped for as many admiring glances as his hero enjoyed. F-51038-1/2, Alexander Turnbull Library, Wellington.

of fitness and national well-being, they could send photographs of their unclothed bodies to magazines, and plaster their rooms with pictures of fellow physical culturists. Given that everyone was aspiring to the Greek ideal, many of these photographs left little to the imagination. The rhetoric of health and national fitness cloaked such activities in respectability, but for some the undressing and displaying of the exercised body seems to have been the drawcard.

Celebrating the body beautiful in this way became far more acceptable after the Great War. Changes in fashion and cultural norms meant that physical culturists who were more concerned with appearance than health no longer had to pretend that they were exercising solely for the

A MODERN APOLLO.

Little indeed is left to the imagination in this
photograph of 'A Modern Apollo'. G-32886-1/2,
Alexander Turnbull Library, Wellington.

good of the nation. Advertisements for physical culture courses reflected
this shift. Whereas previously claims about improved health and national
strength had been to the fore, by the 1920s many advertisements spoke
directly to men's fears that they were unattractive to women because they
were scrawny, and to women's concerns that they were too fat to attract
the man of their dreams. Alfred Briton's 'Be a Man She'll Admire' campaign, and Dorothy Woolley's series of 'Are You Too Fat?' advertisements
are indicative of this trend.[138] Physical culture was now clearly associated
with sexual attractiveness.

Briton's advertisement was adamant that 'Women want he-men for
their husbands and sweethearts'.[139] His magazine, *HPC*, also offered men

The elderly husband, often a figure of ridicule, is seen here joining Professor Samson's gymnasium so that he can 'Be a Man' and retain the affection of his young wife. *Man Junior*, November 1937. Mitchell Library, Sydney.

" . . . and this is my little wife . . . she persuaded me to take the course"

exercises designed to turn them into the 'he-men' that women desired. Summer was an especially dangerous season for underdeveloped men. As swimming costumes became swimming trunks, and men's chests were bared for all to see, remedial action was called for. Briton offered readers advice on how to build up their bodies so that they no longer resembled 'perambulating scarecrow[s]'.[140] Asking men 'How Are Your Legs?', he reminded them that 'Shapely legs are not the prerogative of our girl-friends alone! Oh, no!'[141] If men were going to promenade along the beach, wearing the new season's swimming trunks, then their legs had to be worthy of women's attention.

Month after month, *HPC* offered men advice and specific exercise routines that would enable them to tone their torsos, enhance their beach presence and acquire the sort of body that warranted women's admiring

P. L. Judge of Nelson as The Gladiator. In the caption Briton noted that Judge had 'a physique which reminds us of the classic statuary of the early Greeks. Note the symmetrical leg development.' Judge was clearly able to enjoy admiring glances as he strolled the beaches of Golden Bay. *Health and Physical Culture*, 1 February 1936. Mitchell Library, Sydney.

glances. Hamiltonian Noel Blyth was grateful for all the help he could get. Writing to Briton, Blyth noted that many of his friends had 'rushed into a course of training as a result of hints from their girl friends'. Briton understood the pressure. He replied that 'even we men are vain – and if the girls do prefer straight back and strong arms, it's all the better for us'.[142]

There was always the fear that men would take this too far. In its first issue, *HPC* published 'The Epic of Saint Paddy', a short story about a New Zealander called Paddy Sullivan. Readers of Paddy's tale were greeted with an unusual opening: 'I don't know what Paddy Sullivan's religion was, but I know that he worshipped his sound bodily health, and no girl's curving breast had a second thought to him when it came to his own rippling biceps. He was safe within himself.'[143] At least Paddy's thoughts did not turn to other males. Narcissism was better than homosexuality. But men whose thoughts and desires were directed at other men must have found the physical culture movement a godsend. Every town now boasted a gym, where men regularly stripped down to exercise. Physique contests provided an annual highlight, as attractive, well-built men posed in their drawers, encouraging the admiring stares of others. It was now legitimate to look and marvel. Unwanted touching, though, was still prohibited. Percy Trapp began exercising the Sandow way in the 1890s. By the 1920s, as a 58-year-old, he encouraged two young boys at Auckland's Tepid Baths to join him in his quest for a strong body. Trapp told thirteen-year-old John Mander, and his ten-year-old brother, Norman, to put out their chests and build up their muscles. As John told the court, 'He seemed to want me to go in for exercise and become a big strong man.' Trapp's quest was in vain. He was sentenced to three years with hard labour for indecently assaulting the boys.[144]

For those who chose the safer route of looking but not touching, there was plenty of pleasure to be had in the handsomely illustrated books and magazines spawned by the movement. Descriptions of exercise routines, for example, were accompanied by 'how-to' shots of young, well-developed men, wearing only athletic supports, or by photographs of the latest Hollywood he-man, chest bared and muscles rippling.[145] The text of such articles was sometimes ambiguous. In his piece on toning your torso so that you made an impression on the beach, Horace Grayson noted that these exercises 'will gain a figure which, whether in street clothes or in a swim suit, will demand admiring attention'. Whose attention Grayson did not specify.[146] As with the ubiquitous references to Greek ideals, readers could pick up a homoerotic subtext if they so desired.

Usually, though, physical culture books and magazines stressed the manly, heterosexual virtues of systematic exercise. Perhaps they had to be so insistent because the 'menace of effeminacy' was a well-founded fear.[147] Tamar Garb has noted that as claims grew that modern man was becoming more feminine, so representations of bourgeois men increasingly focused on their health and physique.[148] Garb was writing about France, but the same phenomenon was apparent in New Zealand. Local weightlifter, J. R. Davis, was clear that 'The desire for strength is inherent in man'. For Davis, a man was not 'normal' if he was not strong.[149] And 'normal' men were heterosexual. But these men did not necessarily want to be strong to defend the nation, or even to be good workers, who never took ill on the job. Physical culture magazines make it clear that many men simply enjoyed the power of being strong. With broad shoulders and bulging biceps, they

Pictures such as this one of D. W. Deholm of Napier illustrated physical culture magazines and books. Described as 'Truly a wonderful example of physical culture methods', his photograph must have been truly wonderful for those who wished to gaze upon naked male bodies. *Health and Physical Culture*, 1 June 1930. Mitchell Library, Sydney.

asserted their right to be in control. Big muscles meant that you could defend yourself in a fight or bend a streetlamp if you needed a light for your cigar. The metaphorical power of the exercised body also made you a force to be reckoned with. In his 1926 annual, W. E. Withrow went so far as to suggest that 'There is no human possession that compares in importance with the powers associated with superior physical manhood. A real man is literally the work of the Divinity. He is almost omnipotent in his possibilities.'[150] A little blasphemous, perhaps, but the sales pitch worked for many men. With a toned body, nothing was impossible.

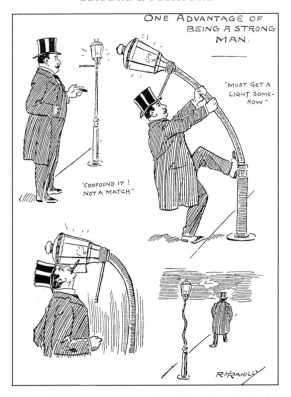

This 'advantage' of being a strong man found its way into *Sandow's Magazine* in 1906. Two years before, a very similar drawing had appeared in the French physical culture magazine, *La Culture Physique*. Even the cartoons crossed geographical boundaries as the physical culture movement swept through the Western world. *Sandow's Magazine*, 25 March 1906.

Readers of physical culture magazines could not have failed to notice that when young women wrote in for male pen pals, they were often explicit about how their new friend should look. Muriel Nicol of Pauatahanui left nothing to chance in her 1934 request. Her pen friend needed to be a 'dark-haired, handsome young man, 18–20, who is fond of boxing, wrestling, hiking, and other outdoor sports'.[151] Photographic evidence was often requested. Once the man had measured up by reshaping and revealing his body, he could be rewarded with sexual attention. Dorothy Harrison did not have to rely on the vagaries of the post or camera tricks when she went looking for a 'he-man'. She enrolled in Garnet Sims' physical culture class and was soon dating her instructor. Unfortunately Sims was already married, and their affair made national headlines when Sims became embroiled in a messy divorce suit.[152] The physical appeal of gym instructors had long been recognised. Back in 1907, *Truth* ran an item about physical culture for school girls, noting that if authorities hired 'a handsome and shapely man', the pupils would find the lessons 'more enjoyable'.[153]

Just as women like Dorothy Harrison and Muriel Nicol found the idea of a physically cultured male body much more enticing than a flabby or weak one, so many men were no longer finding languid, anaemic women attractive. Fashions were changing. To be modern, a woman had to reject the values of the previous generation. Just as she discarded last season's dresses so she had to reject old-fashioned attitudes about exercise and fitness. These new ideas were current long before Dorothy Harrison clapped eyes on Garnet Sims' mighty abdomen.[154] In the first decade of the twentieth century the popular press was full of articles encouraging young women to get into shape. Physical culturists often wrote about the need for women to exercise for the greater good of the nation, but in the mainstream press, and in women's own writings, the focus was more on personal pleasure and fun.

According to Snowy Baker, himself a he-man, physical culture was the best beautifier around. Advocating frequent physical exertion for women, he assured his readers that once they had taken up regular exercise 'all the eligible and discerning young men of [their] acquaintance' would be drawn to them. As Baker wrote, 'Could aught else be desired?'[155] A decade later, Clarence Weber, another physical culture teacher, reiterated Baker's claim:

A girl with a good figure, shapely limbs, graceful deportment and health vitality, should be far more attractive, and stand a much better chance of securing a good husband than the girl who is a slave to fashion and neglects nature's method and resorts to powdering, painting and "dolling herself up" as so many girls do nowadays.[156]

In order to be desirable, women had to reshape their bodies. This might involve reducing the amount of meat they ate, so that they could lose weight.[157] It might require particular exercises to improve 'problem areas'. Articles appeared to help women obtain graceful arms: 'Doubtless many a woman has in secret shed bitter tears over the thin, scraggy appear-

To reduce shoulders and waistline, take this exercise sixty times an hour, being careful not to drink any water before, after or during meals. Do not eat any meat, vegetables, bread, sweets or fruit. In a few weeks your waistline will be perfect, even if your spine be dislocated.

According to this satirical illustrator, women's desire for the perfect waistline motivated them to diet and exercise to extremes. The idea that women might take up physical culture for the nation's good did not figure in their bodily calculations. *New Zealand Graphic*, 21 April 1906.

ance of her arms'.[158] There were exercises to cure flabby hips, abdomens and throats,[159] and 'Beauty Exercises' to develop busts.[160] Sandow invented a piece of exercise equipment specifically for women. The Symmetrion was designed to 'produce symmetry of form' rather than turn women into Amazons. With regular use, women were assured that it would 'Remove double chins', 'Correct scraggy necks', 'Fill out salt cellars', 'Develop the bust' and 'Make the waist slim'.[161] No mention was made of strengthening women's bodies for childbirth. The Symmetrion opened the door to pleasure, not duty. Alongside the patented equipment, booklets were published telling women how they could avoid middle-aged spread and protruding abdomens.[162] Local women wrote books, sharing their secrets on

The SYMMETRION.

This Machine is **not** designed to create **muscular development, but** produce **symmetry of form.**

No woman who values a good appearance should be without this appliance. Its principle feature is that it accomplishes the improvements with a minimum of exertion.

The chart which accompanies the "Symmetrion" shows certain simple movements. They are specially arranged in groups to—

Remove double chins,	Develop the bust,
Correct scraggy necks,	Make the waist slim,
Fill out salt cellars,	Improve the hips,
Create graceful, well	Shape the Calves, and
padded shoulders,	Strengthen the ankles.

Each Machine is neatly packed in box, and contains full instructions as to use.

PRICE: 12/6

Postage, 6d. extra.

APPLY— —:—

SANDOW'S MAGAZINE (Appliances Department), 131, Temple Chambers, London, E.C.

As the text made clear, Sandow's Symmetrion was 'not designed to create muscular development, but produce symmetry of form'. Women were also reassured that 'a minimum of exertion' would achieve the desired results. Men were never let off so lightly. *Sandow's Magazine*, 27 September 1906. David Chapman Collection.

achieving good looks and long life through exercise.[163] In their diaries, women set out their own 'Beauty Physical Culture' regimes, noting the exercises they did to retain their youthful beauty.[164] And if everything went according to plan, then they became the girl admired by men like George from Masterton, and Peter of North Auckland, both of whom wrote about the beauty of the 'present-day athletic girl' with her 'energy and zest for life'.[165]

Being so attractive could be dangerous. The admiration the Georges and Peters felt for these young women could lead to unwanted attention. Luckily the fashion for fitness saw many young women become fighting fit. Some took to fencing, lunging in a graceful manner. A few climbed into the ring, and slugged it out. More sought instruction in the art of jui jitsu. Within a short time of reading about women in London learning how to throw a strongman, women in Auckland were joining Professor Potter's class for instruction.[166] Over the next 30 years, jui jitsu and self-defence were often advocated as important parts of women's exercise regime.[167]

With an exercise book on one side and a bottle of anti-fat potion on the other, this woman has yet to see the results of her efforts. *Truth*, 18 August 1927.

The pleasure women got from being shapely and attractive to men, strong and self-reliant, and able to wear the latest fashions with ease, sometimes extended to the workplace. With new bodies, and a desire to show them off to others, young women sought employment as mannequins and models.

Before the Great War, articles appeared in the local press about women in Paris and London who worked as dress models, parading in fashion showrooms and sometimes in shop windows.[168] After the war, young women in Auckland and Wellington were also aspiring to model for artists and wear the latest fashions for a living. Three young women achieved their goal in 1919, when William Cody, a shopkeeper on Wellington's Courtenay Place, employed them to display stockings. The women stood behind a velveteen curtain in the window of Cody's store, wearing the latest fashion in footwear and hosiery. Three inches above their knees the curtain ended, and their 'leg show' began. Crowds gathered on the pavement to look at the display, but 'whether the many eager eyes scanned the size and shape of the legs, or the style of stockings and shoes, or even the garters is best known to those who happened upon the scene'. The incident was reminiscent of James Young's 1902 performance in the Christchurch department store window, and indeed that event was mentioned in the court case that followed this leg show. Both window displays breached city by-laws, and in both cases the store managers appeared in court. Cody was convicted and fined £4 for causing an obstruction.[169] Whereas in the Young case the magistrate had praised the Sandow system, in Cody's case there was no higher principle for His Worship to note. Perfectly proportioned and symmetrical, these women's bodies were not being exposed in the name of health and racial fitness. Cody's leg show was a commercial proposition, pure and simple.

Stories about mannequins continued to find their way into local papers, encouraging other women to aspire to the glamorous world of modelling.[170] Some found that prospective employers had less than honourable intentions. There were many unfortunate cases where young women were promised work as models, only to find they had been duped by con men more interested in private displays of their bodies than in helping them to secure a career on the catwalk. If Aucklander Hilda Alderton had taken a course in jui jitsu then Albert Lincoln might not have assaulted her. Lincoln promised Alderton work as a model but instead attacked her when she refused to have sex with him.[171] Sometimes having a physically cultured body was not very pleasurable at all.

After Labour was elected to power in 1935, it passed the Physical Welfare and Recreation Act, which made physical culture a state-sanctioned leisure activity. Those in charge were finally seeing systematic exercise as a necessity, not a luxury.[172] It was not difficult for the new government to persuade the populace that they had a duty to get fit. Physical culture was a significant social movement, supported by many leading citizens, and it fitted early twentieth-century New Zealand society in more ways than one. While it turned the previously unhealthy into A1 subjects, capable of fulfilling their destiny as soldiers and mothers, it also allowed individuals to gain control over their bodies in a rational, systematic way. They could practise their own culture of constraint as they reshaped themselves. But constraint did not sit well with everyone. For the men who enjoyed looking and being looked at during Fred Hornibrook's physique contests, and the women who hoped their beautiful bodies would land them a husband or a modelling job, pleasure and personal gain were more attractive motives than national fitness and self-control. They enjoyed the consumerism of physical culture: the new outfits, the equipment, the books and magazines. They relished the sexual energy that could come with exercise and the ways others admired their revealed bodies. They delighted in the power of their new bodies, their literal and figurative strength. While some applauded national health and well-being, others celebrated their bodies beautiful.

New Zealand in these years was not a one-dimensional society, not just a place of constraint and moral harmony. People were open to messages and experiences of both leisure and pleasure. They might dress up their revealed bodies with classical references, or they might simply enjoy flaunting their reshaped bodies. Fred Hornibrook's physique contests did both. As his male pupils stood in the Christchurch Art Gallery, beside the statues of the ancient world, they took their strength and legitimacy from past civilisations. Women were about to do something very similar.

Three **Beautiful Bodies**[1]

As Sandow stood centre stage, flexing his muscles and posing for the pleasure of his audience, he won over many female fans. The women of New Zealand took pleasure in looking at his beautiful body. Sometimes their gazes were direct: in the anonymity of the darkened theatre, they could admire his manly muscles and imagine that he was performing just for them. Sometimes they stole a peek: '[M]any admiring surreptitious female glances' were said to be cast at the statue of Sandow 'adorning' a Wellington shop window.[2] After he left the country, women could still enjoy his body. They bought photographs of him, subscribed to his magazine and purchased his illustrated books. As more local men adopted the Sandow System and entered physical development competitions, women provided an appreciative audience. They may not have been the judges of the men's competitions – often they were not even allowed to see the competitions taking place – but they could take pleasure in the results.

Visitors who disrobed also continued to attract a lot of female attention. Women 'rushed the gate' to see a group of 'Three-quarter-naked' Fijian firewalkers perform in Christchurch in 1907.[3] And some, it seems, were not content just to look admiringly at these 'dusky Don Juans from across the water'. *Truth*, which did not approve of such miscegenation, claimed that several part-Fijian babies were born nine months after the show.[4] Although a few Christchurch women had done more than just gaze upon desirable, exotic men, most were content to accept domestic offerings. But, as Sandow reminded his male readers, if men expected their wives to remain trim and good-looking, women should be able to expect the same. Husbands who acquired 'bay-window waistcoat[s]' and lost their 'pretty curly locks' might also lose their wives' affections.[5]

Whether women viewed men's reshaped and revealed bodies as instructive leisure or pure pleasure, the physical culture movement contained within it a seed for social change, though that seed was rarely allowed to germinate. Sandow's suggestion that men had a duty to maintain themselves 'in order to keep their wives fascinated' was predicated on the understanding that women were already working hard to maintain their looks and figures. Women were still the subject of male looks and comments. Sandow was forthright in his views about women exercising so that they were prepared for their roles as wives and mothers, but he also preached that women needed to attain and retain physical perfection for more aesthetic reasons. *Sandow's Magazine* published many articles on the importance of women looking after their skin, since good skin care aided health and beauty.[6] Exercises were offered so that modern women could achieve the 'column-like throats of the Greek statues'.[7] The goal was for women to become naturally beautiful, rather than relying on artificial assistance. In particular, women were encouraged to strengthen their bodies so that they no longer relied on corsets to produce curves. Like the Venus de Milo, the modern woman's muscles should give her perfect form.

Sandow maintained that if he could achieve the beauty and symmetry of Adonis, then his female followers should aspire to become living Venus de Milos. For Sandow and many fellow commentators, the Venus de Milo was 'The absolute type of feminine beauty' and 'The embodiment of physical development'.[8] She was female perfection, even though – or perhaps because – so much of the statue was missing.[9] In their minds she was complete and with her broad shoulders and large waist they knew that she belonged in a gymnasium rather than a darkened drawing room. Modern woman's body should likewise celebrate her health and vigour rather than artificial styles and standards.[10] Sandow wanted every girls' schoolroom to contain statues of the Venus de Milo and other figures from ancient Greece, so that young women had role models to aspire to.[11] Beauty, Sandow maintained, required 'perfection of face' *and* 'perfection of figure'.[12] The Venus de Milo had both, with the added bonus that her shapely figure was revealed for all to see: she was only partially clad. Sandow did not go so far as to suggest that women should go around with only a little diaphanous drapery to protect their modesty, but he and other like-minded men encouraged women to display their reshaped bodies in public. The male gaze was being reasserted. Women were there to be looked at.[13]

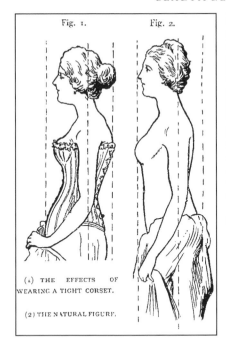

LEFT Illustrating the evil effects of corset-wearing, and the positive outcomes of going free, the picture of 'natural' beauty (Fig. 2) bears a striking resemblance to Sandow's ideal woman, the Venus de Milo (with arms added). *Sandow's Magazine*, June 1900. RIGHT For many women, chocolates, excellent or not, prevented them from achieving the ideal body, but the makers of Queen Anne chocolates nonetheless allied their product with that other symbol of perfection, the Venus de Milo. *Truth*, 30 June 1937.

As muscles and strength were to men, so, increasingly, was beauty of face and form to women. Both were visible signs of the superiority of the racial stock.[14] With strong men and beautiful women, New Zealand no longer had to worry about population decline and degeneration. But in order for the beauty of women's face and form to be recognised and revealed, other cultural shifts had to take place. At the beginning of the twentieth century, women posing as the Venus de Milo, or revealing as much of their bodies as the statue did, were found on pornographic post-cards or on the stage.[15] Decent, respectable women did not parade publicly in a half-dressed state.[16] Plans to hold a physical development competition for women at the 1907 Christchurch Exhibition were cancelled after

ENDURING BEAUTY

The classic beauty of Westcraft Handbags comes of the use, by expert designers, of the very best materials. Westcraft's wartime policy is to insist that all materials comply with pre-war standards. You may find it a little difficult to secure a Westcraft Handbag—stocks are short—but there are still a limited number of Westcraft guaranteed Handbags available.

Westcraft Handbags SINCE 1904

The Venus de Milo did not have arms, and could not hold a handbag, but Westcraft still used this embodied ideal of femininity to hawk their wares. The image was as enduring as they claimed their handbags were. *Truth*, 21 June 1944.

howls of protest. Yet shortly after the Christchurch fiasco local women were entering beauty contests, in the full knowledge that the general public, male and female, was going to judge them on their looks alone. Their bodies and their faces would be scrutinised, commented upon and ranked, in the same way that audiences in galleries viewed paintings and sculptures. What had once been illicit pleasure – looking at indecent post-cards and chorus girls' legs – was becoming a common, even respectable, leisure activity. Sandow's health message helped this process along, as did the predilection for invoking ancient precedents whenever women disrobed in public. If the Greeks had done it, modern New Zealanders could claim that it was artistic and civilised, not crude and brutish.

In this changing climate, beauty contests became an acceptable form of entertainment. At first women posed in photographic competitions, and were judged by experts, but soon they were parading on stages, performing before audiences in much the way that Sandow had done, though beauty rather than strength determined who won. By 1926 beauty pageants were so mainstream that the first Miss New Zealand competition was held. The perfect female form had become a newly repackaged commodity and a form of leisure. In one short generation people had experienced a seismic shift in their everyday attitudes to displaying women's bodies.

A passing reference to ancient statues, and Sandow's body was clothed in respectability. A hint that physical improvement and display benefited the 'race', and no questions were asked. If it was good enough for Sandow, it was good enough for women. If classical associations could be conjured up, and healthful motives suggested, then women's bodies could be revealed, off and on stage, for the leisure and pleasure of others. But if there was no attempt to dress up the display with references to antiquity or racial improvement, then the morality of the performance was questioned.

Most public displays of naked, or almost naked women, played by these rules. The women posed in the manner of works of high culture, so that the purveyors of these pictures could, and did, argue that there was nothing indecent about the display. If the rules were not obeyed, the public, and the press, was indignant. When Frank Sales of Christchurch ignored the convention, he was labelled a 'prurient picture post-card codger'. In 1906 he encouraged three local women to pose for him and the resulting postcards were said to be 'simply horrible and outraged decency in every particular'. For creating such 'filthy, disgusting . . . cards', Sales was sentenced to six months' imprisonment.[17] But it would be a mistake to read the Sales case as typical. Naturally, there were groups in society who were horrified by any display of bodily flesh. Organisations such as the Young Women's Christian Association, or the 'Old Women's Cleansing ASSociation' as some preferred to call them, were adamant that bodies were meant to be covered up.[18] Even statues came in for a fair amount of criticism. A Sydneysider joked that the statue of the Venus de Milo would be put in woolen underwear before it was displayed at the Christchurch Exhibition.[19] Thirty years later the Women's Christian Temperance Union (WCTU) and the YMCA were incensed when Richard Gross's statue of a naked male athlete was erected at the entrance to Auckland's Domain.[20] But plenty of other New Zealanders were selling, buying and looking at bodily displays, and were not disgusted by what they saw.[21]

The law supposedly protected the public from unwanted displays of naked bodies. The Offensive Publications Act of 1892, its amended form in 1905 and the 1910 Indecent Publications Act, could be held up as evidence of a local 'crusade for moral harmony', a desire by puritanical New Zealanders to create a 'Tight' society, where bodies were never on display.[22] The 1892 law stated that it was an offence to publish anything 'intended to have an indecent, immoral or obscene effect'. The existence of such a law indicated, of course, that such material was in circulation. By 1905 the 'Tight' society clamped down on a loophole in the original act. Booksellers had been claiming they did not know that the material they sold was indecent, immoral or obscene. This was no longer an adequate defence. But the mere presence of these laws on the statute books does not mean that the judiciary or the general public behaved as if they belonged to a society of puritans. Indeed, there is plenty of evidence to the contrary.

In the first three decades of the twentieth century numerous charges were laid against booksellers who displayed and sold 'indecent' postcards and magazines containing pictures of naked women. Sometimes the police secured a prosecution and the bookseller was fined,[23] but often the case was dismissed, the magistrate convinced that the pictures were artistic rather than indecent. Just as Sandow managed to reveal his body but retain his respectability, so these booksellers argued that their photographs were aesthetically pleasing and uplifting rather than lewd and vulgar. The key to their successful defence was that the women posed in classical attitudes, imitating great works of art. Venus, after all, was a classical figure, and 'The classical style was viewed as grand and asexual' rather than sensual.[24] Some ran this line for years. A tailor in Napier displayed pictures of naked women in his Tennyson Street shop window for over a decade, arguing that these were works of art.[25] When the police disagreed with such artistic judgements, they often faced resistance from the judiciary. Despite the efforts of the YMCA and the police, for example, Magistrate Kettle found that the picture 'The Bath of Psyche' was not indecent.[26] Lord Leighton's painting, inspired by the statue of Venus Kalipigge at Naples, was saved by its high culture pedigree. The case against Lindsay Bernard Hall's picture, 'Sleep', reproduced in the magazine, *Lone Hand*, was also dismissed.[27] Magistrate Riddell did not find that Hall's illustration of a nude girl reclining caused offence, much to the delight of the magazine's New Zealand distributors and its Australian publishers. The *Lone Hand*, a monthly magazine in the same stable as Sydney's *Bulletin*, was designed to offer Australasians a serious and challenging literary magazine. (One of its early short story competitions was won by Dulcie Deamer of

Featherston, a physical culturist who later also embraced the nudist movement.)[28] It also prided itself on its role as a disseminator of art.[29] Not surprisingly, then, its publishers declared that the nude in art was 'not only not impure, but . . . a force for purity and cleanliness'. Noting that only the 'filthy-minded' could find such a work of art 'objectionable', they anticipated the arguments nudists would make to defend their leisure pursuit a couple of decades later.[30]

Alongside the claim that the pictures and postcards they sold merely reproduced great works of art, booksellers also reminded the public that living displays of the female body had recently been seen on stage, and had not been ruled indecent. In the early 1900s New Zealand audiences enjoyed performances of living statuary: men and women on stage, imitating famous sculptures. These performers took posing to a new level. Unlike Sandow, they did not move a muscle. They painted their bodies to resemble plaster and wore a minimum of clothing. Either alone, or in troupes, they recreated famous statues and scenes to the amazement of the crowds who paid to see them. This was an international craze: *Sandow's Magazine* carried several stories about groups like the Seldoms, who posed on the London stage as 'The Wrestlers' and 'Samson and Delilah'.[31] For Sandow, living statues were a natural and desirable spin-off of physical culture. If people exercised, developed muscles and understood how to control their bodies, then displaying their bodily achievement was to be encouraged. Just as many young men converted to physical culture after seeing his performances, so young women and men who saw the Seldoms 'must be awakened to the advisability of healthy habits and desires'. Only 'utterly degenerate mortal[s]' with 'diseased mind[s]' could find such bodily displays less than uplifting.[32]

Before the Seldoms stormed the London stage, a young woman known as La Milo attracted Sandow's attention. She, too, posed in the manner of famous statues, but alone. Sandow was intrigued by her, and in 1906 made her a cover girl on his magazine.[33] New Zealand subscribers to *Sandow's Magazine*, though, might well have seen La Milo before she achieved international pin-up status. In 1905, after a successful tour of Australia, Melburnian Pansy Montague crossed the Tasman and entertained full houses throughout New Zealand. Known in the Antipodes as the Modern Milo, the 21-year-old covered her body with white enamel paint, added a little drapery for effect and stood on a pedestal, adopting the poses of famous Greek and Roman statues. Her *poses plastique* were a huge success. Australasians were able to enjoy this new performer and

Pansy Montague poses as Hebe, the goddess of forgiveness and youth, daughter of
Zeus and Hera. As Hebe, Pansy Montague was a fine specimen of modern youth,
exhibiting the corporeal control that was cherished in the early twentieth century.
Sandow's Magazine, 3 May 1906. David Chapman Collection.

performance before London theatregoers, but as with so many aspects of
their leisure, they were participating in an international trend.

It has become common in New Zealand history to portray Freda Stark,
the Second World War dancer who entertained servicemen wearing little
more than a coat of paint, as a novel and risqué performer, ahead of her
time.[34] But the Modern Milo was performing to crowded, mixed houses,
night after night, before Stark was born. As with Sandow's tour a couple
of years before, Montague's promoters had to reassure the public that this
bodily display was tasteful and refined, though at the same time pleasurable. Advertisements noted that she performed with 'delicacy and taste',

representing the figures of the Venus de Milo, Sappho, Hebe, Diana and Psyche in a 'chaste and classic style' designed to charm and educate her audience. This was rational recreation, a night of leisure and instruction. The advertisements also claimed that, during her show, 'The Female Form is displayed in all its essential detail'. If the prospective audience was unsure what this meant, the publicity noted that 'Women will Wonder, Men Must Admire'.[35] Women, including members of local physical culture classes, did wonder, and both sexes admired Montague's body and skill.[36] At one Christchurch performance alone 2000 people were said to have been turned away.[37]

The Modern Milo was held up as the perfect embodiment of womanhood. Like Belle Verne, who toured New Zealand a decade later, she was '[t]he hundred per cent eugenic girl'.[38] Montague was not muscle-bound; there were no 'abnormal sinews' on show here.[39] As Sandow insisted, modern women could achieve classical perfection without surrendering their natural beauty. Montague's measurements were given to emphasise her symmetry.[40] The promoters could not resist claiming that she 'sent the audiences crazy over her curves', but at the same time they knew that they had to play up the classical references.[41] No matter how fair and clear her skin was, nor how audacious her posing, artistic merit had to be stressed if the show was to go on.

Other women posed as living statues after Montague, but in the early twentieth century it was the Modern Milo who captured the public's imagination.[42] After her New Zealand tour she did not immediately fade from their gaze. The local press reported on her success at the London Pavilion, and on her growing international reputation.[43] There was the unfortunate incident in 1907, when a man infatuated with her took prussic acid in a tube station lavatory. He committed suicide wearing a false red beard, his disguise when he went to watch La Milo perform.[44] When she appeared as Lady Godiva in a procession at Coventry, New Zealanders first read about it, and then were able to see a film version of the event.[45] The Modern Milo's name and stage show was also invoked in a court case the year after her New Zealand tour. How, the defence lawyer argued, could his client be prosecuted for selling indecent pictures, when a young woman had performed live on stage, coated in paint and little else, and no one had charged her with indecency?[46] If her show could be held up as an artistic triumph, then so could the life studies his client sold.

By 1913 the press was asking where the 'Milonairess' had disappeared to.[47] She was not yet 30, but Pansy Montague's best days were behind her.

In some respects, however, she was lucky to have made a career for herself through living statuary. Although what she did was still daring in 1913, it was not very long before ordinary women on the street would be encouraged to pose on stage in the name of beauty. Wearing little more than the Modern Milo had, these women would also aspire to measure up against the Venus de Milo. The age of the modern beauty contest was about to dawn.

New Zealand women had been exposed to the idea of a beauty contest before Pansy Montague took to the stage. Around the time that Sandow's New Zealand tour came to an end, a 'Persevering Girl' wrote to his magazine, suggesting that he hold a competition for women.[48] For several years Sandow had been running physique contests for men, and even for babies and children. Apart from 'The Great Competition' held in September 1901 at London's Albert Hall, and judged by the artist Sir Charles Lawes and the writer Sir Arthur Conan Doyle, these competitions were based on people sending in photographs of themselves and readers using a coupon in the magazine to vote for the best-developed body.[49] Men tended to wear trunks or athletic supports when photographed, but Sandow encouraged parents to send in pictures of their babies 'with as little clothing [on] as possible', and photographs of children 'nude to the waist'.[50] The question of what women should wear for such a competition perplexed Sandow. He asked readers for advice, and many wrote in, offering suggestions.[51]

In May 1903 Sandow announced that, in response to public pressure, he would hold a 'Competition for Ladies', open to all women in the British Empire. As for other competitions run through his magazine, women were to send in their photographs and readers would judge who had the 'most symmetrical development'. A prize of 1 guinea would be awarded to the woman with the most votes at the end of each month. Unlike his other competitions, though, Sandow did not dictate what these contestants had to wear. The previous month, when the idea of such a contest was discussed in the ladies' pages of the magazine, Sandow noted that 'The chief difficulty seems to be the most suitable costumes for would-be competitors to be photographed in. On this opinions differ considerably, some suggesting bathing costume, others evening dress, and so on, but that is a matter which will have to be dealt with later.'[52] By May he had decided not to make a decision: 'The question of costume for the lady competitors, which has brought in so much correspondence,

I must leave to the choice of the ladies who, no doubt, will discover the most satisfactory costume for the purpose'.[53]

Sandow had hoped that women would flood his office with their photographs immediately, but in the June issue he had to admit that although a 'few' had been sent in, more were required. At this stage he was prepared to make excuses, suggesting that the earlier than usual printing deadline for the magazine meant that women had 'scarcely had time' to forward their photographs. He also reassured women that they could choose what to wear, so long as the outfit gave readers 'a fair idea' of their physical development.[54] By the following month the excuses had run out. Sandow regretted to announce that women had not been forthcoming with photographs, and that he was 'compelled to withdraw the Competition'.[55] One 'lady reader' wrote in to say that women were enthusiastic about the competition, but they knew that they fell short of Sandow's ideal of female beauty. She suggested that in a few years all that might be different, as women became more accustomed both to physical culture and to showing off their bodies in public.[56] Sandow also remained hopeful, noting that he would revive the idea at a later stage.[57] His faith was misplaced. Although *Sandow's Magazine* reported on several other beauty pageants, including contests in Leeds and New York, it never again tried to run a competition for women.[58]

Sandow remained convinced that competitions, run along 'proper lines', were worthwhile, but he worried about the escalating fashion for holding physique and beauty contests for women. Most of the promoters of such competitions, he believed, were more interested in commercial gain and creating a spectacle than they were in encouraging women to aspire to a healthier and naturally beautiful life.[59] This might seem a little rich, coming from a man who printed endless photographs of the Venus de Milo in his magazine, had invited women to send him their photographs so that they could be judged by the general public and who lauded the craze for living statues. But, as Sandow presented it, he was on a quest to improve women's health and the empire's well-being, not make money or exploit his female readers.

Sandow's proposed 'Competition for Ladies', and other quests, such as those held in New York by Bernarr Macfadden, were nascent beauty contests.[60] The physical attractiveness of the competitors was obviously important. Only pretty girls could win. But devotion to physical culture also counted: physique mattered as much as face. And it was not simply that these women had bodies that pleased the male eye. The questions

they were asked about their lifestyle, particularly whether they wore corsets, what sorts of exercises they did and what their diet was like, made
it plain that *how* they had achieved their perfect form was crucial. By the
time beauty contests arrived in New Zealand such questions were still
being asked, but commercial considerations soon rivalled physical culture concerns.

The first local beauty contest for which I have discovered plans
was associated with the New Zealand International Exhibition held in
Christchurch over the summer months of 1906-07. This was the same
exhibition where the Fijian firewalkers performed and the suggestion was
made that a statue of the Venus de Milo would have to be clothed. Perhaps
there were earlier contests. There was certainly a lot of interest in the
early 1900s in specifying the measurements of the perfect female figure.[61]
Stories of overseas beauty competitions were also being regularly reported
in the local press.[62] New Zealanders were well aware of this international
leisure development. In 1903 H. J. Priestley, a member of the *Graphic*'s
'club' for girls, wrote an amusing story for the magazine about a beauty
competition. Lizzie Bryant and 'Baldy' Grubb were selected as Waihora's
Queen of Beauty and handsomest man, and won prizes for their efforts.
In the tradition of all good fairy tales, Waihora's Venus and Hercules married and lived happily ever after.[63] Locals were also familiar with wom-
en's bodies being judged in physical culture competitions, since contests
for women had been held within the confines of local gymnasia. But now
something quite different was proposed.

On Tuesday 12 March 1907, the good citizens of Christchurch woke
to find a new event being advertised at the International Exhibition.[64] As
part of the 'Wonderland' entertainment programme, patrons were promised that on 22 March a 'Beauty Show and Physical Culture Competition'
would be held.[65] On a specially raised platform, 'So that Ten Thousand
Persons Can See in Comfort', men and women would be judged by
experts to see who had the 'Best Physical Development'. The women who
entered were informed that, if they wished, they could wear a mask in
order to retain their anonymity.[66] This was to be a contest about bodily
development, rather than facial attractiveness. Its organiser envisaged
'Sandow girls' standing on stage, posing in draped costumes much as the
Modern Milo had. Beauty of form, rather than 'prettiness of feature' was
the focus, so the faces of the women did not matter. What counted was
showing how everybody could develop their physique, and thus improve
the nation's racial fitness.[67]

Two other competitions for women were also announced. The first was for the 'Best Shaped Arm and Shoulder' and the 'Neatest Foot and Ankle (bare)'. The women would stand behind a curtain, and thrust their arms through a slit in the curtain. The curtain would fall short of the ground, so that the women's feet and ankles, but nothing else, would be revealed. Such a contest departed from the norms of a physical culture competition. No equivalent for men was suggested. In the second competition the audience would be invited to vote for the 'Prettiest Girl in Christchurch'. This was a beauty contest, pure and simple.

The announcement provoked outrage among some sections of Christchurch society. The local branch of the WCTU carried a unanimous resolution strongly protesting against 'The proposed beauty show':

> While in full accord with every legitimate effort to promote physical culture among both men and women, the Union considers the proposed public exhibition of women, as set forth in the advertisement, will neither conduce to the encouragement of physical development nor to the modesty of our young people.

The idea that women physical culturists would display themselves in public, even with the aid of a mask, was seen as undesirable, while the 'prettiest girl' contest was simply 'vulgar'.[68] J. C. Martin agreed: such contests would 'appeal to the lowest instincts of the mob'.[69] Newspaper editors noted that the proposed arm and ankle displays 'cannot by any stretch of imagination be regarded as a demonstration of the benefits of physical culture'.[70] The contest was merely designed to make money for its organisers by commodifying women's bodies.

Others defended the event. The most vocal supporter of the entire competition, at least during the initial period, was George Munro, the general manager of the exhibition. He pointed out that the entertainment at the exhibition was designed to appeal to a wide section of the community, rather than just pander to the interest of groups like the YMCA and WCTU. He also ran the line that the contest would have an educative value, as the audience gazed upon exercised bodies.[71] Rather more tongue-in-cheek was the suggestion of 'The Whole Hog or None' that since the contest was about celebrating the human form divine, the beauty show should be conducted 'wholly in a state of nature'.[72] Although this was an outrageous suggestion in 1907, by the early 1950s nudists in New Zealand, like their overseas counterparts, were holding nude beauty contests at their annual

TWO SIDES OF THE CURTAIN: A NEW BEAUTY SHOW.

Although such a contest was not permitted in Christchurch, readers of the
local press were able to look at photographs of ankle contests held overseas.
The excitement of the event did not make for a very clear photograph, but in
the top half of the picture happy contestants are seen safely behind the curtain,
while in the bottom half their stockinged feet are displayed for their public.
Canterbury Times, 10 November 1909. Christchurch City Libraries.

rallies. Kathleen from New Plymouth, the first Queen of the Nudists, was
judged on 'her all-over tan, general good health and appearance'. In 1907,
though, suntans were not yet in fashion.[73]

The vocal minority who opposed the beauty contest won the day. The
organisers were forced to abandon their plans for both the 'prettiest girl'
contest and the arm and ankle competition. The exhibition's managers
decreed that arm and ankle displays were not standard in physical culture
contests, so had no place in the Christchurch show. Ironically, a couple
of years later a similar contest in England was not only reported in the
local press, but also illustrated with a blurry photograph of the proceed-

ings.[74] Although the physical culture competition was allowed to proceed, it, too, was shrouded in controversy. The contest's organisers named several prominent local artists as the judges for the competition, only to have them claim that they had not agreed to perform this role.[75]

Those behind the contest tried to make the best of an increasingly bad situation. They offered a half-guinea prize for the cleverest answer to the question 'Why Didn't the Beauty Show?'[76] But the Wonderland experience they offered was less than magical. The show they managed to put on was proclaimed in the press to have been a failure and a farce. Punters who had not been following the controversy in the newspapers were especially disappointed. They paid an extra sixpence so that they could get close to the stage, all the better to see the arms and ankles of Christchurch's finest, only to learn, too late, that no hosiery would be on show. Instead, they saw men 'exhibit[ing] themselves in well-known Sandowesque poses', and one woman posing on a pedestal. The organisers had had to engage her specially for the evening; no local women were willing to risk their reputations by taking to the stage.[77]

The Christchurch contest had become a joke. The exhibition's own magazine included a cartoon of manager Munro measuring the calf of a muscular woman, an entrant in the aborted contest. It also suggested that if a men's beauty contest was held, Munro would win for 'prettiest nose', while other prominent men would scoop the prizes for 'best leg', 'smallest waist', 'finest moustache' and 'prettiest walk'.[78] Yet within a few months of the Christchurch débâcle, young women were being urged to enter the Australasian 'leg' of an international beauty contest. Organised by the *Chicago Tribune*, this beauty contest also involved women throughout the United States and England.[79]

'The World's Beauty Challenge', as it was known, was administered in Australasia by the *Lone Hand*. Its beauty contest was open to all women over the age of sixteen, except actresses and professional models.[80] Women had to be nominated on the official entry form, found in the magazine, and had to send in a recent photograph. If they wished, they could also send in their 'particulars': age, height, weight, waist and bust measurement, glove and shoe size, colour of hair and eyes, and details of their complexion. If they chose, they could withhold this information until asked for it at a later date. Either way, they were reassured that their particulars would not be published without their specific consent. The entry form made it clear that single and married women could enter, and that in each state of Australia, and in the 'Dominion of Maoriland' (as the *Bulletin* and the

From the exhibition's own magazine, this cartoon has fun at the expense
of general manager George Munro while also questioning whether beefy
or beautiful women would enter the proposed Christchurch contest.
Exhibition Sketcher, 23 March 1907. Canterbury Museum, Christchurch.

Lone Hand liked to call New Zealand), a board of judges would make the
final selection. The judging panels would be composed of five 'experts'.
Alongside a journalist, the judges would be 'a prominent gentlewoman',
'a doctor of repute', 'an artist of repute' and a 'physical culture expert'.
The propriety of the contest was being stressed. This was not going to be a
tawdry affair.[81]

Having announced the contest, the magazine's team sat back, waiting
for the photographs to flood in. But as Sandow had found a few years earlier, they discovered that women were reluctant to participate. In December
the magazine offered the same excuse Sandow had used: women had not
yet had a chance to send in their entry forms. They had received only a 'few'
photographs, but unlike Sandow they published these, along with more
information about the contest, in the hope of encouraging other women
to enter.[82] Readers learned, for the first time, that the winner of the contest
would not receive any monetary prize, since women were entering 'for the

good reputation of Australia' (they forgot to mention the Dominion of Maoriland).[83] Contestants were reassured, though, that the winner would receive an all-expenses paid trip for herself and a chaperon to the world beauty final, to be held in either Europe or the United States.

By February women were still being urged to send in their photographs, with the added incentive that the contest would close on 31 March.[84] Although women from Tasmania, South Australia and 'Westralia' sent in few photographs, the women of 'Maoriland' were more forthcoming. Kathleen McCarthy of Paeroa, Edna Hayes of Gisborne and Mary Yates of Palmerston North had their photographs reproduced in the pages of the *Lone Hand* as readers waited for the judges to decide.[85] They were not to be rushed. It took until October 1908 for the decisions in Victoria and New South Wales to come through, and it was February 1909 before readers learned the names of the winners in Queensland and New Zealand, and found out who the supreme winner was.[86]

The *Lone Hand* claimed the expectation had always been that the New Zealand finalist would win, but Baby Mowat of Blenheim, judged by the panel of experts to be the most beautiful of the New Zealand entrants, did not go on to claim the overall prize. That honour went to the Victorian winner, Alice Buckridge. Both women had indeed been judged by a panel of experts. The New Zealand judges included physical culture expert Royd Garlick, and the portrait artist, H. Linley Richardson.[87] The Victorian panel relied on beauty advice from Helena Rubinstein and the physical culture expertise of Clarence Weber. They decided that 21-year-old Alice Buckridge was the Venus of the South Seas. A statuesque, brown-haired natural beauty, she never used cosmetics, did not touch alcohol and enjoyed exercise. She played tennis, went roller-skating, walked for miles and worked dumb-bells at the local gymnasium. Although she claimed she was not a 'Sandow girl', she epitomised all that Sandow and his followers preached: a balanced lifestyle with a healthy dose of exercise.[88]

There was, not surprisingly, a commercial aspect to the *Lone Hand*'s contest. Entrants had to fill in a form found only in the magazine; the whole affair was spun out over sixteen months. The publishers surely hoped that it would boost circulation. But although the *Lone Hand* published the photographs of many of the entrants, it did not trust the general public to judge the competition. This was not a popularity contest. Their expert judges arrived at a rigorous, scientific decision, based on comparing measurements. An aesthetic judgement was also being made, but by an expert artist, who could recognise classical features, rather than by people who just chose a pretty face. In this regard, the *Lone Hand* contest was on the cusp. It was more than a physical development contest, where a woman could wear a mask and still win, but it was not quite a fully fledged beauty contest, where an attractive face and a shapely body would win, regardless of how the woman had achieved her curves. Such contests, though, were not far off.

The *Lone Hand* had not long announced its winner in 'The World's Beauty Challenge' when a new type of beauty contest appeared in New Zealand. In association with Pathé Pictures theatres throughout the country began to hold photographic beauty contests.[89] It was 1909 and going to the movies was becoming an increasingly popular leisure pursuit.[90] To make it even more popular, audiences were lured not only by the promise of the excitement of *The Mohawk's Revenge*, the exotic appeal of *Zambesi Falls* and the charm of *The Little Flower Seller*, but also by the power of the vote.[91] Every night, alongside Pathé's latest offering of short films, they would see pictures of pretty local girls on the big screen. During the week-long season, the audience would vote for the prettiest, and at the end of the week the girl with the most votes would win a 'valuable' prize, and have her photograph sent to the English illustrated newspapers to show 'Types of New Zealand beauty'.[92] The final tally was not a complete surprise. During the week the theatre's management published the running results for the six leading candidates in the daily press and full results were available daily at a local shop.

These contests were modelled on beauty competitions held in English theatres but there was a New Zealand twist to the proceedings. In England, competitors were judged in the flesh. In New Zealand, the movie distributors paid for women's photographs to be taken, and threw these up on the big screen, with a number in the corner so that the competitors retained their anonymity.[93]

In Christchurch, two years after the International Exhibition beauty contest had had to be abandoned, 64 young women put themselves forward to be judged 'Prettiest Girl'.[94] On the first night alone, over 1000 votes were cast and by the final night the Theatre Royal's manager was so pleased with the success of the competition that he broke into verse:

> Where are you going, my pretty maid?
> To see how I look, kind sir, she said!
> May I come with you, my pretty maid?
> Yes, if you'll vote for me, sir! she said.[95]

By 1911, photographic beauty contests at movie theatres had become commonplace. Here a group of Auckland women pose for the camera, their faces soon to be projected onto the big screen downtown. *Auckland Weekly News Illustrations*, 6 April 1911. Hocken Library, Uare Taoka o Hakena, University of Otago, Dunedin

In the end, 'Lady Competitor No. 8' was triumphant, with 900 votes, closely followed by contestant number 52, who secured 890 votes.[96] The contest was a huge success, with the management declaring that they would soon also hold a 'Baby Beauty Competition'.[97]

These competitions, and others held by picture companies in the following years, did not generate the hue and cry that had surrounded the proposed Exhibition contest. No doubt showing anonymous photographs of the women, rather than expecting the competitors to parade on the stage, helped to quell concerns about threats to female modesty. The appeal of cinema, the new leisure technology, was also part of the attraction. The only concern such contests seemed to raise was one of national pride. During a 1910 contest, 'A New Zealander' suggested that the local competitors were of 'a very indifferent type of beauty' and worried that when the photographs of the winners were sent to the English papers, they would present 'a very poor advertisement for New Zealand beauty'.[98] Pretty local girls were now being encouraged to submit their photographs for scrutiny in the name of civic and national pride.

Many women entered these photographic competitions, and most retained their anonymity. The identity of Christchurch's winning 'Lady Competitor No. 8' was not revealed, unlike her Auckland counterpart,

'Lady Competitor No. 21', usually known as Bessie Foy of Upper Queen Street.[99] 'Lady Competitor No. 8' was probably Ivy Schilling, a music hall star from Australia who happened to be performing in Christchurch at the time of the contest. A couple of years later, in an advertisement for Rexona, 'The Rapid Healer', Schilling, who had also gone on to win West's Pictures Surf Sirens' Competition in Australia, claimed that she had won a beauty contest in Christchurch. Like Bessie Foy, she had received a 'valuable' gold watch and chain.[100]

Ivy Schilling was a very athletic young woman, noted for both her acrobatic dancing and her surfing prowess. Her figure was said to be 'perfect', a 'model of athletic symmetry and grace'.[101] Yet she was advertising a skin cream, rather than a piece of exercise equipment. Lizette Parkes, another 'Australasian favourite' on the stage, won two beauty contests in New Zealand, and a contract to endorse Dr Sheldon's New Discovery for Coughs and Colds.[102] Millicent Mahy, winner of 'The Venus Competition', also provided a testimonial for Rexona, in this case for Rexona Skin and Facial soap.[103] A few years before these young women would have been interviewed about their diet and exercise regimes, and held up as the embodiment of what systematic physical culture programmes could achieve. But by the outbreak of the Great War they were advertising beauty potions. Their clear complexions were assumed to come from a bottle rather than from exercising in the fresh air. Their curves were supposedly natural, with no assumption that nature needed a helping hand in the form of a Symmetrion or dumb-bells. The hand of Sandow was fast losing its grip on female beauty contests.

Beauty helped New Zealand to fight the Great War, as young – and not so young – women entered patriotic Queen Carnival contests and raised hundreds of thousands of pounds for the war effort. Such competitions had more in common with charity fundraisers than with the movie contests. Although the community contests were a huge success, there was still room for more commercial competitions and in 1916 the *Lone Hand* announced that it was going to hold another Australasian quest. This time, though, there was no need for physical culture experts and artists of repute. Readers were entrusted with the task of voting for the most beautiful girl. In order to vote, though, they had to fill in the coupon in each month's issue.[104] This competition was clearly designed to boost the *Lone Hand*'s flagging circulation.

Like the magazine's earlier contest, the wartime competition was based on women sending in recent photographs. There was no age limit

VETERANS' HOME GARDEN FETE, WELLINGTON COLLEGE GROUNDS, FEBRUARY 10.

The wartime Queen Carnival contests had more in common with early twentieth-century fundraisers. Back in 1903, around the time Sandow was trying to organise his competition for ladies, these women dressed up to raise money for the Veterans' Home in Wellington. As living posters for everything from 'Kola Nip' to 'Zealandia Shirts', they helped raise funds for others. *Canterbury Times*, 25 February 1903. Christchurch City Libraries.

and married women were also eligible for the £50 first prize.[105] Numbered photographs were reproduced in the magazine: this time the identity of the women was not revealed, although the name of the photographer was, so observant readers could work out that contestant No. 10 was from New Zealand, as was contestant No. 45.[106] In total, 135 women entered. Voting was intense and even soldiers in France and Palestine followed the results with great interest. Again, the magazine made a beauty contest last for sixteen months: the final results were not announced until November 1917. Readers were clear that No. 45 was the most beautiful woman in Australasia. Enid A. Sharpin, of Mangapapa, Gisborne, was the grateful recipient of the £50 winner's cheque.[107] At last a girl from Maoriland had won.

The *Lone Hand* attempted one more 'Patriotic Beauty Competition', in 1918, but by this time the magazine was in its death throes, and it seems unlikely that any Australasian girl was awarded the first prize of £40 worth of War Bonds.[108] Other magazines, though, were quick to pick up on the idea of running a photographic beauty contest. When the *Pictorial News* began in 1924, it announced in its first issue that it was going to hold a 'Fair Sex Competition', open to all women in the dominion except 'Professional beauties'. Women were to send in their photographs, along with ten nomination coupons.[109] Each issue of the magazine contained one coupon. Readers, voting on the official voting coupons, would then decide who was the fairest of them all. For six months the *Pictorial News* kept up the pretence that it was offering a £100 prize, before quietly dropping any references to its competition.

Queen Carnival and photographic beauty contests continued throughout the 1920s. Young women and their 'courts' raised money to build tennis courts and swimming baths at New Lynn, and to improve the school grounds at Ohaupo.[110] The women who entered competitions run by their local movie theatres were usually motivated by less altruistic goals, though the women who entered the Strand Arcade's 1925 photographic beauty contest might have been spurred into action in order to defend the reputation of their sisters.[111] Just after the Strand announced it was to hold yet another contest, a single man, who had been living in New Zealand for two years, wrote to the press to complain about the number of 'ugly women in Auckland'. Their broad and long feet (the result of going barefoot as children), hairy arms (from wearing sleeveless dresses) and brown necks (the result of too much sun on their exposed skin) disgusted him.[112] His claims provoked many defensive replies,[113] and a tailored advertisement for the Strand Beauty Contest, suggesting that the 'cure' for his woes could be found nightly at the Strand, where photographs of beautiful local young women were on display.[114]

Alongside the carnival queens and the women who submitted their studio portraits for public scrutiny, a new type of contestant took to the stage, and appeared on film during the 1920s. She was the bathing beauty, the future body (and face) of beauty contests.

When Baby Mowat, Bessie Foy and Enid Sharpin entered beauty contests they put on their prettiest dresses and went along to a portrait photographer. In the privacy of his studio, they sat and smiled. Head and shoulder shots later appeared in magazines or on the screen at their local cinema. Although the women were subjecting themselves to the public's gaze, they did not have to endure full public scrutiny. A physical culture expert judged Baby Mowat's body, in private, but for the most part, beauty contestants' bodies remained out of bounds. In the 1920s this changed. Following the international trend (swimsuit parades had fast become essential in American contests), young New Zealand women were increasingly expected to put on this season's bathing costume, and strut their stuff.[115] At Auckland's Summer Carnival in 1923, for example, a 'Venetian Carnival' was held at Devonport's Calliope Dock. The promise of a 'bathing dress competition' drew hundreds to the ferry gates, eager to make it across the harbour to witness the contest. The police had to be called

By the mid-1920s, bathing beauty contests had become commonplace. This
American cartoon was reproduced in an Auckland newspaper. The joke about
women's vanity and men's desire to gaze upon semi-clad female bodies worked
just as well on this side of the Pacific. *Auckland Star*, 18 April 1925.

in to assist harbour officials with the crush at the terminal. Once at the
dock those in the crowd struggled for the best positions. Some climbed
onto roofs to ensure an uninterrupted view of the two dozen or so young
women who had entered the contest. Whether they agreed with the judges
that Miss Mudgway looked best in her bathing suit is not recorded.[116]

A couple of years later a slightly different bathing beauties' contest was
held. The Grand Theatre in Auckland arranged for motion pictures to be
taken of young women in their swimsuits at Auckland's main beaches.
This film then screened nightly at the Grand, and the audience got to vote
for 'Auckland's Most Beautiful Bathing Girl'. The claim that the competition was run on 'Refined and Dignified Lines' was neither explained nor
defended, but the prize was a first-class return ticket to Sydney. Perhaps
the status of the ticket reassured the public.[117] Or perhaps the fact that
those who bought the most expensive seats at the Grand had more voting
clout ensured the contest was refined. Patrons who purchased a 2s ticket
had ten votes at their disposal; those who settled for a 1s 6d ticket had to
be content with five votes; and those who could only afford a 1s ticket
had to think carefully about how they cast their two votes. Like so many
aspects of New Zealand society, judging beauty was not classless.[118]

The Grand's competition also offered the audience the delight of
seeing 'Auckland's Mermaids' in the flesh. Each night, alongside the film
of young women in their bathing attire, the contestants stood on stage,
in their swimsuits, before their public.[119] This was very different from the
photographic contests the public had grown used to. Women were not
only appearing in moving pictures, they were also performing in public,

parading in what were becoming increasingly briefer bathing costumes. No wonder cartoonists began to speculate on the attractions of such competitions.[120] Up to now, these contests had been local. In late 1925, though, the organisers of the Lyall Bay Beach Gala decided to go national. They announced that over the Christmas holidays they would be staging the county's first 'National Bathing Beauty Contest', open to all women over the age of seventeen who had lived in New Zealand for at least a year. The winner would be crowned 'Miss New Zealand' and would receive a silver cup for the year of her reign.[121] Atlantic City – the birthplace of the Miss America quest – was thousands of miles away, but its influence was clear.

However, a single advertisement in a national newspaper, even if the paper had as wide a circulation as *Truth*, does not a national contest make. Although the 'bathing beauty' contest attracted a large amount of interest, this was a local gala and a local competition. The judges declared Mrs Scales of Lyall Bay the winner, and her neighbours, who made up the 'large crowd of interested spectators', agreed. The other place-getters had not travelled much further than Mrs Scales. Runner-up Miss G. I. Smith hailed from Petone, while the third-placed woman, Miss H. Eglinton, lived in Featherston.[122]

The official crowning of Mrs Scales as Miss New Zealand, and the handing over of the silver cup, took place in early 1926.[123] Later that year, though, the first 'real' Miss New Zealand contest was held. Unlike the Lyall Bay gala, this was a truly national competition.

On Monday 30 August 1926 a dominion-wide beauty contest was launched to find Miss New Zealand. In conjunction with New Zealand Entertainers Ltd, daily newspapers in the four main centres set about finding the prettiest girl in their province. The woman chosen as Miss Auckland or Miss Otago would win £50 and her runner-up £25. But, more than that, the chosen eight (the four regional winners and their maids of honour) would then assemble in Auckland – all expenses paid – and one lucky woman would be crowned Miss New Zealand. Among her prizes was a cheque for a further £250. At the time, few qualified women school teachers earned £250 a year.[124] The 5s entrance fee paled into insignificance when the chance of winning up to £300 was dangled before the young women of Maoriland.[125] As with the Lyall Bay contest, married women could vie for the title of Miss New Zealand.[126]

It is difficult to convey the sense of excitement and expectation generated by this contest. By the late twentieth century one Miss New Zealand

Mrs Scales, winner of
the Lyall Bay 'Miss New
Zealand Contest'. *Auckland
Weekly News Illustrations*,
7 January 1926. Hocken
Library, Uare Taoka o
Hakena, University of
Otago, Dunedin.

knowingly referred to herself as 'Miss Anonymous',[127] but in 1926 the finalists and the eventual winner, Dunedin's Thelma McMillan, were household names, their faces (and bodies) known throughout the land. The first real Miss New Zealand contest ran for almost three months. Day after day, the participating newspapers ran columns, explaining the rules, encouraging local girls to enter and reporting on the contest to date. The young women of Auckland were quick to answer the call. The day after the contest was announced completed entry forms began to arrive at the *Star*'s office. One aspiring beauty got down to the official photographers by 9.30 a.m. that day, determined to be first to have her picture taken.[128]

The reluctance shown by women in the past was noticeably absent in 1926. Within a week, over 100 women had entered the Auckland section of the contest.[129] In total, 656 young Aucklanders put their names, faces and bodies on the line.[130]

When aspiring Miss New Zealands filled in the entrance form, and paid over their 5s, they bought the right to have their photograph taken by the contest's official photographer. Hundreds of these head and shoulder pictures appeared in the newspaper over the next weeks and months. Alongside the upper body shots, the contestants also had a full body photograph taken, for the benefit of the judges. The pictures appearing in the daily press showed the girls in their finest frocks, but for the full body shots they wore their bathing costumes. Contestants also had to leave their measurements with the photographer. Since this was a contest judged on 'beauty of face and form', it was important that their bodies measured up. The judges needed to know the height and weight of each contestant, as well as her bust, waist, hip, thigh, neck, arm, calf, ankle and wrist measurements. The young women could compare themselves with the current Miss Australia (Beryl Mills) and Miss America (Fay Lamphier): their measurements were given as a point of comparison, as were the particulars of the Venus de Milo.[131]

The notoriety of becoming the nation's bathing beauty discouraged some women from entering.[132] It also encouraged some of the strongest opposition to the contest. The Auckland District Methodist Synod declared its

> deep regret at the promotion in this city of beauty competitions and at some of the displays associated therewith. We regard these as calculated to lower the sense of modesty and self-respect of the young womanhood of the Dominion and earnestly request the newspapers and business firms of the city to discourage further competitions of this nature.

The mover of the resolution, the Reverend G. S. Cook, 'also condemned "bathing costume parades of physical charm" before crowds at least some of whom gloated over the exhibition. Herodotus said when woman begins to leave off her clothes she begins to leave off her modesty.'[133] Although some other religious bodies agreed with the Auckland Methodists,[134] most seem to have viewed even the bathing beauty aspect of the contest as either harmless (the standard refrain of 'To the pure-minded all things are pure' was echoed again[135]) or good for the nation.

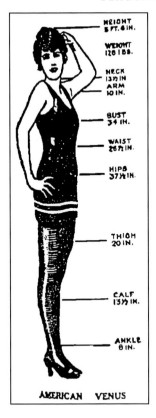

HEIGHT
5 FT. 6 IN.

WEIGHT
128 LBS.

NECK
13½ IN
ARM
10 IN.

BUST
34 IN.

WAIST
26½ IN.

HIPS
37½ IN.

THIGH
20 IN.

CALF
13½ IN.

ANKLE
8 IN.

AMERICAN VENUS

After Fay Lamphier became Miss America, she won a role in the Hollywood film *The American Venus*. By the time of the Miss New Zealand contest, she had simply become the 'American Venus', with measurements to match the legendary Venus de Milo. *Auckland Star*, 1 September 1926.

In the build-up to the contest, and in its initial announcement, two aspects of beauty pageants were stressed. The first was that they offered young women new career opportunities, especially in the field of entertainment. Winners of contests in Australia and the United States had gone on to be successful on stage and screen. The implication was clear: local girls could use the pageant as a springboard to fame and fortune.[136] The second spoke to national pride. Organisers claimed that this contest would help to bring New Zealand 'into line with other countries of the world who are stimulating the love of the beautiful by means of annual beauty quests'.[137] New Zealanders did not want to be behind the times. The number of reports indicating that Australians knew about and were following the Miss New Zealand contest encouraged those who feared that New Zealand did not register on the international map.[138] But though

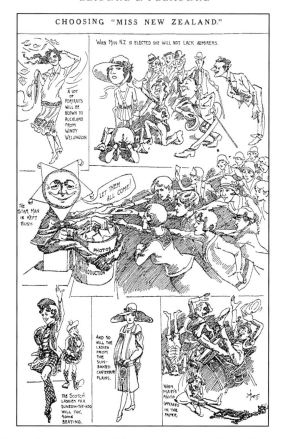

When Auckland readers contemplated choosing Miss New Zealand, they were well aware
that contestants from Wellington, Dunedin and Christchurch were also vying for the
honour. As a measure of their civic pride, they had to rush to the '*Star* Man', and give him
their entry forms and photographs. *Auckland Star*, 18 September 1926.

pride played a part in the contest, it was more regional than national in
focus. Given that the eventual winner was not going to go overseas to
compete as Miss New Zealand, national concerns were not to the fore.[139]
Whether she came from Auckland or Christchurch did matter, though.
Provincial loyalties were used to encourage 'local' girls to put themselves
forward, for the good of their town or city.

As the contest got under way, however, another value emerged, and
became a refrain throughout the ensuing months. The first Miss New
Zealand quest reinforced the link between beauty, health, exercise and

a natural lifestyle: it was as though the spirit of the recently deceased Sandow were hovering near. For years commercial considerations had been to the fore as young women posed for movie companies and in bathing beauty parades, but with Miss New Zealand Sandow's original intent was restored. Only the healthy could be beautiful, and to be healthy girls had to eat well, live right and exercise regularly. Although cosmetic companies had been telling women that their creams and lotions were aids to beauty, the connection between exercise and perfection of face and form had not disappeared. Even in the ill-fated *Pictorial News* beauty competition, readers had gazed upon pictures of international beauties like Alice Knowlton, 'An American girl who claims that physical culture and exercise make for beauty'.[140] It was not surprising, then, that when a tobacco company offered 1000 of its cigarettes as part of Miss New Zealand's prize package, and 200 for each of the other provincial winners, the organisers remarked that none of the finalists indulged.[141] On the other hand, the winner and her maid of honour were quick to take up Masco's offer of a bathing suit knitted to order by their Karangahape Road firm. Within days of the final, they were visiting Masco's premises, being measured for their new costumes.[142]

Many of the contestants were avid physical culturists. One father who went to the *Star*'s office to pay his daughter's entrance fee claimed that 'If she has any luck at all, it will be due to physical culture . . . My girl is the picture of health . . . she is a wonderful specimen. She eats, works and plays all kinds of games for health's sake.'[143] The finalists were also committed to systematic exercise. After Miss Canterbury and her maid of honour had been chosen, they visited Dunedin to assist with the Otago competition. While there, both underwent 'a rigid course of training' so that they remained in top physical form.[144] Miss Canterbury's advice to other young women was simple: 'Live naturally, girls, and exercise. Do your daily dozen—it's great fun. Eat chocolates if you like them, and if they make you fat, well, stop eating them. That's what I would do, but chocolates have never made me fat.' Perhaps the cold shower she took each morning, or the track running she did, helped keep off the pounds, or perhaps the fact that she was only sixteen explained her youthful figure.[145] Whatever her secret, the advice she offered was similar to that given by contest winners the world over: 'live right, eat right, exercise, and you will be beautiful'.[146]

The Auckland finalists were also keen on fresh air and exercise. Distin Strange, who made it to the final four in the Auckland contest, was a

Pro: " Your form is terrible—you don't keep your knees in place—
your wrists are weak—you don't use your eyes and your
shoulders droop when you—"

Pupil: " Sir! I'll have you know I won a Beauty Contest last week."

—" Judge."

By the mid-1920s, even the cartoonists knew that health and beauty went
hand in hand. Here a young flapper, with her fashionable hair and clothes, is
reprimanded for her poor golfing form. But as she reminds her coach, she is a
beauty contest winner. *Auckland Star*, 11 September 1926.

'physical culture enthusiast', her 'splendid figure said to be a result of her
"daily dozen" activities'.[147] With the other finalists, she enjoyed swimming
at the Parnell baths in the lead-up to the contest's grand finale.[148] The overall winner, Thelma McMillan, was a keen swimmer. Years later, when she
was in her 70s, she still swam every day in summer.[149] Back in 1926, she
swam, played tennis and was attentive 'To health-giving exercise'.[150]

Despite the glamour of Hollywood, and the insistence of cosmetic
companies, these young women personified the healthy, racial ideal
Sandow had advocated before they were born. In a few years, they would
become perfect wives and mothers, their fit young bodies ready and willing
to give birth. It was no surprise that Mrs W. H. Parkes was one of the judges
of the Auckland competition. As the president of the Plunket Society she

knew a potential Plunket mother when she saw one.[151] This eugenic, racial ideal meant that the competitors had to be local girls: the rules stated that casual visitors and immigrants were not allowed to enter.[152] Despite a suggestion that 'The candidate must be of British birth', Maori women entered the contest, though none made it through to the final eight.[153] Beauty was still white. It was also natural. When the finalists appeared on stage, before a packed auditorium, their skins were unadorned by paint, powder or pencil.[154] Miss New Zealand relied on soap and water, not patented potions and creams.

Given this focus on health and beauty, and the assumption that in order to be beautiful you had to be healthy, the swimsuit component of the contest made sense. It was not, the organisers could claim, designed to excite the audience, debase the women or boost the newspaper's circulation. While some, especially *Truth*, disputed this, if the public accepted that this was a contest about beauty of face *and* form, asking the finalists to parade in their bathing costumes did not seem unreasonable.[155] Once twelve young women had been chosen by a panel of judges as the fairest Auckland had to offer, the organisers took them off to Takapuna Beach, put them in their bathing costumes and had them pose on the sand for the *Star*'s photographer. A large crowd gathered to watch the proceedings.[156] A couple of days later, full body shots of the finalists in their swimsuits were printed in the newspaper. Their 'physical grace' was clear for all to see.[157]

These photographs appeared while the public was deciding which four of the twelve finalists they wanted to go forward to the Miss Auckland final. Using voting coupons from the newspaper, Aucklanders cast over half a million votes,[158] and the swimsuit photographs helped them to make up their minds. Before Miss Auckland was announced, though, the final four Aucklanders, and the six regional winners (Miss Wellington, Miss Canterbury and Miss Otago, with their maids of honour), gathered nightly in a beauty parade. On the second night the women paraded in their bathing suits, enchanting many: 'Much as the girls charmed the audience when they appeared in their evening frocks, the sight of the shapely figures, clad in chic bathing suits, roused those present to still greater enthusiasm'.[159] Thelma McMillan later recalled that, in her day, 'The bathing suit parade was done in private only in front of the judges. Women used to be a lot more mysterious.'[160] Although she did not parade in her swimsuit during the grand final, in the parades leading up to the final, and in the week-long show at the Majestic after the final, she and the other contestants put on their bathing costumes and revealed their form.[161]

The first 'real' Miss New Zealand, Dunedin's own Thelma McMillan.
Otago Witness Illustrations, 2 November 1926. Hocken Library,
Uare Taoka o Hakena, University of Otago, Dunedin.

Many years before, Sandow had argued that beauty required perfection of face and form. Since then, there had been undue attention to the attractiveness of young women's faces, but by the time Thelma McMillan became the first Miss New Zealand, having a beautiful body was no longer something to hide. One female columnist understood the change: 'In Victorian times it wasn't quite nice for a girl to think of herself as good-looking. Now, however, good looks are so much identified with health and hygiene that a girl will discuss her own chances in that way just as easily as if a hockey test were under discussion.'[162] Thelma McMillan could remain modest and unaffected, but still impress local judge A. P. Roydhouse, a physical culture instructor with the Education Department.[163] With measurements rivaling the Venus de Milo's (Thelma's ankles were a little thicker), she lived up to 'Mere Man's' expectations that a local girl could be 'as perfect as the famous Greek goddess'.[164] As Sandow had been to Adonis, so Thelma was now to Venus.

In 1927, the excitement of the Miss New Zealand contest was repeated. The winner was Dale Austen, another Dunedinite.[165] After that, Miss New Zealand was held intermittently, until Joe Brown bought the franchise and began to hold annual quests from 1960.[166] Other beauty competitions, including many bathing beauty beach contests, were held along the way. Between the wars these were often concerned with health and fitness. For example, New Zealand's first de facto nudist magazine, *Health and Sunshine*, ran a 'beauty of form' contest in the mid-1930s.[167] Women readers of *New Zealand Health News* were also encouraged to send in photographs of themselves, posing in their swimsuits. The editor of *California Health News* wanted to reproduce the pictures, to show his readers what 'New Zealand feminine health and beauty' looked like.[168] Although Dr Sheldon's Gin Pills claimed that their product would help women achieve health, beauty, power and therefore happiness, it seems many New Zealand women continued to put their faith in exercise rather than patent medicines.[169]

Beauty pageants had become a legitimate leisure pursuit. A few religious types worried about the moral effect of swimsuit contests, but most New Zealanders seem to have enthusiastically embraced this new form of entertainment. It is impossible to know whether contestants believed that the competitions were about racial health and fitness, or whether they used this as a convenient excuse, a way to justify parading their bodies. Likewise, we cannot know if the spectators viewed the contestants as eugenic role models, or whether they just enjoyed eyeing the offerings on stage. Certainly, though, the rhetoric of health was used to explain these cultural phenomena and that same rhetoric was also brought into play at beaches and swimming pools, as more and more people took off their clothes and put on their swimsuits.

Four In the Swim

In December 1956 Yvonne Christian and Lucy McClement were moved to write to Auckland's town clerk, praising the city for hosting a hair, beauty and fashion parade at the Parnell swimming pool. Christian considered herself 'fortunate' to have seen the show, 'The most glamorous beauty parade' she had ever witnessed: 'It was something like the type of show you see on the movies'.[1] McClement was also adamant that it was 'The most professional show that has ever been held in this country'. For her, too, the movies were the yardstick when it came to measuring glamour: 'I felt I was in Hollywood for that one hour.'[2] Just as the organisers of the inaugural Miss New Zealand contest had encouraged their contestants to frolic on the beach and pose in their bathing costumes, so the backers of the Parnell show sited their parade at one of the homes of bodily display, the municipal swimming pool. In 1956 the council approved this use: back in 1914, when the pool was opened, the city fathers would not even have entertained the suggestion.

In the early years of the twentieth century the men of the Parnell Borough Council had plans drawn up for sea baths to be built for the exercise and enjoyment of locals. Their ratepayers, however, decided that the expenditure outweighed the health returns of swimming and the plans were put on hold.[3] But by 1914, under the auspices of the Auckland City Council, the Parnell baths were built, allowing locals to enjoy saltwater pools in their own neighbourhood, rather than have to travel into the city to take their daily dip.[4]

In 1914, though, people did not go to the Parnell pool to laze in the sun and watch others parade around in skimpy swimsuits. The price of admission bought you the right to swim, not loiter. Swimming was touted as one of the healthiest forms of exercise, though the condition of the

The Parnell Baths. Although the scene of fun in the sun for many, they were
designed by the city's fathers as a health-giving, respectable leisure site.
A1195, Special Collections, Auckland City Libraries.

pool sometimes belied that claim. In 1919 a Mr Cornes dived into the
pool and was most surprised to find a dead man floating beside him. The
water was so murky that Cornes did not notice the body before he began
his swim.[5] When Cornes contacted city administrators the response did
not flatter the unidentified corpse: the town clerk noted that the Parnell
baths were cleaned out several times during the year, and that from now
on 'every endeavour will be made to keep the water as f[r]ee from scum as
possible'.[6] Such incidents did not seem to faze many swimmers. They saw
and felt the bodily benefits of swimming, and every summer season they
plunged into the Parnell pool and swam their laps. By the late 1920s, over
30,000 people visited the pool each season. In the 1930s that figure sometimes climbed to over 50,000.[7]

When city councils took it upon themselves to build swimming pools,
they justified the expenditure by pointing out their civic obligation to
ratepayers' health. Swimming, declared the Mayor of Dunedin, W. P.
Street, as he opened the St Clair baths in 1884, is 'one of the healthiest and

most invigorating of recreations'.[8] This was not Dunedin's first swimming pool – locals had been bathing at the Pelichet Bay baths for some time – but the St Clair pool was part of a new attempt to encourage Dunedinites to embrace this most beneficial pastime. Up in Auckland the council also invested heavily, providing saltwater baths in Customs Street West and a freshwater pool in Albert Street.[9] They knew that this investment might not pay off in monetary terms. As Walter Bush, the city engineer, noted, swimming pools might not provide a 'profitable investment' in the ordinary sense, but they were 'very valuable' when it came to building up 'healthy citizens'.[10] Christchurch's mayor agreed. Opening the city's new tepid baths in Manchester Street, he told the assembled crowd, to applause, that the baths were expected to run up a 'small deficit', but that 'would be more than counterbalanced by the benefits that the community would derive from the institution'.[11]

This mania for building public swimming pools was not peculiar to New Zealand. Across the Tasman exactly the same pattern can be found,[12] and at 'Home' in Britain most major towns had erected municipal baths by the turn of the twentieth century.[13] Mayors and councillors were prepared to strike special loans for municipal baths because they believed in swimming. In the mid-nineteenth century bathing and swimming had been fringe activities, indulged in by health fanatics, but regarded by many as unsafe and unseemly.[14] By 1900, that view was fast giving way to an acceptance of the health benefits of swimming. Just as physical culture became mainstream, so swimming came to be regarded as a sensible, systematic, rational form of exercise, which developed respiration, aided circulation, strengthened the digestive organs and generally purified the body.[15] Local authorities now accepted the claims of doctors like W. A. Chapple, the eugenicist, when he proclaimed in 1894 that 'There is absolutely no exercise at once so pleasurable, so invigorating, so healthful, and so productive of physical development as swimming. Every other exercise to which the human body can be subjected pales into utter insignificance when we contemplate the far-reaching advantages of this health-giving recreation.'[16] The councillors read and were swayed by articles about turn-of-the-century champion swimmers like Agnes Beckwith, who swam miles every day, despite having been a sickly child. Eugen Sandow might have been made strong by lifting weights, but for Beckwith 'constant bathing and swimming have made me healthy'.[17] They listened when physical culturists like Sandow and Fred Hornibrook sang the praises of swimming.[18]

From the 1890s, being able to swim and save lives became new markers of good citizenship. Men, women and children who could do both were taking responsibility for their personal physical health, and were also prepared to do their civic duty, and save those who got into trouble in the water. Hornibrook favoured compulsion when it came to swimming: he suggested that it made more health-sense for swimming instruction to be compulsory than for vaccinations to be required. He also suggested that learning to swim was 'fair'. No one should be expected to risk their life to save yours, so he encouraged everyone to learn to swim, and to focus on endurance and life-saving rather than speed.[19]

The health and safety message caught on. Governments subsidised school programmes in swimming and life-saving.[20] Articles appeared in the press, asking 'Can You Swim?', and encouraging everyone to learn.[21] The governor-general suggested that everyone should become 'Thoroughly at home in the water'.[22] The Royal Life Saving Society taught thousands how to swim and save lives.[23] Advertisements for swimming aids began to appear.[24] And local bodies built pools and staffed them with swimming and life-saving instructors.

Swimming had traditionally taken place in the sea, and many of its advocates still sang the praises of the briny. They delighted in the fresh air and cold water, found the breakers exhilarating and enjoyed the challenge of swimming against the current. Local authorities understood the attractions of the beach. The sea air refreshed the jaded office worker and saltwater was 'nectar' compared with 'The sickly, lukewarm municipal fluid' inside tepid baths.[25] But rather than surrender to the lure of the sea, local bodies built open-air or partially covered pools on the edge of the foreshore. Swimmers could still enjoy the bracing effects of sea air and saltwater, but they were protected from the dangerous freedoms of the beach.

That the beach was free was a problem for local authorities. Their concern was not about revenue – they knew that municipal baths would never pay their way – but within the pool's walls they could control what went on, and protect their ratepayers. They could determine opening hours, regulate costumes and impose other restrictions on behaviour. The baths' custodian could also make sure that people were safe as they swam. The sea was an uncontrolled and uncontrollable mass, the beach a morally and physically dangerous zone where anything might happen.

Local authorities passed by-laws to try to restrict beach use and prohibit sea bathing. In 1895 swimming at Dunedin's St Clair Beach was forbidden, but with no custodian to enforce the prohibition, hardy locals still rushed into the surf.[26] Up in Auckland, by-laws were passed to restrict sea bathing, limiting where and at what time bathers could take to the waves, and stipulating what they must wear at the beach.[27] But the swimmers defied the rules. They entered the water when and where they wanted, and often did not bother to wear anything when they did so. After a number of passers-by came across a group of naked young men enjoying a North Shore beach in 1893, the local press suggested that if the problem continued 'bathing will probably be completely prohibited'.[28] It was not, but swimming pools were built, and locals were encouraged to take their daily dip in the physically, and morally, safer municipal baths.

The beach was a genuinely dangerous place for many New Zealanders. Every now and again there were shark scares,[29] but the real problem was the fact that so many people could not swim. Every summer newspapers contained reports of numerous beach drownings, stories of inexperienced swimmers getting into trouble and warnings about undertows and rips.[30] Baths, though, had shallow ends for those who had not yet built up their confidence, ropes at the side for the nervous to grab, and custodians, trained life-savers who were often champion swimmers to boot. On top of all that, at your local baths you could also take swimming and life-saving lessons.

Whether the instructors were pool staff, who made extra money from teaching swimming, or self-employed teachers, who paid councils a fee or percentage of their take for the use of the pool, local authorities were ultimately in control of what went on. If they were happy with the services provided, instructors could enjoy long careers. 'Professor' Anderson, for example, taught swimming in Auckland's pools for over 30 years.[31] But if instructors overstepped the mark, and did not uphold the healthy credo espoused by council, then they would be dismissed. This is what happened to Malcolm Champion, a member of the Australasian swimming team at the 1911 Empire games and the first New Zealander to swim at an Olympic games.[32]

Soon after his international appearances, Champion was appointed caretaker of Auckland city's new tepid baths (the Teps) in Hobson Street. At first, he seems to have done his job well, teaching swimming and generally keeping the baths in good order. He ran into some controversy in 1920, when he banned Indian men from washing in the slipper baths, which were provided (as they were at many public pools) for those who did not have a bath at home. Champion, and other (white) patrons at the baths held that the 'Indian coolies' were 'unclean . . . in their habits [and] in person', so he refused the men admission.[33] After one of the men complained, the council decided that one bath was to be set aside for 'Hindoos', and other 'coloured people'.[34] Champion's racism did not unduly worry the council. A few years before they had asked Mrs Champion to apologise for insulting some 'half caste' Fijian children who had swum at the pools. Mrs Champion had apparently told them that she did not want 'girls like them', that 'she only wanted respectable people there and not their sort' and that she would not allow them to return to the tepid baths.[35] Apology or no, Chapman and his wife were allowed to stay on. Keeping non-white bodies away from the fair swimmers of Auckland seems to have met with tacit approval. Certainly, European swimmers did not stay away. Crowds flocked to the Teps. By the mid-1920s annual attendance was well over the 100,000 mark.[36] Champion continued to hold swimming classes, and his pupils were claimed to be champions in name and ability.[37]

In 1928 Champion was promoted to baths supervisor, but trouble was brewing. There were complaints about his swimming lessons, and the council decided he could no longer take private classes. He was still allowed to teach, but as part of his salaried job. It seems, though, that the private lessons, with their private fees, continued, and when the council found out that he was still charging for lessons, was still taking female pupils despite his contract forbidding this, and that his hand was in the till, they took action. Champion found himself in court, was convicted and sentenced to twelve months' probation.[38]

Champion's life unravelled at the Teps, but most swimmers and most swimming instructors left the water refreshed and energised, secure in the knowledge that they were doing their duty by learning to swim and by teaching others.

But the numerous rules at council pools riled some users. At the beach by-laws could be flouted, but at the baths you were always under the watchful eye of the caretakers. They could, and did, refuse admission to anyone who was drunk or who was known to be suffering from an infectious or contagious disease. They threw out patrons who behaved in an indecent, improper or disorderly manner.[39] They enforced Sabbatarianism, closing pools early on Sundays, and the rules only after swimmers like Arthur E. Toye complained. Toye pointed out that Sunday was the one day in the week that most people were free to use the pools, and the one day when the council decided to enforce early closing.[40]

Frederick George Radcliffe's photograph of the crowds at Wellington's Lyall Bay shows how popular the seaside was in inter-war New Zealand, and how by-laws could be flouted at unpatrolled beaches. Although the dressing shed's sign makes it clear that 'Children under 14 are not admitted in this shed', the two girls in the doorway are obviously under age. R1782, Special Collections, Auckland City Libraries.

Councils had hoped that they would also be able to separate the sexes, and keep men and women bathers apart in a way that was never feasible in the sea. But, despite their best intentions, the public soon tired of sex-specific swimming. When public pools were first built there was no assumption that men and women would swim together. Such an idea was morally outrageous and dangerous. Wet costumes, even if voluminous, clung to bodies, and also showed more flesh than was deemed proper in mixed company. The murkiness of the water in most baths also raised concerns: who could tell what was going on under the surface? Sex-segregated swimming was the name of the game, and though provisions were made for women to swim, the assumption was that the 'sterner sex' would be the main patrons of the pools. At Auckland's Albert Street baths, for example, women were able to swim for two hours every morning except Sunday, whereas the pool opened at sunrise for men, and apart from the time set aside for women, men could continue to swim until an hour after sunset. They were also able to take a dip on Sunday mornings. To remind women that the baths were not really for them, a red pennant with the word 'Females' emblazoned on it in white was hoisted over the baths during the women's session.[41]

At the same time that women were being denied easy access to swimming pools, they were being bombarded with messages about the health-giving properties of swimming. Readers of the *New Zealand Graphic*, for example, learned that

> Swimming will do more to develop perfect health in woman than any other
> form of exercise. It develops the whole body symmetrically, loosens the
> joints, gives free action to the limbs. It increases the lung capacity, inducing
> deep breathing; straightens the frame, throwing the chest forward and the
> shoulders back. The woman who swims gains all this, and in the gaining has
> much pleasure.[42]

The pleasure came from knowing that swimming was not only good for her, it also made her look good. From the turn of the century women were reading about the benefits of swimming for their figures and complexions.[43] The promise was that they could emerge from the pool toned and slender, their reshaped bodies as enticing as young Annette Kellermann's.[44]

Kellermann was one of the swimming sensations of the twentieth century. She came to New Zealanders' attention in the early 1900s, when she wore a tight black swimming costume in a stage production. As one reporter noted, her bathing suit was 'not too near the neck nor too close to the knee', and when the 'Australian Mermaid' stood on the springboard, her costume wet and clinging, 'The bald heads [in the audience] gr[e]w pink with emotion'.[45] The parallels with the Modern Milo are obvious: both were young Australian performers with loyal local followings, who found success in Britain and the United States.[46] Both displayed their physically cultured bodies for a living. Like Pansy Montague, Kellermann was measured against the Venus de Milo and not found wanting.[47] The difference was that Kellermann's fame rested on her aquatic abilities. According to her 1918 book, *Physical Beauty: How to Keep It*, she was crippled as a child and swimming gave her strength, beauty and a perfect figure.[48] With such a role model to inspire them, it is little wonder that the women of New Zealand began to protest about the restricted hours set aside for their enjoyment of municipal swimming pools.

Douglas Booth has pointed out a positive, but unintended consequence of sex-segregated swimming for women: it increased their confi-

Pansy Montague as La Milo, swimming as a woman's life-saver. Annette Kellermann was famously arrested in the United States for wearing a similar costume. *Sandow's Magazine*, 31 May 1906. David Chapman Collection.

dence. Without having to worry about men, they learned how to swim and got used to seeing themselves and others in their costumes.[49] Once they felt at ease in the pool, though, they started to agitate for longer and better swimming times, and for mixed bathing.

Within days of the official opening of the Parnell baths, Miss E. M. Swallow was writing to the Auckland City Council, complaining about the times allocated for women's swimming. Already a keen swimmer, Swallow was not happy that women were denied access to the pool before work and on Saturday afternoons, when shop workers enjoyed their half-day holiday. She was outraged by the council's response that women could now swim on Wednesday afternoons too: Wednesday was not a half-day holiday for most working women. To her it seemed 'a most scandalous thing that women can be ousted from their just rights in matters of this kind, and have no remedy'. But then the mayor decided that mixed bathing should be permitted at Parnell. The baths had not been open a month, and already the moral control the council had hoped to enforce was crumbling.[50]

By the outbreak of the Great War the red pennant had been lowered and mixed bathing was permitted in pools around the country. It was a popular move. Reports suggested that attendance at the Napier swimming pool increased ten-fold when mixed bathing was allowed. Many paid the price of admission 'merely to look and enjoy the spectacle'.[51] New by-laws were passed to reassure the public that municipal baths were still morally safe: swimmers had to keep to their own changing rooms, wear regulation costumes, and at some pools those who attended mixed bathing sessions had to be accompanied by a member of the opposite sex, a rule nudist camps later adopted.[52] The rules were based on those used in pools overseas, but councils everywhere were fighting a losing battle.[53] The fresh air and saltwater of their seaside pools may have been refreshing, but the rules and restrictions they enforced diluted the swimmers' pleasure. Mixed bathing, which was now commonplace on the beach, was policed at the pool. And because women were present, men could no longer lie around the pool after their swim, soaking in the sun, as they had done in the days of sex-segregated swimming. Their 'sun-baths' were 'a thing of the past' at the pool, whereas at the beach the dunes beckoned.[54]

By 1914 the freedoms of the beach were attracting more New Zealanders but municipal baths still had appeal as physically and morally safe spaces to indulge in healthful leisure. But for those who did not want to be constrained, and who were as interested in pleasure as leisure, surf and sand seemed so much more inviting than pools and rules.

In nineteenth-century New Zealand, no 'right minded' person deliberately acquired a suntan. Many were browned as they went about their daily lives, but few deliberately stripped off in the midday sun. 'Savages' and navvies were brown, not settlers and those who aspired to the middling classes. Yet within a few years Pakeha New Zealanders were being told that it was their national duty to get into the sun and bake their bodies. Like swimming, sunbathing was about to become a mark of good citizenship. And the best place to perform this duty was at the beach.

New Zealanders had been going to the beach long before sunbathing became the norm. Whether for annual holidays or afternoon picnics, most people lived close enough to the sea to allow them occasional ocean visits. Improved public transport in the late nineteenth century made paddles and seashore promenades even more accessible.[55] The benefits of the bracing sea air were often remarked: the office worker could return from his seaside holiday 'bronzed and with an unwonted elasticity in his muscles which tides him over [for] another year'.[56] But it was not until about 1910 that swimming at the beach, rather than just dipping one's toes in the waves, started to become a popular pastime. Obviously some people swam in the sea before then. Maori had swum in the ocean for centuries, and some Pakeha had already embraced the briny, much to the consternation of city councillors, who passed by-laws restricting and sometimes prohibiting sea bathing. But before the First World War swimming in the sea began to become a general, rather than a fringe, activity.[57] The advent of surf life-saving clubs was an important impetus for this: beaches long considered too dangerous for swimming appeared much safer if trained guards were on patrol and life-saving equipment was at hand. The number of people who could swim was also increasing, thanks to the provision of municipal and (slowly) school swimming pools. Emboldened, these new swimmers joined those who had long believed in the power of the surf, and began to enjoy the freedom of the beach.

With no entrance fee to pay, all-day access on Sundays and no restrictions on how long you were allowed in the water – many municipal pools set a half-hour limit for each swim – the beach opened up new opportunities for leisure and pleasure.[58] And for many swimmers, one of the great pleasures of the beach was lying in the sand dunes after their swim, luxuriating as the sun's rays baked their bodies. One Christchurch beachgoer wrote a homage to sunbathing in his 'sunny couch among the dunes' after the 'paradise' of his ocean dip:

> The sand is deliciously hot and grateful to the wet, cold body, and the bather, sufficiently removed from the prudish eye, strips down the wet costume and revels in the warm, smooth blanket. He lies back and is somnolent. . . . The sun beats down and dries the body, and paints it a golden brown shade, and the warmth of it penetrates into the blood and fills it with fresh stores of the youthful warmth and eagerness and energy, sapped by the strenuous city.[59]

As this 1912 advertisement for cigarettes makes clear, the idea of a dip in the sea was now a regular activity for a growing number of men and women. Mabel rues the fact that she is denied the added pleasure of indulging in one of Three Castles' fragrant cigarettes after her swim. Mixed sea bathing was enough of a challenge to social conventions without women smoking in public as well. *Lyttelton Times*, 3 September 1912.

What was paradise for some was a problem for others. As swimming at the beach became commonplace, and as more swimmers made themselves at home in the dunes, peeling down their wet costumes while they did so, other members of the community objected to their behaviour. Like their counterparts in Australia, they wrote letters to the editor, complaining about the men who rolled up the legs of their costumes and folded down their tops so that they could lie in the sand 'in as near a state of nature as they very well can'.[60] When the sunbathers did not even bother with costumes, the letters became particularly heated. The sight of two men lying on Napier's Marine Parade with only a towel covering their hips appalled 'One Disgusted'. To make matters worse, this incident took place on a Sunday, the letter writer was with his wife when they came across the men, and one sat up as they passed, leaving nothing to the imagination.[61]

C. Beken's photograph of New Brighton Beach was taken around the time of the
mayor's outburst. As the picture shows, a number of men lie on the sand, wearing
less than a neck-to-knee costume. Most of the women in the shot are fully dressed,
though. Only one strides down the beach for a swim wearing full regulation
costume. 586/1, Canterbury Museum, Christchurch.

Indignant citizens contacted their local councils, and found that their
mayors and councillors were also seething at the public indecency of it all.
The Mayor of New Brighton (a Christchurch seaside township) was especially incensed. He did not approve of mixed sea bathing, worried about
the insufficient clothing the swimmers were wearing and was particularly
disturbed by what the bathers did when they left the water. He, in turn,
incensed a fair number of locals when he told a journalist that 'Some of
the women who went into the water were immodest sights, and after they
came out they lay about on the sand like a lot of pigs. There were some
men who were also very offensive.'[62] Fred Hornibrook likened the may-
or's outburst to the intemperate comments men had made when women
first took to riding bicycles. He was sure of the benefits of a sun bath on
the beach.[63] The 'pigs' also replied, informing the mayor that 'One of the

In 1926 an Auckland newspaper reproduced this Australian cartoon. In both countries 'seaside Bumbles' tried to prevent the young from having fun in the sun. The first of the 'Rules for Bathing' on the side of the inadequate changing shed reads 'No Sun Bathing Will Be Tolerated'. The shackles and 'Irksome Restrictions' did not deter beachgoers and sunseekers. *Auckland Star*, 16 October 1926.

pleasures that was most enjoyed by many bathers was the "sun bath" in the sand at the conclusion of a swim, and the suggestion that this should be prohibited was utterly absurd.'[64]

Absurd or not, it was common for councils and domain boards to prohibit sunbathing. In Auckland, the council decreed that

> No person shall be or remain dressed in bathing costume only upon any beach or on any street or public place adjoining any beach, for a longer time than is reasonably necessary for enabling him to pass from the dressing place to the water, or from the water to the dressing place, as the case may be, and all persons bathing or intending to bathe on any beach shall proceed directly from the dressing place to the water on undressing and directly to the dressing place on leaving the water, and shall then dress in ordinary costume.[65]

There were similar by-laws in many parts of Australia.[66] Down in Timaru, sunbathing structures were specially constructed to keep swimmers from flaunting their bodies on the beach,[67] and the local constable was instructed to take action against those who dared leave the sunbathers' com-

Auckland's Mission Bay Beach, Anniversary Day 1938. Hundreds gather to
bathe and bake their bodies in the summer sun. A14530, Special
Collections, Auckland City Libraries.

pound.[68] These by-laws were still in place in the 1920s, but as *Truth* noted,
'no one, excepting . . . old maids, male and female, takes any notice of a
mid-Victorian old ruling like that, and, after all, who the deuce wants to
see old and grumpy maids sunbathing?'[69] As with mixed bathing in municipal pools, councils had not been able to prevent sunbaking from becoming a commonplace activity. The constraints they had tried to impose
faded faster than a summer tan.

By the summer of 1930 it was more common to see people 'lazing on
the beach than rolling in the waves'.[70] Sunbaking had become something
of a national (and international) obsession, and a sanctioned obsession
at that. Local authorities were still cautious, insisting that poolgoers cover
up, but even they were coming to realise that they could not fight the
'attraction of sunbathing and the comparative freedom on the sands'.[71]
Within a few years sundecks were built at pools like Parnell to lure back
lost patrons.[72] But while councils were wrestling with the morality of sunbathing, many New Zealanders had already woken up 'To the value of
sunlight'.[73] They had taken to visiting 'The dispensary of Nature' for a regular dose of sunshine.[74] Just as doing their 'daily dozen' exercises or going
for a daily dip made them fitter, better citizens, so getting a daily dose of
sunshine and acquiring a tan became a measure of their good health and
ability to be productive members of the community.

The cultural shift, from believing that civilised and proper people were
pale, to accepting and even expecting that people would be bronzed and
glowing, took place quite rapidly. It followed a similar trajectory to the

embrace of physical culture, though without a figurehead like Sandow to spearhead the movement. As with the spread of the physical culture gospel, supporters gave the movement legitimacy by referring back to the Greeks and Romans. They also needed to prove that this was a modern, scientific response to the problems of the day. Prominent citizens had to be seen to be supporting the cause, and overseas precedents and experts were cited. With the health, welfare and future of the nation at stake, no stone (or sunbather) could be left unturned.

Ancient precedents were important in establishing the long, lost history of the benefits of sunbaking. Journalists noted that 'The ancients' had recognised the importance of sunlight as a cure for disease; now modern New Zealanders had to do the same.[75] Sir Frederic Truby King, founder of the Plunket society and by the mid-1920s the Director of Child Welfare, reminded his listeners that the Greeks and Romans had understood the power of the sun. With rhetorical flourish he claimed that the fall of the Roman Empire had seen the world 'plunged into darkness'. He worried that this darkness continued: modern parents were letting their children go to the cinema on sunny afternoons, rather than taking them to the beach.[76] The citizens of tomorrow needed fresh air and sunshine, not Hollywood westerns and comedies. Professor James Shelley, the popular WEA lecturer and well-known supporter of open-air schools, took a more aesthetic approach to the subject. He informed listeners of the Greek ideal of beauty, and the importance they had placed on sunlight.[77] Rather than being a marker of savagery, being tanned was touted as a sign of civilisation.

But tanning advocates faced the important hurdle of the association of brown bodies with 'savages'. There was local resistance and distaste at the idea of 'white women endeavouring to become brown women'.[78] Supporters of sunbaking, though, pointed out that native peoples had been far healthier before being colonised, 'civilised' and forced to cover their bodies with western-style clothing. This was the case with American Indians and with Maori.[79] The desire for better health meant that certain racial prejudices had to be overcome. Being brown could be celebrated if it was associated with ancient civilised societies and if it was proved to be healthier than being pale.

In the early twentieth century people were worried that, even in God's Own Country, ill-health defined the nation. Before the Great War some individuals pointed out the health benefits of lying on the beach and letting the sun work its magic. And there was a sense of magic about sunbathing. With little idea of how a tan could be built up through slow exposure, sunburn was described as 'a miracle, a protection to mankind'.[80] 'M.E.T.' thought it was a protection Aucklanders in particular needed. The city sapped bodily strength, but the power of the sun restored those who had learned about its health-giving rays.[81] After the war fears about the health of the nation intensified and sunlight was widely promoted as a saviour, a cure-all for the complaints of the modern age.

By the mid-1920s it was impossible to pick up a newspaper or maga-zine without seeing an article extolling the virtues of sunbathing. As one reporter put it, 'The glories of New Zealand sunshine and the wonder of New Zealand fresh air hav[e] been expounded to us until we can almost feel the freckles pop up'.[82] There were reports on the 'sunlight cure' in England, and similar experiments in Europe.[83] Plans were afoot to build a solarium in Napier and a health and rest home in Takapuna with a glassed-in upper storey so that the convalescents could sunbathe their way back to health.[84] The government passed an act allowing for daylight saving, the extra hour of sunshine welcomed by those who believed in the sunlight cure.[85] Open-air schooling was advocated as a way to increase the amount of fresh air and sunshine young New Zealanders could enjoy. Such schools would be hygienic and 'modernist', both very desirable characteristics.[86]

Modern man was a rational, scientific creature, swayed by intellect rather than emotion. Fortunately there was plenty of scientific evidence to persuade him of the benefits of sunbathing. With over 1000 scientists said to be studying the 'curative and preventative virtues of sunlight', he could read about the various rays that emanated from the sun, and the benefits of ultra-violet light.[87] He could listen to the rector of Waitaki Boys' High School as he discoursed on the importance of fresh air and sunshine:

> Sunlight is not only a powerful disinfectant and germicide, but it is also a stimulant. Now that the tonic effect of sunshine on the phagocytes has been established as well as its general beneficial influence on the whole system, we should teach our young people to place no reliance on the artificial stimulants of drugs such as alcohol, but to find invigoration in sunshine, exercise, and perspiration. The half octave of ultra-violet rays next to the violet in the solar spectrum is the precious essential for the maintenance of life upon the earth. The relationship of sunlight to vitamines has been amply demonstrated by recent scientific research.[88]

If the word of the headmaster of a prominent boys' school was not good enough, there were always overseas experts to turn to.

In the early twentieth century a Swiss doctor called Auguste Rollier set up a sun-therapy clinic at the town of Leysin, high in the Swiss Alps, to treat sufferers of tuberculosis, rickets and infantile paralysis. In the fresh mountain air, exposed to the health-giving properties of the sun, his patients were cured of their debilitating diseases. News of Rollier's success spread around the world, and by the 1920s his reputation was well established in New Zealand. Reports of the beneficial effects of sunlight often mentioned his work, and there were even suggestions that the Southern Alps could play the same health-giving role here as the Swiss Alps did in Europe.[89] Of course, most people did not suffer from tuberculosis, and the beach was handier than the Alps. But whether the body needed a little dip or a long soak in a sunbath, New Zealanders, too, believed in the restorative and curative powers of ultra-violet rays.[90]

If modern man was meant to be scientific and rational, modern woman was assumed to be a caring mother who put her children's health first. She, too, turned to experts for advice and guidance, and her guru was Truby King. A great advocate of the value of ultra-violet rays, he promised mothers that if they took their children to the beach, the sun would strengthen their young bodies against the 'poisonous microbes' that threatened their good health.[91] Aware that in the economically straitened late 1920s it might not be possible to take a holiday at the beach, Plunket reminded mothers that sunshine was a 'child's natural birthright', and that by the end of the summer their children should be as 'brown as a berry', even if the tan was acquired in the back garden, rather than at the seashore. 'Sunraying The Baby' was encouraged from the time the child was two months old, with '[e]xposure, not protection' required for young bodies.[92]

In this climate new organisations were formed, set on spreading the word about the health-giving properties of the sun. A Sunshine Health Club was formed in Auckland in 1927, and in 1931 the Sunlight League of New Zealand held its inaugural meeting in Christchurch.[93] This was not a fringe movement. Anglican Archbishop Churchill Julius was in the chair and he was joined on stage by the Minister of Health, the Mayor of Christchurch and prominent physicians including Renfrew White and Dr Elspeth Fitzgerald. Cora Wilding, the instigator of the league, was also to the fore that night.[94] Founded along the same lines as Dr Caleb Saleeby's Sunlight League of England, the New Zealand organisation aimed to edu-

The mothers of these three girls clearly believed that exposure, not protection, was required in order for their daughters to grow up healthy and strong. As the children of nudists, the girls probably exposed rather more than Truby King thought was appropriate. *Australian Sunbather*, January 1951. Mitchell Library, Sydney.

cate the public to appreciate 'sunlight and fresh air as a means to health'.[95] As Renfrew White noted in his speech that night, they wanted to 'promote national efficiency by improving national health'.[96]

There was more than a eugenic tinge to all of this, and quite a hard-line, genetically determined tinge at that. Professor John Macmillan Brown, Chancellor of the University of New Zealand and a supporter of the Sunlight League, wrote an article on 'Eugenism' at the time the league was formed. Urging New Zealanders to 'cultivate as an instinct [a] regard for posterity', he advocated compulsory sterilisation of those he considered unfit to breed.[97] At the league's annual meeting in 1934, Dr F. Montgomery Spencer of Wellington spoke about the need to arrest the deterioration of the British race, and suggested that sterilisation of the unfit was a kindness rather than a cruelty.[98] That year the league emphasised its commitment to the eugenic movement by publishing a booklet that reprinted nine articles on the subject.[99] The horrors of the Nazi regime did not dissuade them. Like many New Zealanders in the early 1930s, league members spoke and wrote in favour of the German love of fresh air and sunshine.[100] Montgomery Spencer praised the Nazis for their promotion of civic worth and their valuing of racial purity. This, he argued, was something for New

The Sunlight League's Rules for Sunbathing. The instructions were clear and precise,
although some of the advice may seem dubious today. Varnished copies of these rules
could be found at holiday spots around New Zealand in the 1930s. H1, 35/27/1 35217,
Archives New Zealand/Te Whare Tohu Tuhituhinga o Aotearoa, Wellington.

Zealanders to aspire to.[101] The league's 1934 booklet noted with approval
German measures to prevent diseases 'from tainting future generations'
and suggested that Mussolini also was both insightful and right-headed.[102]
Even as the war came to a close the league's objects still included 'To educate people through the medical and scientific advisers of the League, in
the knowledge of the laws of heredity, the importance of civic worth and
racial value, and by the study of eugenics to exchange racial deterioration
for racial improvement'.[103]

Sunbathers were advised that patented products like Sydal, alongside baking soda and rose-water, could help keep their skin cool after a day in the hot sun. By the 1920s, mixed sunbaking was as common as mixed bathing. *Truth*, 19 January 1924.

There were clearly many disturbing aspects to the Sunlight League and its scientific claims, but it is important to remember that these views were not considered extreme in their day. Nor were they peculiar to New Zealand.[104] As James Walvin and Richard Rutt have noted, the sunbathing bug bit Englishmen in the 1930s thanks to ideas imported from Germany.[105] It is also important to note that the league was responsible for a number of other health measures. Members of the society gave regular radio talks, informing New Zealanders of the health benefits of fresh air and sunshine.[106] During the winter, when the sun was not shining, league members ran 'keep fit' classes for unemployed girls.[107] And during summer, when New Zealanders were flocking to the beach, the league produced and distributed its famous 'Rules for Sunbathing'.

By the 1920s, New Zealanders knew why they had to acquire a suntan. Scientists, doctors, government ministers and headmasters had all told them that it was their individual and civic duty to strengthen their bodies through sunlight. The question was, how? How could they turn their lily white bodies a rich shade of brown without suffering the agonies of

SUN bathers are warned against the practice. Their ignorance is blistering.

With the advent of the Sunlight League in 1931, and its Rules for Sunbathing posters, sunbakers had no excuses. But in 1929, when this cartoon appeared, the ignorance of these young flappers is said to be blistering. Despite their caps and parasol, they are still spending too much time in the midday sun, their bodies covered in olive or coconut oil. *Truth*, 3 October 1929.

– and even death from – sunburn? Early reports warned of the dangers of sunbathing and advised 'extreme caution', but went no further.[108] But slowly more practical articles began to appear, stressing the importance of taking a gradual and systematic approach to sunbathing.[109] The advice to cover your body in petroleum jelly, coconut or olive oil to prevent burning might have misled some, but if they spent only five to ten minutes in the sun on the first day, and then gradually built up their tolerance, the damage was probably not too severe. If it was, remedies were at hand. Smearing a thick paste of baking soda on burnt skin was said to provide instant relief, while rose water relieved redness.[110]

The Sunlight League, though, did not believe that anyone should suffer sunburn on the way to getting a healthy tan. Members were aware that doctors had warned those in poor health not to overexpose themselves to the sun, and that others were debasing the movement by referring to it as a 'cult'.[111] They also heard of cases where children had been badly burnt after sunbathing for too long at the beach. Worried about such developments, the league printed up posters of their sunbathing rules. In their first summer they sent 200 of these varnished posters to life-saving and surf bathing clubs around New Zealand.[112]

Beachgoers had no excuses. Everywhere they turned, a Sunlight League poster, leaflet or booklet spelled out the rules for safe sunbathing:

> Sunlight Leagues' Rules for Sunbathing
> 1. Head and Neck must always be protected by sunhat.
> 2. 'Hasten Slowly.' Remember, the whole body is unaccustomed to the light. To commence sunbathing, let child wear just knickers and vest for five minutes. The next day, discard the vest. The third day, give sunbath of ten minutes; while for each successive day, give a few minutes longer.
> 3. Blistering of skin is thus avoided. **'Sunburning is not Sunbathing.'**
> 4. In summer, the best hours for sunbathing are before 11 o'clock.
> In winter, however, the best time is between 11 and 2 o'clock. It is not the heat rays, but the light rays (which produce chemical action), which are the more important.[113]

League members also gave radio talks on safe sunbathing.[114]

Sunbathers, though, were slow learners, and every year people suffered serious burns from overdoing their daily dose. The league worried that these people gave sunbathing a bad name, and asked them to take responsibility for their own actions:

> In future will the novice who chooses to commence sunbathing with one or two hours' exposure to a hot summer sun, instead of a few minutes, blame himself for the consequent disastrous results, and not condemn sunbathing. The result of his lack of common sense may help to prevent others from making use of this powerful promoter of health and fitness.[115]

Disappointed with those who continued to ignore the rules and showed a 'complete disregard of commonsense, and the necessity of commencing gradually', they struggled on, reprinting 500 copies of their poster and hoping for the best.[116] Goodness only knows what they thought of the women who took to wearing cellophane 'sun-tan slips' on the beach. The claim that wrapping your body in clear viscose allowed you to 'acquire a smooth, even coat of tan without the attendant discomforts of sunburn' seems doubtful.[117] At least league members could take comfort from the official support they received. The Minister of Railways, Dan Sullivan, asked that their posters be displayed at all seaside railway stations and the

As this advertisement for Q-Tol makes clear, the less sunbathers wore, the more
they needed after-sun remedies to relieve their sunburn and promote their
suntans. In the early 1930s a new fashion for backless costumes meant women
had to rely on others to slather on their Q-Tol. *Truth*, 7 November 1934.

Minister in Charge of Physical Welfare and Recreation, Bill Parry, congrat-
ulated them on the wise counsel they offered sunbathers.[118]

The health claims of sunbathing swayed government ministers like
Sullivan and Parry, and were clearly important in legitimising sunbaking as a leisure activity, but it would be a mistake to think that sunbathers regarded going to the beach in the same light as a visit to the doctor or
chemist. The beach meant pleasure as well as leisure, and sunbathing was
about sensuality and fashion, as well as health and national well-being.

It is not always possible to distinguish between what was leisure and
therefore good for you, and what was simply pleasurable and enjoyable.
When Wellington physical culture instructor Garnet Sims performed gymnastics on the beach with his pupil and 'lady friend', Dorothy Harrison,
they were both exercising and having fun – so much fun that he found
himself in court, embroiled in messy divorce proceedings.[119] Beach gymnastics became something of a fashion by the 1930s. New Zealand never
experienced the institutionalised beach sports clubs of France or the organisation of Santa Monica's Muscle Beach, but young people were using
beaches as outdoor gyms.[120] Couples went down to the sands to practise
adagio, a combined form of dance and gymnastics in which young men
lifted and flipped their flexible young women partners as though they
were as light as feathers.[121] Muscular men tossed one another through the
air, and human pyramids could be seen on beaches throughout the dominion.[122] The Sunlight League approved of these developments. After all,
the ancient Greeks had taken their exercise outdoors, exposing their skin
to the sun's rays as they did so.[123] The league was less impressed, though,
by those who enjoyed the beach and sunbathing for the sensual and
sexual pleasures they offered.

Even in the days of neck-to-knee costumes, voyeurs flocked to the seaside. When surf-bathing became common at Dunedin's St Clair Beach,
sales of fieldglasses and telescopes 'boomed'.[124] For those who wanted a

NOW THEN, AUSTRALIANS, CAN YOU BEAT THESE NEW ZEALAND LADS? IF YOU THINK YOU CAN, DON'T HANG FIRE—JUST SEND YOUR PHOTOS ALONG!

Every Physical Culturist Should Sport Their "H. & P.C." Badge or Brooch. Send 2/6 in Stamps for Yours Now!

At the beach, and at beachside parks, young New Zealand men worked together to show off their strength and agility. In the centre shot Mr C. Tucker supports Miss Coligrave on his left forearm. This spread appeared in the Sydney-based magazine, *Health and Physical Culture,* and editor Alfred Briton threw out a challenge to his Australian readers to better the efforts of their Kiwi counterparts. *Health and Physical Culture,* 1 December 1941. Mitchell Library, Sydney.

closer look, strolling along the sands could be very rewarding. They might stumble across young men who had rolled the legs of their costumes up as high as they could, folded down the tops of their swimsuits 'Till there was only a narrow band round them, and there they lay stretched full length on the sand, or ran races on the beach'. It was not a sight the Auckland City Council wanted its ratepayers exposed to, but it was there for all to see.[125] By the 1920s the sight of 'bold, bad lads and lasses' lying on the sands together had become so common that such images found

Gordon Burt's 1940s campaign for Jantzen swimwear played on the idea of bathing
beauties. In first place, at the top of the podium, is Joan Archer (Ongley).
Barbara Taylor (Shand) stands to her left, while June Allison poses on her right.
Gordon Burt Collection, F-36937-1/2, Alexander Turnbull Library, Wellington.

their way into advertisements.[126] The penny-in-the-slot machines found at
local beaches were tame compared with what could be seen in the flesh.[127]
Popular verse was composed to the 'Beach Girls' who 'strew the beach'.
There were 'The seems-they-could-be-had ones', 'The love-you-for-your-
cash ones' and 'The shout-us-to-the-show ones'.[128] These 'sirens of the sea'
were portrayed as sexual temptresses, lying in waiting, ready to ensnare
any man who passed by.[129]

   The girls on the sand were not sunbathing for the good of the nation;
rather, a key to their motivation was the changing idea of beauty. To be

considered beautiful, a woman now required 'sun-tinted' skin. White skin was no longer acceptable.[130] Tan lines were frowned upon, but older women were advised to cover up: 'They neither look well tanned nor do their skins have the resiliency necessary for an autumn come-back'.[131] To be beautiful a woman had to be young, tanned and look good in the latest bathing costume. And every season that costume got briefer, and more of her body was revealed for all to see. Scientists and doctors might proclaim that this was all in the name of good health, but for those putting on the new season's swimwear, and those watching the parade of bathing beauties, other considerations were often paramount.[132]

In 1904, a popular weekly magazine published a short tale about a misunderstood bathing suit. Determined to prove its modesty, the costume asked a violet how it had gained its reputation as a shy, retiring flower. The violet answered 'I shrink!' and so the bathing costume 'went away and began to shrink, and the more it shrank the more it got itself talked about, until at last there was an unbearable scandal'.[133] The author of this little story might have thought turn-of-the-century costumes were scandalously brief, but within a generation bathing suits had shrunk so much that people began to wonder if it was worth putting them on at all. Over the first half of the twentieth century swimwear all but disappeared as sunbathers tried to tan as much of their bodies as decency would allow, and men and women enjoyed displaying as much of their reshaped bodies as they could get away with. It was a tale of bodily performance, of people dressing up in costumes designed to catch the eye and attention of other beachgoers. It was a tale of modesty, decency and sexual desire.[134]

There was an unappreciated irony to the shrinking violet story, in that wearing bathing costumes at all was a relatively recent development. Until the mid-nineteenth century it was still common for Englishmen to swim naked. Public baths in London did not require men to wear any form of costume until 1860. Even then, if men swam away from public view then no one objected if they did so in the nude.[135] These were the standards brought to New Zealand by the early settlers. If people – for the most part, men – wished to swim naked, and kept out of public sight, then they were not deemed to be breaching any moral or legal code.[136]

Nude swimming continued into the early twentieth century. Around the time the shrinking bathing suit story appeared, the *New Zealand Graphic* noted that men who swam on the Auckland foreshore during day-

HE FELT IT KEENLY.

Elderly Spinster (horrified) : "Little boy, aren't you ashamed to go in
bathing in such a public place with such a bathing-suit as that on ?"
    Small Boy : " Yes'm ; but me mother makes me wear it. I'll take it off,
though, if you'll promise not to say nothing to her about it.

Not quite naked, this small boy wishes that his mother would not make
him don his swimming trunks. Adult men at the time were required
to wear neck-to-knee costumes, though many flouted the by-laws.
New Zealand Graphic, 17 November 1900.

light hours should be required to wear a neck-to-knee bathing costume.[137]
Clearly, many were wearing considerably less. Down at New Brighton
Constable Rowe was having to tell off 'kiddies who swam without the for-
mality of putting on bathing trunks', while at Onehunga men bathed off
the wharf wearing 'scanty attire' at best: many still swam naked.[138] As late
as 1913 cases were still noted of men who swam naked at local beaches.
A group of women on Takapuna Beach were said to have been shocked
when some young men left the water, their naked bodies exposed for all
to see.[139]

   When it came to women's bathing attire, though, the shrinking violet
story contained more than a grain of truth. In the late 1890s, women had
been encouraged to bathe in a three-piece suit: a serge jacket, loose drawers that tied below the knee, with a skirt over the drawers. Up to 36 yards
of fabric were required to make one of these outfits.[140] By the time the
violet story appeared, bathing costumes had become knee-length,[141] but

FOR THE RUSH TO THE SEA.

In these elaborate outfits it was difficult for women to rush anywhere. The costume
on the left was made of black pongee silk, trimmed with lace and silk braid and
fastened with mother-of-pearl buttons. The middle outfit was a simpler creation
of blue serge trimmed with cream wool. Before and after their swim, women were
encouraged to wear beach capes, such as the one on the right. Fastened with red
satin ribbons, the red molleton cloak with its hood and high collar encased her
body and protected her modesty. *New Zealand Graphic*, 2 January 1904.

they were still elaborate and expensive fashion statements, with names
like the 'Promenade' (which had a sailor collar and puffed sleeves, and
could be yours for 10s 6d), rather than practical swimsuits.[142] But as more
women took up swimming, tightly laced, heavily skirted bathing dresses
had to give way to sleeker, form-fitting suits.[143] Skirtless and sleeveless
outfits were recommended for women who took their health and responsibilities seriously, and learned how to swim.[144]

The health benefits of swimming helped to dampen concerns about
the indecency of shrinking bathing suits. Swimming clubs further aided
the cause by imposing strict costume requirements on their members.
Local swimming clubs adopted the costume regulations of the English
Amateur Swimming Association: navy or black neck-to-knee suits, with

Although it was not required on all beaches, most of these 1910 swimmers chose
to wear trunks over their one-piece swimming costumes. By this time most bathing
suits were sleeveless and were cut off at mid-thigh rather than the knee. Indeed,
when councils tried to impose neck-to-knee regulations they were informed that it
was impossible to buy costumes that conformed to their by-laws. Steffano Webb
Collection, G-9066-1/1, Alexander Turnbull Library, Wellington.

shoulder straps at least 2 inches wide, the legs of the suit not higher than 3
inches above the knee and the neckline not more than 2 inches below the
pit of the neck.[145] Costume stewards were on hand to ensure that the rules
were adhered to. For those who did not belong to a club, local authorities
were happy to step in and act as costume stewards at pools and beaches.

In the days of single-sex swimming, costume regulations at pools were
fairly relaxed. In the 1880s, the Auckland City Council required swimmers
to wear short bathing drawers, rather than a swimming suit, at its Albert
Street pool.[146] When the Teps were opened in 1914, boys and men could
hire a pair of brown trunks when they went for a swim.[147] As at Albert
Street, most of their bodies were revealed, but since no women were present this was deemed permissible. At the council's mixed-bathing pools,
though, everyone had to wear regulation neck-to-knee costumes, and the
men were also required to wear trunks over their bathing suits. The trunks
were not required on the beach, but proper costumes were.[148]

Custodians enforced costume requirements at pools, but on the beach the absence of an ever-present constraining force meant swimmers and sunbathers could bend the by-laws. Women took to wearing bathing suits 'of a distinctly Continental cut and texture', described as 'elegant' by those who opposed the by-laws, and 'scarcely sufficient or decent' by those who supported the culture of constraint. The women enjoyed wearing and being seen to wear their figure-hugging costumes.[149] Men also rejected the councillors' moral code as outmoded and unflattering. Their necklines plunged more than the regulation 2 inches, and the legs of their suits crept well above the 3-inch limit. This was 'Nature so lightly clad that one can guess the rest'.[150] Having got their bodies into shape, these swimmers did not want their hard work to go unnoticed.

Constable Rowe of New Brighton certainly noticed three bathers in breach of the borough's bathing by-laws in 1909. He arrested the men for not wearing regulation costumes, and for loitering on the beach (instead of dressing immediately on leaving the water, they had gone up to the sand dunes to sun themselves). A test case was taken against one of the accused, Herbert Withall, the authorities hoping that a quick conviction would warn others to obey the standards of decency their by-laws represented. The magistrate who heard the case, though, was not impressed with the charges. He accepted that it was impossible to buy a costume that went from neck to knee and that the bathing suit Withall had worn was standard attire on the beaches of Europe and England. The charges were dismissed.[151]

The decision did not deter local authorities. They continued to pass neck-to-knee regulations, and in some cases extended the rules so that men had to wear trunks over their costumes at the beach as well as the pool.[152] Beachgoers fought back. At New Brighton a group decided to stage a mock protest at the council's desire for a 'clean beach'. Wearing overcoats, hats, sou'westers, and full-length nightgowns, they marched up and down the beach carrying signs declaring 'We want a clean beach' and yelling slogans to the assembled crowd. They then dashed into the water, where many of them lost their top hats and bowlers as the waves crashed around them.[153] Their procession echoed a demonstration by 250 bathers at Sydney's Bondi Beach a couple of years before, where swimmers had also protested against similar costume regulations. As Douglas Booth has written, 'Humour and laughter are potent strategies of resistance'.[154] Mayors who tried to enforce neck-to-knee regulations deserved to be mocked, and when magistrates agreed with the bathers, and refused

to enforce the by-laws, swimmers took heart, rolling the legs of their costumes up even further. Men also began to unbutton the tops of their suits
and fold down the jersey part of their costumes, all the better for the sun
to work its magic on their torsos.

Perhaps this is what Ernest Clay was doing when he was arrested
at Lyall Bay in 1915 and charged with breaching the city's bathing by-
laws. His offence: 'exposing about three inches of his manly bosom'. Clay
claimed that a button was missing from his costume, but the police acted
as though far more than a piece of thread was at stake. At their insistence
Clay was made to put on his costume in court, although the magistrate
drew the line at dousing him with water to replicate the conditions at the
beach (the police inspector explained that when the costume was wet
it sagged and even more of Clay's chest was exposed). Clay enjoyed the
same outcome as Withall: the magistrate dismissed the case.[155] Beaches
could be awash with bathing by-laws, but swimmers, and magistrates, felt
no compunction to follow them.

Tensions between the letter of the by-laws and common practice intensified after the Great War as more people took to swimming and sunbathing at the beach. Councils continued to dictate what beachgoers should
wear and how they should behave. Although they enjoyed some public
support, the beach became increasingly free. The surrounding streets and
suburbs were places of respectability and responsibility, but in the water,
and on the sands, rules and regulations were toyed with.

Although it was impossible to buy a costume that actually went from
neck to knee, local authorities managed to ignore this consumer conun-
drum as they revised their bathing by-laws. In Auckland, for example, the
neck-to-knee requirement was repeated in 1912, 1917 and 1925.[156] The
Napier City Council continued to insist that swimmers wear neck-to-
knee suits into the late 1920s.[157] Down in Canterbury the New Brighton
Borough Council clung to the regulation, surrendering only when the borough merged with the city of Christchurch in 1941.[158] In New Plymouth
the requirement remained in place into the mid-1950s.[159]

The regulations may have been on the books, but it was increasingly
rare that they were enforced. When they were, the public protested and
the press had a field day. 'Seaside Visitor', for example, was indignant
when a 'gigantic dragoon in [an] imposing uniform' was employed to
stalk Auckland's beaches in 1926. The visitor was not impressed when
'The stormy petrel' reminded swimmers that they were meant to be wearing neck-to-knee costumes, and that sunbathing breached city by-laws.[160]

Running along the beach without the covering of a cape or overcoat and wearing costumes well above their knees, these young New Zealanders were not concerned that they were flouting local by-laws. The bathing suit worn by the woman on the left would have been considered especially risqué: light in colour it revealed far more of her body than the darker suits favoured by local authorities. In 1929 she is still wearing a skirted costume. Within a few years this protective covering would be removed and even more of her body would be on show. *Health and Physical Culture*, 1 November 1929. Mitchell Library, Sydney.

Bathers at Sumner in 1929 were similarly shocked when the local constable told them to put on their beach wraps or coats before they walked along the beach. Although this was required by the by-laws, 'it is not very often that it is enforced'.[161] Sumner's mayor, W. H. Nicholson, was scorned for encouraging the police to revive the regulation, and reminded that in this modern age, seeing scantily clad young bodies on the beach was 'so familiar that it passes almost unnoticed'.[162] Costume requirements and sunbathing bans were not much in force at Lyall Bay either, but in 1935 the police decided to take down the names of men who had stripped to the waist to sunbathe, and those who wore bathing shorts rather than a neck-to-knee costume. Remembering earlier cases, the press suggested that 'If any prosecution follows the Police Department runs an excellent

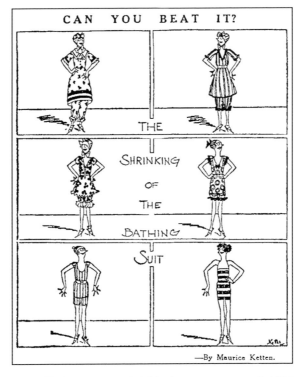

CAN YOU BEAT IT?

THE SHRINKING OF THE BATHING SUIT

—By Maurice Ketten.

Council by-laws were not shrinking but costumes were. In 1926
cartoonist Maurice Ketten asks, 'Can you beat it?' Within a few years, with
the introduction of the two-piece, and then the bikini, the answer was a
resounding 'yes'. *Auckland Star*, 2 October 1926.

chance of failing dismally to prove the alleged indecency, and of convict-
ing itself of being right out of touch with public opinion'. All over the
country, men and women were baking in the sun, wearing costumes that
made little contact with their necks and had not even a passing acquaintance with their knees. As the journalist wrote, 'The antiquated neck-to-
knee rule is enduring a living death'.[163]

The general public may have shown complete disregard for the bathing by-laws, but swimming clubs continued to uphold costume constraints and practise 'safe competing'. Costume stewards were on hand
to ensure that regulations were adhered to, and that 'lady competitors'
wore a cloak as they made their way to the starting blocks, and when they
left the water. The sport that had brought about swimwear reform, and

provided a public occasion for bodies to be revealed, remained true to its nineteenth-century origins, despite the fact that by the mid-1930s most men on the beach were wearing bathing shorts and a fair few women had adopted shorts and a brassiere top as their preferred beachwear.[164]

A variation on neck-to-knee costumes could be found on most beaches around New Zealand into the 1930s. The neckline was not as high as councillors desired, and the length not as low, but the basic outfit remained true to its swimming club origins. Because the costumes were dark in colour, women had to rely on bright bathing caps to add a touch of fashion and individuality.[165] But in the 1920s, as beachgoing became such a popular pastime, and both sunbathing and swimming were encouraged, new beach fashions made their way into the shops and onto the sands. In this postwar hedonistic climate, even designers like Chanel produced swimsuits.[166] Consumerism was paramount, and Hollywood was set to play an important role. Mabel Normand's post-war film *The Venus Model*, for example, showed viewers that a new bathing dress design could save an ailing business, and flatter a young woman's figure. In one scene Mabel donned a body-hugging outfit and was said to have provided the men in the audience with a vision worth dreaming about.[167]

Women were assumed to be the natural consumers of fashion, eager to know what colour this year's costume should be, and whether their towelling beach wrap should have sleeves.[168] But women were not portrayed as slaves to fashion; rather, it was recognised that 'The beach . . . allows women a freedom they are denied anywhere else, and they make the most of it'.[169] It was also recognised that the beach offered men far more clothing freedom than they enjoyed in the city. Despite the brave efforts of a few men in Christchurch (including physical culturist Dr Thacker), who formed a Summer Dress Reform League, encouraging men to wear 'saner and healthier clothing', most men clung to their collars and ties and dark coloured suits. They were not ready to saunter down the street in an open-necked shirt.[170] But at the beach, 'mermen' were prepared to reveal their personalities as well as their bodies in brightly coloured and patterned swimwear. In the mid-1920s many men still donned navy and black suits, but others took to wearing more striking outfits. One young man strolled along Takapuna beach in 'a crushed strawberry creation with mauve and orange stripes', while a 'dandy' at Devonport put on a green and yellow suit. Even if they wore regulation costumes reporters noted that '[i]t is a striking fact that the men with the best figures wear well-fitting bathing raiment' unlike the 'human hairpin' men, who wore old cotton costumes that flopped below their knees.[171] It was not only women who aimed to be bathing beauties and show off their bodies and tans before an admiring audience.

As the popularity of sunbathing grew, swimwear manufacturers began to cut away sections of bathing costumes, all the better to let the sun shine on previously covered parts of the body. Whether they were responding to the scientific health claims of ultra-violet light research, or the growing desire of many to show off their bodies, costumes began to appear that further defied neck-to-knee by-laws. In the late 1920s costumes were designed with a deep V cut into their backs. These were already popular in Hollywood, 'and where Hollywood leads the rest of the world soon follows'. New Zealand was no exception. If health claims provided a justification for this, so be it. The fact was backless evening gowns were in fashion and women needed to be able to tan their backs.[172]

Within a couple of years the deep V had given way to an even 'briefer, snappier and more backless bathing suit'. Medical and scientific justifications were still offered in defence of this risqué fashion statement, but despite the qualms of moralists the 'modern miss' was wedded to her revealing suit.[173] Local manufacturer, Roslyn, sold many of its new 'sunshine back' costumes, even though New Zealand was in the grip of a major economic depression.[174]

New Zealand men were not ignored in this changing swimwear climate. They were also encouraged to buy a new suit each season so that they, too, wore the latest colours and styles. Otherwise, Jantzen pointed out, they would feel 'shabby' next to their friends.[175] And it would be obvious if they had resisted the lure of the most up-to-date Jantzen. Made of wool and cotton, costumes quickly lost their shape and colour: a few dips in the sea and a few hours lying in the sun, and bathing suits became saggy, baggy, faded rags. Not only that, but men's styles were changing, and fast. The V back had been replaced by the 'sunshine back', and then Jantzen brought out 'The Topper' and 'The Sun-Suit'. Both had detachable tops: men could unzip the top half of their 'Topper' and sun both their chests and backs.[176] Men's costumes had not just shrunk, they had been cut in half.[177]

Joanna Bourke has noted that the English Men's Dress Reform Party, which boasted the support of sunlight advocates Caleb Saleeby and Fred Hornibrook, was not a particularly successful organisation, except when it came to beachwear. By the early 1930s the party had persuaded 38 English seaside resorts to allow men to wear bathing shorts as they

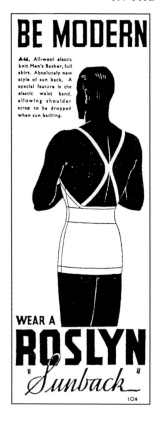

The modern man wore a 'Sunback' costume, made of an all-wool elastic knit so that his curves were shown to best advantage. The shoulder straps on the 'Sunback' were designed to be dropped down, allowing for an all-over tan. *Truth*, 26 September 1934.

sunned and swam.[178] The Christchurch movement did not make any pronouncements on bathing attire, but members such as R. Atkinson Reddell were well-known advocates of suntanning. Reddell ran an 'Electrical Health Institute' in Christchurch, where clients could strip off and enjoy the benefits of artificial sunlight treatment.[179] Now at local beaches, too, men were casting off their tops. Even the New Zealand Surf and Life-Saving Association agreed that the time had come for men to bare their manly bosoms. In 1934 they declared that if a man wore a pair of woollen bathing shorts on the beach, without a top, he should be considered 'decently' attired. The association argued that such an outfit was considered acceptable in England and Europe, and on some Australian beaches too, and that it was time for neck-to-knee regulations to be removed once and for all.[180] Many men seem to have agreed. Within a very short time

UNDOUBTEDLY.

HAROLD—"They tell me, Ethel, that your aunt, Miss Thinly, will not go in bathing until after dark. Is it a fad?"
ETHEL—"No: it's a matter of form with her, I believe."

She is not too fat but Ethel's aunt, Miss Thinly, will still not be seen in her
bathing costume. Ethel and her friends, though, are happy to parade in front
of Harold and his mate. *New Zealand Graphic*, 10 December 1904.

men all over the country were wearing bathing shorts as they swam and
sunbaked.[181]

Women's fashions also continued to evolve, ensuring that new outfits were bought each season. Aided by revolutionary elastic yarns such
as Lastex, swimwear designers were able to produce costumes that clung
to dry as well as wet bodies.[182] In 1936 one of their innovations was to
remove the slight skirted front on women's suits which acted as a thin veil
over their pubic area.[183] By then some women had already decided to do
away with one-piece suits. They did not go topless, as the men had, but
took to wearing a brassiere top with their shorts. Drawing on the customs
of Europe and some – but not all – English beaches, they decided that
their stomachs as well as their backs deserved to be coated in tan and seen
by other beachgoers.[184]

The cost of these more revealing outfits was not just financial. Putting
on any bathing costume exposed the wearer to the glances and comments
of others. Wet costumes clung to bodies, and even if the outfit was neck-
to-knee, the swimmer's body was still revealed. Before backless and two-
piece suits had made an appearance, critics were noting that it was a 'pity
. . . that all the ladies' who wore figure-hugging outfits 'have not the shape
of Venus'.[185] As more women took to sea bathing in the 1920s, wearing

The Girl: "How could you tell it was me at that distance? You couldn't see my face!"

The Man: "Oh, that didn't matter; I'm very quick at figures."

—The Humorist.

Her costume is still skirted, but the neck is low and the leg high. More importantly, she has the right figure to catch his eye. *New Zealand Herald*, 17 October 1925.

abbreviated, shrunken bathing suits, commentators noted that the sight before them was 'very pleasing to the eye, especially the masculine eye'. But if the bather was 'plump' then she became the object of derision, said to have come rather too far through her costume.[186] When backless suits came in, the stakes were raised:

> Get into a clinging one-piece bathing suit and see how much disguising you can do to your figure. You'll be revealed to the world as Nature and your own slackness made you. Firm muscles and graceful lines do not develop unaided, and if you've been shirking the truth about your own figure, have a dress rehearsal before a mirror early in the summer, and enlist an outspoken brother to tell you what's wrong.[187]

If nothing else worked, shame was used to encourage New Zealanders to reshape their bodies before revealing them on the beach.

By the late 1930s controversies over shrinking bathing costumes had begun to recede. Trunks were *de rigueur* for men, and women were often seen in backless suits, with some exposing their midriff as they took to wearing brassiere tops and shorts. After the war, though, a new controversy exploded on the beaches of New Zealand as Louis Réard's bikini

With the men in their trunks and one of the women in a two-piece, this young group
epitomises the carefree beach attire of the 1940s. Unlike Mabel in the Three Castles
advertisement of 1912, women could now be seen smoking at the beach. Ironically,
Clifton Firth shot this photograph as part of a campaign for Korma sweaters.
34-K145A, Special Collections, Auckland City Libraries.

sent shockwaves through polite society. Before the war French women
had been seen on the beach wearing 'The tiniest of brassier's [*sic*] and
brief shorts', but their tops still had straps, and their shorts came up well
over their hip bones.[188] All this changed after the war, as the tops became
skimpier and lost their shoulder straps, and shorts gave way to very brief
knickers that sat well below the hips. After the Great War hedonism had

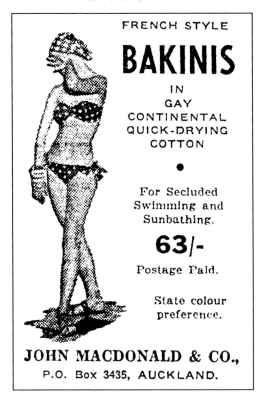

FRENCH STYLE

BAKINIS

IN
GAY
CONTINENTAL
QUICK-DRYING
COTTON

•

For Secluded
Swimming and
Sunbathing.

63/-

Postage Paid.

State colour
preference.

JOHN MACDONALD & CO.,
P.O. Box 3435, AUCKLAND.

If they were not available at their local clothing store, women could mail order
French bathing costumes from an Auckland company. The woman wearing
her polka-dot 'bakini' is not confident enough to face the camera or wear her
outfit in public. It would not be long, though, before New Zealand beaches were
covered in women wearing bikinis. *Truth*, 2 October 1956.

led to colourful, backless costumes. Now swimwear shrank further, and
was named after the site of atomic tests.

By late 1945 bikinis were on display in the window of a Christchurch
shop, and reports of controversy abut the new 'French style' bathing costume were coming in from Sydney (it took some time before the name
bikini became common).[189] When a Wellington store decided to dress
some mannequins in a bikini, '[t]he footpath was blocked with curious,
critical crowds–even the nearby point-duty inspectors found it difficult
to keep their eyes off the models'.[190] In 1902 it had been James Young's
window performance that caused a stir; in 1919 a leg model display had

"I SHOULD have bought this
new swimsuit much earlier in
the season!"

By the 1950s bikinis were commonplace in beach cartoons.
Within a summer this woman's swimming costume has shrunk
considerably, as her tan lines reveal. *Truth*, 28 January 1953.

done the same; now in 1945 the bikini brought traffic (and traffic cops) to
a standstill.

It took some time, though, for local women to feel comfortable enough
to wear a bikini on the beach. Early reports noted that many women did
not have the figure to wear such a revealing costume.[191] And though it was
possible for women to wear bikinis on local beaches – the town clerk at
Northcote, for example, said he could not see that anyone would worry
if women wore them – most women were not prepared to be quite so
continental.[192] As late as 1951, bikinis were not on sale in New Zealand
shops.[193]

The tide was turning, though, and by the end of the decade bikinis had
become commonplace.[194] Cartoonists drew them, women bought them,

and every year they seemed to shrink just a little bit more.[195] Men's bathing shorts also shrunk. Soon after the war men started to wear briefer trunks, with side laces rather than a solid, material panel. Although banned in some swimming pools, these 'hippies' remained popular. Those who worried about their laces coming undone opted for lower cut briefs, with only an inch or two of material at the side, rather than the pre-war average of 6-8 inches.[196] Claims about the health benefits of swimming and sunbathing were a distant memory. Pleasure was the focus at the beach.

Encouraging everybody to learn how to swim, and teaching them how to sunbathe revealed New Zealand bodies to the public's gaze in an unprecedented way. In the name of health and good citizenship, New Zealanders had entered a 'light era', with the promise that soon 'The superman will be almost an accomplished fact'.[197] The trickle of reports raising concerns about the long-term effects of sunbathing and its association with an increased risk of cancer had yet to make much of an impact.[198] The focus was on becoming tanned all over, because '[t]he browner we are the happier' we are.[199] Leisure was giving way to pleasure, just as neck-to-knee costumes were giving way to hippies and bikinis. For some, true leisure and pleasure could be achieved only if costumes were discarded altogether. From the late 1920s New Zealanders could read about the freedom Germans enjoyed as they sunbathed in the nude and swam without the hindrance of a costume.[200] These were not stories about midnight nude bathers who stripped off as a dare, or because they had drunk too much – though plenty of stories along these lines also appeared – but accounts of people who, for their health's sake, and for the sake of national and racial fitness, believed in taking off all of their clothes whenever possible.[201] The same cultural and scientific climate that encouraged swimming and sunbathing and bathing suit reform, also gave a certain legitimacy to the gymnosophists, the men and women we normally refer to as nudists.

Five Indecent Exposure?[1]

Around the same time that Roslyn's new backless swimsuits were making waves, another story about the body at leisure hit the headlines. 'New Zealand Does Not Want Cult of Nakedness: Nudism Invades New Zealand' proclaimed the weekly, *Truth*.[2] The newspaper was responding to stories that a group of hardy southerners had formed the Dunedin Gymnosophy Club, modelled on the 'best' clubs in England and the United States. Its founders were looking for land so that those who wanted to sunbathe, swim and do their physical exercises in the nude would have a place to go. The founding committee sent a circular outlining their intentions to various swimming clubs in Dunedin. They felt that swimmers would be especially interested in nudism, and hoped that a large number of women would join. Perhaps not surprisingly, this opened them up to a fair amount of 'ridicule and criticism', with some club members taking offence at the suggestion that swimmers were inclined to nudism. Many advocated rational swimming costumes, but they had no intention of taking their togs off. The nudists may have been hiding behind the 'euphemistic' name of gymnosophy, but the Dunedin swimmers intended to keep themselves nice by swimming with their costumes on.[3]

The very idea that organised nudism should arise in such a cold part of the country gave *Truth* plenty of opportunity for jibes about frostbite and chilblains, but the newspaper also declared that 'This extraordinary cult should be banned in New Zealand'. Noting that nudism had 'definite potentialities for evil', *Truth* interviewed clergymen to bolster its claim. Eric Flint, the honorary secretary of the Dunedin Gymnosophy Club, was also interviewed. Admitting that Dunedin was a little cool to be an ideal nudist retreat, Flint set out the club's aims and rules. *Truth* was impressed with Flint's sincerity but remained unconvinced about nudism's benefits

– except when it came to selling newspapers. Over the years it published many stories about nudists in New Zealand and elsewhere, happy to award them front-page status if the story generated sales.[4] Nudism should be banned, but stories about nudists could be banner headlines.

Nudism has not sparked the curiosity of many New Zealand historians. Like so many aspects of the story of the body at leisure, it barely rates a mention. Yet, like beauty contests and changing swimwear fashions, nudism raises many questions about when, how and why New Zealand bodies were revealed for display. To its advocates, nudism was as legitimate a leisure activity as physical culture and swimming. It shared their quest for health; it, too, was a form of corporeal control. To its opponents, though, nudism was the antithesis of bodily constraint. The health claims of nudists were clearly a front for pure, illegitimate pleasure. But many New Zealanders believed that, as a form of leisure and pleasure, nudism had much to recommend it. To find out why we have to leave the beach and enter the bush, the home of New Zealand's nudist camps.

Long before the formation of the Dunedin Gymnosophy Club there were nudists in New Zealand. One, Francis B. Hutchinson, had been a physician at Wellington Hospital in the late nineteenth century. In a guest editorial in *Sandow's Magazine*, Hutchinson recommended exercising in the nude, and also making the nude body 'honourable' again, as it had been in the time of the ancients. Like Dudley Sargent at Harvard, Hutchinson had been photographing and measuring the bodies of his pupils. He illustrated his article with two of these photographs, both showing young naked men in classical poses. Hutchinson suggested that all gymnasia proudly display nude pictures of their most beautiful and symmetrical members and that books of honour, *Libri d'oro*, be made containing pictures of the most beautiful naked, male bodies.[5]

Hutchinson's nude young men were there to be enjoyed but also to educate. Just as statues of David and the Discobolus in art galleries gave pleasure *and* instruction, so his photographs showed the public physical perfection and gave them something to strive towards. It was the same logic Sandow used to justify his stage show: the *Sandow Season* entertained, but it also gave him the opportunity to preach the benefits of the Sandow System. Sandow, though, did not appear on stage in the nude.

By holding up the classical ideal, Hutchinson dampened claims that there was anything coarse or tawdry about his celebration of the naked

One of the two young men photographed to illustrate Hutchinson's first article. He was naked when the shot was taken: his fig leaf was added for this public showing. *Sandow's Magazine*, June 1899. David Chapman Collection.

body, although his next contribution to Sandow's magazine might have raised some eyebrows. Recommending that the publication should include more photographs of young, naked men, he noted that it would give him 'pleasure' to exchange copies of such photographs with others.[6] Whether he managed to set up an international trade in photographs of naked men is unknown. Francis B. Hutchinson was not the sort of advocate New Zealand nudists wanted.

There was little public advocacy of nudism in early twentieth-century New Zealand. Occasionally stories about nudists made it into the newspapers, but these were about 'cranky . . . religious maniacs' like the Doukhobors in Canada who used nudity as a form of religious expression

Illustrating Hutchinson's second article, this 'Beautiful Study' was entitled 'After a Portion of the Frieze of the Temple of Apollo'. The classical references abounded, but Hutchinson was also keen to point out that the two men in the photograph were both 'eminent athletes, the elder a representative footballer, the youth ha[ving] carried off a shopful of prizes'. He claimed that he valued this photograph above all others that he had taken. Whether he valued it more highly before the fig leaves were added is not stated. *Sandow's Magazine*, May 1901. David Chapman Collection.

– returning to the simplicity of Adam and Eve – and as a way to protest against civic authority. Mass public nudity had strategic potential. When a group of Doukhobors went on a nude march in the winter of 1907, they probably did not anticipate that they would become objects of ridicule in the New Zealand press.[7] Besides religious fanatics, the public read about people in the nude being charged with indecent exposure and about the trade in indecent pictures.[8] There was, for example, the nude cyclist in

Christchurch, who sped through North Park and the golf links. Startled players at first thought he was dressed in white, until he got a little closer.[9] But before the Great War there was little public discussion that spelt out the case for and against the practice of nudism.

By the 1920s, though, nudism was attracting more attention. Sometimes this was unwelcome. When George Anderson took off his bathing suit after a swim at the beach he ended up in court, charged with indecency. Anderson claimed he was unaware that a group of women was able to see him drying off, but pleaded guilty to the offence and was fined for his carelessness. He also had to suffer the editorialising of *Truth*, under the heading 'Anderson Apes Apollo':

> In the good old days when the world was young, and Greece the centre of culture, nudeness was considered the height of art, and [t]he 'human form divine' is mentioned in many of the ancient classics. But those days are far distant, and although we treasure the memory of much of the finest in Grecian art and literature, we do not now conform to their custom regarding the naked body as the most beautiful thing in existence. Whether we have advanced or retarded is, of course, a matter of opinion, but the old saying, 'when in Rome do as the Romans,' still holds good, and it is as well for one to conform to the standards of the present day world, and always appear in public with one's understandings well obscured–that is, of course, if one desires to lead a peaceful existence, and keep clear of the law courts.[10]

Anderson's exposure of his 'understandings' may have been unintentional, but a growing number of people decided, contrary to *Truth*'s assertions, that the naked body was a thing of beauty and that the Greeks were right when they disrobed and celebrated the human form divine. Like Sandow and Hutchinson a generation before, many turned to the classical world to dress their support of nudism in respectability. It was no accident that the Dunedin organisation called itself the Gymnosophy Club.

Although the Dunedin group received a fair amount of attention in 1933, it is unlikely that this was the first attempt at organised nudism in New Zealand. There are suggestions that fifteen people started a club in Te Aroha in 1927. It lasted only a couple of years, but shortly afterwards a club was formed in Auckland. It, too, was short-lived.[11] But individual New Zealanders, and groups of friends, were practising nudism at home and on holiday. And once talk of nudist camps started, plenty of people were prepared to put up their hands as potential members.

It is impossible to say how many people practised nudism within the privacy of their own homes and gardens since they came to public attention only when their activities caused offence. This was the case with Riversdale farmer August Leitze, who appeared in court in 1931, charged with assault and obscene exposure. The magistrate noted that Leitze seemed to be '[i]ntroducing the nude cult' to the area, given his habit of working on his farm without the protection of clothing. Leitze's lawyer argued that his client believed that 'The healthiest way to live was to go about without clothes', but felt that this was taking the 'sunshine cure' too far. So did the magistrate, who remanded Leitze for medical examination.[12]

Most nudists, though, did not end up in court. Like Norman Gibson and Roy Ayling in Kaimiro, they managed to enjoy nudism without offending anyone, largely because they took great care not to be seen by others.[13] Three young women who 'dared to go nudist' during their summer holiday in February 1932 also took such precautions. They arranged to rent a whare on an isolated beach, and spent much of their time enjoying nude sunbathing and the 'invigorating feeling . . . [of] the waves against our bodies, unhampered with bathing costumes'. During a hailstorm they ran along the beach, the hailstones 'stinging' their bare bodies. This was illicit pleasure, yet the young women approached their holiday with the rigour and discipline one might expect at a health camp or a military base, rather than in a beach hut. Each day they rose at 5.30 a.m., and after a cup of milk and a biscuit exercised for half an hour before running along the beach and having an invigorating swim. After a hearty breakfast they returned to the beach to sunbathe, swim and 'ramble along the beach'. They continued to sunbathe after lunch, to ensure that they acquired 'as heavy a coating of tan as possible'. In the middle of the afternoon they swam again, and played a healthy game of cricket or rounders with the young men who provided them with fresh milk each day. Such games required that the young women put on their shorts, although after a few days they decided, 'by common consent', to swim in the nude with the young men. All of this was chaste: 'There was never once any mention or suggestion of sex during the whole time'. Dinner and 'yarning' followed, and the young women went to sleep about 8 p.m. When their month-long holiday was over, they left their nude beach 'feeling better and fitter than we had ever felt in our lives'. None had suffered a cold since returning to the clothed world, and like the children who attended health camps, all had put on weight. On average, their calves and thighs increased by over three-quarters of an inch and their busts by well over an inch.[14]

No member of the Wakatipu camping party was allowed to take photographs of their fellow campers, but nudist magazines were full of outdoor shots of young women in 'natural' surroundings. This picture, taken by I. J. Petterson of Akaroa, was used to illustrate an article on nudist 'Pioneers in New Zealand'. *Australian Sunbather*, March 1950. Mitchell Library, Sydney.

Although they had contact with their milk boys, the young women had decided on a single-sex nudist holiday. Other New Zealanders, though, holidayed in unsegregated nudist camps. In the late 1920s a group of fourteen southerners began an annual 'sun-bake camp' on the shores of Lake Wakatipu. One of the campers, T. W. Holland, wrote about the experience after their fourth trip. Unlike the young women, these campers were only semi-nude: the men wore athletic supports under their swimming Vs and the women Vs or short shorts and brassieres. But in other respects their camp was very similar to the young women's. The southern campers also rose at 5.30 a.m. for a swim or a run before tidying up their bedding (one rug per person) and going on 'parade' at 6 a.m. Half an hour of drill prepared the campers for breakfast, which was followed by 'free time': fishing, hunting, hiking, botanical and geological expeditions. The group reassembled in the late afternoon for a swim and rest before dinner 'which [wa]s held punctually at 6 o'clock'. After eating and clearing away dinner, they sat around the fire recounting their day's exploits, singing and telling stories. At 9 p.m. a light supper was served and by 9.30 they snuggled down in a 'sheltered nook among the thick native bush . . . and in two jiffs' were all sound asleep. The Wakatipu campers also recorded the health benefits of nudism:

> There is no doctor like Old Sol and no tonic like the fresh, exhilarating wind tanning the skin to a golden brown, and those who have never known the unparalleled freedom of swimming without cumbersome woollen tights, or the thrills of running and leaping through the sparkling freshness of a golden sunrise, have never known what it is to feel grandly and beautifully alive.

Playing to the stereotype that southerners were a little tight with their money, Holland also noted how much cheaper their camp was than any holiday resort; and it 'pays better dividends in splendid health and spirits'.[15]

Whether a daily way of life for individuals, or an annual experience by single or mixed sex groups, nudism was clearly being practised in New Zealand by the early 1930s. Nudists and would-be nudists were encouraged in this by reading overseas literature on the nudist movement. These books and magazines spelled out the increasingly popular nudist creed, and the press picked up on this interest, publishing stories about American plans for a nudist utopia in the South Seas,[16] women seeking divorces from husbands who insisted on practising nudism at home[17] and articles about nude beaches and nudist clubs in Spain, the United States and South Africa.[18] Cartoons also began to appear. The very first issue of *Man* magazine, an Australian monthly widely available in New Zealand, lampooned the 'Healthville Nudist Camp'.[19] The weekly press also poked fun. A cartoon by Gilmour noted that although nudism was booming in England, wintry conditions in the southern hemisphere meant it was making little headway in New Zealand.[20]

By the middle of 1935 Gilmour's claim that nudism was making 'no progress in N.Z.' was not quite true, as the publishers of his cartoon were well aware. *Truth* may have laughed at the nudists but it recognised that they were a growing force. The previous year it had announced that 'Nudism, like the trousers of the weaker sex has come to stay. In fact, an announcement is expected at any moment that the cult has been placed under State Control.'[21] Although support in New Zealand did not reach Germanic proportions, it was becoming increasingly clear that New Zealand was not go-

"*I've been sent by 'The Herald' to cover you*"

In its first issue, *Man* poked fun at nudists and the embarrassment of men sent to 'cover' them. *Man* was the *Playboy* of its day, full of cartoons and pictures of scantily clad women. The nudist movement provided it with much material for many years. *Man*, December 1936. Mitchell Library, Sydney.

ing to 'lag behind the rest of the world in the gymnosophical spheres'.[22] The time was ripe for the formation of nudist camps and organisations. In late 1934 E. W. Flint – or Brother Flint, as *Truth* preferred – announced plans to revitalise the Dunedin club. During the winter he and some enthusiasts 'went gymnosophising' in the snow, but now the hope was that men and women would 'form themselves into a real nudist club for the summer'.[23] Other clubs followed, in Auckland, Wellington, Napier and Gisborne.[24] Soon the mainstream press was noting that the weather was 'ideal' for 'Titirangi nudists'.[25] New Zealand nudists also started to send reports of their activities to international nudist magazines. The British magazine *Health and Efficiency* published articles describing nudist camps in New Zealand, where devotees, 'surrounded by the beauty and majesty of mountain, bush and sea' cast off their clothes and 'walked, swam and played, clear, cool sea breezes caressing [their] naked bodies, restoring health and vigor to constitutions undermined by weeks of indoor activity'.[26] Some New Zealand delegates attended the annual convention of the United States National Nudist Association.[27] It is not so surprising, then,

A local cartoon questions the suitability of New Zealand's
(winter) climate for nudism. *Truth*, 31 July 1935.

that in 1934, when a man was spotted by a group of boy scouts near Red
Rocks, on the Wellington coast, clad only in shoes and black bowler hat,
that *Truth* suggested he was 'a representative of one nudist club on his
way to start negotiations for the amalgamation, or affiliation of all clubs
throughout the Dominion'.[28] This was overstating the case – there was no
national organisation until the 1950s – but the joke contained a kernel of
truth. Nudism was becoming a widespread movement.

The growth of organised nudism in 1930s New Zealand had parallels in
England, the United States and Australia. New Zealand nudists took their
lead from these countries. Although the German movement had a much
longer history, most New Zealand nudists learned of it indirectly, through
English and American sources.[29] New Zealand nudists were not trailblaz-
ers, but they did not lag far behind other Western countries either. The
first nudist camps were formed in England in 1927,[30] in the United States
in the dying days of 1929[31] and in Australia in the early 1930s.[32] In all of
these countries, nudism was a minority pursuit, and one that came in for
a fair amount of negative comment. So it became important to nudists

to publish articles, books and magazines to explain, justify and defend their leisure pursuit. They also hoped that this literature would convert others to the nudist way of life. New Zealand nudists read these works and echoed the central ideas in their own writings. Regardless of whether the literature was imported into New Zealand or created here, it contained two central messages. First, nudism was about health. It was a positive social movement, aimed at improving the race. Second, there was nothing erotic or sexual about nudism. Indeed, the reverse was claimed. Nudists maintained that current fashions were far more tantalising and likely to incite licentious behaviour than the nude body. Nudism was part of the culture of constraint.

By the late 1920s New Zealanders interested in nudism were able to read about it in magazines devoted to health and physical culture. Alfred Briton's *Health and Physical Culture* (*HPC*), was especially important. It began to publish articles on nudism in 1929. The first, about the German movement,[33] was illustrated with a photograph of nudists, as were all of its subsequent articles on the 'nude cult'. Throughout the 1930s, *HPC* published numerous articles on Australasian nudism and on the inter-national movement.[34] Most of these were reprinted in Briton's 'fully illus-trated' 1939 book, *Mixed Nudist Camps Throughout the World*.[35] Alongside the *HPC* articles, New Zealanders were reading the British naturist mag-azine *Health and Efficiency*, articles by expatriate nudists such as Dulcie Deamer (who features on the back cover of this book) and books pub-lished by nudists and those advocating nudism.[36] In the early 1930s these included Frances and Mason Merrill's *Among the Nudists* and *Nudism Comes to America*, Julian Strange's *Adventures in Nakedness* and the works of British naturist William Wellby.[37] Wellby's ideas in particular influ-enced New Zealand's most prominent advocate of nudism in the 1930s, Trevor G. Bain.

In 1936 29-year-old Trevor Bain founded *Health and Sunshine*, a mag-azine devoted to improving the bodies and health of New Zealanders. During its brief existence *Health and Sunshine* carried several articles and many letters on nudism. It was, de facto, the first nudist magazine in New Zealand, providing a forum for nudists to make contact with other like-minded people.[38] In the first issue, Bain, 'The Man With a Purpose', asked the question 'Nudism: Is It Desirable?' and he repeatedly raised the subject in subsequent issues.[39] Although posed as a question, the text made it clear that Bain supported the nudist movement. In 1937 he pub-lished New Zealand's first monograph on nudism, also entitled *Nudism–*

Is It Desirable? He began the book by noting that he had never been in a 'nudist colony', but that he had had 'a good deal to do with Nudists from all over the world',[40] and this contact had convinced him that nudism deserved support. Bain's book explained why nudism was desirable, and why its critics were wrong to denounce it.

Bain's central claim was that nudism was a healthy movement. He had surveyed nudists, asking them why they decided to disrobe, and most had replied that they did so for health reasons.[41] This made perfect sense to Bain, since the sun's rays are 'essential food' for the healthy body, and sunlight 'will repair the ravages of light starvation in human life'.[42] In order to strengthen these claims, Bain quoted William Wellby, who had written extensively on the importance of the skin receiving sunlight.[43] Wellby offered 'scientific' reasons to support nudism, arguing that rays of light could not reach the sexual organs through clothing, yet such rays were essential to stimulate the 'endocrine secretions which are absorbed directly into the blood and so increase the vitality of all other organs'.[44] Bain mimicked his master, writing about the layers of the epidermis, and about melanin, keratin, amino acids and endocrine glands.[45] The appeal to science was not new, but nudists hoped it would convince the clothed of their seriousness and legitimacy.

According to Wellby, the healthiness of nudism did not come just from exposure to the sun and fresh air, but from the fact that nudists moved about while unclothed. This allowed the sun's rays to reach all parts of their bodies, and 'The currents of air [to act] as mild insulation from the infra-red or heat rays which are liable to scorch the skin'.[46] It also meant that nudists were engaging in healthful activity, rather than just lying in the sun. This was important. Wellby and Bain stressed that in nudist camps people were out in the fresh air engaged in exercises and games designed to improve their physiques. The ubiquitous medicine ball came into play, as did physical culture.[47] The organiser of the planned Napier sun club noted that 'Physical culture would be one of the principal objects of the club . . . Members would have the opportunity of building up their bodies and rendering themselves less subject to the physical ills which beset the human race.'[48] And collective activities would help here, since 'physical exercises carried out by groups are pleasanter and more efficacious than those performed alone'.[49] There was also recognition that without clothing to hide in, nudists had a real incentive to improve their bodies.[50] One woman nudist suggested that mixed skinny-dipping 'would be a public benefit in that it would compel woman to pay as much atten-

Brandishing what looks more like a beach ball than a medicine ball, these two
women epitomise the nudist movement's ideal: they are young, healthy, fit and
happy. This photograph, used as an illustration in Bain's book, was altered so
that no pubic hair or genitalia were revealed. This legal requirement led some
women to believe that in order to join a nudist organisation they had to shave
their pubic hair. Trevor G. Bain, *Nudism – Is It Desirable?*, Auckland, 1937.

tion to her body as to the clothes that cover it'.[51] If concerns about health
were not enough, then vanity might lead to an improved 'race'. Like the
proponents of the physical culture movement, physique contests and
swimming and sunbathing, nudists claimed that they were acting in the
best interests of the nation's bodies.

Such ideas did not go unchallenged. One wag suggested that she would
become a plastic surgeon when nudism became universal, since most

bodies could not stand such exposure.[52] Occasional voices were raised about the increased cancer risk faced by nudists.[53] But the nudists were undeterred. Nudism, they claimed, could even save your life. The wife of a New Zealand doctor maintained that she was destined to die from tuberculosis until she discovered the benefits of nudism. 'Dr Sun' was her saviour.[54] Others made lesser claims, but nonetheless stressed that nudism improved everyone's health and well-being.[55] Not only that, it also improved the mind. Bain claimed that just as nudists' bodies were of a higher than average standard, so was their mentality. The organiser of the Hawke's Bay Sun Club agreed. He was sure that nudism improved the IQ.[56] A super-race could emerge if everyone embraced nudism.

Most nudists gave health as the main reason for their decision to disrobe, but they were also prepared to draw on ancient precedents and religious justifications. Like Sandow and Hutchinson, they held up the ancient Greeks as the embodiment of high culture and physical perfection. Many supporters of nudism noted that young Greek athletes had performed in the nude, and that their society had encouraged this.[57] Christianity was also brought into the debate. 'If we are created in God's image,' Bain asked, 'what's indecent about the human body?'[58] 'H.G.K.', a nudist from New Plymouth, was clear about the answer: 'We are taught that God made man in the nude after His likeness . . . It is the way that God meant us to live, otherwise He would have clothed us in the first place when He made man. He wants us to live a clean, sweet and beautiful life.'[59] Many others agreed. If nudity was good enough for Adam and Eve before the fall, it was good enough for them. [60]

Although Bain and his supporters claimed that nudism was a 'sane and healthy' response to the problems besetting the bodies of the nation, not everyone agreed.[61] Despite the appeals to science, ancient civilisation and religion, many argued that nudism was nothing more than a cranky cult, peopled by perverts and exhibitionists. Nudism was really about sex: all the talk about health was a smokescreen. As one contributor to *HPC* put it, the health claims of nudism were 'ALL BOLONEY' and nudists were 'MORONS and EXHIBITIONISTS', a mere 'species of fungoid growth'.[62] Some historians of nudism, using more restrained language, have made similar suggestions.[63] Bain was familiar with this sort of response, and claimed that he had once shared such views, until he managed to 'break through the thick veil of prejudice and stupidity' underpinning the claim.[64] His book was in large part a refutation of the argument that nudism was really about sex. In this respect, he was part of a long and

HEALTH—STRENGTH—PHYSIQUE.
The perfect combination for the human machine.

One of the few photographs of men illustrating Bain's book. Wearing a 'V', he poses
as a work of art, a living statue, yet at the same time is a very modern man, a 'human
machine' strong enough to withstand the pressures of the contemporary era, thanks to
his nudist lifestyle. Trevor G. Bain, *Nudism – Is It Desirable?*, Auckland, 1937.

large tradition. As one historian of nudism has noted, 'Legion have been
the tracts which dissociate nudity from sexuality'.[65] There were certainly
many articles and letters in *HPC* through the 1930s denying that there was
anything sexual about being a nudist.[66] Critics were unimpressed, though.
While many dismissed nudism as an indecent fad, others took its health
message seriously, but raised questions about the way nudism was carried
out. They did not understand why the entire body had to be exposed to
the sun and air, why nudists had to practise their nudism in groups, rather

The 'colony' (a term many nudists rejected) may be called Paradise, but these men have decided that the girl wearing the latest Jantzen is far more enticing than what they can see through their peep-holes. Ironically, this was exactly what the nudists claimed: the nude body was natural and unremarkable, the partially unclad body was sexualised and erotic. *Man*, October 1937. Mitchell Library, Sydney.

than by themselves, and why these groups had to contain both men and women.

Some dismissed as 'ridiculous' the notion that the whole body had to be exposed to the sun. New season swimwear, they felt, was scanty enough. The few inches of flesh still covered by the latest Jantzen could not possibly interfere with the healthful effects of the sun. They argued that the nudists' desire to remove even such small garments indicated that their true goal was not health but perversion.[67] These critics also worried that the unclothed would revert to a primitive state. In their minds nudism was associated with savagery, clothing with civilisation.[68]

Nudists disagreed. They argued that clothes were far more likely to arouse curiosity and sexual interest than the nude body. They often claimed that in 'primitive' societies, where there were no clothes, moral standards were far higher than in so-called civilised societies.[69] They worried that modern fashions, especially in women's clothes, were designed to excite and entice the opposite sex. Partial concealment, rather than the full revelation of the body, was the problem. Readers of *HPC* were well versed in this argument. Back in 1931 Jonothan Harles had written an article on 'The Charm of Concealment', in which he asked whether nudity or concealment was more conducive to a sense of shame. He reminded readers of Anatole France's novel, *Penguin Isle*, in which a young woman used shells and bits of seaweed to adorn her body. When she was nude, she never received a second glance from the boys in her village; now she became the centre of attention. Her concealment aroused their curiosity, and led to the downfall of their community.[70] Even those who practised only semi-nudity agreed that clothes were far more provocative than the nude body.[71] Wearing Vs and bras, they claimed, attracted attention to the differences in men's and women's bodies.[72]

Nudists distinguished between being undressed, and therefore naked, and being natural, that is, being nude. While the nude was pure, the half-dressed was a vulgar creature.[73] For this reason, nudists condemned strip-tease and burlesque shows featuring semi-clad showgirls. They found such displays as 'disgusting' as the clothed found their nudism.[74] Wellby worried that a young couple in a darkened movie theatre watching the latest Hollywood love story, or in the stalls at a music hall revue where the chorus girls were only partially clad, would be 'susceptible to erotic urgings'. He felt that they would be far safer at a nudist camp, surrounded by family groups, exercising in the fresh air.[75]

The idea that nudism should be practised in a group setting, though, concerned many. They could accept that nudism offered some genuine health benefits, but they could not see why it required an audience. As H. J. Burrand pointed out, 'One does not need company to enjoy God's air, His sun and His pure, rippling streams.'[76] Nudists were simply posing, and such posing was distasteful. Yet when Trevor Bain asked a nudist if the same benefits could be gained through solo, backyard nudism, his informant answered with an emphatic 'No'. Practising nudism alone would make a man

feel like a naughty little boy, afraid that he is going to be found out any minute. And, besides, there is a social aspect of Nudism which has helped in a large measure to make it what it is . . . Man cannot live unto himself alone. That goes for Nudism.[77]

The secretary of the Hawke's Bay Sun Club echoed these sentiments.[78] Opponents, though, were not convinced by this line of reasoning, especially since these social groups were mixed.

Many were outraged by the idea of women and men together in the nude. Even if the nudists were exercising in the fresh air, such a development was unhealthy:

> there is a great deal of objection to the practice of nudists who do their sunbathing together in colonies, play games with medicine balls and conduct the activities of a sports club in the nude, with the sexes commingled. Any reasonable person must admit that nudists are simply developing a cult for the manifestation of sex, and little else.[79]

F. Winter of Masterton blushed at the very thought of undressing in front of the opposite sex and did not relish the idea of his 'best girl' being ogled by other men. Quick to point out that his body could withstand the scrutiny of nudists, he still maintained that 'If one must tear around in one's birthday suit, at least make it exclusive to your own sex'.[80] It was a common sentiment: many could accept the health benefits of nudity, or being almost nude, but believed it was abnormal to want to do this in front of the opposite sex. Such a desire revealed the nudists' true motive.[81] If they were sincere about the health claims, suggested 'Modern Mother, White and Civilised', then they would not mind occupying separate camps: 'The sun would shine as brightly on both camps, but somehow I don't think they would last very long'.[82]

The nudists dismissed such suggestions. The reason the camps were mixed, they explained, was not to encourage illicit sexual behaviour, but to prevent it. Time and again they declared that the mixing of the sexes without clothing on dispelled the 'pruriency and psuedo [sic] eroticism' of modern life.[83] Clothes fostered 'seductiveness and coquetry', but once these were dispensed with men and women could rise above such thoughts.[84] Nudists were not posing, they were engaged in a purposeful reshaping of and rethinking about the modern body. Individuals recounted their own experiences, to reinforce the claim. R. E. Ellis wrote about his first nudist holiday and his love for Clare. He was worried about how he would react when he first saw the woman he loved unclothed, but as he 'looked at these girls running and jumping in a state of near-nudity, he felt no atom of untoward sexual excitement. They were just comrades in the sun.'[85] Lorraine Esmond claimed that mixed skinny-dipping was the best way to 'sweep away that sniggering false modesty which is an insult to all at whom it is directed'.[86] Douglas Reeder agreed. He argued that within the camp it was natural to be nude. At his camp, one young woman had put on her swimsuit, but soon 'stripped it off shamefacedly, as if it were a visible sin'. Reeder was writing for *Man Junior*, a magazine devoted to sexual innuendo, so his poetic recounting – 'Light and shade freckle the pretty bosoms of the girls – which, exposed like this, hold no more "sex suggestion" than a flower-curve'– is all the more remarkable.[87]

To Reeder, nudism was a 'moral bath': it allowed the relationships between the sexes to be cleansed.[88] Agreeing with Freud that most people had sexual inhibitions, Wellby argued that joining a mixed nudist camp would free them from feelings of shame, secrecy and hypocrisy.[89] Children, therefore, especially benefited from the camps, since they grew up with a wholesome attitude towards bodies and sex. By the 1950s, New Zealand parents were being urged to join a nudist club so that they could help their children to 'grow up with a sane view on life'.[90]

While vehemently denying that mixed nudism was morally improper, nudists were happy to concede that their philosophy celebrated the beauty of the nude body. For Bain this was one of the higher goals of nudism. He concluded his first column on the desirability of nudism with a homily:

> When men and women can gaze upon each other's nudity and see nothing but the beauty and splendour of the human machine, then and only then will we have surmounted one of our greatest problems and our imaginations will conform to only one impression, 'A thing of beauty is a joy forever.'[91]

For Bain, preaching a message of bodily beauty and healthful, modern leisure, nudism was as natural as breathing. If the body was not as beautiful as it could be, then nudism would help. It would give the flabby and thin opportunities to exercise in the fresh air and sunshine, and the members of the camps who already had impressive physiques would act as role models for those whose bodies had yet to be reshaped into beautiful specimens of humanity.[92]

Nudist camps were clearly central to the movement, since the nudist philosophy stressed the benefits of communal sunbathing and exercise, and the positive spin-offs if the sexes mingled in a safe environment. But as 'Brother Flint' had discovered, establishing a camp exposed you to a fair amount of scrutiny and ridicule. Perhaps if he had read Bain's article, 'How to Form a Nudist Club', he could have avoided some of the pitfalls.[93] Bain's practical little piece provided a blueprint for others to follow. Most of the nudist clubs formed in the 1930s, and those that emerged after the Second World War, followed Bain's three key precepts.[94] He offered nudists sound advice, but at the same time limited the transformative potential of nudism.[95] Nudism could have challenged ideas and attitudes about the human body. It could have called into question heterosexual assumptions and expectations. It contained within it the seeds for a sexual leisure revolution. Yet the rules Bain laid out, and nudists followed, were essentially conservative.

The first golden rule concerned membership of nudist clubs: 'Be very selective in dealing with members. Make sure they are 100 per cent. genuine.' Since clubs were about clean, healthy living, undesirables had to be kept out. Prospective members were interviewed, sometimes several times, before they were allowed to join. One Wellington club rejected over 70 per cent of applicants.[96] Once a member, anyone who did not observe club rules and regulations could be expelled.[97] News about disgraced members travelled fast: clubs informed one another of miscreants. By the 1950s, New Zealand clubs were part of an international network of nudist clubs. If a member was expelled from any club in 25 countries, New Zealand nudists knew about it.[98]

Bain also stressed that women should be encouraged to join clubs, as should families:[99] the presence of children would deter 'erotic or unseemly behaviour' in the camps.[100] Most New Zealand clubs followed this international pattern, many retaining their family focus through into the 1980s.[101] But like clubs elsewhere, they faced the 'single male' problem: a disproportionate number of single men wished to join clubs. Some clubs refused such men membership, unless accompanied by a sister, a fiancée or a female friend.[102] Others made the men join a 'men only' group first, so that their behaviour could be monitored. Once they were deemed genuine nudists, they were allowed to join the mixed group.[103] If men had the idea that joining a nudist club offered them unbounded voyeuristic pleasure, the committees in charge had news for them.

That nudism was about wholesome leisure rather than unlicensed pleasure was Bain's second rule: 'Be sure that all your activities comply with the requirements of the law, and, above all, stipulate wholesomeness and decency. This is most important. The object of Nudism should be to lift the value of the human machine, not lower it.'[104] Abstaining from alcohol was a common way nudists maintained a wholesome lifestyle, at least while at their camps. Until the 1960s, most clubs prohibited the consumption of alcohol within club grounds.[105] Physical culture,

"This is Mr. Wilson . . . one of our new members!"

Bain's rules meant Mr Wilson would never have been admitted into a nudist club. Men who joined knew that they were not allowed to stare at fellow members. But cartoonists could not resist suggesting that the Mr Wilsons of this world joined only to ogle shapely women members. *Man Junior*, June 1947. Mitchell Library, Sydney.

on the other hand, was encouraged. Immediately after the Second World War, a Sydney nudist, Ron Ashworth, began to publish the region's first, dedicated nudist magazine. Like Briton's *Health and Physical Culture*, Ashworth's *Australian Sunbather* had many New Zealand readers and subscribers. Although Ashworth did not bow to New Zealanders' requests that the title be renamed 'Australasian Sunbather', he did start *Australasian Sunbathing Quarterly Review* especially for New Zealand nudists. In all of Ashworth's many magazines, New Zealand nudists were reminded that nudism was about more than taking their clothes off. It was a way of life, and a healthier one than that practised by their clothed friends. Besides spending as much time as possible in the fresh air and sunshine, nudists were also implored to watch their diet, increase their circulation by scrubbing their skin with a stiff brush, spend at least 20 minutes a day exercising, walk to and from work, sleep in a well-ventilated room and make sure that they brushed their teeth.[106] It was the sort of advice Sandow had offered 50 years earlier. In winter, when the weather prevented nudists taking to the great outdoors, they were encouraged to exercise in the nude inside. In Sydney they could even attend nude physical culture classes

Cartoonists could not depict men who might be sexually aroused by seeing so many nude women, but they could hint at this by showing blushing men. *Man Junior*, January 1946. Mitchell Library, Sydney.

"If he intends remaining in the club, he'll have to get over his blushing habits."

taken by Diana O'Dea.[107] Regardless of whether they exercised alone or in a group, nudists were reminded that it was their duty to develop and improve their bodies until they were trim and healthy. Then they could act as an advertisement for the nudist movement. No matter what their critics claimed, nudists were adamant that they were spending their leisure time following the sort of corporeal control that non-nudists claimed embodied good citizenship.[108]

Although nudists were encouraged to exercise at home and in the camps, most clubs enforced a strict 'no touching' rule: wholesome sport and exercise should be carried out without bodily contact. In general, body contact was discouraged in clubs, as it was in camps overseas.[109] Many clubs, for example, did not allow hand holding and hugging.[110] The fear of being labelled sexual perverts was clearly behind this restriction. Nudists had to practise bodily control, and when they looked at other nudists, their thoughts were meant to be wholesome. Bain was very worried about this. As a nudist camp virgin, he could not see how young men could be in a club with young women and not be sexually aroused. He asked a nudist friend:

'Did your embarrassment not increase when you came face to face with other members of the club, especially those of the opposite sex?' Naturally, I had in mind what does seem obvious to the majority of us, that a man, when faced with a woman in the nude, must have a certain stimulated response. This, I must confess, was the reaction I was anxious to hear about. 'Well, although I did feel a bit strange, I was amazed at the absence of any direct feeling of sexual stimulus. On the contrary, I felt that what I was doing was quite right and proper. There was I, a sane, full-grown and matured man, standing just as Nature had produced me, and yet I had no feeling of guilt. The warm sun kissed my bare body, and believe me, the satisfaction was great. I felt as though I was a man–a real, honest-to-goodness man.'[111]

Bain's friend had proved his masculinity by controlling his sexuality. Over the years the erection question continued to rear its ugly head, so to speak. But even non-nudists, on their first visit to a camp, agreed that the men did not become aroused at the sight of nude females.[112] Likewise, there was never any sexual talk. Bain's friend claimed that 'one's mind never strays to such thoughts', just as the three girls who 'dared to go nudist' could swim with their milk boys safe in the knowledge that nothing untoward would take place.[113]

The wholesomeness of activities within nudist camps may have been upheld, but many non-nudists argued that nudist literature was far from decent. In the 1950s, when concerns about juvenile sexual delinquency reached epidemic proportions, nudist magazines were denounced as mere pornography.[114] Juvenile sex offenders were said to be 'ardent readers' of *Health and Efficiency* and other publications.[115] These young men were not reading the magazines for their articles on healthy living. Photographs of shapely young women, rather than homilies about the wholesome activities of nudists, were said to be the drawcard.[116] Even the nudists had to agree that their magazines might be used for 'other' purposes, although they hoped that the young men seeking relief in the magazines would end up reading some of the articles and thus convert to a healthier way of life.[117] Indeed, the nudists went further, arguing that nudism offered a cure for the sexual ills of the young. Bodgies and widgies should be packed off to a nudist camp where, 'After a few days with us in such surroundings, they would be much too tired to spend their evenings in milk bars and other so-called meeting places.' A little bit of bush walking would turn the bodgies around.[118] As New Zealand nudists often noted, there had never been a case of juvenile delinquency in a local nudist camp, or in an English

LEFT Moralists condemned nudist literature from the outset. In Ashley Hunter's
cartoon from Bain's magazine, the 'wowser' is the figure of fun, eagerly looking at
Health and Sunshine, and wondering how he can lay his hands on back issues. *Health
and Sunshine,* 1 July 1937. S-L 523-457, Alexander Turnbull Library, Wellington.
RIGHT By the 1950s, the nudists' idea that people read the magazines for the articles
had become a visual joke: the 'studious type' is more interested in the articles than
the pictures, or in the women behind him. The joke foreshadows the claim that men
bought *Playboy* for its articles. *Truth,* 4 December 1956.

or American one.[119] So though the importation of some international
nudist magazines was prohibited, and the New Zealand Broadcasting
Service banned Bobby Darin's song 'Splish Splash' because it 'gave the suggestion of nude bathing parties', the nudists knew that there was nothing
immoral going on in nudist camps.[120]

Bain's final rule for nudist camps helped to ensure that they were
wholesome, decent places. When it came to selecting the site for a nudist
camp he was both practical and poetic. Secluded spots had to be chosen.
If the nudists could not be seen by others, they could not be charged with
indecent exposure or obscene behaviour. But above that, nudists should
go for sylvan surroundings. Bain suggested that they seek out bush areas,

Not exactly a natural bush setting, but nonetheless a safe place for nudists to swim
and sunbathe away from prying eyes. Bain thought beaches were too exposed
for nudist camps. They may have been natural settings, but they were peopled by
sunbathers wearing scanty costumes, drawing attention to their partially clad bodies.
Trevor G. Bain, *Nudism – Is It Desirable?*, Auckland, 1937.

rather than beaches. The bush should have a stream running through
it, since 'Bathing and Nudism are inseparable', but he saw no reason to
look out to sea for this.[121] He, and the nudists who followed him, instead
looked inland, buying or leasing tracts of native bush. While for the most
part nudists argued that their leisure habit embodied modernity, when it
came to locating their camps they turned back the clocks.

The members of nudist clubs tended to live in towns and cities, rather
than in the countryside. 'Spartan', a 'country person' from the Central
Hawke's Bay township of Onga Onga, recognised this. In the summer
of 1938 he entered into the debate about proposals to establish a nudist
camp outside of Napier. 'Spartan' was not a nudist, but he knew that in

Ted and Mavis Richardson, two New Zealand nudists, enjoying themselves in
the Australian bush. As regular readers of Ashworth's many publications, the
Richardsons felt at home when they visited Sydney. This photograph was taken by
Ashworth's main photographer, Lawford White, who was also a New Zealander.
Australian Sunbather, October 1949. Mitchell Library, Sydney.

the country men could work out in the fresh air, bare to the waist, without
comment, and that after work the lads could strip off and plunge naked
into the local river. He understood the nudists' desire for this sort of freedom, which did not exist in city life.[122] Nudism was seen as a cure for the
'frets and strains of an over-mechanised civilisation'.[123] People needed to
go back to nature in order to become natural again.

While some people took to tramping and camping in order to re-
connect with the landscape, nudists went into the bush and took off
their clothes. Some, like Ormond Wilson, managed to combine the two,

Percy W. Cousins, a man at home in the bush. Cousins was New
Zealand's most prominent nudist in the 1940s and 1950s.
Sunbathing Quarterly Review, Winter 1948. Mitchell Library, Sydney.

spending their leisure time nude tramping.[124] Regardless of whether they
tramped or not, nudists were always keen to stress that there was nothing sexual or immoral about nudism. They presented the bush as a pure,
wholesome land of plenty.[125] As Bain's nudist friend said of his camp, 'This
was paradise. I felt like Adam in the Garden of Eden.'[126] It was a popular
sentiment among New Zealand nudists. Percy Cousins, the public face of
New Zealand nudism through the 1940s and 1950s, wrote a couple of articles for the British magazine *Health and Efficiency* about the 'Naturist's
Paradise' he had created in the bush outside Wellington. His first piece was

Percy Cousins tending his bush garden. Although the photograph echoes
earlier poses of Sandow and his followers, this seems unintentional. Cousins
is not tensing his muscles to look like a Greek god. *Australian Sunbather*,
September 1949. Mitchell Library, Sydney.

entitled 'New Zealand Eden'. With his family and friends, 'in the midst of
lovely surroundings, ourselves blending with the peace and quiet of it all,
we recuperate and revitalise in Nature's own way'.[127] This was the garden
before the fall, where the body could 'blend in perfect harmony with natural surroundings'.[128] Like their British and Australian counterparts, who
were also 'idyll-izing' the rural landscape, New Zealand nudists sought
solace in the unspoiled splendours of the bush.[129]

The buxom blonde protects herself with two fierce dogs.
Man Junior, October 1959. Mitchell Library, Sydney.

To the clothed, however, nudist camps were places of sexual excess. Despite the social and moral conservatism of nudists, the clothed equated nature with animalistic sexuality, and nudist camps with debauchery. Nudism was about illicit pleasure, rather than wholesome leisure, so cartoon after cartoon depicted the members of the 'Fairview Nudist Camp' and the 'Seemore Nudist Camp' as exhibitionists and voyeurs.[130] Cartoonists could not believe that new male nudists were not embarrassed by the riches of flesh before them, so they drew them blushing so furiously that bulls chased them.[131] Nor could they accept that men could resist staring at the nude bodies of young women: men were shown receiving black eyes after they had ogled women's bodies, and women nudists armed

Sun, surf and sand were associated with saucy humour and sexual excess, so it was not surprising that cartoonists often drew nudists at the beach, even though most nudist camps were safely in the bush. *Man Junior*, December 1959. Mitchell Library, Sydney.

"Pardon, miss . . . we have an honorary membership available!"

themselves with fierce bulldogs as protection from lecherous male nudists.[132] They also discounted the idea that male nudists' intentions were pure, instead portraying them trying to lure clothed young women into nudist camps.[133] In all these cartoons, women nudists were depicted as being as young and shapely as those who posed for nudist magazines. On this at least the nudists and the clothed were agreed.

In the 1930s, during Bain's heyday, the clothed saw nudism as a daring and provocative contribution to the quest to reveal and reshape the modern body. A man who sold copies of *Health and Sunshine*, for example, ended up in court charged with exhibiting and selling an indecent document, since the magazine encouraged nudism and published pictures of naked women. The defence claimed that *Health and Sunshine* was 'a serious and honest effort to improve the welfare of the nation: it was aiming at objects to which the Government had recently subscribed'. The nudist movement was depicted as a product of the era: 'Had anyone founded a nudist cult at the beginning of the century they would have been arrested. But if people want to be nudists today, let them, providing they don't offend against the Police Offences Act. The world wags on just the same!'[134] But in the 1930s many New Zealanders were not prepared to wag on. The seller of *Health and Sunshine* was fined.[135] A similar case in 1950, against a shopkeeper who supplied *Health and Efficiency*, failed.[136] Attitudes were changing. But a 1975 legal decision really brought nudism into the open when the Supreme Court quashed the conviction of a man who had been found guilty of offensive behaviour after he swam naked at a Waiheke Island beach. The judge declared that in order for the behaviour to be offensive, it had to offend representative members of society in that place, at that time, and in those circumstances. Since others at Little Palm Beach had not batted an eyelid at the nude swimmer, no offensive behaviour had taken place.[137] After years of seclusion in the bush, nudists could take to the beaches. Many had long called for this, although in some ways these 'free beaches' were a death knell for nudist clubs.[138] Rex Matheson had suggested back in 1939 that once nude bathing on public beaches was legal, nudity would become 'mundane'.[139] Now that the courts had seen sense, there was no need for nudist clubs per se.[140]

Of course there were critics of this development. Patricia Bartlett and her Society for the Promotion of Community Standards believed that 'Next thing they'll be fornicating on beaches'.[141] Society might have changed, but she was adamant that biology had not: 'normal' men could not look at naked women 'without being aroused'.[142] But her petition to the Minister of Police, requesting that the police keep beaches 'safe' from nudists, fell on deaf ears.[143] By this time the police no longer initiated prosecutions of nude swimmers and sunbathers, and most of the people polled on the question of 'open beaches' supported the right of people to swim and sunbathe in the nude, alongside those who chose to wear swimsuits.[144] Revealing all of the body had become so commonplace that the *New Zealand Woman's Weekly* declared that 1978 'has been a nude New Zealand summer'.[145]

Some of the reports on nudity at public beaches echoed the rhetoric of the earlier nudist movement. The *Woman's Weekly* article stressed that family groups were enjoying open beaches, and reassured readers that there was nothing sexual about nudity on beaches. Other stories reported the efforts of genuine nudists to keep voyeurs away from the free beaches, and how the nudists removed people whose behaviour was offensive.[146] But in other respects the movement out of the bush and onto the beach was indicative of the changing nature of the nudist movement. The emphasis on physical culture and fitness, so central to the movement in the 1930s and 1940s, had gradually faded. Now people were happy to laze around on the beach, achieving an all-over tan. The body beautiful was a distant memory. Surviving nudist clubs became more lax about behaviour: alcohol was allowed within the camps, and some even permitted public touching. Although occasional articles about the nudist movement continued to appear in mainstream magazines, the novelty had worn off.[147] Now the main criticism was directed at nudists' increased risk of skin cancer.[148] Far from being a challenge to the nation's bodies, this once illicit movement had become an everyday leisure pursuit. Nudism had indeed become mundane.

Six Swings and Roundabouts

One of the nudists' great claims was that social nudism was positive for children. If they attended nudist camps they would not be cursed with the sexual hang-ups of their clothed peers. They would regard the nude body as natural; they would not be ashamed of their own bodies and those of the opposite sex would hold no mysteries for them. Nudist children would grow up to be healthy, sane members of the body politic. Although most people, especially before the Second World War, were not as tolerant of nudism as the nudists wished, many shared their concerns and hopes for young people. Long before the first nudist camps had established their rules and regulations, adults were anxious about the physical and moral welfare of young New Zealanders, concerned that they were not developing into the ideal citizens of tomorrow. And though they preferred youngsters to remain clothed, they agreed with the nudists' desire that young bodies be reshaped in the name of national health and well-being.

For the most part, the concerns raised about children's bodies were the same as those raised about adults: young and old were drawn into discussions about 'race suicide' and racial degeneration. Whether these were turn-of-the-century conversations, fears raised after the horrors of the First World War, or musings on the impact of the Depression, every body was discussed, and a fair few were measured and photographed too. But children's bodies differed in the degree of control and compulsion that was imposed on them. For adults, reshaping their bodies through physical culture was a matter of individual choice and, for the most part, physical culture was not state-imposed. When it came to young bodies, though, central and local government officials intervened and, along with parents and other adults, assumed the right to direct and control children's leisure and thus their bodies. They imposed on children what David Kirk has referred to as 'corporeal regulation'.[1] Of course adults did not always achieve their aims when it came to children's leisure. The government's focus might have been state-sanctioned, licensed pleasure for children, designed to improve their mental and moral well-being and turn them into productive, controlled citizens, but for many children physical education at school was a chance to play games, and council-provided parks were places to meet up with friends and have fun. For the adults in charge, it may have been all about control and discipline, but for the children it was often a case of playing on the swings and roundabouts.

During his New Zealand tour Eugen Sandow made a point of visiting Sandow classes for children, inspecting school pupils and preaching a message of bodily improvement. But he was not the first to utter such sentiments. Politicians, government officials and concerned citizens had long been worried about the health and physical well-being of young New Zealanders. In the 1860s the Auckland YMCA imported gymnastic equipment from the United States and Harold Palmer opened a public gymnasium in Christchurch.[2] When the government decided to make primary schooling free, secular and compulsory for Pakeha children, they included the provision that 'whenever practicable there shall be attached to each school a playground of at least a quarter of an acre', in which physical training might be offered.[3] That was in the 1870s. It was not until the 1890s, though, that compulsory schooling was enforced for these children, and even then physical education was not required, although some local education boards made it mandatory.[4] Schooling itself was only made compulsory for Maori in 1894.[5] By that time, the state was becoming more concerned about children's healthful recreation, as were many of its citizens. W. A. Chapple, who later gained fame for his eugenic treatise, *The Fertility of the Unfit*, burst into print in the mid-1890s with a booklet on the need for compulsory physical education in state schools. For Chapple it was a matter of '[c]ommon justice' that all primary schools teach physical education.[6] He regarded ample space for a playground, a well-equipped school gymnasium and a scientific, regular, systematic curriculum of exercise as essential.[7] As with so many who went on to advocate reshaping the bodies of young New Zealanders, Chapple saw physical training as a means to an end. Stronger, fitter bodies would make for better workers in the years to come, and would also raise the moral tone of society. He maintained that 'one well-equipped gymnasium exerts a

V. —MOST EXTRAORDINARY ! THIS AFTERNOON FITZMAURICE GRABBED ME, HIS FATHER, WITHOUT ANY WARNING, AND PITCHED ME UP TO THE CEILING, EXCLAIMING, UPSY-DAISIES !

The consequence of having an 'athletic baby': this junior Sandow uses his father as a piece of exercise equipment, tossing him effortlessly into the air. *Sandow's Magazine*, August 1898.

greater influence against social vice than one sensational sermon'. It was clear to him that if young people's leisure time was 'properly utilized', and their 'physical energies' were channelled in 'useful' ways, the individual and the community would benefit.[8] Such sentiments were echoed again and again over the next 50 years.

For Chapple and other concerned citizens, such as dress reformer J. R. Wilkinson, who organised a games club for Christchurch children at this time, the focus was on school children.[9] But for Sandow and his followers it was never too soon to start an exercise programme. Sandow was a great advocate of the 'athletic baby', the child who knew his way around a combined developer and was not afraid to show his rocking horse or his father who was boss. He admired babies who did sit-ups before they could walk and played with dumb-bells rather than rattles.[10] From the outset his magazine ran articles on physical culture in childhood, dispelling fears that exercise placed undue strain on the young, and arguing instead that parents had a moral responsibility to exercise their infants. If parents held out their thumbs for a baby to grab hold of, and then lifted the baby, using

The header for the new children's page in Sandow's magazine. The advice
contained in the monthly column was firmly directed at parents and teachers,
rather than the children themselves. As the illustration indicates, girls were
encouraged to exercise alongside boys, and it was never too soon for babies to be
given their first set of dumb-bells. *Sandow's Magazine*, November 1900.

only the infant's grip for support, they were told that they were helping
their child to develop his or her muscles and organs, as well as improving
'mental capacity and activity, and so [encouraging] greater self-control,
self-reliance, and healthful influence upon the moral side' of their baby's
nature.[11] With this in mind, Sandow published pictures of exercised and
exercising children, from babies to toddlers to school boys and girls.[12]
He ran monthly competitions in his magazine, with 1 guinea prizes, for
the best-developed baby under two years of age,[13] best-developed child
between three and eight[14] and best-developed child between eight and
twelve.[15] The magazine contained a children's page 'for the reading of parents and teachers'.[16] In his books he also provided exercise programmes
for children, advocating that boys and girls under the age of fifteen follow
the same routine.[17]

Through his various writings, Sandow declared that the current system
of physical training offered in schools was 'useless'.[18] Worse than that,
he claimed the drill often did 'serious and vital harm' to young bodies.[19]
The potential for bodily improvement was great. As he wrote in one editorial, 'Any teacher will tell you that the vicious boys in the class are uni-
formly boys who mope and loaf; these are the boys who bring dry-rot into
a school, a moral and physical dry-rot that eats into the very heart of the
institution.'[20] With systematic, modern, rational exercise the rot could be

removed, and replaced with hard wood – fine, upstanding young citizens of tomorrow. Sandow was adamant that the state, with the support of parents, had a duty to remove the rot.

Sandow brought these ideas and motivations with him on his New Zealand tour along with his dumb-bells and barbells. He was pleased to find that New Zealand led the way when it came to instructing children in physical culture. Although the 1877 Education Act had allowed for the possibility of physical training at school it was not mandated, but by the time Sandow disembarked a new, compulsory physical drill scheme was being put in place. In 1901 a bill had been introduced into parliament to make physical instruction compulsory for all children at state-funded schools. There was to be no gender differentiation. As John McLachlan, the member for Ashburton, made clear: 'We want Amazons in this colony, and from the Amazons we will breed soldiers. We could not have anything better for our girls than physical training if we wish to rear New Zealand soldiers.' Girls, he went on to note, 'are citizens, and they deserve any benefit that we may have it in our power to confer on them'.[21] The 1901 Physical Drill in Public and Native Schools Act made it compulsory for all children over the age of eight to be taught physical, as opposed to military, drill, unless the head teacher thought an individual child was not capable of joining in. It applied equally to boys and girls and to Maori and Pakeha. The act came into effect for the 1902 school year and by year's end over 94,000 children were receiving physical instruction at school.[22] In this regard, New Zealand was ahead of England, Wales and Australia, none of which had yet introduced a national physical education scheme.[23]

Some education boards embraced the new legislation as vigorously as Sandow converts gripped their dumb-bells. But, like the Sandow devo-tees, they wanted to be sure that they were receiving the maximum ben-efit from the instruction they offered their pupils. In Wanganui, 'The New Zealand Sandow', Dick Jarrett, was able to persuade the local education board to conduct an experiment as to which system of physical training was most beneficial for school children. In the middle of 1902 two teams of boys were formed, and their measurements taken. One team spent the next eleven weeks being instructed in the 'free movement' system cur-rently used in Wanganui's public schools. Three times a week, for no more than 50 minutes a session, these pupils swung clubs and marched around the playground. The other team, under Jarrett's instruction, spent their time practising Sandow's exercises. At the conclusion of the trial the pupils were measured and their results compared: 'The result was a most

Dick Jarrett, the 'New Zealand Sandow'. A sickly young man who had built up
his body through systematic exercise, Jarrett was the perfect poster-boy for the
Sandow system. Through his work with the Wanganui Education Board, he
spread Sandow's gospel and converted many young men and boys to the Sandow
way. *Sandow's Magazine*, April 1901. David Chapman Collection.

decided win for the Sandow system'. Jarrett's boys' muscular development
was far greater than that enjoyed by the boys instructed under the free
movement system.[24] When Sandow visited later in the year, he inspected
Jarrett's young boys and was most impressed with the results achieved.[25]

Jarrett's experiment also impressed the authorities at Wanganui Collegiate. The young men who attended the school spent half an hour each
day in the gymnasium doing Sandow exercises.[26] When Sandow visited he
declared the boys the 'best lot' he had seen.[27] They were living proof of his
contention that if the body was in shape, strength of mind would follow.

When Sandow visited other parts of the country, though, he expressed
concern that educational authorities were not training their pupils in a
systematic or rational way – that is, they had yet to adopt his system.
In Christchurch he was disturbed that the headmaster of a local school

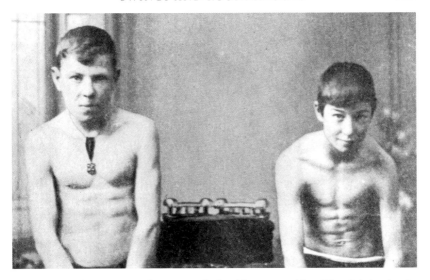

As winner and runner-up in the Wanganui school-boy competition, Edgar Pritchard and Laurence Healey enjoyed the ultimate prize: their photographs appeared in Sandow's magazine. *Sandow's Magazine*, May 1903. David Chapman Collection.

could not explain the scientific basis behind the exercises he was requiring his pupils to do. He was unimpressed with the headmaster's plea that 'We must have exercises that will make a good display before the public'. According to Sandow, schools should not be 'playing to the gallery'. Teachers, and parents, should realise that the goal was healthy, strong, disciplined bodies, not mass displays and end-of-year spectaculars.[28]

Once Sandow left the country it was up to men like Jarrett to continue the good work. Private classes for children and young men and women continued to be led by Sandow-trained and influenced instructors like Jarrett in Wanganui, Hornibrook and Tankard in Christchurch and Carrollo in Auckland. These men instructed boys and girls, Maori and Pakeha, and encouraged their pupils to put on the sort of displays that would have impressed Sandow. At their performances these young Sandowites showed off their individual strength and precision, rather than simply swinging Indian clubs in time to music. They were often rewarded by seeing their pictures in local newspapers.[29]

Within the school system, though, Sandow's legacy was not always so assured. The minority of pupils who attended secondary school fared quite well in the immediate post-Sandow years. The boys at Nelson College and

Master D. Cox of
Christchurch was taught
by Fred Hornibrook, who
was proud to record that
his pupil was capable of
expanding his chest by
3¾ inches. Hornibrook
sent this photograph to
Sandow's Magazine, where it
was reproduced, but before
he achieved international
recognition, Master Cox's
photograph appeared in a
local newspaper. *Canterbury
Times*, 26 April 1905.
Christchurch City Libraries.

King's College, for example, were encouraged to develop their gymnastic skills.[30] At Christchurch Boys' High the instructors introduced a modified version of the Sandow system, and were pleased to note the improvements in the boys' chest measurements after a course of instruction.[31] In Auckland, girls at Mount Eden College took to their dumb-bells.[32] Down in Wellington, Mr Harrison was busy instructing pupils at Wellington Girls' High School, St Mary's Convent and Chilton House Girls' School in the Sandow system.[33] At Christchurch Girls' High School a drill instructor put the girls through their paces twice a week, and more than half of the girls attended Mr Tankard's gymnasium over the winter months for instruction outside school hours.[34]

In primary schools, however, the picture was less impressive. Although the number of children receiving instruction in drill increased each year, questions were raised about the quality of the instruction.[35] The Wanganui Education Board continued to insist that drill was taught in all schools, and for the most part followed the Sandow system, but in

To ensure that the physical drill being taught to children in Christchurch's primary schools was appropriate, members of the Christchurch Physical Culture Society took it upon themselves to inspect the children as they exercised. Local education boards often welcomed such assistance. *Canterbury Times*, 21 March 1906. Christchurch City Libraries.

other areas of the country teachers complained that they had not received instruction in physical education. Lacking training, they often resorted to mass drill exercises and displays of the very kind Sandow had decried as farcical.[36] Fred Hornibrook despaired that 'The pretty uniforms' worn by the children seemed to be of greater concern than the 'physiological value of the work done' and was disparaging of the 'ridiculous, aimless lunging exercises' encouraged by so many teachers.[37] In the Native School system, too, physical instruction was often inadequate. As late as 1910 the inspector of Native Schools had to report that 'in a few schools the exercises are done in so perfunctory a manner as to be almost barren of results'.[38] The same problem plagued the public schools of Taranaki, the inspector there noting that in some schools 'The exercises seem to be somewhat aimless in character and execution'.[39] The girls who ended up in the Caversham Industrial School were not even provided with instruction. When this was drawn to the authorities' attention they approached the school's matron to rectify the situation, but she declared that she knew little about drill and was far too busy to learn.[40] The boys at the Burnham and Weraroa training farms were in a similar situation.[41] Despite the lofty aims of bodily and moral improvement through physical drill, and despite the best intentions of some school boards and training colleges, the standard of instruction offered in primary and industrial schools was often woeful.[42]

Yet the belief persisted that physical instruction was important for the minds and bodies of young New Zealanders. In 1907 Sir John Gorst, the one-time mission teacher and resident magistrate in the Waikato, wrote that 'it is the duty of the education authorities to see that every child

Royd Garlick, long-time follower of the Sandow System, was
appointed as the inaugural Director of Physical Education in 1912.
Sandow's Magazine, 3 May 1906. David Chapman Collection.

reaches that standard of health which Nature and heredity allow'. His sentiment was shared by many of his former countrymen.[43] Sir John alleged
that parental neglect or ignorance was having a devastating impact on
the bodily welfare of the young. He advocated state, rather than parental, responsibility for young bodies, and the New Zealand government
agreed. In 1908 Fred Hornibrook claimed that in the recent elections
almost every man who stood for parliament 'included in his manifesto his
belief in a proper system of physical culture in the school'. Hornibrook
perhaps went a little further than many of the parliamentarians, suggesting that it was more important to teach children about good health than
dates in history or Greek grammar, but the men in power acted on their
beliefs.[44] A few years earlier a politician had suggested that the government
appoint 'at least one competent man to go round the schools and see that
the physical training was properly carried out'.[45] In November 1912 the
government did just that, appointing Sandow-trained Royd Garlick as the
country's first Director of Physical Education.

Garlick had been involved in training young bodies for several years.
As we have already seen, he offered postal courses in physical culture and
by 1907 was the director of the Wellington School of Physical Culture.[46] In

As director of the Wellington Physical Training School, Royd Garlick was responsible for mass displays and individual programmes. Photographs of his pupils often appeared in the local press, and he sent many pictures to Sandow, who dutifully published them. Before this shot appeared in *Sandow's Magazine*, it graced the pages of a local weekly. *Canterbury Times*, 9 November 1906. Christchurch City Libraries.

1909, just as B. Dovey's *Manual of Physical Exercises* became popular with teachers around the country, Garlick was appointed to the Wellington Education Board. Dovey, who had also taught at the Wellington School of Physical Culture, advocated age-specific training and placed much emphasis on deep breathing.[47] Garlick agreed. He and his wife were firm believers in targeting exercises to the specific needs of the individual. As the president of the Wellington Council of the Girls' Peace Scout movement, Mrs Garlick had advocated the need for a 'comprehensive scheme' to improve the bodies of the next generation.[48] Within a couple of months, her husband was appointed by the government to implement such a scheme. It was a controversial decision.

In 1912, as part of a wider inquiry into the education system, an advisory committee had been established to investigate the physical training of school children and report to cabinet. Of particular concern was the operation of the military training young boys did at primary school, known as the Junior Cadet scheme. It was decided to demilitarise the junior cadets and introduce a new physical education scheme which all children at primary school should do every day. For the most part boys and girls were to do the same exercises, just as Sandow recommended.

From the age of twelve, boys might also do some squad and company drill, but the general focus was on a shared physical exercise programme.[49] The Inspector-General of Schools, George Hogben, recommended that the government appoint Royd Garlick to the new position of Director of Physical Education in public schools, and that he take up the position 'as early as possible'. His brief was 'To initiate and organize physical education in the public schools, and (as directed) in other schools. To issue, direct, and supervise the work of the Instructors and Inspectors of Physical Training.' Although his focus was to be on public schools, he was required to consult with the inspectors of Native Schools, and make sure that Maori children did not miss out on improved physical training.[50] Garlick was appointed without the job being advertised, and the decision did not please the Opposition.[51] They were further enraged when, immediately after getting the job, Garlick left the country on a fully funded trip to Australia to learn how physical education was taught there. If the government was prepared to pay him the very generous salary of £600 a year, surely he already knew how best to instruct local children?

By appointing Garlick the government signalled its intent to further improve the bodies of young New Zealanders. Following the lead of England and the Australian state of Victoria, it had already established a school medical service.[52] Children were now subject to regular health checks, and by Garlick's time they could also expect to be measured and weighed by state officials, their statistics recorded and tabulated in the name of national improvement.[53] As James C. Scott has argued, the collection of such statistics allows governments to describe society, and from there it is but a small step to 'a design and manipulation of society, with its improvement in mind'.[54] As the Minister of Education noted in his annual report for 1913:

> Recognizing that one of the highest aims of State education is to fit the child for a useful and active life of citizenship with a well-balanced personality in which the physical, mental, and moral qualities are equally developed and disciplined, the Government decided to introduce a sound system of physical education more complete than had been in existence before.[55]

Through systematic exercise, young bodies could be disciplined and strengthened, all the better to cope with the vagaries of the modern era. The man who had been a regular correspondent to *Sandow's Magazine*, had been brought in to modernise and rationalise the state system.

Garlick did just that during his brief stint as director. In 1913 new regulations for physical education and military drill were gazetted. Public
school teachers now had to spend at least fifteen minutes a day taking
all the boys and girls in their charge through the exercises in the English
Board of Education's *Syllabus of Physical Exercises*. (The English syllabus
was, in turn, based on the Swedish system of physical education.)[56] In
addition, after each classroom lesson, or at the end of each teaching hour,
teachers were to instruct their students in approved breathing exercises.[57]
To aid teachers in these new tasks ten instructors of physical training were
appointed in Garlick's first year.[58] Along with the director, these men and
women trained school teachers in the new syllabus, inspected how they
carried it out and offered instruction to pupils. Teachers who had trained
under the athletic Herbert Milnes, at the Auckland teachers' training college, required less instruction than most, but the instructors found they
had much work to do.[59]

By the time of Garlick's sudden death, in February 1915, the vast
majority of primary school teachers had attended a training camp led by
one of his instructors.[60] The new scheme was not without its critics – some
education boards felt that they had been offering their charges a more systematic and scientific programme than Garlick's – but there was a general
feeling that young bodies were being reshaped along the right lines.[61] As
the Great War took its toll, the government could be heartened that the
next generation would be in better shape than the men who failed their
medical examination, or returned from the front maimed and disfigured.

Garlick's death created an opportunity to bring the School Medical
Service and the Physical Education Branch into closer alignment. During
the war years, doctors and physical instructors often visited schools together, measuring and assessing pupils, instructing teachers and lectur-
ing parents on the correct way to bring up their children. During a visit to
Christchurch primary schools in 1916, for instance, a male and a female
physical instructor joined a doctor from the School Medical Service. Together they inspected the children, selected the 'worst three cases' in each
school, and in front of the teachers stripped the pupils to the waist and
compared them with children deemed to have a 'normal development'.
With their human specimens on show, the doctor and instructors then
pointed out the defects suffered by the children, and demonstrated corrective exercises.[62] The whole performance was not too dissimilar to Sandow's use of James Young in his turn-of-the-century 'expositions', or the
'before and after' photographs that illustrated his magazine.

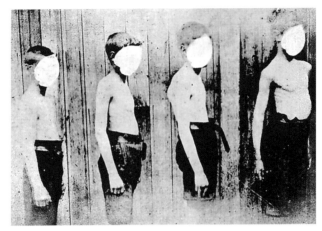

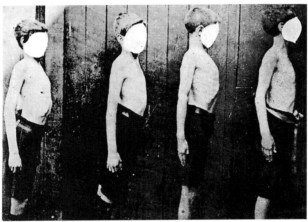

'Before' and 'after' photographs of primary school boys. After a year
of corrective exercises, they could, and did, stand tall. *Appendices to the
Journals of the House of Representatives*, 1917, E-11.

The Minister of Education insisted on special classes in large city
schools for children classified as 'physically defective'. Since medical
records were kept, teachers could easily determine who had failed their
physical.[63] In these classes, children with hollow chests and stooped shoulders were shown exercises that would rectify their particular 'problems'.
Photographs were taken of the children at the beginning of their special
course of exercises, and at the end of the year's treatment.[64] Sandow would
have been proud. Here was a state-run scheme, based on a scientific, ratio-

nal approach to young bodies. The children were measured and photographed; before and after pictures were compared. Programmes were tailored to the needs of individuals. It was everything he had called for over
a decade before.

All this measuring and monitoring revealed that all was not well with
young New Zealanders. These were not new problems, but tabulating and
reporting them brought home how far from ideal God's Own young were.
War only intensified concern. The school medical inspectors began their
lengthy 1917 report noting that 'It has for some time been recognized that
the physical condition of the race is very far from satisfactory. Recently the
war has emphasized this lamentable fact, and has aroused the public as
nothing else could have done to the fundamental importance of physical
fitness.'[65] The war had also, however, 'demonstrated as nothing else could
have done the improvement in physical development and bodily health
that is attainable by systematic exercise'.[66] This was the lesson that the
authorities took into the 1920s.

During that decade the School Medical Service moved from the
Education to the Health Department, and a replacement for Garlick was
finally appointed, but in many respects it was a period that consolidated
state involvement in the bodily welfare of the young. Sometimes this
overstepped the mark. In 1920 H. E. Longworth, the new Chief Physical
Instructor, issued a very strange edict to the head teachers of all public
schools.

> It is . . . considered necessary that after every assembly the children should
> walk into school on their tip toes. By this means the tendency to flat feet will
> be counteracted, and children will become much more sprightly by reason
> of the fact that the weight of the body will be carried on the balls of the feet
> rather than on the heels.[67]

This was taking bodily control too far. It seems unlikely that many
teachers encouraged children to damage their toes and overdevelop their
calves just because Bert Longworth had suffered from a rush of blood to
the head. The new *Syllabus of Physical Training for Schools*, issued by the
Education Department in 1920, certainly did not mention walking on
tiptoe. It built on the earlier programme introduced by Garlick, encouraging boys and girls to participate in the same exercises, so that 'The
boys will learn gentleness, forbearance, and courtesy, [and] the girls will
learn to "play the game"'.[68] Bodily control was still to the fore: the new

syllabus was designed to develop 'healthy physique[s], keen intelligence, and sound character' in every child.[69] Teachers maintained that the goal was achieved, claiming that physical education benefited their students' physiques and also aided 'discipline, self-control, and concentration'.[70] The approach did not, however, reinforce gender differences in the playground. Like Sandow before it, the state was not using physical education per se to reshape pre-pubescent bodies in gendered ways.[71] Concerns about national welfare and racial survival took precedence at the primary school level.[72]

The race did, of course, survive, and teachers reiterated the message that physical welfare was crucial to good citizenship. When she left Wellington's Mount Cook primary school in 1925, Mary Jermsen received a copy of the school's standard leaving letter, a small pamphlet wishing pupils well, encouraging them on to further education and stressing the need to pay attention to 'The physical side of [their] nature'. Before the school committee reminded her to work hard, be thrifty, moral and loyal to the Union Jack and her parents (in that order), she was implored to 'exercise regularly'.[73] Thanks to the efforts of teachers at schools like Mount Cook, and the instructors provided by the state, inspectors could point to some marked improvements in the welfare of young children. In his 1927 report the Chief Physical Instructor noted that when the physical training scheme began, in 1913, over 40 per cent of children suffered from general physical defects, a third had obstructed breathing and almost a quarter had stooped shoulders. By 1927 only 20 per cent were afflicted with a general physical defect, the breathing of less than 3 per cent was obstructed, and only 1 in 20 still had stooped shoulders.[74] For these men and women of science, the statistics did not lie. Through the school system, the state had stepped in and saved young bodies. There were still concerns that parents were not taking due responsibility for the physical well-being of their offspring, and had failed to realise that physical culture was 'The moral salvation' of the young, but at least the central government could heave a sigh of relief (using approved breathing techniques) and congratulate itself.[75]

By the late 1920s, though, a new challenge had to be faced: the Depression. Bodily improvements were even more important now. Down in Oamaru, Arthur Roydhouse, a Dunedin-based physical instructor who had recently acted as a judge in the inaugural Miss New Zealand pageant, inspected and measured the boys attending a local special school. He was pleased to note that these 'backward' boys exhibited 'first class

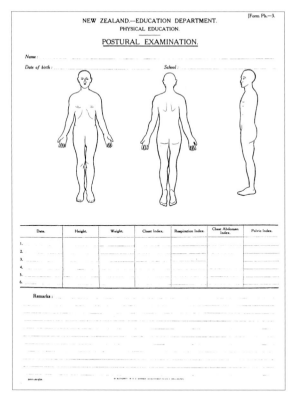

Prepared by the Department of Education, Form Ph.—3 indicated that a young body
might be examined by school physical instructors six times. The fact that the categories
of chest, respiration, chest abdomen and pelvic were an index indicates that there were
standard measurements to judge these young bodies against. This department's fixation
with measuring and recording individual children's physical statistics began in Garlick's
time and continued long after his untimely death. Education, W773, 38/9/1, Archives
New Zealand/Te Whare Tohu Tuhituhinga o Aotearoa, Wellington.

posture': well-arched chests, straight backs and well-formed abdomens.[76]
The boys may have faced many disadvantages in life, but Roydhouse was
determined that they would not be physically handicapped too. The following year instructors like Roydhouse were issued with a new form to
complete for each child they inspected. Form Ph.—3 allowed for quite
specific monitoring of children's bodies, and helped inspectors to determine which bodies needed special attention.[77] The pupils at Otago Boys'
High School who were found wanting were put into a remedial class,

where they received special attention for two hours a week. Alongside their regular classmates, they also spent fifteen minutes a day exercising in the school grounds under the watchful eye of Hornibrook-trained John Northey.[78] Sandow was dead and gone but his legacy lived on in Depression-era New Zealand.

But while the physical instructors were patting themselves on their very straight backs, pleased with the results they were achieving, others were growing dissatisfied with the physical training scheme, and worrying that not everyone was benefiting from it. A 1929 report by Dr Harold Turbott, the Medical Officer of Health and School Medical Officer for Gisborne, on the comparative health of Maori and Pakeha school children was a wake-up call for many. Turbott's study of 1423 Maori and 146 Pakeha children from East Cape suggested 'That the sturdiness of the old Maori warrior is not yet lost in his children. They compare more than favourably with the white child.' Maori children may have suffered from more anaemia and heart trouble than their Pakeha counterparts, and been infected with scabies and septic sores more often, but their teeth were sounder and their physiques far superior. Overall, their bodies were in better shape, even though physical instruction was not as closely monitored in Native Schools as it was in public schools. The only ray of hope for Pakeha was that Maori children had much flatter feet. Clearly the teachers at Native Schools had not heeded Longworth's instruction and forced their charges to walk on tiptoe each day.[79]

Turbott carried out his study in the latter half of 1928. At the same time one of the school medical officers was recommending that the state set up Sunlight Clinics at Napier schools, where malnourished children could be sent for a dose of sunshine and a hearty exercise programme.[80] The Depression was taking its toll on young bodies. They needed even more attention than in the past. James Renfrew White, an orthopaedic surgeon from Dunedin, claimed that at the very time when young bodies required extra attention, they were actually receiving less instruction than before. White worried that children left schools with poorer not better physiques.[81] Others shared his concern.[82] Demanding to know the full extent of the problem with young bodies, White suggested a 'census of the physical condition of children'. He also acted on his concern. In 1928 White was appointed to the Dunedin Training College to supervise its physical education programme. In his first year he instructed twelve young teachers in a year-long special course in physical education.[83] One of his pupils, Miss D. Garratt, was appointed to the Valley Road school in Auckland's

Mount Eden, where she tried to ensure that her young charges left school with better bodies than they had arrived with.[84]

White's programme focused on attaining and maintaining correct posture. On a visit to the United States in the early 1920s he had been impressed with the work of an orthopaedic surgeon called Joel Goldthwaite who had written a book on the importance of good posture.[85] On his return to New Zealand, White began a campaign to improve postural defects, which he regarded as the 'result of perverted and subnormal forms of living'. He aimed to offer children a complete system of living, one that overcame the deficiencies they brought with them from home, and prepared them as they left the school grounds and entered the wide world beyond.[86]

To assist his campaign, White wrote two books. *The Growing Body* was approved by the Minister of Education as the prescribed text for New Zealand school teachers.[87] In it, White offered teachers specific exercises to rectify their pupils' poor posture and flat feet, improve breathing and generally build up muscle and flexibility. But before the teachers reached the exercise charts and tables they had to wade through 200 pages of theory and background. On top of that, they had to buy their own copy of this new textbook. Depression cutbacks meant the Department of Education was unable to supply teachers or even schools with White's book.

Although White was not as fond as Sandow of publishing pictures of his own, exercised body, *The Growing Body* and its companion volume for parents, *Your Children's Health and Physique*, can be read as updated versions of Sandow's *Strength and How to Obtain It* and *Body-Building, or Man in the Making*.[88] Like Sandow, White stressed the importance of understanding the science and rationale behind each exercise. It was not enough simply to exercise the body: the mind had to be engaged as well. He also repeated the message about moderation: everybody needed a good diet, plenty of rest and fresh air, and a daily dose of systematic exercise. He noted the importance of dental hygiene – advocating the daily use of 'floss silk' (dental floss) – and exercising in loose clothing. He reminded readers of the classical link, holding up the bodies of the ancient Greeks as the modern ideal. And following in Sandow's footsteps, he maintained that for the most part boys and girls should do the same exercises.[89] There were exceptions – games such as Jockeys and Horses, where the 'jockey' had to dive through the open legs of the 'horse' were recommended for either boys only or girls only[90] – but generally his programme was not gender-specific.

Muriel Banks's parents did not seem to worry that their daughter was exercising
in her bare feet. Posed in the 'wrestler's bridge', Muriel was photographed
supporting her 130-pound instructor, David Andrews, who claimed this was a
record-breaking feat. His delight in Muriel's achievement was short-lived.
In 1938 he was arrested and charged with indecently assaulting young boys.
Health and Physical Culture, 1 October 1932. Mitchell Library, Sydney.

With the opening of the 1932 school year, White's system was introduced into primary schools around the country.[91] The first lesson teachers
had to impart to their pupils was the importance of good posture. This
was central to White's philosophy, as it was to physical education systems
around the world at the time.[92] Once again, there was nothing distinctive
or local about White's approach. He was concerned with offering the best
possible advice to teachers. He did not claim that his system was unique,
just that it was the best practice of the day.

Although many parents shared the sentiment behind White's programme, they sometimes questioned the method. Some were suspicious

THE PHYSICAL CULTURIST'S CHILD.

Like Fitzmaurice before him, this young Sandowite was soon outperforming
his physical culturist father. *New Zealand Herald*, 18 April 1925. I am grateful
to Tim Frank for bringing this cartoon to my attention.

of his enthusiasm for getting children to lie on the ground and exercise,
and his desire that they exercise in bare feet. What if the ground was
damp? Why did they have to take off their shoes?[93] Was White simply
offering the latest among many fitness fads?[94] Despite the reservations,
though, parents and the public were vocal in their support of the general
principle of the need to reshape young bodies. They called for workers'
housing to be on blocks of land large enough for the 'nippers' to play outside.[95] Fitness magazines instructed parents to '[r]ig up a gymnasium in
the garden' for their school-aged children, and take their babies through
a daily programme of calisthenics.[96] Those who bought White's book for
parents received instructions on how to build swings and see-saws for
the garden.[97] Organisations like the National Council of Women passed
resolutions urging the authorities to build open-air schools, and newspapers carried article after article on physical welfare and primary school
children.[98] Local department stores, such as Hay's in Christchurch, set up

clubs for children, where the young could do gymnastics and strengthen their bodies.[99] Society may have been in economic disarray, but there was no reason why Depression-era bodies could not be ordered and orderly.

Compulsion and control may have dictated the movements of some bodies, but many children seem to have liked their daily dose of drill. Despite the focus on discipline and order, physical education meant being outside, in the fresh air, away from their desks and books. Some enjoyed it so much that they joined extra-curricular gym classes, which they continued after their schooling had ceased. Many young men found it difficult to attend physical culture classes and gyms once they began work, as long hours of employment and compulsory territorial training left them with no free time. But when the territorial programme was suspended owing to Depression cutbacks, young men were free to join a gym and sign up for a course of physical instruction. That so many did so indicates that the young themselves were keen to reshape their own bodies.[100] Perhaps the same reasons encouraged young men and women to join the Australian and New Zealand Legion of Gymnasts, the 'Legion of the Fit', and later Alfred Briton's youth league.[101]

This last concept was heavily indebted to the Hitler Youth Movement. In the 1930s the most important new international influence on children's physical training came from Nazi Germany. Without any sense that the hard-line eugenic flavour of the message was inappropriate, newspapers carried articles praising the German example and likening the attention the Nazi authorities placed on developing bodily 'harmony, beauty, physical, and moral courage' to the values espoused by the ancient Greeks. The Germans added a scientific approach to the classical system – a pleasingly modern dimension – but they never lost sight of their aim: to create the perfect race and the perfect civilization.[102] As late as August 1938 readers of *Health and Physical Culture* were being told how Hitler had stopped the German race's physical decline. The rigorous system of physical education enjoyed by the Germans came in for a large amount of praise. The fate of Gypsies and Jews was not mentioned.[103]

State authorities also portrayed the Nazis as role models in how to improve young bodies. For instance the Director of Education drew his minister's attention to the German practice of appointing special organisers of physical education who instructed both school pupils and members of the general community.[104] With the election of the first Labour government something along those lines took place, but before Labour took office the state's focus remained on reshaping children's bodies. Although the efforts within the education system were extensive, outside school, too, adults took on the roles of play time supervisors and directors of young bodies.

Even after war had been declared in 1939, New Zealand officials still turned to Germany when they sought a world leader in raising healthy, fit young men and women. In 1940, attendees at the Parks' Superintendents' Conference learned that in 1882 Germans set aside playgrounds in all their major cities to 'inculcate the young with the play spirit'. In these children benefited from the 'physical, mental and manual' stimulation of playing on the equipment, under the watchful eye of adult supervisors.[105] Although the German example was cited, when it came to extra-curricular playgrounds in New Zealand, it was the United States, rather than Germany, that had provided the role model.

In the late nineteenth century, as the northern and eastern seaboard cities of the United States became larger and ever more industrial, groups of concerned adults worked together to provide safe parks for children to play in. These were not mere open spaces. Although it was considered desirable that the children play outside, those behind the playground movement wanted to create playgrounds where everyone participated, where there were dedicated spaces for all ages and where all children's play was supervised. That was the essence of the playground movement: supervised play.[106] Just as teachers watched over their pupils while they did their physical drill and breathing exercises, so playground supervisors would monitor the children when they were out of school. There was to be no unlicensed pleasure for these youngsters.

Knowledge of the American playground movement made its way into New Zealand through various avenues. There were articles in academic journals outlining the movement and its benefits.[107] Readers of *Sandow's Magazine* were treated to a series extolling the virtues of supervised play for children. They discovered that at Chicago's Armour Square there was a playground for young children, supervised by a woman instructor, and separate open-air gymnasiums for young girls and women, and for young boys and men. The children who went to the play area were promised a safe and 'wholesome' environment, away from the dangers of the street and the 'questionable amusements' that might otherwise tempt them.[108] Readers were also informed of how quickly the playground movement had spread in the United States, and the considerable cost New Yorkers

Auckland's Myers Park, open for business and very popular with local children.
W. A. Price Collection, G-1353-1/2, Alexander Turnbull Library, Wellington.

were prepared to pay in order to ensure that their children had access to proper playgrounds.[109] By 1908 even readers of the mainstream press in New Zealand were learning about the Playground Association of America, and its efforts to provide safe, supervised outdoor spaces for all city children.[110]

It took a few years before knowledge of this international movement was translated into local action. But around the time that the government was appointing Royd Garlick as the country's inaugural Director of Physical Education, a former Mayor of Auckland, Arthur Myers, donated enough money to allow the Auckland City Council to purchase a large block of inner-city land. He wanted the council to buy up slum properties around Grey Street, clear the land and build a 'health-giving park' for the children of Auckland.[111] The result was Myers Park, with its see-saws, 'Rock-a-bye swing', slides and 'Giant Stride'. But when the park opened it was under the direction of a caretaker, rather than a dedicated playground supervisor. The town clerk and city engineer were aware of the supervised play movement, though, and felt that the children of Auckland would

The Rights of Childhood League.

Led by unionist Edward Hunter, aka Billy Banjo, the Rights of Childhood League was
one of many post-Great War public organisations, campaigning on behalf of inner-city
children. Series 275, Box 29, Item 19/215, Auckland City Council Archives.

benefit from having a qualified playground instructor. But until there was
enough money for such an appointment, they recommended that the
caretaker be put in uniform and given a slight pay increase to encourage
him and his wife to supervise the play area.[112]

Other Aucklanders, too, wanted children's play to be properly controlled and directed. In 1919 a group of concerned citizens formed the
Rights of Childhood League, an organisation dedicated to protecting and
advancing the cause of childhood.[113] Their letterhead conveyed their message: a ragged girl gazed wistfully into a gated park, where other children
enjoyed supervised play. The league was principally concerned with improving public education, but other individuals and groups concerned themselves more specifically with children's out-of-school activities. John Court,
founder of one of the city's department stores, donated a large amount of
recreation equipment to Victoria Park. Although some suggested he had
an ulterior motive – the children would wear out their clothes playing on
the swings and slides, forcing their mothers to visit his store – this seems
churlish. Like many of the leading citizens of his era, Court had a strong

sense of civic duty, and a firm belief in the need to improve the bodies of young Aucklanders. He was also involved in the Community Sunshine Association's health camp movement.[114] Nellie Ferner, a member of the Auckland Education Board, was also civic-minded. She took herself off to Sydney, Melbourne and England to investigate children's play areas, and returned home singing the praises of Lady Astor's supervised playground in Plymouth.[115] Deputations of the Auckland Play Association, led by Ferner, were soon descending on the council, demanding more inner-city play spaces for the young. Echoing Chapple's 1890s plea, they reminded the council that 'The question of having sufficient and suitable playing areas was one of extreme importance for the physical, mental, and character development of future generations'.[116] The Labour Party's Boys' Club was more verbose, but shared the sentiments of the Play Association:

'The Child without play is the father of the man without a job,' or in other words, the Child who has not been given ample opportunity to play is not likely to reach the high state of Physical and Mental development, for it is chiefly in its play that the child developes [sic] its faculty of observation, initiative, courage and perseverance.

The boys' club had over 100 members, all 'drawn from the poorer children in the crowded parts of our City'.[117] The Auckland Community Welfare Council also petitioned the city council to provide more playing grounds.[118] Local journalists were sympathetic to the cause, pointing out that in 'all the great cities of the world consideration is given to the problem of finding space, off the streets, where, under efficient control, children can take part in those games and contests which are so essential to their well-being'.[119] If Auckland was to be a great city, it too needed to create more supervised, inner-city play areas.

Nellie Ferner was not the sort of woman to sit around and wait until the council sprang into action. As the Honorary Superintendent of the Auckland Civic League she was behind its Summer Vacation Playground Movement. Following similar schemes in England and the United States, Civic League volunteers supervised the children playing in the Victoria Park playground. Each session began with the children singing a verse of the national anthem before the supervisors directed the children into purposeful play, boys on one side, girls on the other. Unlike school physical education classes, these volunteers followed international play movement recommendations, and separated the sexes. They also divided chil-

They take their turn and take their chance

SEE-SAW! Marjorie Daw! Now the yellow head is silhouetted against the sky, now the brown. Good for them? Of course.

But Mother, the health doctor, will see to it that their health does not suffer unnecessary ups and downs. She will fight the stray germs lurking in the dust and contacts of the playground with Lifebuoy Soap. Dirt and disease germs cannot remain after the cleansing Lifebuoy lather has done its work. Lever Brothers (N.Z.) Limited Petone.

Mother the Health Doctor says

Lifebuoy Soap
FOR HEALTH

By the 1920s, even advertisers recognised the importance of bodies being ordered and orderly in the playground. *Auckland Star*, 18 December 1926.

dren by age. 'Proper' organisation required such intervention, but the 200-odd children who flocked to the park each day do not seem to have minded. They were there to play on the equipment and have fun with their friends, and they seem to have managed to do just that, despite adult intervention.[120]

By the mid-1920s the Auckland Play Association was providing regular supervision in parks and school playgrounds during the summer holidays.[121] This was also a voluntary effort, funded by street appeals and the like. Although volunteers like Ferner were motivated by the desire to 'develop child citizenship along sane and healthy lines', they nevertheless reminded the council that 'in practically all American and Canadian cities it was recognised as a civic duty to provide playing spaces and to appoint [council funded] supervisors'.[122]

Councils and other institutions around the country responded to such pressure by following their North American counterparts and employing women supervisors to children's play areas. Auckland's first Supervisor of Children's Games, Osyth Davies, was appointed in 1921. She spent time at both Myers and Victoria parks, but resigned after an altercation with the caretaker at Myers Park.[123] She was replaced by Gertrude Armstrong, who spent the next 20 years supervising Auckland's inner-city children.

Whether you were a lady supervisor at Myers Park in Auckland or Moore Park in Sydney, your role was very similar. Each day you made sure that the children playing on the swings and roundabouts were well behaved and orderly. You organised games like baseball and rounders, to instill the right values in children and to encourage them to participate. You tended to the cuts and bruises that plagued the knees and elbows of your charges, and occasionally escorted a wounded child to hospital. And when it was too wet for outdoor play, you ran activities in the park's shelter sheds, or sometimes visited children in their homes.[124]

Gertrude Armstrong was universally declared to be doing an excellent job – so good, in fact, that when councillors questioned the expenditure during the lean Depression years, her supporters rallied and saved her job. The Stipendary Magistrate of the Auckland Children's Court, local JPs, members of the Auckland Branch of the National Council of Women, and prominent citizens such as John Court all contacted the council, anxious that Armstrong's services be retained. Members of the judiciary said that her presence in the parks had been 'an important factor in keeping down the number of children brought before the Auckland Children's Court'.[125] Another deputation declared that in 'The interests of morality and public welfare' Armstrong must not be dismissed.[126] Even council officials agreed:

> There is no question as to the ability of the Lady Supervisor to instruct and organize the various games. Her kind nature and influence with the children are most marked and one cannot but admire the respect which is shown her by the boys and girls from the poorer quarters of the city.[127]

Their pleading did not fall on deaf ears. Armstrong enjoyed continuous employment through the Depression years.

The strength of support she received was testament to the growing belief among prominent citizens that children, especially those from poorer, inner-city areas, needed adult supervision at all times. Parents could not be relied on to provide this and it was the responsibility of government – local and national – to step in and control and reshape young bodies. Even the working-class Rights of Childhood League ran this line, arguing that the state had become a 'Social-Parent'.[128] In areas like Auckland's

The barefoot boys sitting on the roundabout in Auckland's Victoria
Park were prime candidates for Gertrude Armstrong's attention.
W1657, Special Collections, Auckland City Libraries.

Freeman's Bay, mothers could be out at work all day. Supervised play areas
meant free after-school and holiday care for their children.[129] This eased
the minds of working-class mothers, and reassured the middle classes.
Instead of running wild, these children would go to the park and learn
how to be good citizens.

While hundreds of children enjoyed the swings and roundabouts
each week, Armstrong maintained tight control over her playground.
Sometimes she failed: children fell off equipment and injured themselves
– one or two even died as a result.[130] There were also occasions when she
had to bring in other agencies to achieve the bodily constraint she deemed
appropriate. If children were playing truant from school and running wild
in her park she would report them to the Child Welfare Department.[131]
But for the most part she was able to instill the 'right' values in her charges
through leadership and discipline. She appears to have been the sort
of playground supervisor whose triumphs the manuals lauded: a positive role model who led by example and managed to keep the mischief-
makers at bay.[132]

Under Armstrong's watchful eye school-aged children were encouraged to play in the fresh air, building up their muscles as they swung on
the bars and ran from the see-saw to the swings. They were taught the 'play

spirit' as they joined in team games, and competed with one another. Armstrong was delighted with the 'fine sporting spirit' the children displayed when they won the Play Association's cricket cup.[133] When the older boys took an interest in coaching younger players she was thrilled by the 'excellent spirit of sportsman-ship . . . shown among the children throughout all their games'.[134] And although she found her job strenuous, she knew 'That this work is well worth while. The whole hearted enjoyment of the children together with the definite character training they receive in having to co-operate is of infinite value to the children.'[135]

In her regular reports to the council Armstrong reminded her superiors that her presence checked the larrikin tendencies in working-class children. Time and again she wondered what 'mischief' these children would get up to if she was not there to 'absorb their energies and hold their interest'.[136] Like the parents and passers-by who praised the work of the supervised play system, Armstrong maintained that with her 'strict but kindly discipline and a great deal of patience' she was mother to a 'large family' of playground goers.[137] Her children were good children.

Whether by making sure the children lined up for their turn on the swings, stood to attention and saluted the flag, or learned how to play rounders, women like Gertrude Armstrong were constantly monitoring and directing young bodies. They did this with the best of intentions: they wanted inner-city children to grow up to be healthy and strong, loyal and hard-working. But even so, they were interfering in children's pleasure and turning it into leisure. Unless it was a Sunday. Until the mid-1930s the Auckland City Council made sure that all the swings and other equipment in their playgrounds was tied up and out of action on the Sabbath. It seems that children were not meant to enjoy either pleasure or leisure on a Sunday.[138]

But Armstrong was also there to protect her charges. And in inter-war Auckland, there were plenty of dangers lurking behind the shelter sheds. The Great War was blamed for some of these. Adults worried that young people had become 'a thought too casual' in their behaviour. Young women were too free with their charms, and young men were far too happy to 'loll long days away in the parks'.[139] Such young people were not suitable role models for the city's children. Steps had to be taken to protect the children from these influences. Before playground supervisors were appointed, park caretakers suggested passing by-laws to keep the nuisance-makers away from the swings.[140] Once supervisors were appointed, they took it upon themselves to caution and chastise the unemployed youths

"There's nothing about it in the by-laws . . ."

The 'casualness' of young people after the Great War was only intensified by the Second World War, if this cartoon is to be believed. The constraints imposed by the numerous by-laws are not enough to deter this young couple. Gertrude Armstrong would have been appalled. *Man*, May 1946. Mitchell Library, Sydney.

and girls who gathered in the playgrounds. If they ignored Armstrong's requests to leave she called the police. Several arrests were made.[141]

Armstrong was concerned that these youths shouted and swore, and generally behaved inappropriately. Sometimes this was alcohol-induced, which gave her particular concern,[142] but her biggest fear was the sexual danger that men – young and old – posed for her charges. It was a fear many shared. The press, individuals and community groups regularly reminded the council of the need for measures to protect children from the sexual predators who skulked around the city's parks.[143] Whether these men were covering the park's toilet walls with 'invitations & acceptances to sodomy etc. and other kinds of filth', or offering children money for sex, they were taking an unhealthy interest in young bodies.[144]

From her reports, it is clear that Gertrude Armstrong shared these community concerns. She went so far as to claim that the most important part of her work was keeping undesirable men away from the playgrounds and the children.[145] This led her to suggest that the council paint 'For Ladies' on the seats opposite the swings in Victoria Park. Armstrong was not impressed that old men usually occupied these park benches.[146]

Safely covered by shorts and rompers, three young gymnasts
show coach Alfred Jenkins what sturdy young bodies can achieve.
F-3701-1/2, Alexander Turnbull Library, Wellington.

It was obvious to her that they were not just there to enjoy the children's laughter. Perhaps she was right. There were men who followed children around the park, encouraged them to sit on their knees, and who pestered adolescent girls until they shook with fear. Such men disappeared when Armstrong or her assistant appeared, but just to make sure that the playgrounds were safe, the park supervisors always contacted the police and encouraged them to patrol the parks on a more regular basis.[147]

Armstrong's desire to protect young bodies from the prying eyes and undesirable bodies of these park predators echoed what was happening in the school system. Whereas at the beginning of the century it was commonplace to expect young children to strip off to be inspected by teachers and other experts, by the 1920s – at the very time that the nudist movement was beginning to take off – the message was that young bodies might need to be reshaped, but they should not be revealed for all to see. The revised physical education syllabus of 1920 instructed teachers that when 'undisciplined' children were being taught games and exercises, care should be taken to 'avoid all positions or formations in which the children can touch each other'.[148] Students at teacher training colleges were also reminded that 'in no circumstances' were they to examine nude or semi-nude children. Similarly, when they took physical education classes they were to ensure that the children's modesty and propriety were not offended. The warning came after a teacher conducted examinations of completely nude children, a practice the ministry regarded as 'very dangerous' indeed.[149] As the first nudist camps were being set up in New Zealand, young bodies were being firmly encased in cotton shorts and gym tunics.

Until the election of the first Labour government in 1935, the leisured bodies of children and adults in New Zealand were on increasingly divergent paths. Although some held that everyone needed attention, there was no sense that adult bodies could be compelled to get into better shape. Wider social pressures and desires might encourage grown men and women to join a gym and reshape themselves, but the state sat back, and hoped that informal cultures of constraint would motivate its citizens. When it came to young bodies, though, the state and local authorities asserted their rights and responsibilities. They made sure that children's bodies were monitored and measured, that they were ordered and orderly. Physical fitness and well-being became a national goal for the country's young.

With Labour's electoral success came a new focus on every body. For children, little changed. Physical education remained an important part of the school system. Playground supervisors continued to direct and control them. But for adults, a new fitness fad was about to be unleashed.

Seven State Experiments

In November 1936 the Honourable W. E. Parry, Minister of Internal Affairs, declared that 'The foundation of every nation should be a proper course of physical education, or, if you like, the commonsense use of leisure'.[1] Well known for his prowess with the punch bag in the parliamentary gymnasium, Parry, like his Labour colleagues, was convinced that the workers of New Zealand deserved more leisure time. They acted on this belief, introducing a shorter working week for many wage earners. But they were mindful that this increased leisure time should be employed in a useful, health-giving way. Within a year, Parry introduced a bill to achieve this goal. The Physical Welfare and Recreation Act provided for the establishment of a National Council of Physical Welfare and Recreation, chaired by Parry, to advise the government on how to maintain and improve the physical well-being of all New Zealanders.[2] It also allowed for the formation of district committees, local organisations to implement the training programmes and initiatives recommended by the national council. Parry was putting the machinery in place to reshape, if not reveal, every body in New Zealand. In 1936 he had spoken of the need to 'deify the body';[3] in 1937 he fathered legislation that did just that.

Parry's and Labour's interest in building up the health and strength of the nation through physical exercise had a long history. Back in 1919, Parry had reassured 'followers of the "Manly Art"' that Labour men supported the physical as well as moral and intellectual development of the people.[4] A few years later Labour leader Harry Holland argued that healthy athleticism was 'one of the finest elements of our national life'.[5] While in Opposition these Labour men could do little to improve the bodily well-being of the workers, but once they were elected their ideal could be translated into reality.

Early in 1937 Parry held a meeting with members of sporting organisations from around the country to discuss how the government could best encourage citizens to deify their bodies. Concerns were aired that the proposed National Council of Sport smacked of compulsion. Hackles were raised when Parry asked 'What is better than a practical demonstration of the health and strength by our young people, properly and fittingly uniformed for the occasion?' Was the minister suggesting that New Zealand needed its own version of the Hitler Youth Movement? But Parry reassured his audience when he claimed that school children needed to be taught physical exercises based on scientific principles, rather than rote-learned 'physical jerks'. Despite the religious overtones of his notion of deification he also promised that he 'would brook no interference from any wowseristic element in regard to Sunday sport'. The young might be regimented in a slightly disturbing way, but at least working men would be able to enjoy sport on a Sunday.[6]

In August Parry held another conference with members of sporting organisations, and then in November introduced his bill into parliament.[7] He claimed that the legislation, which had received so much of his attention since he assumed office, was 'necessary work'. Despite improvements in medicine, the health of New Zealanders continued to worsen. This could not be blamed on the Great War: it was the result of 'everyday living-conditions'. Physical fitness would give individuals confidence, it would strengthen the moral fibre of the nation and it was the best legacy that could be left to the next generation.[8] Eugen Sandow had made such claims at the turn of the century; Bill Parry echoed them as the shadow of war began to lengthen. The Opposition could not disagree with the general principle behind the bill, but they worried about ministerial interference in sport and the question of compulsion.[9] Public concern that Parry would become the nation's 'Dictator of Sport' was dismissed as scaremongering.[10] Parry assured MPs that there was nothing compulsory about the proposed legislation. If compulsion was involved, he pointed out, the activity would cease to be recreation. He also reminded his opponents that the act would give him very similar powers to those granted to the British minister under the Physical Training and Recreation Act, passed by the conservative-led House of Commons in July that year.[11]

Parry made it clear, however, that the British legislation was not the impetus behind his bill. It had provided some practical guidance, but his conversations with sports bodies had taken place long before the British bill entered their parliament.[12] International precedents were important:

Harvey Sutton's pronouncement on the importance of using increased leisure time
appropriately inspired this cartoonist to show how men were not going to enjoy a rest if
their wives had their way. Sutton, a prominent eugenicist, would have been pleased to see
that this man's leisure now included pushing the pram. *Dominion*, 19 November 1937.

he had studied what was happening elsewhere and was familiar with the
German model, as were other speakers in the debate.[13] Italy, Scandinavia
and Czechoslovakia were also mentioned.[14] Everywhere governments
were introducing measures to encourage their citizens to use leisure time
in a profitable manner (and facing accusations of militarism and dictator-
ship).[15] New Zealand's first Labour government was no exception.

Across the Tasman, Australia had yet to pass a similar measure. In 1939
commonwealth and state National Fitness Councils were formed and in
1941 a National Fitness Act was passed.[16] But as Parry introduced his legislation, Professor Harvey Sutton from the School of Public Health and
Tropical Medicine at the University of Sydney arrived in New Zealand.
Sutton was a leading advocate of state intervention in the physical well-
being of its citizens (and a former champion athlete), and Parry was keen
to talk with him. Scheduling problems prevented this, but Sutton was
interviewed by the local press and made clear his desire to devise ways
of using leisure in a profitable manner. Local cartoonists were not so sure

that husbands and wives shared the same ideas about what activities left one healthier and fitter, but everyone seemed to agree with the goal of creating better citizens through a rational use of leisure time.[17]

That general agreement did not mean, however, that everyone was happy for the state to take a leading role in directing New Zealanders' leisure lives. State intervention in children's physical welfare was long established, and seemed to meet with universal approval, but when the state started to intervene in adults' lives, warning bells were sounded. Some accused the new government of overstepping the mark and interfering where it was not wanted.[18] There was a hollow ring to these concerns. The Physical Welfare and Recreation Act enshrined in statute what countless individuals and groups had argued for over the previous 35 years: New Zealanders needed to get fit and stay in good physical shape for the sake of their health and that of the nation. They had already imposed a culture of bodily constraint on themselves. The state was merely supporting their efforts, creating the Physical Welfare Branch of the Department of Internal Affairs, a centralised body to co-ordinate fitness programmes throughout the country. Branch officers spent their time doing what volunteers had previously done: teaching others how to exercise. The only difference was that the state now picked up part of the tab.

The Physical Welfare and Recreation Act has not received a lot of attention from the historians who study the first Labour government[19] – or, indeed, from any historians at all.[20] Here it takes centre stage, not as a brave new measure of applied Christianity by far-thinking Labour leaders, nor as a sign of excessive state interference in people's lives, but as the next, logical step in people's long-term concerns about the physical well-being of New Zealanders.

Throughout the 1930s and into the early 1940s, governments around the world introduced fitness legislation and other measures to improve the bodies of their citizens. They did so for the same reasons as Parry. Modern life was creating what the eugenicists classified as a C3 nation. Telephones, cars, even the radio were encouraging people to become more and more sedentary while advances in science and engineering meant that they had more and more leisure time.[21] The eugenic concerns of the early twentieth century had not abated. When a previous government had introduced daylight saving, editorials lamented that the devil found work for idle hands. Leisure time was a problem if people were not taught how to use it

The advent of the 40-hour week opened up the possibility for more leisure
and pleasure, and became another worry for the gloomy wowsers. Still
campaigning to keep the Sabbath holy, they now had to contend with even
more snakes in the grass. *Truth*, 25 November 1936.

wisely.[22] With Labour's election the problem intensified. Working hours
were reduced and two-day weekends became the norm for a growing
number of workers.[23] Fearing the consequences of the 40-hour week, the
editor of the *New Zealand Medical Journal* cautioned: 'Unless the people
are educated to appreciate the potentialities of added leisure hours and
their steps guided to utilise them to some productive purpose, a spirit of
discontent and indolence may be engendered in our nation'.[24] We could
not escape C3 status, let alone achieve an A1 ranking, without some serious re-education.[25] This was not just the view of the medical élite. Sports
broadcaster Bill Hindman maintained that when a nation forgot how to
play 'There is disaster ahead for its people'. He thought the appointment
of a Minister of Sport was required to prevent this national catastrophe.[26]
Fitness magazines such as *Health and Physical Culture* ran the same line.
Increased leisure was a modern social scourge that would rival the problem of unemployment unless action was taken.[27] And the appropriate
agency to take that action was the state. Recreation was recast as the 'life-
blood of democracy', rather than just something people did when not

at work. Therefore, democratic governments had a responsibility to take over the nation's sport and leisure activities, rescuing them from the grip of commercial exploiters.[28] New Zealanders faced a tough match against modern indolence, but Parry was prepared to kick for touch.

Although Parry stressed that there was nothing compulsory about his legislation, and that his aim was to aid existing sporting organisations rather than usurp them, the sporting democracy he put in place was not as democratic as his legislation had suggested. The main advisory body established under the act, the National Council of Physical Welfare and Recreation, was never allowed to perform its proper function. It met at the minister's behest, and Parry rarely summoned it.[29] In effect he became the Minister of Sport, aided by his loyal under-secretary at Internal Affairs, Joseph Heenan. Rather than taking advice from the national council, the minister saw that the Physical Welfare and Recreation Branch carried out his wishes, spreading the physical fitness gospel throughout the country. Its physical welfare officers provided recreational programmes for men, women and children, trained volunteers to become fitness leaders, provided information on sports and other activities and generally promoted the rational use of leisure time.

Although the Physical Welfare and Recreation Act was passed in 1937, and the first physical welfare officers were appointed in 1938, the Physical Welfare and Recreation Branch did not make an impact on the leisure lives of New Zealanders until February 1939. Aided by local committees of volunteers, branch officers instituted a major campaign to teach everyone how to use their increased leisure time in a sensible, worthwhile way. National Fitness Week was an extravaganza of activities that would have exhausted even an A1 citizen.

Under-Secretary Heenan provided local authorities with a glimpse of what their National Fitness Week should look like. He suggested a carnival on the opening Saturday, with mass demonstrations by schools and other groups. The Sunday could begin with church services in which youth and recreational organisations took part, followed by an afternoon at the beach, with surf life-saving, or hiking out in the bush. During the week, there would be activities each lunchtime and in the evening. These might include health talks, recruitment campaigns by clubs and sporting groups, learn-to-swim classes, sports meetings and even military parades. On the final Saturday another mass rally and sporting carnival would bring the week to a close.[30] Every district was to have its own fitness week, but everyone would exercise to a national agenda.

Echoes of the Hitler Youth Movement. The caption for this picture noted that the
girls from Dunedin's YWCA gave the 'Olympic Salute' as they marched with pride
during National Fitness Week. *Auckland Weekly News Illustrations*, 22 February 1939.
Hocken Library, Uare Taoka o Hakena, University of Otago, Dunedin.

Celebrities and statesmen, from broadcasting personality Aunt Daisy
(Maud Basham) to the governor-general, were co-opted to boost interest
in the inaugural National Fitness Week. The Labour government is well
known for using the radio to get its message across. In 1936 it began to
broadcast parliamentary debates, in part because it felt that the Tory press
did not give it a fair go.[31] In 1939 it was delighted that Aunt Daisy agreed
to promote fitness week, 'in her inimitable style', during her morning
radio show, which was listened to by tens of thousands of women every
day. Her endorsement was an important publicity coup.[32] Parry also took

to the airwaves to launch the week, trying to unite the country by declaring that '[i]n this case there is only one party – the people of New Zealand – and only one platform – New Zealand itself'. The activities of the week would place New Zealanders in 'The vanguard of a great health army which will rout such enemies of body and mind as laziness and slackness'.[33] If Parry was too partisan for listeners, the Governor-General Lord Galway's address the next night may have spurred them into action:

> History shows cases of decay and ruin of great empires when the people lapsed into laziness and sloth, and suicidally took the line of least resistance . . . A sense of responsibility towards personal fitness is one of the qualities of individual citizenship which should be fostered and developed by every means at our command. The maintenance of health is indeed a social, as well as a personal duty, for completeness of citizenship calls for completeness of physical and mental health . . . The old view that the whole destiny of man was work, more work and still more work, with only a very meagre measure of play, has passed away, without regret by the great majority of the public. The beneficial effects of sports, physical training clubs and other fitness movements for the welfare of men and women engaged in business and industry extends far beyond the development of balance and alertness, for they have a great value in building character and in assuring sanity, serenity and cheerfulness in life. Even from a cold, hard, economic viewpoint, a proper proportion of health-giving recreation has its definite value in a national balance-sheet.[34]

National Fitness Week could save the modern nation from decay. An economically and socially responsible programme, it promised to reshape all bodies and recreate them as better citizens.

Come Monday morning, even before Aunt Daisy had a chance to say 'Good morning everybody', the radio was pressed into action. At 7 a.m. listeners could tune in to the fitness week exercise programme. Armed with newspaper diagrams explaining the moves, families were encouraged to do their 'daily dozen' together, in time to the music coming out of the wireless.[35] Radio exercise shows were not new: the previous year 1ZB had run a Saturday morning 'Physical Culture' programme, and later replaced it with 'Leah Taylor's Exercise Club'. What was novel was the state's involvement in the fitness week shows, the daily broadcasts scheduled at a time when all family members could participate.[36] The Australian government took very similar measures at the same time, although the

They may not have spent much money on illustrations, but at least the instructions were clear. Exercise 7 required everybody to 'Stand feet astride – body upright. Count 1: Keep the knees braced; bend downward and grasp the left ankle with both hands. Count 2: Stand upright again, arms at the side. Count 3: Bend down and grasp the right ankle. Count 4: Body erect.' After Exercise 7, participants were encouraged to practise their posture to music, shoulders back, head erect, eyes forward. The military stance was especially appropriate as war grew closer. *Auckland Star*, 18 February 1939.

BBC lagged somewhat, owing to bureaucratic procedures. Morning exercise programmes were also common on radio stations around Europe.[37]

Publicity stills of young people exercising in their pyjamas did not silence the sceptics. Critics of National Fitness Week wondered how much could really be achieved from a week of activities. But even they accepted the need for such a programme, given the disturbing tendency of people to use their increased leisure time loafing around, watching rather than doing.[38] 'Spectatoritis' was a modern disease; National Fitness Week might just be part of the cure.[39]

There was plenty to watch and do that week in Auckland. Following Heenan's suggestion, the week was launched with a display at Eden Park. Teams from various business houses around the city marched and exercised in front of a large, appreciative crowd.[40] The national Surf Life Saving championships were held at Milford Beach that weekend, and enjoyed 'record entries'.[41] For those not yet in championship class, there was free admission to city swimming pools and instruction in swimming and life-saving. The learn-to-swim campaign also extended to many of the city's beaches.[42] During the week Aucklanders were also offered free classes in gymnastics, fencing, dancing, table tennis, badminton, American basketball, tap-dancing and boxing.[43] The last named proved especially popular. The Boxing Association made sure that each evening at least one of the city's many gyms offered free admission, a display bout and a lesson

A staged publicity shot of pyjama-clad exercisers. Like all good physical culturists, they exercised in front of an open window, but since they were in a mixed group they had to make sure that their pyjamas were securely fastened. Internal Affairs, 1, 139/59, Archives New Zealand/Te Whare Tohu Tuhituhinga o Aotearoa, Wellington.

in how to box. Whether it was Wally Williams's gym in Avondale, Ted Caughey's in High Street or the Leys Institute in Ponsonby, young boys crowded these sweaty sanctums of masculinity and enrolled for classes. Women may not have boxed, but fencing at the YWCA was popular among the fair sex. On the opening night of fitness week the YWCA held a Robin Hood Party, where women took part in an archery competition, country dances and other games, before enjoying a 'forest feast'.[44] During the week there were free lessons and fencing displays that rose above mere technical demonstrations. They were two-scene plays, which nicely combined the leisure and pleasure fencing afforded women. In the first scene, the two fencers met in an 'old-time café', an insult was offered and a duel declared. In the second scene the duel took place in a forest setting.[45] Participating in a sport such as fencing may have been women's national duty as good citizens but, like boxing for men, it also offered them personal opportunities for pleasure. The young men of Auckland could reap

At the beginning of Fitness 'Weak' Sam is not able to withstand the onslaught of
all these approved activities. Despite years of physical encouragement, many male
bodies remained objects of derision. *New Zealand Herald*, 18 February 1939.

the benefits of toning up their torsos; the women could enjoy a rich fan-
tasy life of damsels in distress and dawn duels.

Auckland's fitness week closed as it began, with a mass display, this
time at Carlaw Park. Three thousand sporting individuals marched into
the park, where the mayor, Sir Ernest Davis, took the salute. He praised
those before him: 'In appearance, deportment, spectacle and character,
this parade will remain in our minds as an event. It represents the genesis
of what I hope will be an institution in Auckland.'[46] It was wishful thinking. The outbreak of war put an end to the fitness week initiative.

Early morning radio exercise programmes did not cease when fitness
week was over. The senior physical welfare officers at the Physical Welfare
and Recreation Branch, C. Ruxton Bach and Helen Black, produced an instruction manual for morning exercises and a booklet indicating suitable
music to play while doing your 'daily dozen'.[47] Each week they sent newspapers new exercise routines, so that listeners to the morning YA shows
could follow the instructions.[48] When the programmes ended, letters
flooded into the Minister's office, asking for their resumption.[49] The public
may have been keen, but when it came to leaflets setting out the exercises,
and special sheet music to exercise by, the government rather overesti-
mated demand. In the end they had to give away most of the 10,000 leaflets they produced, and Begg's found it very difficult to sell all 1500 copies
of the sheet music.[50]

Propaganda efforts on radio and in the daily press continued, despite
such setbacks, but war priorities and rationing saw a slight shift in emphasis. Now that physical welfare officers had been appointed to districts
around the country, activities on the ground took on new importance.

By the end of National Fitness Week Gordon Minhinnick's focus has changed from making fun of puny male bodies to political satire. Minhinnick often portrayed elections as physical quests, placing political leaders in the boxing ring. Here the joke revolves around Minister of Finance Walter Nash and the 'financial jerks' he has planned for New Zealand taxpayers. *New Zealand Herald*, 25 February 1939.

Local officers were able to build on work already done by councils and other organisations, especially when it came to children's recreation, and introduce new programmes for the men and women of their area. National Fitness Week had been a trial run, limited in scope. It was time for a concerted, year-round campaign. With the outbreak of war, that became a campaign for the duration.

The appointment of physical welfare officers built on the work done within the school system, but they could not directly intervene in these efforts. The 1937 act and the machinery it set up did not allow for a working relationship between the departments of Internal Affairs and Education.[51] So when teachers like Emmie Cannell of Ngunguru School wrote to the Physical Welfare and Recreation Branch, reporting on the work they had done, officers could not take these developments and replicate them around the country. Cannell's efforts did not go unacknowledged, however. Parry was delighted to hear that the girls at her school had formed their own physical culture class and that Maori and Pakeha girls gathered in the hall to do their physical jerks together. This was especially pleasing since the school had previously had 'a clearly marked colour bar'.[52] Physical fitness could lead to racial harmony, but such initiatives were off-limits to welfare officers. Instead they concentrated on finding out what boys and girls did once the final school bell of the day had rung.

School medical officers measured bodies. Physical welfare officers surveyed leisure activities. Neither was impressed with what they found. Welfare officers discovered that team games were popular in winter and summer, but that few young people were involved in other leisure activities. They needed to get children and youths involved in 'approved activities', warning that if they did not everyone would pay the price for the young's 'harmful idleness in leisure hours'.[53]

Municipal authorities had been working for many years to create 'approved activities' for children in their areas. As we have seen, in cities like Auckland councils had invested heavily, providing parks and paying lady supervisors to guide inner-city children into healthful leisure. Now in areas like Timaru and Te Kuiti land was being given back to the people so that more playgrounds could be built.[54] A new era in supervised play was about to dawn, led by energetic and committed physical welfare officers.

Branch officers explained the need for supervised play in the same ways as supervisors like Gertrude Armstrong had done: children needed fresh air and sunshine; playgrounds in parks encouraged them to participate rather than just watch; supervision reassured parents that their children, especially their daughters, would be safe outside; and supervision ensured that the children's leisure would be directed into approved activities.[55] By training volunteers to assist them, branch officers were able to extend the supervision scheme. In Auckland this meant providing park leaders – who tended to be young women from groups like the Girls' Life Brigade – to the working-class suburbs of Grey Lynn and Point Chevalier.[56] The latter had the advantage of a beach next to the park: while mothers were taught to swim by branch-trained instructors, branch-trained play leaders could supervise their children.[57] The use of volunteers also meant that hours of park supervision could be extended. This was something Helen Black had contemplated after a research trip to Sydney in 1940, where she studied play programmes and camps. She returned to New Zealand convinced of the need to provide night lights in parks so that youngsters at work could also benefit from the scheme.[58] At Auckland's Victoria Park, long the scene of supervised play, branch-trained play leaders began to hold evening sessions in summer, aimed at children who had paper runs after school.[59] Once the last issues of the *Auckland Star* were delivered, the children could relax in the park, playing team sports or enjoying themselves on the swings and roundabouts. Wartime blackout restrictions, though, prevented any night light schemes.

War did, though, give new impetus to the idea of supervised play. In the park, children could be encouraged to celebrate their nationalism each day, as they participated in flag-raising ceremonies, sang the national anthem and other patriotic songs and performed patriotic pageants. Other values were not lost sight of, however: girls were taught dancing and gymnastics, which developed grace and poise; boys were encouraged into such manly, practical hobbies as woodcraft.[60] The gendered nature of supervised play was not disrupted by war, nor was the belief that supervision curtailed juvenile delinquency.[61] This was important for school children, but was even more of an issue with school leavers.

Physical welfare officers were very keen to direct school leavers into approved leisure activities. With money in their pockets these young workers could indulge in far too much pleasure if someone did not keep an eye on them. Before the branch was formed, groups like the YMCA, YWCA and various scouting organisations played an important role in directing young people's leisure time. Even the editor of *Health and Physical Culture*, Alfred Briton, began a League of Youth movement in the mid-1930s, to encourage school leavers of both sexes to gather into small local groups for wholesome recreation. *HPC* readers in Auckland, Napier, Wellington and Christchurch responded to the instruction 'We Want You With Us!' and formed groups.[62] At the same time, young women banded together into athletic associations and held regular meets. Minie Inman from the Berlei team was awarded the distinction of being named Miss AGAA at the Auckland Girls' Athletics Association carnival in October 1937. Whether her undergarment provided her body with the requisite 'symmetry, grace and deportment', or whether marching and physical exercise led to her perfect form, we do not know.[63] But the commitment to physical culture shown by young women like Minie Inman, and the members of the League of Youth, made them perfect recruits for the Physical Welfare Branch's volunteers programme. The young people who liked to loaf on street corners, though, or went to parks to watch rather than participate, posed a major challenge for local welfare officers. As war loomed even trade unionists wrote to the minister arguing for some sort of compulsory leisure activities for youth. Railway worker Charlie Dawson could not see why these youngsters should be allowed to abuse their bodies and become a burden on the rest of society.[64] His was not a lone voice.

Although Dawson did not mention the Hitler Youth Movement, members of the branch often looked to Germany for inspiration. During National Fitness Week, for example, senior physical welfare officer Bach told a group of Rotarians that the Hitler youth were 'a healthy, whole-some, intelligent appearing lot'.[65] The following month, under the aus-pices of the Department of Internal Affairs, Noel Gibson visited Germany to study 'The organisation and activity of the Hitler Youth Movement, particularly as to the State control of the physical training of the young people'.[66] The threat of war did not overshadow the praise meted out to Nazi youth schemes.

The local ideal may have been in keeping with the German reality, but branch officers were a practical people. They needed to make sure that young people did not disappear into a world of pleasure once they left school, so they set up a system to keep track of them. All school leavers were required to fill in a card with their personal contact details and indi-cate the sort of winter and summertime activities and clubs they were in-terested in joining. Welfare officers then forwarded the information to the appropriate sporting bodies. Some clubs were not interested in babysit-ting youths: the Auckland Tramping Club returned a list of 30 keen school leavers, stating that they were 'unable to cater for them'.[67] Most clubs, though, were happy that the branch was so busy recruiting for them, espe-cially when many of their older members were being called away on war service.[68]

The cost of war on bodies, young and old, was an ongoing concern. Everyone needed to be strong enough to cope with the rigours of war, and mentally and morally able to withstand its pressures and temptations. Physical welfare officers were warned that those aged between fourteen and eighteen were especially vulnerable. Wartime friendships were often fleeting, and could place young people, particularly young women, in compromising situations. The arrival of American troops in 1942 only intensified the problems. Reconstruction could not wait until war's end. A confidential report suggested that all young people under the age of eighteen who were in paid employment should be required to attend an annual camp. These camps would have four main aims:

> (a) To restore their spent (or wasted) energy, (b) perhaps to cleanse and heal the tastes of life, (c) to inspire them with a desire for healthy activity born of a new sense of well-being, and (d) to start training in earnest sufficient, we hope, to grip them with the joy of achievement.[69]

The proposal was all about leisure, rather than pleasure, but welfare offi-cers could not necessarily control how individuals viewed and experi-

enced branch activities. This was as true for adults as it was for children
and young people.

In 1902 women had been told that necessity was the mother of invention
and that their flat-irons made admirable substitute dumb-bells. In 1935
they read about German researchers who had discovered that housework
exercised the same muscles as dance and keep fit programmes. Weekly
window washing strengthened abdominal muscles and daily dusting
was good for spinal stretching.[70] The message that exercising made them
attractive to men and allowed them to wear this season's swimwear was
also ever-present.[71] Reshaping and revealing men's bodies also remained
on the agenda. By the late 1930s Kenneth J. Webb's Kelvin School of
Physical Culture on The Terrace in Wellington had replaced schools run
by the likes of J. W. M. Harrison and Royd Garlick, but Sandow's legacy
was still clear in the advertising copy:

> [the school] is founded on body building and the development and
> fulfilment of the old Roman motto, 'mens sana in corpore sano.' It specialises
> [in] the orderly and cognate development of mind and body, Mr. Webb
> believing most emphatically that the physical culture without reference to the
> mental is all wrong and quite lopsided.[72]

Even his grasp of the English language was positively Sandowesque.

For the women who believed in the physical benefits of dusting and
the men who enrolled at Webb's gym, Parry's legislation and the advent of
the Physical Welfare and Recreation Branch were welcome developments.
Finally the state was recognising that it should be involved in the leisure
lives of its citizens. But for those whose involvement with physical culture
did not extend beyond buying a ticket to George Formby's new comedy,
Keep Fit (in which George, playing a barber's assistant, entered a newspaper's keep fit contest in order to impress a young manicurist), the idea of
state intervention in their recreation time must have come as something
of a shock.[73] Some may have been placated by government 'spin' that, far
from being a totalitarian measure, this was in fact 'The other side of Social
Security' – an opportunity for individuals to develop the habits and skills
which would ensure that they were 'self-sufficient and independent under
almost any conditions'.[74] The pre-war activities of branch officers probably also reassured sceptics.

In the small window between the appointment of physical welfare officers and the outbreak of war, the new appointees worked hard to show that what Parry said was true: there was nothing compulsory about this scheme. Rather, the state was there to assist established, voluntary organisations and help those who wished to form new groups. So the branch organised training courses for women who led the physical recreation programme in girls' clubs,[75] liaised with established groups over activities and information[76] and encouraged those who were already 'doers' rather than mere spectators.[77] The outbreak of war, though, changed the terms of the debate.

One of the radio talks given by the branch in the early days of the war was entitled 'Physical Welfare and Recreation – A Modern Crusade'. The idea that the populace was entitled to fritter away its leisure time was anathema. The word compulsion was still not used, but listeners were reminded that 'There must now be a note of grim realism in view of the implications of a physical fitness programme for national defence and the maintenance of morale in the face of war'.[78] It was everyone's duty, as patriotic citizens, to get fit and stay fit. And that meant branch officers had a big job ahead of them.

Physical welfare officers seem to have been determined to leave no body unreformed. Even visitors could be reshaped: branch officers thought that they were best placed to work with American forces stationed in New Zealand.[79] Groups who were normally ignored in such campaigns, such as rural Maori, also received some attention. Branch officers asked who could best harness the interest Maori in Ruatoria had recently shown in physical welfare,[80] and whether it was time to appoint a dedicated Maori physical welfare officer to serve the Maori community.[81] But while they pondered such questions, most of their time was spent trying to reshape the bodies of Pakeha women and men.

Women whose war service was carried out in the home were reminded that their bodies had to be recreated, just as soldiers' bodies did. They were invited to lectures and demonstrations by branch officers, where they learned how and why they should exercise.[82] The message was repeated in radio broadcasts telling them that it was their 'national service' to attend regular keep fit classes.[83] Branch officers led such classes, and tailored the programme to suit older women who did not appreciate having instructions barked at them.[84] If the campaigns of recent decades had washed over them, they were also encouraged to learn to swim as a sign of their commitment to national defence. Hundreds of women in

Auckland responded to the call, joining the 'Splash Club' where Gladys Gebbie taught them how to swim and dive.[85]

The branch was also there for the women whose war service took them outside the domestic sphere. In the early days of the conflict physical welfare officers provided keep fit instruction to the many women's groups formed to support the war effort. Whether it was the Masterton Women's Emergency Corps, the Hamilton Women's Army Volunteer Company, or the Auckland branch of the Women's War Service Auxiliary (WWSA), physical training was led from the front by Physical Welfare and Recreation officers. As the machinery of the WWSA was put in place, the branch found it no longer had a leadership role in its keep fit efforts, but the work they began continued to have good effect. A 1941 radio broadcast reassured the New Zealand troops in the Middle East that though their women were exercising for national fitness the classes were 'also the way to glory in the shape of renewed slimness and vigour'.[86] It may have been done in the name of leisure, but the men could hope for some bodily pleasure on their safe return.

The branch also played a minor role in reshaping fighting bodies. It helped out with training cadets of the Air Training Corps and with the Home Guard.[87] The death of a Home Guardsman during an exercise session served as a timely reminder that physical welfare officers needed to pay more attention to the age and physique of their pupils, but for the most part their keep fit classes were uneventful.[88] While the armed forces took the leading role in making its men and women fighting fit, the branch concentrated on its own army, the bodies of the women and men who stayed in New Zealand to work in essential industries.

Even before war was declared many workers were convinced of the benefits of exercise. A number of Wellington public servants attended physical culture classes on a regular basis and many others declared that they would do so if better facilities were available.[89] Keen to capitalise on the willingness of state employees 'To take up physical training for the sake of fitness itself', Joe Heenan arranged for the government to pick up the costs of hiring a hall for these keep fit classes.[90] Hundreds of men and women turned up to the lunchtime and early evening classes and exercised to music.[91] Once local branch officers had been appointed, they took the lead in such classes, providing instruction for public servants, the police force, and even the girls employed to work in the railway tearooms at Mercer.[92] Bach was very interested in a New South Wales scheme that required all new youths entering the public service to spend at least two

If You Are Unable to Join the Forces
GET FIT AND KEEP FIT

Public Service ᴬᵀ Gymnasium

WELLINGTON.

(Branch of the Public Service Sports Society, Inc.)

NOTE.—All officers under the control of the Public Service Commissioner; General Manager, Railways; Director-General, Post and Telegraph; Governor, Reserve Bank; and Army, Navy, Air and Police personnel are eligible.

Classes are now being held in the Anglican Hall, Sydney Street, East (near Tivoli Theatre) at the following times and under the stated direction.

Attendance at Classes will not be permitted during office hours and all travelling time for attending Classes must be done in the officer's own time.

MEN	LADIES.
TUESDAY and THURSDAY LUNCHEON HOURS, 12.15 to 1.45. (3 Classes of ½ an hour each.)	EVERY MONDAY & WEDNESDAY EVENING 4.45 to 6.30 p.m.
TUESDAY & THURSDAY EVENINGS 4.45 to 6.30 p.m.	
INSTRUCTORS:—MR. ALF. JENKINS AND FIRST ASSISTANT—MR. RON. MARTIN.	INSTRUCTRESS:— MISS M. M. MEREDITH-JONES.

EXTRA CLASSES WILL BE HELD AS MEMBERSHIP GROWS.

Subscriptions

Ladies .... 5/– per term

Gentlemen .... 7/6 „ „

Through the interest and enthusiasm of the Hon. W. E. Parry, Minister of Internal Affairs the Government has granted the hall rent free. This is the reason that the Society is able to make the fee so reasonable and trusts that all Public Servants will **Support Their Own Enterprise.**

The Class work is graded according to the physical capacity of members. All Government Servants who are interested in Physical Training or desirous of keeping in the best possible physical condition are earnestly invited to join the Gymnasium.

Full particulars may be obtained from:—

E. JENKINS,
Honorary Secretary,
Sydney Street, West.

Phone 45-030.   c/o Native Land Court,

H. & P.C. Print.

DO YOUR BIT----KEEP FIT.

As this poster for the Public Service Gymnasium makes clear, the minister's support of physical culture meant the government provided the exercise venue for its civil servants. One of the gym instructors was Alfred Jenkins, a leading physical culturist in Wellington, known for his work with children and adults. Internal Affairs, W2578, 139/33, Archives New Zealand/ Te Whare Tohu Tuhituhinga o Aotearoa, Wellington.

hours a week on physical training.[93] They might be just clerical workers, but if branch officers were allowed to train them they could be fit, strong, productive clerical workers.

Promises of increased productivity helped district officers convince private employers that their workers, too, needed time out for exercise. In Auckland welfare officers contacted the local Employers' Association, pointing out that they could enjoy increased production if their workers were engaged in some 'relaxing' recreation during their lunch break.[94] Down in Wellington branch officers put their bodies on the line in an experiment at Amos's softgoods factory. Mr Amos agreed to allow his workers an extra half-hour a day for lunch if they used the time to attend the physical fitness class organised on site by a Mr Mitchell from the branch. The six-week trial was declared a success, with productivity having 'increased considerably'. Happy, healthy workers were better workers. The New Zealand Manufacturers' Federation was also pleased, and recommended the scheme to its members.[95]

Managers of department stores could have told Mr Amos that an exercised workforce was a productive workforce. They had long supported their staff's extra-curricular sports programmes, and were keen to now boost these activities with the help of branch officers.[96] Gladys Gebbie, for example, was invited to speak to the Welfare Committee at Milne & Choyce in Auckland, to advise them on how best to implement the idea of 'Physical fitness for Home Defense [sic]'.[97] She also worked with the staff of the Queen Street branch of chain store Woolworths, leading keep fit classes in their lunchroom.[98]

Lunchtime classes had their place, but even during the war many workers were seen to be suffering from a surfeit of leisure time. Were they using their weekends and holidays to best advantage? They were if branch officers had anything to do with it. Alongside workplace classes, physical welfare officers began to organise recreation camps for workers. Joyce Thomson of the Otago office ran week-long 'pep' camps for factory girls. After skiing and playing games during their week in Queenstown or Wanaka they returned to Dunedin 'full of vim and determined to hit up new records at work'.[99]

As with so many of the schemes carried out by branch officers, the idea of state-sponsored holiday camps for workers pre-dated the war. A group in Christchurch led the way, organising weekend recreation camps in the Port Hills for urban youth. Joe Heenan heard of the programme, and suggested to Parry that something similar be established throughout the country.[100] Heenan was aware of similar movements in Britain and Germany and could see the benefits. The Nazis' plan to build a massive holiday resort at Rügen, a Baltic Island off Stalsund, was perhaps a little beyond the resources of the New Zealand Labour government – known as the Colossus of Prora, the German resort stretched 4.5 kilometres down the coast – but huts and camps in the bush and at the beach seemed feasible.[101] Before and during the war Labour Party members lobbied the minister for such facilities, arguing that workers and their families needed a refuge where they could 'recuperate from the city' and rest their minds and bodies.[102] Parry was sympathetic, but wartime constraints meant no resources for such a programme.[103] He did suggest, though, that military camps might be available after the war for such a purpose.[104] As the fighting came to an end, though, he sang a different tune, suggesting that bodies like the Auckland Trades Council should set up and control their own camps, rather than expect the government to intervene.[105] It was an interesting turnaround. Unionists were asking for more state intervention in their leisure lives; the Labour government was backing away. For a decade central government had intervened in adults' leisure lives to an extent previously reserved for children's recreation. But the heyday of this state experiment was passing.

But 1945 did not signal an end to requests for state-funded holiday camps run along approved lines. War bride Ruby Keedwell was concerned by the high cost of family holidays in New Zealand. Just before the war she had enjoyed a week at a Butlin's holiday camp at Skegness, on the northeast coast of England. For 16s a day, she pointed out, women could relax, knowing that trained nurses were taking care of their children, waiters would serve their food, chamber maids were cleaning the bedrooms and entertainment would be provided. Keedwell painted a picture of women at pleasure, relaxing in their deckchairs with nothing to worry about or do.[106] Perhaps not surprisingly, the government did not follow Billy Butlin's lead, but there was interest in the notion of family health camps. One branch officer suggested that all workers who agreed to attend a state-run family health camp be given an additional two weeks of annual leave. As they entered these camp all members of the family would be given a medical examination, and then be issued with their kit (blankets, cooking utensils etc.). Babies and young children would be cared for by 'competent child nurses' (rather than incompetent ones), leaving mothers free to participate in physical activities. During the day, families would be divided by age, each group engaged in activities best suited to their levels of health and fitness. In the evening they would gather together to sing, dance, watch films and generally recover from their day of swimming, hiking, boxing, tennis, sunbathing and skittles. By this method, the officer noted, '[w]e could . . . really educate the people to sane living as once they had tasted the fruits of living a healthy life the people themselves would become the torch bearers of a Health and Fitness campaign and they would foster and promote the cause of a healthy nation'.[107]

During and after the Second World War young women lined up for physical
training. Originally captioned 'A leg change', this 1944 photograph proved that
with proper instruction A1 status was attainable. John Pascoe Collection,
F-976-1/4, Alexander Turnbull Library, Wellington.

Parry maintained a polite interest in such suggestions, but was not
swayed by the arguments of his officers, the pleas of individuals, or the
requests of the Federation of Labour.[108] In New South Wales labour organisations were investigating establishing their own chain of family holiday
centres.[109] The minister suggested that local labour bodies do the same.

As government enthusiasm faded, branch officers carried on their pre-
war and wartime work. They supervised children's playgrounds and continued to train volunteer play leaders.[110] This took them into new state
housing suburbs like Naenae, where they also helped to set up a local
'recreation week', to boost physical activities in the new suburb.[111] Female
officers continued to work with women's groups around the country,
using the radio to help spread the physical fitness message.[112] Officers
of both sexes also made a 'fresh effort' among industrial workers, visiting factories and workshops to provide workers with information and
instruction on how best to build up their bodies.[113] In Christchurch alone

LEFT By 1945 the Department of Health was issuing announcements 'for a healthier nation'. The state still regarded it as appropriate to encourage bodily self-control among its citizens, here reminding women of the importance of good posture. Such a message had previously been the domain of the Physical Welfare and Recreation Branch. Now another arm of government preached the gospel of physical culture. *Truth,* 26 December 1945. RIGHT In the 1930s voluntary organisations like the Sunlight League taught New Zealanders how to sunbathe. By the 1940s the state was taking over the task. Whether it was the Department of Health or the Physical Welfare and Recreation Branch, non-governmental leisure programmes often provided the basis for the state's initiatives. *Truth,* 23 January 1946.

this effort involved over 9000 employees.[114] Otago officers organised further trips for 'business girls' to Queenstown, Wanaka, Glenorchy and Stewart Island, and Auckland officer Gladys Gebbie continued her efforts among department store workers.[115] The Second World War might have been won, but the war on workers' bodies was still being waged.

Most of the workers who found themselves attending lunchtime keep fit classes or weekend sports tournaments were Pakeha, but physical welfare officers also took a keen interest in the bodies of post-war migrants.

POLITICAL JERKS

National may have been lukewarm about the survival of the Branch, but with
their Labour colleagues they were happy to use the new gym at parliament.
Sid Holland cycled his way to victory in the general election held soon after
Minhinnick drew this cartoon. *New Zealand Herald*, 17 August 1949.

Their work with refugees at Pahiatua was important, they maintained, 'in
initiating new settlers into the New Zealand way of life through social and
recreational activities'.[116] Among Maori, too, they argued for the importance of well-funded fitness schemes, noting that in new settlements such
as Murupara it was important to set up suitable programmes for the for-
estry workers' leisure time. If the branch was not a presence, the door
would be wide open 'To drunkenness, gambling, and to the other social
ills which afflict a discontented community'.[117] District officers claimed
that the state still had a role in imposing a culture of constraint on lei-
surely bodies.

Although branch officers continued to perform this controlling function into the 1950s, they increasingly found themselves in disputes over
jurisdiction. Was it the role of district officers to provide leadership and
recreation training to Maori in their area, or was this a task for members
of the Department of Maori Affairs?[118] Should branch officers step aside at
Arohata Women's Borstal, where they had been running regular physical
and recreational training session for the inmates, because the Department
of Education had decided to take over the programme?[119] The 1937 act

did not cover the relationship between the branch and other arms of government;[120] by the 1950s this was becoming increasingly problematic. A committee appointed in the late 1940s to investigate the workings of the branch had recommended that it should be co-ordinated with the Department of Education's physical education efforts, but the government did not follow this up.[121] The new National government simply starved this state experiment of money and personnel. Funding was slashed and departing branch officers were not replaced. By the late 1950s only two staff members remained.[122] The 20-year experiment was over.

In 1973, after the election of the third Labour government, round two of the state's experiment with adult recreation began. With Joe Walding as the minister, Labour created a Ministry of Recreation and Sport and passed the Recreation and Sport Act. The parallels with Parry's era were strong, right down to the running of a 'Come Alive!' campaign in 1975, the modern equivalent of National Fitness Week.[123] When Labour lost office, its physical welfare ideal went into abeyance, only to be revived in 1987, when the Hillary Commission for Sport, Fitness and Leisure was established. This 1980s version of the Physical Welfare and Recreation Branch was designed to promote and develop New Zealanders' leisure habits, broadly defined. The act that established the commission was amended in 1992. As had happened in 1937, politicians argued that the Sport, Fitness and Leisure Amendment Act would promote the moral and physical welfare of the nation. If citizens had strong, healthy, reshaped bodies, they would be able to withstand the threats of modern life.[124] It was as if Parry had never left the House.

Conclusion

A decade after Daisy Martin received her Sandow statue in the mail Frank Sargeson published *Memoirs of a Peon*, a novel about the early life of Michael Newhouse, who, as a young man, was awed by his very own encounter with Sandowism. One cold autumn night Newhouse found himself down at the local rugby club, ready to be instructed in the finer arts of the game. One of his new coaches – the man dedicated to ensuring that the players were physically fit – was known as Spots. As Newhouse told his tale, Spots was a man 'so remarkably smooth and muscular that he positively invited comparison with any one of Michelangelo's supermen one cared to name'. Newhouse was familiar with Spots's body because his coach wore only a leopard skin and sandshoes. It was not quite the Auckland City Hall theatre where Sandow had performed, but Spots was as determined as his hero had been to impress his rugby protégés.[1] Thirty-five years later Sandow reappeared in our literature, this time in Lloyd Jones's prize-winning novel about the 1905 All Blacks, *The Book of Fame*. Just after the triumphant rugby players have enjoyed Annette Kellermann's performance at the London Hippodrome, Jones introduces them to Sandow, making it clear that the New Zealanders are now the centre of attention and cause of awe. In the sparse prose that defines the novel, he writes of 'world strongman Eugene [*sic*] Sandow and his assistants studying us in our baths following victory over Middlesex'.[2] Given how prone Sandow was to fictionalising his life story, it seems appropriate that he should end up as a character in a novel. But Sandow was much more than a literary creation. Declared the ideal modern man at the turn of the twentieth century, he toured New Zealand at the height of his fame. He was a strongman on stage, but the strength of his message meant he had an enduring off-stage presence too. So strong, in fact, that 100 years later he stands at the centre of this book.

No leopard-skin knickers for these Wellingtonians, but like Sandow they had reshaped themselves through exercise and were now revealing their bodies, and their weightlifting prowess, for all to see. F-57016-1/2, Alexander Turnbull Library, Wellington.

If Sandow had not existed, or had not visited New Zealand in 1902–03, a book like this might still have been possible. Someone else would have taken his place. Sandow appealed to his contemporaries because he was both extraordinary and 'just a MAN!'[3] Bernarr Macfadden in the United States and Edmond Desbonnet in France performed the same role.[4] All became mouthpieces and bodies for their generation, and all left behind a physical culture legacy.

Like Macfadden and Desbonnet, Sandow was real, unique and yet at the same time representative of a general cultural phenomenon. Thousands of New Zealanders saw him perform. In his leopard-skin knickers, muscles rippling, he performed feats of strength the like of which had never been seen before. In 1955 a group of young men similarly set out to surprise the crowds around them. On Wellington's Oriental Parade they gathered around their barbell, ready to impress and entertain fellow beachgo-ers. Their attire was somewhat more demure than Sandow's, but the in-tention was not too dissimilar. The pleasure they took in revealing their reshaped bodies stands in stark contrast to a 1911 cartoon that appeared in *Truth*. 'The Wowser's Dream' included no sport, no betting, no dancing and no 'Xmas cheer'. In the wowser's God's Own there would be 'no plea-sure'. The joke is often made that, until a few years ago, New Zealand was

THE WOWSER'S DREAM.

The wowser's dream was the hedonist's nightmare, a land where everything pleasurable, including pleasure itself, was outlawed. *Truth*, 25 November 1911.

20 years behind the rest of the Western world. It is tempting to read these two images as visual evidence of an even longer time lag. At the turn of the century the visiting strongman could stand on stage, displaying his body for all to see; it took 50 years before New Zealanders caught up. I have rejected such an interpretation in this book. Although change over time is important, especially for historians, such a straightforward reading of the two pictures glosses over the richness and complexity of our history.

Wowsers could only dream of a land without vineyards and mixed bathing because in 1911, despite their best efforts, many New Zealanders still enjoyed alcohol, and a growing number were learning of the delights of mixed bathing. Herbert Corder, an Englishman who had just spent six months in New Zealand, was adamant that New Zealanders were less reverent than their English counterparts and were not conventional in behaviour. He concluded that there was altogether 'Too much striving after pleasure' in New Zealand.[5] If Corder is to be believed, New Zealand was a living nightmare for wowsers. Hedonism ruled the day.

Social histories of New Zealand tell us that 1911 was remarkable as the year when over half of the electorate voted for national prohibition.[6] As this book has shown, it was also a time when the government was very intent on reshaping young bodies through a new physical education syllabus, and when many other New Zealanders took themselves to their local gym and took their bodies in hand. But 1911 was also the year the first national physical development competition was held, with C. Clifford Jennings becoming, in effect, the first Mr New Zealand. It was the heyday of photographic beauty contests for women, organised by movie houses motivated more by revenue than improving the racial stock. The era of Annette Kellermann was a time when more and more men and women flocked to the beach, revealing their bodies for all to see. Sales of binoculars soared as swimming and sunbaking became typical Sunday fare.

W. Norman Kerr nicely represents what was going on. Kerr offered Aucklanders private courses in physical culture. He treated nerve and muscular diseases, and provided instruction in breathing techniques. As his letterhead explained, he offered 'Health, Strength, and Physical Development'. His letterhead also noted that he was a 'Society Entertainer in Original Posing, Living Statuary, Muscular Control'.[7] He embodied leisure and pleasure just as Sandow had through his stage show and the Sandow System.

From the turn of the twentieth century through to the 1950s we can find other Kerrs and other ways that New Zealanders were able to blur the boundaries between sanctioned leisure activities and pure pleasure. Some, of course, had no intention of blurring any boundaries. There were high-minded, serious citizens who were genuinely persuaded by the rhetoric of health and racial fitness. When they watched Sandow or the Modern Milo, went to the beach or even joined a nudist club, they sincerely believed that they were acting in the country's best interests. Others only ever wanted to pay an extra sixpence to get close to the beauty contestants' bodies, buy nudist magazines for the pictures and stroll beaches in search of costume violations. For them the modern focus on reshaping and revealing the body was a very pleasurable dream indeed, all the more so as the dream became a reality.

But as Leisure & Pleasure has shown, many New Zealanders were comfortable when boundaries were blurred. They needed to be reassured that looking at Sandow was 'above board', and welcomed the classical references that gave legitimacy to his show.[8] His off-stage preaching also aided their enjoyment of his on-stage performance. When they took up physical culture they could congratulate themselves for rebuilding their bodies at the same time as they revelled in the attention their new physiques received. Beauty contestants, especially those who were judged by physical culture experts, could tell themselves that they were role models for other women, while hoping that success would lead to a profitable career on stage or screen. Pool and beach enthusiasts accepted that it was 'fair' that they learn to swim and save lives, and to lie in the sun in their rapidly shrinking costumes.[9] Nudists turned their skins brown in the name of health and racial improvement, and wrote about the pleasure of exercising and sunning in groups. Children followed the play supervisor's instructions as young bodies were ordered and made orderly, all the while having fun on the swings and roundabouts. Even the government's attempts at corporeal control recognised that all leisure and no pleasure did not make for happy citizens and productive workers.

These blendings of leisure and pleasure both reflected modern New Zealand life and had consequences for the shape of society. Like their counterparts elsewhere, New Zealanders were trying to cope with the transition from traditional to modern society. Modern society offered unparalleled freedoms. These were welcomed by some, but many found the relaxation of social controls confusing and frightening. The potential results were terrifying: a society where the 'fit' were so intent on having fun that they left the 'unfit' to populate the country; where 'spectatoritis' rather than participation ruled the day;[10] where good health gave way to lethargy and perversion. Cultures of constraint were called for to survive and thrive in this new age. The leisure pursuits discussed in this book were part of this desire to curb the worst excesses of the era while also enjoying the greater freedoms available.

The ways New Zealanders blended leisure and pleasure had an important consequence for the role recreation played in society. They muted its transgressive, transformative potential. Modern New Zealand could have been a haven for hedonists: a society that celebrated the pleasures of the flesh, of Sandow, the Modern Milo, and physique and beauty contestants; that welcomed the development of swimming and sunbathing for the bodies they revealed; that encouraged nudists to step out from the bush and play in the open. But the leisure message tempered the pleasure of these activities. The higher purposes of leisure, which some held dear and many others hid behind, limited how much pleasure, pure and simple, New Zealanders could enjoy.

This book has not set out to make particular national claims. New Zealanders seem to have regarded modern society with the same worried eyes as the rest of the Western world. And their solution – a desire to strengthen themselves physically and morally – was not unique. They looked overseas for role models and reassurance, and were pleased when their gaze fell on Sandow and the physical culture movement. They shared experts such as Auguste Rollier and William Wellby, and associations like the playground movement. Sometimes they led the way, welcoming the Modern Milo before she achieved international fame; more often they followed trends. The time lags were very small. New season costumes on the beaches of Los Angeles in June could be seen at Takapuna and New Brighton in December. Modern New Zealanders were part of an international recreation culture. As local beauties entered global quests, nudists travelled to conventions overseas, and government officials searched the world to find out how best to reshape New Zealand bodies, they were active participants in a movement that went far beyond national boundaries. The only thing that marks New Zealand's leisure and pleasure history off from countries elsewhere is that historians here have not shown much interest in revealing it. I hope *Leisure & Pleasure* will act as a catalyst, encouraging some to reassess my interpretation of this period and these activities, and others to explore the myriad other aspects of our leisure history not touched on here.

I have drawn this book to a close in 1960. The year was not particularly significant in terms of New Zealand leisure, apart from Joe Brown's relaunch of the Miss New Zealand contest. It was not a watershed year, a move from modern to post-modern bodies. Rather it represents the widespread acceptance of what the ideal modern body should look like. I could just as easily have chosen 1955, when Daisy Martin received her unexpected Christmas present, or 1965, when Sargeson published *Memoirs of a Peon*. The choice of 1960 is as idiosyncratic as the rest of this book.

I am convinced, however, that the modern body discussed in these pages came under increased challenge as the 1960s gave way to the 1970s and hippies became something people were rather than wore. Glam rock and punk, New Romantics and Goths created new ambiguities about the body at play. By the 1990s heroin chic sat alongside he-men whose bodies were fit to burst as they pumped ever more steroids into them. The post-modern body was as confused and confusing as the ideology that came with it. It could well make one long for the certainty of Sandow and an age when leisure and pleasure blurred in the quest to reshape and reveal New Zealand bodies.

Notes

INTRODUCTION

1 *New Zealand Herald* (*NZH*), 22 Dec. 1955, p.13.

2 *Sandow's Magazine*, July 1898, p.79. Note: Sandow began the magazine in July 1898 as *Physical Culture*. By April 1899 the magazine was renamed *Sandow's Magazine*. In Sept.1900 it became *Sandow's Magazine of Physical Culture and British Sport*. In 1901 it was *Sandow's Magazine of Physical Culture* before reverting to *Sandow's Magazine of Physical Culture and British Sport*. In 1903 it changed to *Sandow's Magazine of Physical Culture, Sport and Fiction* and in 1905 became *Sandow's Weekly Magazine of Physical Culture & Sport*. For the sake of simplicity it is referred to here as *Sandow's Magazine*.

3 *Sandow's Magazine*, Oct. 1901, pp.286-91.

4 *NZH*, 22 Dec. 1955, p.13.

5 Unless otherwise noted, the information on Sandow's life and career is taken from the most comprehensive biography of Sandow, David L. Chapman's *Sandow the Magnificent: Eugen Sandow and the Beginnings of Bodybuilding*, Urbana and Chicago, 1994.

6 For other accounts of Sandow's arrival on the London stage see Chapman, *Sandow the Magnificent*, pp.23-32; Eugen Sandow, 'How I Came to London and Defeated Samson', in *Strength and How To Obtain It*, London, 1897, pp.93-99; 'How I Became a Strong Man', in *The Gospel of Strength According to Sandow: A Series of Talks on the Sandow System of Physical Culture, by its Founder*, Melbourne, 1902, pp.11-15. Chapman refers to the French strongman as Sampson, while Sandow's own accounts give his name as Samson.

7 Such references are numerous. See, for example, *Adelaide Register*, 2 Aug. 1902, p.10 and 15 Aug. 1902, p.6; *Adelaide Advertiser*, 9 Aug. 1902, p.14; *NZH*, 18 Nov. 1902, p.7; *Wanganui Chronicle*, 22 Nov. 1902, p.7; *Daily Telegraph* [Napier], 29 Nov. 1902, p.5.

8 For his New Zealand tour see Ch. 1 and Caroline Daley, 'Selling Sandow: Modernity and Leisure in Early Twentieth-Century New Zealand', *New Zealand Journal of History*, 34, 2, 2000, pp.241-61. The run-in with the Land and Income Tax Department is discussed on pp.249-50 of the article. For his Australian tour see Caroline Daley, 'The Strongman of Eugenics, Eugen Sandow', *Australian Historical Studies*, 33, 120, 2002, pp.233-48. On his tours in other parts of the world see Chapman, *Sandow the Magnificent*.

9 Many of the histories of rugby take their lead from two key works of the 1980s, Keith Sinclair's history of New Zealand's national identity (*A Destiny Apart: New Zealand's Search for National Identity*, Wellington, 1986) and Jock Phillips's history of mateship (*A Man's Country? The Image of the Pakeha Male – A History*, Auckland, 1987, revised edition 1996). See also Geoff Fougere, 'Sport, Culture and Identity: The Case of Rugby Football', in David Novitz and Bill Willmott (eds), *Culture and Identity in New Zealand*, Wellington, 1989, pp.110-22. Greg Ryan's work on the history of rugby is notable in bucking this particular national story. See in particular Greg Ryan, 'Rural Myth and Urban Actuality: The Anatomy of All Black and New Zealand Rugby 1884–1938', *New Zealand Journal of History*, 35, 1, 2001, pp.45-69.

10 It is clear that New Zealand has performed more than credibly on the world rugby stage, small though that stage be. However, James Belich's recent claim that New Zealand is a 'world superpower' when it comes to sport seems like another attempt to tell a unique national tale. James Belich, *Paradise Reforged: A History of the New Zealanders From the 1880s to the Year 2000*, Auckland, 2001, p.368.

11 For a recent plea for New Zealand historians to eschew national stories and instead place New Zealand's history in a world systems framework see Peter Gibbons, 'The Far Side of the Search for Identity: Reconsidering

New Zealand History', *New Zealand Journal of History*, 37, 1, 2003, pp.38-49.

12 See Charles S. Maier, *In Search of Stability: Explorations in Historical Political Economy*, Cambridge MA., 1987; Anson Rabinbach, *The Human Motor: Energy, Fatigue, and the Origins of Modernity*, New York, 1990; James C. Scott, *Seeing Like a State: How Certain Schemes to Improve the Human Condition Have Failed*, New Haven and London, 1998, esp. Ch. 3.

13 For a useful overview of the rational recreation idea see Peter Bailey, 'The Politics and Poetics of Modern British Leisure: A late twentieth-century review', *Rethinking History*, 3, 2, 1999, esp. pp.131-3. On bodily control matching the control of the workplace see Tim Armstrong, 'Introduction', in Tim Armstrong (ed.), *American Bodies: Cultural Histories of the Physique*, Sheffield, 1996, esp. pp.10-11; Julia L. Foulkes, *Modern Bodies: Dance and American Modernism from Martha Graham to Alvin Ailey*, Chapel Hill & London, 2002; Tamar Garb, *Bodies of Modernity: Figure and Flesh in Fin-de-Siecle France*, London, 1998.

14 On the 'modernist preoccupation with physicality' see Harold B. Segel, *Body Ascendant: Modernism and the Physical Imperative*, Baltimore and London, 1998. The quote is from p.1.

15 Sandow often told the story of his trip to Italy and how it inspired him. He related the tale several times during his time in New Zealand. See *New Zealand Graphic*, 15 Nov. 1902, p.1243; *Wanganui Chronicle*, 24 Nov. 1902, p.2; *New Zealand Mail*, 10 Dec. 1902, p.46; *Press*, 19 Dec. 1902, p.5; *Oamaru Mail*, 25 Dec. 1902, p.1; *Otago Daily Times* (*ODT*), 27 Dec. 1902, p.8; *Weekly Press*, 31 Dec. 1902, p.41; *Southland Daily News*, 6 Jan. 1903, p.3. The quotes are from the account in the *Press*.

16 Michael Anton Budd, *The Sculpture Machine: Physical Culture and Body Politics in the Age of Empire*, New York, 1997, p.147, fn.34.

17 On the Alexander technique see Armstrong, 'Introduction', p.11; on dieting see Peter N. Stearns, *Fat History: Bodies and Beauty in the Modern West*, New York and London, 1997; on physical fitness see Mary Lynn Stewart, *For Health and Beauty: Physical Culture for Frenchwomen, 1880s–1930s*, Baltimore and London, 2001.

18 *Timaru Herald*, 29 Dec. 1902, p.3.

19 Armstrong, 'Introduction', p.11.

20 Bailey, 'The Politics and Poetics of Modern British Leisure'. The discussion of the limitations of rational recreation can be found on pp.141-2; the suggestion of the need to place the body into leisure history on pp.152-3; the quote about fun on p.153.

21 *Ibid.*, p.141.

22 For a useful overview of modernization in New Zealand 1890-1940, see Erik Olssen, 'Towards a New Society', in Geoffrey W. Rice (ed.), *The Oxford History of New Zealand*, 2nd edn, Auckland, 1992, pp.254-84.

23 Belich, *Paradise Reforged*, esp. Ch. 5, 'Moral Harmony: A New Crusade', pp.157-88.

24 On the connections between Sandow and Tarzan see John F. Kasson, *Houdini, Tarzan and The Perfect Man: The White Male Body and The Challenge of Modernity in America*, New York, 2001.

25 Scott, *Seeing Like a State*, pp.89-90.

26 For Foucault, of course, discipline was not a crude state-imposed set of rules, but 'a multiplicity of often minor processes, of different origin and scattered location, which overlap, repeat, or intimate one another, support one another, distinguish themselves from one another according to their domain of application, converge and gradually produce the blueprint of a general method'. Michel Foucault, *Discipline and Punish: The Birth of the Prison*, translated from the French by Alan Sheridan, New York, 1977, p.138.

27 Mike J. Huggins, 'More Sinful Pleasures? Leisure, Respectability and the Male Middle Classes in Victorian England', *Journal of Social History*, 33, 3, 2000, p.587.

28 Rob Shields, *Places on the Margin: Alternative geographies of modernity*, London and New York, 1991, p.96. Emphasis in the original.

29 Belich entitles Part 2 of his book, which contains his Ch. on moral harmony, 'The Great Tightening'. Belich, *Paradise Reforged*, pp.121-240.

30 Historical geographers often use the term 'liminality' when describing such potentially transgressive and transformative spaces. See Shields, *Places on the Margin*.

31 Garb makes a similar point when discussing physical culture in France. Garb, *Bodies of Modernity*, esp. pp.55-79.

32 See, for example, Bronwyn Dalley, 'Lolly Shops "of the red-light kind" and "soldiers of the King": Suppressing One-Woman Brothels in New Zealand, 1908–1916', *New Zealand Journal of History*, 30, 1, 1996, pp.3-23; P. Fleming, 'Fighting the "Red Plague": Observations on the Response to Venereal Disease in New Zealand 1910–45', *New Zealand Journal of History*, 22, 1, 1988, pp.56-64; Charlotte Macdonald, 'The "Social Evil": Prostitution and the Passage of the Contagious Diseases Act', in Barbara Brookes, Charlotte Macdonald and Margaret Tennant (eds), *Women in History: Essays on European Women in New Zealand*, Wellington,

1986, pp.13-34; K. V. Parcell, 'The 1922 Committee of Inquiry into Venereal Disease in New Zealand', Research Essay, University of Auckland, 1970; Barbara Brookes, 'Reproductive Rights: The Debate over Abortion and Birth Control in the 1930s', in Brookes, Macdonald and Tennant (eds), *Women in History*, pp.119-36. Even the book that bucks this trend, Stevan Eldred-Grigg's *Pleasures of the Flesh: Sex and Drugs in Colonial New Zealand 1840–1915*, Wellington, 1984, is preoccupied with attempts to thwart the pleasures of the flesh.

33 On violence and drink see Miles Fairburn, *The Ideal Society and its Enemies: The Foundation of Modern New Zealand Society, 1850–1900*, Auckland, 1989. On temperance and prohibition see A. R. Grigg, 'Prohibition, the Church and Labour: a Programme for Social Reform, 1890–1914', *New Zealand Journal of History*, 15, 2, 1981, pp.135-56; A. R. Grigg, 'Prohibition and Women: The Preservation of an Ideal and a Myth', *New Zealand Journal of History*, 17, 2, 1983, pp.144-65; Paul McKimmey, 'The Temperance Movement in New Zealand, 1853–1894', MA Thesis, University of Auckland, 1968; Jock Phillips, *A Man's Country? The Image of the Pakeha Male – A History*, revised edn, Auckland, 1996, esp. Ch. 2; Craig Turney, 'The New Zealand Alliance and Auckland, 1905–1920', MA Thesis, University of Auckland, 1996.

34 There are exceptions, of course. Bronwyn Dalley's *Living in the 20th Century: New Zealand History in Photographs 1900–1980*, Wellington, 2000, is an excellent example of a book that takes pleasure as seriously as work.

35 The body at leisure is the focus of much of the writing about women's sport, where team games are to the fore. Sport and team games are not the focus in this book, but for those interested in them, see Sandra Coney, *Every Girl: A Social History of Women and the YWCA in Auckland, 1885–1985*, Auckland, 1986 and *Standing in the Sunshine*, Auckland, 1993, pp.238-59; Ruth Fry, '"Don't let down the side": Physical Education for New Zealand Schoolgirls, 1900–1945', in Brookes, Macdonald and Tennant (eds), *Women in History*, pp.101-17; Margaret A. E. Hammer, '"Something Else in the World to Live For": Sport and the Physical Emancipation of Women and Girls in Auckland 1880–1920', MA Thesis, University of Auckland, 1990; Charlotte Macdonald *et al.*, 'The Unbalanced Parallel', in Anne Else (ed.), *Women Together: A History of Women's Organisations in New Zealand/Nga Ropu Wahine o te Motu*, Wellington, 1993, pp.403-44.

36 Histories of leisure activities such as knitting might well make some claim at comprehensiveness, but the body at play is too large and diverse a topic for me to make any such claim. On knitting see Heather Nicholson, *The Loving Stitch: A history of knitting and spinning in New Zealand*, Auckland, 1998.

37 On tramping see Chris Maclean, *Tararua: the story of a mountain range*, Wellington, 1994; Kirstie Ross, 'Signs of Landing: Pakeha Outdoor Recreation and the Cultural Colonisation of New Zealand', MA Thesis, University of Auckland, 1999, and '"Schooled by Nature": Pakeha Tramping Between the Wars', *New Zealand Journal of History*, 36, 1, 2002, pp.51-65. On mountaineering see Freda du Faur, *The Conquest of Mount Cook, and Other Climbs: An Account of Four Seasons' Mountaineering on the Southern Alps of New Zealand*, London, 1915; Sally Irwin, *Between Heaven and Earth: the life of a mountaineer, Freda Du Faur 1882–1935*, Hawthorn, Vic., 2000; Graham Langton, 'A History of Mountain Climbing in New Zealand to 1953', PhD Thesis, University of Canterbury, 1996.

38 This description was often used in press reports announcing the *Sandow Season*. See, for example, *Budget and Taranaki Weekly Herald*, 22 Nov. 1902, p.17; *Wanganui Herald*, 22 Nov. 1902, p.6; *Manawatu Evening Standard*, 26 Nov. 1902, p.2; *Manawatu Daily Times*, 26 Nov. 1902, p.2; *Hawke's Bay Herald*, 28 Nov. 1902, p.2; *Timaru Herald*, 20 Dec. 1902, p.4.

ONE THE STRONGMAN COMETH

1 Eugen Sandow, *Body-Building, or Man in the Making: How to Become Healthy & Strong*, London, 1904, p.115. Emphasis in the original.

2 *Budget and Taranaki Weekly Herald*, 29 Nov. 1902, p.22. Report on opening night in New Plymouth.

3 *Evening Star* [Dunedin], 2 Jan. 1903, p.6.

4 Sandow, *Body-Building*, p.110.

5 *New Zealand Graphic*, 8 Feb. 1908, p.29.

6 *Auckland Star* (AS), 19 Nov. 1902, p.2.

7 *Canterbury Times*, 24 Dec. 1902, p.50.

8 *Budget and Taranaki Weekly Herald*, 29 Nov. 1902, p.22.

9 *Otago Daily Times* (ODT), 6 Jan. 1903, p.6.

10 *Manawatu Daily Times*, 1 Dec. 1902, p.2

11 References to Sargent's endorsement of Sandow can be found in several New Zealand newspapers. See *Budget and Taranaki Weekly Herald*, 22 Nov. 1902, p.17; *Wanganui Herald*, 24 Nov. 1902, p.5; *Manawatu Daily Times*, 26 Nov. 1902, p.2; *Wairarapa Daily Times*, 27

Nov. 1902, p.3; *Timaru Herald*, 20 Dec. 1902, p.4; *Evening Star*, 24 Dec. 1902, p.6.

12 *Manawatu Daily Times*, 1 Dec. 1902, p.2.

13 *Weekly Press* [Christchurch], 24 Dec. 1902, p.45.

14 *Oamaru Mail*, 30 Dec. 1902, p.4.

15 *Evening Post* [Wellington], 9 Dec. 1902, p.4.

16 *Wairarapa Daily Times*, 2 Dec. 1902, p.2.

17 *Budget and Taranaki Weekly Herald*, 29 Nov. 1902, p.22.

18 *Manawatu Evening Standard*, 1 Dec. 1902, p.2.

19 *Evening Post*, 9 Dec. 1902, p.4.

20 *Budget and Taranaki Weekly Herald*, 29 Nov. 1902, p.22.

21 *AS*, 19 Nov. 1902, p.2; *Lyttelton Times*, 19 Dec. 1902, p.5.

22 *Wanganui Chronicle*, 27 Nov. 1902, p.4.

23 Lois W. Banner, *American Beauty*, New York, 1983, p.170.

24 This argument is explored in Ch. 5.

25 Kenneth R. Dutton and Ronald S. Laura, 'Towards a History of Bodybuilding', *Sporting Traditions*, 6, 1, Nov. 1989, p.33.

26 Maurizia Boscagli, *Eye On The Flesh: Fashions of Masculinity in the Early Twentieth Century*, Boulder CO, 1996, p.106.

27 Edison's film was part of a package of films screened when the movies were first introduced in New Zealand. See *Evening Post*, 27 Oct. 1896, p.2; *Canterbury Times*, 12 Nov. 1896, p.43.

28 *New Zealand Graphic*, 15 Nov. 1902, p.1243. See also *Auckland Weekly News*, 13 Nov. 1902, Supplement p.8; *New Zealand Mail*, 10 Dec. 1902, p.43.

29 *Weekly Press*, 17 Dec. 1902, p.45.

30 *Manawatu Evening Standard*, 27 Nov. 1902, p.2.

31 *Wanganui Chronicle*, 27 Nov. 1902, p.4.

32 *Ibid.*

33 For example, in New York Sandow played at Koster & Bial's Music Hall, 'one of the best and most prestigious variety theatres in America', David L. Chapman, *Sandow the Magnificent: Eugen Sandow and the Beginnings of Bodybuilding*, Urbana and Chicago, 1994, p.70.

34 *Weekly Press*, 17 Dec. 1902, p.54.

35 *Evening Post*, 20 Dec. 1902, Supplement p.3.

36 *Weekly Press*, 7 Jan. 1903, p.54.

37 Report of the New Plymouth performance in the *Taranaki Herald*, reprinted in *Wanganui Chronicle*, 27 Nov. 1902, p.4.

38 On women looking at Sandow, and Sandow looking back at them, see Caroline Daley, 'The Body Builder and Beauty Contests', *Journal of Australian Studies*, 71, 2001, pp.55-66.

39 *Evening Post*, 13 Dec. 1902, Supplement p.2.

40 On women touching Sandow see Chapman,

Sandow the Magnificent, pp.60, 75, 78.

41 *Evening Post*, 13 Dec. 1902, Supplement p.2.

42 *Southland Times*, 10 Jan. 1903, p.2.

43 *Press*, 20 Dec. 1902, p.8.

44 *Wanganui Chronicle*, 28 Nov. 1902, p.5.

45 See Daley, 'The Body Builder and Beauty Contests', pp.59-60.

46 This label was used several times during the tour. See *Wanganui Chronicle*, 22 Nov. 1902, p.7; *Daily Telegraph* [Napier], 29 Nov. 1902, p.5; *Canterbury Times*, 17 Dec. 1902, p.41; *ODT*, 1 Jan. 1903, p.6.

47 *Wanganui Chronicle*, 28 Nov. 1902, p.5.

48 *Ibid.*

49 *Budget and Taranaki Weekly Herald*, 22 Nov. 1902, p.17; *Wanganui Herald*, 22 Nov. 1902, p.6; *Manawatu Evening Standard*, 26 Nov. 1902, p.2; *Manawatu Daily Times*, 26 Nov. 1902, p.2; *Hawke's Bay Herald*, 28 Nov. 1902, p.2.

50 *Wanganui Chronicle*, 27 Nov. 1902, p.4; *Evening Post*, 9 Dec. 1902, p.4; *Timaru Herald*, 27 Dec. 1902, p.4.

51 *Wanganui Chronicle*, 28 Nov. 1902, p.5.

52 *Ibid.*

53 *AS*, 19 Nov. 1902, p.2.

54 *NZH*, 19 Nov. 1902, p.6; *Oamaru Mail*, 30 Dec. 1902, p.4; *Wanganui Chronicle*, 27 Nov. 1902, p.4.

55 Aucklanders had been able to view a statue of the Discobolus for some time, thanks to an 1878 donation to the Auckland Institute. Sandra Chesterman, *FigureWork: The Nude and Life Modelling in New Zealand Art*, Dunedin, 2002, p.6.

56 Cited in *Wanganui Chronicle*, 27 Nov. 1902, p.4.

57 *Evening Post*, 10 Dec. 1902, p.4.

58 As Tohunga noted, he was 'teuton but fair-haired'. *Auckland Weekly News*, 4 Dec. 1902, p.10. For other comments on his Teutonic good looks, see *Evening Post*, 10 Dec. 1902, p.4; *New Zealand Mail*, 17 Dec. 1902, p.25; *Weekly Press*, 31 Dec. 1902, p.41.

59 Measurements of his chest, arms, thighs, calves and waist were given in several reports. See *Manawatu Daily Times*, 25 Nov. 1902, p.2; *Manawatu Evening Standard*, 25 Nov. 1902, p.2; *Yeoman*, 6 Dec. 1902, p.6; *Southland Times*, 7 Jan. 1903, p.2. For references to Harvard Professor Sargent's endorsement of Sandow as the best developed man who ever lived, see footnote 11 above.

60 *New Zealand Graphic*, 1 Nov. 1902, p.1101.

61 *Lyttelton Times*, 19 Dec. 1902, p.2.

62 *Auckland Weekly News*, 4 Dec. 1902, p.10. Other reports supporting Sandow's scientific claims can be found in *Evening Post*, 10 Dec. 1902, p.4.

63 *Evening Post*, 10 Dec. 1902, p.4.

64 *Lyttelton Times*, 19 Dec. 1902, p.2.

65 On the popularity of athletics, see Caroline Daley, 'A Gendered Domain: Leisure in Auckland, 1890–1940', in Caroline Daley and Deborah Montgomerie (eds), *The Gendered Kiwi*, Auckland, 1999, pp.87-111.

66 *Weekly Press*, 31 Dec. 1902, p.41.

67 *Lyttelton Times*, 19 Dec. 1902, p.2.

68 The first New Zealand reference in the magazine came in a story 'Strong Men of the Church', which included Bishop Selwyn. *Sandow's Magazine*, April 1899, pp.256-7. Later in the year William Pember Reeves contributed an article on 'Native Races from a Physical Standpoint. The Maoris'. *Sandow's Magazine*, Aug. 1899, pp.143-50. Francis B. Hutchinson contributed several articles to the magazine. See *Sandow's Magazine*, June 1899, pp.413-17; April 1900, pp.364-8; May 1901, pp.371-2. Early New Zealand photographs included one of the sixteen members of the Christchurch Sandow Team (*Sandow's Magazine*, Nov. 1900, p.368), Charles J. Ward of Wellington, with flexed biceps (Dec. 1900, p.444), athlete A. T. Norton (Feb. 1901, p.112), H. Cutting and W. H. Trengrove, pupils of Fred Hornibrook (Feb. 1901, pp.122, 124) and one of R. O. Garratt [*sic*] (April 1901, p.287). In total, 20 photographs of New Zealanders appeared in the magazine before Sandow's visit.

69 *Budget and Taranaki Weekly Herald*, 22 Nov. 1902, p.17; *Wanganui Herald*, 22 Nov. 1902, p.6; *Manawatu Evening Standard*, 26 Nov. 1902, p.2; *Manawatu Daily Times*, 26 Nov. 1902, p.2; *Hawke's Bay Herald*, 28 Nov. 1902, p.2; *Timaru Herald*, 20 Dec. 1902, p.4.

70 *Wanganui Chronicle*, 22 Nov. 1902, p.7.

71 *Ibid*.

72 *Wairarapa Daily Times*, 27 Nov. 1902, p.3.

73 *Hawke's Bay Herald*, 3 Dec. 1902, p.3.

74 *Daily Telegraph*, 29 Nov. 1902, p.5.

75 *ODT*, 31 Dec. 1902, p.6.

76 On concerns about infant mortality see Erik Olssen, 'Truby King and the Plunket Society: An Analysis of a Prescriptive Ideology', *New Zealand Journal of History*, 15, 1, 1981, pp.3-23; Philippa Mein Smith, 'Truby King in Australia: A Revisionist View of Reduced Infant Mortality', *New Zealand Journal of History*, 22, 1, 1988, pp.23-43.

77 Penelope Ann Gregory, 'Saving the Children in New Zealand: A Study of Social Attitudes Towards Larrikinism in the Later Nineteenth Century', BA (Hons) Thesis, Massey University, 1975, p.10.

78 For useful summaries of contemporary fears, see Bronwyn Dalley, *Family Matters: Child Welfare in Twentieth-Century New Zealand*, Auckland, 1998, esp. pp.1-63; Gregory, 'Saving the Children in New Zealand'; Margaret Tennant, *Paupers and Providers: Charitable Aid in New Zealand*, Wellington, 1989.

79 *Auckland Weekly Press*, 4 Dec. 1902, p.10.

80 *Lyttelton Times*, 18 Dec. 1902, p.4.

81 *Otago Witness*, 7 Jan. 1903, p.27.

82 For references to Sandow as a high priest see *New Zealand Graphic*, 1 Nov. 1902, p.1101; *Auckland Weekly News*, 4 Dec. 1902, p.10. For references to his gospel of strength and physical culture see *Auckland Weekly Press*, 4 Dec. 1902, p.10; *Evening Post*, 10 Dec. 1902, p.4; *Timaru Herald*, 29 Dec. 1902, p.3; *Otago Witness*, 14 Jan. 1903, p.60.

83 The 'apostle of physical development' label was used in *New Zealand Mail*, 17 Dec. 1902, p.25; *Canterbury Times*, 17 Dec. 1902, p.41. He was also called an 'apostle of physical culture' (*Lyttelton Times*, 19 Dec. 1902, p.2) and a plain 'apostle' (*New Zealand Mail*, 10 Dec. 1902, p.46). The labelling of his followers as 'disciples' was used in *Wanganui Chronicle*, 29 Nov. 1902, p.7; *ODT*, 31 Dec. 1902, p.6.

84 *New Zealand Mail*, 10 Dec. 1902, p.46.

85 *New Zealand Graphic*, 20 Dec. 1902, p.1579.

86 *Press*, 18 Dec. 1902, p.5

87 *Evening Post*, 8 Dec. 1902, p.6.

88 Sandow also gave a lecture at a school in Wanganui, which was very similar to his regular exposition format. See *Wanganui Chronicle*, 29 Nov. 1902, p.7. He also gave a lecture and demonstration to firefighters and the police in Wellington. See *Evening Post*, 13 Dec. 1902, p.5.

89 *NZH*, 21 Nov. 1902, p.6; *Evening Post*, 9 Dec. 1902, p.4; *Press*, 20 Dec. 1902, p.8; *ODT*, 1 Jan. 1903, p.7.

90 For example, in Wanganui Young performed in the window of H. I. Jones & Son, which stocked Sandow's equipment and was the ticket agent for his Wanganui shows. He was in the shop window between 11 a.m. and 12.30 p.m., and again between 3 and 4.30 p.m. *Wanganui Herald*, 24 Nov. 1902, p.6.

91 *Press*, 24 Dec. 1902, p.4.

92 *ODT*, 3 Jan. 1903, p.7.

93 *ODT*, 1 Jan. 1903, p.7.

94 *NZH*, 21 Nov. 1902, p.6.

95 *Press*, 20 Dec. 1902, p.8.

96 *Wanganui Herald*, 28 Nov. 1902, p.6.

97 *Wanganui Chronicle*, 29 Nov. 1902, p.7.

98 *Timaru Herald*, 29 Dec. 1902, p.2.

99 *Weekly Press*, 31 Dec. 1902, p.41.

100 *New Zealand Mail*, 10 Dec. 1902, p.46.

101 *Ibid*.

102 *Lyttelton Times*, 19 Dec. 1902, p.2.

103 *Otago Witness*, 7 Jan. 1903, p.27.

104 *New Zealand Mail*, 10 Dec. 1902, p.46.

105 *Auckland Weekly News*, 4 Dec. 1902, p.10.

106 *Ibid.*

107 *ODT*, 1 Jan. 1903, p.7.

108 *Timaru Herald*, 29 Dec. 1902, p.3.

109 See, for example, William Pember Reeves, 'Native Races from a Physical Standpoint. The Maoris', *Sandow's Magazine*, Aug. 1899, pp.143-50.

110 *New Zealand Mail*, 10 Dec. 1902, p.46.

111 W. A. Chapple, *The Fertility of the Unfit*, Melbourne, 1903.

112 The marriage certificate idea had currency for several years. See, for example, the report of the Eugenics Education Society in the Women's Christian Temperance Union's monthly magazine, *White Ribbon*, 18 Dec. 1913, p.12.

113 Chapple, *The Fertility of the Unfit*, p.xii. See also Philip J. Fleming, 'Eugenics in New Zealand 1900-1940', MA Thesis, Massey University, 1981.

114 *Otago Witness*, 7 Jan. 1903, p.27.

115 *Weekly Press*, 31 Dec. 1902, p.41.

116 *Otago Witness*, 7 Jan. 1903, p.27. When visiting the Dunedin Sandow School he repeated this message. *ODT*, 7 Jan. 1903, p.5.

117 *Timaru Herald*, 29 Dec. 1902, p.3.

118 *Otago Witness*, 7 Jan. 1903, p.27.

119 *Weekly Press*, 31 Dec. 1902, p.41.

TWO SANDOW'S LEGACY

1 *New Zealand Mail*, 17 Dec. 1902, p.25.

2 These were the prices in Christchurch during Sandow's stay in that city. *Press*, 23 Dec. 1902, p.7.

3 *Auckland Weekly News*, 19 Jan. 1900, p.6.

4 Sandra Coney, *Standing in the Sunshine: A History of New Zealand Women Since They Won the Vote*, Auckland, 1993, p.298.

5 *Sandow's Magazine*, 27 Dec. 1906, p.820.

6 *Sandow's Magazine*, July 1898, pp.3-7.

7 Lois W. Banner, *American Beauty*, New York, 1983, p.203.

8 Caroline Daley, 'Taradale Meets The Ideal Society and its Enemies', *New Zealand Journal of History*, 25, 2, 1991, pp.135-8, 141-2.

9 *AS*, 15 Mar. 1900, p.3.

10 *AS*, 26 Nov. 1903, p.5. The Leys Institute gymnasium opened in July 1906. For a photograph of Potter's class at the Leys Institute see *New Zealand Graphic*, 4 Jan. 1908, p.3.

11 *AS*, 2 April 1904, p.8.

12 *AS*, 15 July 1904, p.8.

13 *AS*, 9 Sept.1905, p.8.

14 *Sandow's Magazine*, 27 Sept.1906, p.414; 30 May 1907, p.695.

15 *Sandow's Magazine*, May 1901, pp.371-2.

16 *Health and Physical Culture* (*HPC*), 1 Sept.1940, p.50.

17 He wrote to Sandow in Jan. 1901. *Sandow's Magazine*, April 1903, pp.289-90. For 'The New Zealand Sandow' label see *Sandow's Magazine*, 11 Oct. 1906, pp.451-2; *HPC*, 1 Sept.1940, p.50.

18 *New Zealand Listener*, 15 Dec. 1939, p.38.

19 *Sandow's Magazine*, 6 Dec. 1906, p.725; 11 April 1907, pp.470-1.

20 *Cyclopedia of New Zealand, Volume 6, Taranaki, Hawke's Bay, and Wellington Provincial Districts*, Christchurch, 1908, p.597.

21 *Sandow's Magazine*, 13 June 1907, p.758.

22 *Sandow's Magazine*, 25 April 1907, p.533.

23 *Sandow's Magazine*, Dec. 1903, pp.419-20.

24 *Sandow's Magazine*, 19 July 1906, p.90.

25 *Sandow's Magazine*, 14 June 1906, p.763.

26 *Sandow's Magazine*, 28 Dec. 1905, pp.743-4; 31 May 1906, p.689.

27 *Sandow's Magazine*, Dec. 1900, pp.449-50, 481. See also *New Zealand Graphic*, 9 Jan. 1904, p.36; *Sandow's Magazine*, 2 Feb. 1905, pp.127-8.

28 *Canterbury Times*, 9 Mar. 1904, p.24; Robert Parker Papers, MS-Papers-5303-1, Alexander Turnbull Library, Wellington (ATL).

29 *Sandow's Magazine*, Aug. 1903, pp.173-4. See also 6 July 1905, p.27.

30 *Sandow's Magazine*, 3 May 1906, p.559.

31 *Truth*, 3 Aug. 1907, p.4.

32 For the letter from 'Too Hairy', see *Sandow's Magazine*, 17 May 1906, p.639. On the New Zealand Amateur Athletics Association see *Sandow's Magazine*, Aug. 1904, p.144.

33 For an article on boxing, by Mr C. de C. Williams of Tinakori Road, see *Sandow's Magazine*, 31 Jan. 1907, pp.138-9. A photograph of Frank Hatch, and his measurement, appeared in the issue of 28 Dec. 1905, p.744.

34 *Sandow's Magazine*, June 1901, p.446. See also the photograph of Ward on p.445. *Press*, 18 Jan. 1901, p.1; 19 Jan. 1901, p.9.

35 Ward was taking Sandow classes in Christchurch by early 1901. *Sandow's Magazine*, June 1901, p.446. A photograph of Ward's Sydenham Sandow School appeared in the Oct. 1902 issue, p.290.

36 See the report of the sixth such display, *Press*, 15 Oct. 1903, p.6.

37 *Press*, 3 April 1900, p.1; 19 April 1900, p.1.

38 *Press*, 3 April 1900, p.1.

39 *Sandow's Magazine*, Feb. 1901, pp.122-4.

40 *Sandow's Magazine*, Nov. 1900, pp.369-70; Feb. 1901, pp.122-4.

41 See, for example, *Sandow's Magazine*, May 1902, p.387; 14 Feb. 1907, p.203.

42 *Kennaway's Fun*, Oct. 1903, p.12.

43 *Sandow's Magazine*, Nov. 1900, p.400.

44 *Sandow's Magazine*, Feb. 1901, pp.122-4.

45 F. A. Hornibrook, *Without Reserve*, London, 1935, p.14.

46 Guy H. Scholefield and E. Schwabe (eds), *Who's Who in New Zealand and the Western Pacific, 1908*, Wellington, 1908, p.167.

47 *Cyclopedia of New Zealand, Volume 3, Canterbury Provincial District*, Christchurch, 1903, p.250

48 *Press*, 16 Oct. 1901, p.8.

49 A contest was held in 1902, but no information on it has been located.

50 See, for example, his lecture on 'Health by Natural Means', *Press*, 6 Oct. 1904, p.1.

51 *Press*, 13 Nov. 1903, p.10.

52 *Press*, 11 Oct. 1904, p.4; 18 Oct. 1904, p.4; 25 Oct. 1904, p.4; 1 Nov. 1904, p.4; 3 Nov. 1904, p.6.

53 *Press*, 9 Nov. 1905, p.6.

54 *Kennaway's Fun*, Dec. 1904, p.31.

55 *Lyttelton Times*, 6 Nov. 1907, p.6.

56 *Lyttelton Times*, 31 Oct. 1907, p.7.

57 *Lyttelton Times*, 16 May 1911, p.3.

58 *Canterbury Times*, 14 June 1911, p.56.

59 *Lyttelton Times*, 28 Oct. 1911, p.10.

60 *Lyttelton Times*, 23 Oct. 1911, p.7; 28 Oct. 1911, p.10.

61 *Press*, 6 Nov. 1905, p.6. Hornibrook also acted as the judge at the competitions held at Miss B. Whichello's Kaiapoi Physical Culture Class for ladies. *Press*, 6 Nov. 1905, p.6.

62 In 1909, 42 women entered. *Press*, 28 Oct. 1909. In 1905 'over fifty' entered. *Press*, 6 Nov. 1905, p.6.

63 *Lyttelton Times*, 27 Oct. 1910, p.6.

64 *Press*, 23 Dec. 1902, p.1; 24 Dec. 1902, p.3.

65 On Hornibrook's war service and subsequent career in London as a physiotherapist, see Jane Tolerton, *Ettie: A Life of Ettie Rout*, Auckland, 1992.

66 On the first gymnastic and athletic display by the Ashburton Gymnastic Club and School of Physical Culture, see *Press*, 4 Nov. 1903, p.5.

67 *Sandow's Magazine*, Oct. 1899, p.382; Feb. 1901, pp.122-4; *ODT*, 7 Jan. 1903, pp.1, 5.

68 On Hanna see *Sandow's Magazine*, Mar. 1902, pp.214-15. The Otago Gymnastic Association was formed in 1900. *Cyclopedia of New Zealand, Volume 4, Otago and Southland Provincial Districts*, Christchurch, 1905, p.204.

69 T E Y Seddon, Sports Programmes and Newspaper Clippings re Sport etc, Seddon Family Papers, MS-Papers-1619-195, ATL.

70 For a photograph of Charles Kouffe, see *Sandow's Magazine*, Mar. 1901, p.212. Thomas Fogarty wrote to Sandow twice, sending in his before and after measurements,

and a photograph of his improved body. See *Sandow's Magazine*, Mar. 1903, p.230; 12 Jan. 1905, p.39. Zwicker began reading the magazine in 1904, and wrote to Sandow in 1907. *Sandow's Magazine*, 25 April 1907, p.532.

71 *Southland Daily News*, 12 Jan. 1903, p.2.

72 *Cyclopedia of New Zealand, Volume 1, Wellington Provincial District*, Wellington, 1897, p.1229.

73 *Cyclopedia of New Zealand, Volume 1, Wellington Provincial District*, Wellington, 1897, p.863.

74 *Sandow's Magazine*, 14 Mar. 1907, pp.342-3.

75 On Pentecost and Amos see *Sandow's Magazine*, May 1902, pp.343-8; on Anderson see *Sandow's Magazine*, June 1904, pp.453-7; on Murphy see *Sandow's Magazine*, Aug. 1903, pp.192-7.

76 On the legislators, see *New Zealand Graphic*, 23 May 1903, pp.1470, 1437, 1439; 6 June 1903, p.1568. On the All Blacks exercising on their voyage see the voyage entries in George Henry Dixon, 1905 All Black Tour, Tour Diary 1905–1906, Folder 1, MS 748 (1), Auckland Museum Library. I am grateful to Greg Ryan for the reference to the All Blacks exercising the Sandow way.

77 On pig hunters see *Sandow's Magazine*, 6 April 1905, p.338.

78 On his police class see *Appendices to the Journals of the House of Representatives* (*AJHR*), 1906, H-16, p.8. Photographs of his gymnasium class appeared in *New Zealand Graphic*, 16 June 1906, p.38. I am grateful to Judith Binney for information on Skinner and his subsequent career. Further information can be found in Judith Binney, Gillian Chaplin and Craig Wallace, *Mihaia: The Prophet Rua Kenana and His Community at Maungapohatu*, Auckland, 1979.

79 *Truth*, 27 Oct. 1906, p.9.

80 *Auckland Truth*, 2 Feb. 1918, p.4. The report claimed that Sandow had been shot, and that his tour of New Zealand had been a spying mission for the German government. The reporter dismissed the latter claim as 'bunkum', but the execution story was allowed to stand. Sandow's actual death, in 1925, was reported in the New Zealand media. See, for example, *NZH*, 16 Oct. 1925, p.11.

81 *Sandow's Magazine*, 6 Dec. 1906, p.725.

82 *Health and Physical Culture*, 1 June 1934, p.19.

83 *New Zealand Graphic*, 15 July 1905, p.16. See also the article 'Kitchen Gymnastics: By A Woman Doctor', *Canterbury Times*, 25 Aug. 1909, p.76.

84 *Journal of Physical Culture & Health*, 15

Sept.1910, p.4; 16 Oct. 1911, p.4.

85 See, for example, *Journal of Physical Culture & Health*, 16 Jan. 1911.

86 *New Zealand Graphic*, 2 Feb. 1907, p.29.

87 *Gisborne Times*, 26 July 1910, p.6.

88 *Truth*, 1 Oct. 1910, p.3. Sims's real name was revealed when he was involved in a particularly messy divorce case in the early 1920s. *Truth*, 20 May 1922, p.6.

89 Veitch began mail-order courses in 1910. *Truth*, 13 Aug. 1910, p.2; 3 Sept.1910, p.7.

90 *Truth*, 23 Mar. 1912, p.3.

91 By 1911, Baker was including testimonials from 'W.R.' of Napier and 'E.C.' of Waimamuka in his advertisements. *Lone Hand*, 1 April 1911, n.p.; 1 Dec. 1911, p.xxxvii. By the early 1920s, Baker was advertising in the New Zealand press. See, for example, *Auckland Truth*, 10 Sept.1921, p.8.

92 *AS*, 5 Jan. 1927, p.11.

93 Briton also operated out of Sydney. *Truth*, 25 Oct. 1928, p.15.

94 The first advertisement for Charles Atlas's Dynamic Tension system I have found in the New Zealand press was in *Truth*, 5 May 1937, p.11. It showed a photograph of Atlas, with his measurements, rather than one of his famous comic strips. On Atlas see Elizabeth Toon and Janet Golden, 'Rethinking Charles Atlas', *Rethinking History*, 4, 1, 2000, pp.80-4.

95 See, for example, *Pictorial News*, 6 May 1924, p.4; 25 April 1925, p.11.

96 *New Zealand New Health Journal*, Nov. 1926, p.23.

97 *HPC*, May 1929, p.5.

98 *HPC*, Jan. 1930, p.4.

99 The necessity not luxury claim was made in a *Truth* article advocating doing 'That Daily Dozen', *Truth*, 6 Nov. 1930, p.21.

100 F. A. Hornibrook, *The Culture of the Abdomen: The Cure of Obesity and Constipation*, 12th edn, London, 1938. The first edition of this work appeared in Jan. 1924. In 1927 an Australian edition was produced. By 1958 the book had enjoyed 20 editions in English, been translated into Danish, Finnish, Italian, Polish, and Swedish. In 1957 alone a new print run of 90,000 copies sold out. See *Truth*, 11 Feb. 1958, p.26. Ettie A. Rout (Mrs. F. A. Hornibrook), *Sex and Exercise: A Study of the Sex Function in Women and Its Relation to Exercise*, London, 1925. She used the term 'bedroom gymnastics' on p.23.

101 Hornibrook, *The Culture of the Abdomen*, p.16.

102 Rout, *Sex and Exercise*, p.61.

103 Peter N. Stearns, *Fat History: Bodies and Beauty in the Modern West*, New York and London, 1997, p.53.

104 *Truth*, 14 Aug. 1909, p.8.

105 *White Ribbon*, Dec. 1902, pp.10-11.

106 *New Zealand Graphic*, 18 July 1903, p.212.

107 See, for example, *Sandow's Magazine*, Sept.1904, p.222; 10 Aug. 1905, p.154; 7 Dec. 1905, p.648; 28 Dec. 1905, pp.744; 17 May 1906, p.630; 21 June 1906, p.795; 19 July 1906, p.90; 6 Sept.1906, p.318; 27 Dec. 1906, p.820; 25 April 1907, p.532; 30 May 1907, p.695. See also the article on the need for young city men to 'Get Out of Doors', *Young Man's Magazine*, Sept.1907, p.393.

108 *Canterbury Times*, 3 June 1908, p.54.

109 *New Zealand Graphic*, 23 Feb. 1907, p.44.

110 *New Zealand Graphic*, 7 Oct. 1905, p.59.

111 See, for example, concerns about the impact of office work on young women's health, *Auckland Truth*, 13 Aug. 1921, p.4; worries about 'modernity's nerve-killing ways', *Truth*, 27 Oct. 1922, p.4; and fears about the impact of cars on health, *HPC*, Dec. 1929, p.26.

112 *New Zealand Graphic*, 2 July 1907, p.24.

113 *Canterbury Times*, 1 July 1908, p.53.

114 *Sandow's Magazine*, July 1904, pp.28-31.

115 See, for example, *Sandow's Magazine*, Dec. 1904, pp.406-7.

116 See, for example, *Canterbury Times*, 29 July 1908, p.56.

117 See, for example, *Canterbury Times*, 26 Aug. 1908, p.32.

118 *Sandow's Magazine*, 7 June 1906, pp.730-1.

119 *Canterbury Times*, 1 July 1908, p.53.

120 *Canterbury Times*, 13 Jan. 1909, p.31.

121 *Ibid.*

122 See, for example, Eugen Sandow, *Body-Building, or Man in the Making: How to Become Healthy & Strong*, London, 1904, esp. pp.8, 31. See also *Sandow's Magazine*, July 1898, pp.3-7; Dec. 1898, pp.414-20; June 1899, pp.413-17; April 1900, pp.364-8; Feb. 1903, pp.115-21; Aug. 1903, pp.167-9; Dec. 1904, p.403; 2 Mar. 1905, p.222; 18 Jan. 1906, pp.84-6; 1 Mar. 1906, p.266; 12 July 1906, p.40; 10 Jan. 1907, pp.33-7.

123 *Canterbury Times*, 13 Jan. 1909, p.31.

124 *Canterbury Times*, 6 May 1908, p.34; *Sandow's Magazine*, Jan. 1903, pp.3-4; 17 Aug. 1905, pp.169-70.

125 F. M. B. Fisher, Physical Needs of The Empire, MS 0772, ATL. This was a lecture, given to the Christchurch Physical Culture Society in 1905. Ettie Rout typed the lecture for Fisher. The 40 per cent figure can be found on p.9 and the quote on p.25.

126 *Press*, 13 July 1909, p.6.

127 *Press*, 13 July 1909, p.8. See also his response to a similar outcry in 1911: *Lyttelton Times*, 7 June 1911, p.11; 15 Aug. 1911, p.5.

128 Paul Baker, *King and Country Call: New Zealanders, Conscription and the Great War*,

Auckland, 1988, p.111. I am grateful to Deborah Montgomerie for drawing my attention to this reference.

129 *Auckland Truth*, 15 April 1916, p.8.

130 For a discussion of these issues see Philip J. Fleming, 'Eugenics in New Zealand 1900–1940', MA Thesis, Massey University, 1981; Erik Olssen, 'Towards a New Society', in Geoffrey W. Rice (ed.), *The Oxford History of New Zealand*, 2nd edn, Auckland, 1992, esp. pp.254-66.

131 *Canterbury Times*, 17 Mar. 1909, p.54.

132 *New Zealand Graphic*, 21 Feb. 1903, p.550; 19 May 1906, p.7.

133 See, for example, *Sandow's Magazine*, Oct. 1898, pp.298-9; Dec. 1898, pp.414-20; Aug. 1899, pp.99-104; Dec. 1900, pp.403-8; Feb. 1902, pp.83-7; June 1902, pp.420-5; Feb. 1903, pp.83-9; 25 May 1905, pp.521-2; 27 Sept.1906, pp.412-13; 31 Jan. 1907, pp.147-8.

134 *Lyttelton Times*, 23 Oct. 1906, p.5.

135 For Hornibrook's anti-corset sentiment see *Canterbury Times*, 10 Mar. 1909, p.54; 17 Mar. 1909, p.54. Articles advocating dress reform for women, arguing against the corset, appeared in Sandow's magazine from the outset. See, for example, *Sandow's Magazine*, Aug. 1898, pp.92-9, 121-5; July 1899, pp.49-55; July 1899, pp.87-91; June 1900, pp.489-91; Dec. 1900, pp.403-8; Feb. 1903, pp.83-9; Mar. 1903, pp.163-5; July 1903, pp.86-7; April 1904, pp.301-3; May 1904, pp.351-2; 4 Jan. 1906, p.21; 18 July 1907, pp.78-9. Sandow's views on the 'Cult of the Corset' were also aired in the local press. See *New Zealand Graphic*, 8 Aug. 1903, p.363.

136 Sandow often made this point. See, for example, *Sandow's Magazine*, Aug. 1899, pp.99-104; May 1904, pp.351-2; Aug. 1904, pp.85-92; 19 Jan. 1905, pp.62-6; 25 May 1905, pp.521-2; 1 June 1905, pp.547-8; 16 Nov. 1905, pp.534-6; Eugen Sandow, *Body-Building, or Man in the Making: How to Become Healthy & Strong*, London, 1904, esp. Chapters VIII and XII.

137 The 1920s advertising campaign for Grape-Nuts, for example, used the slogan 'A Nation's Strength – its Women's Health'. *New Zealand Health First Journal*, 29 Mar. 1929, p.18.

138 Woolley's advertisements were clearly aimed at women and often appeared on the women's pages of magazines and newspapers. See, for example, *Pictorial News*, 8 Nov. 1924, p.16, where the advert appeared on the 'What to Wear' page, and the issue of 7 Mar. 1925, p.17, when it occurred on 'The Home' page, beside a recipe for kidneys with haricot beans and tomatoes.

139 *Truth*, 25 Oct. 1928, p.15.

140 *HPC*, 1 Mar. 1937, pp.16-17.

141 *HPC*, 1 Sept.1938, pp.36-37.

142 *HPC*, 1 Mar. 1936, p.2.

143 *HPC*, May 1929, p.6.

144 Rex v Percy Coupland Trapp, 30 Oct. 1924. J. Herdman, Notes of Evidence, Civil Criminal and Circuit, 1924, Volume 3. BBAE A304 412; *New Zealand Police Gazette 1924*, p.719, BBAN 5803 48a. Archives New Zealand, Auckland. I am grateful to Matt Wilcox for this information.

145 See, for example, the illustrations accompanying the article on 'Torso-Toning for "Beach Presence"', *HPC*, 1 Jan. 1937, pp.14-15, and the photograph of MGM star Johnny Weismÿller, in trunks, illustrating an article on building the body by bending, *HPC*, 1 Mar. 1937, pp.16-17.

146 *HPC*, 1 Jan. 1937, p.15.

147 See the article 'The Menace of Effeminacy', *HPC*, 1 Jan. 1932, pp.14-15, 40.

148 Tamar Garb, *Bodies of Modernity: Figure and Flesh in Fin-de-Siecle France*, London, 1998, p.35.

149 *HPC*, April 1930, p.23.

150 *Withrow's Physical Culture Annual 1926*, p.4.

151 *HPC*, Sept.1934, p.43.

152 *Truth*, 20 May 1922, p.6.

153 *Truth*, 16 Feb. 1907, p.7.

154 See, for example, *New Zealand Graphic*, 26 May 1906, p.60.

155 *Journal of Physical Culture*, 15 Dec. 1911, p.3.

156 *Withrow's Physical Culture Annual 1921*, pp.29-30.

157 See, for example, 'What to Eat to Be Thin', citing a French woman physical culturist. *New Zealand Graphic*, 3 Nov. 1906, p.31.

158 *New Zealand Graphic*, 3 June 1905, p.60.

159 *New Zealand Graphic*, 5 Mar. 1904, pp.64-5; 26 May 1906, p.42.

160 *New Zealand Graphic*, 5 Nov. 1904, p.60.

161 *Sandow's Magazine*, 27 Sept.1906, p.v.

162 Health Culture Association, *Secrets of the Toilet: How to Become & Remain Beautiful*, Melbourne, 1916, esp. p.48.

163 See, for example, Jacqueline Gore, *Good Looks and Long Life: A Guide to Beauty and Health in Australasia*, Melbourne, 1913; Annette Kellermann, *Physical Beauty: How To Keep It*, London, 1918.

164 See, for example, Monica Brundall Diary 1926–30, Folder 1529, ARC 1998.113, Canterbury Museum, Christchurch. Brundall used the term 'Beauty Physical Culture' and illustrated her diary with stick figure drawings of exercises such as the 'Egyptian' and the 'Venus'. See also Lucy Taylor, Papers, 90-262, ATL.

165 *HPC*, 1 Jan. 1936, p.2; 1 Aug. 1936, p.4.
166 For reports on women in London see *New Zealand Graphic*, 22 April 1905, p.16; 9 Dec. 1905, p.60. For Professor Potter's class see *New Zealand Graphic*, 18 Aug. 1906, p.6.
167 See, for example, *Auckland Truth*, 10 Jan. 1914, p.6; 21 Feb. 1914, p.6; *NZH*, 12 April 1926, p.11; *New Zealand Illustrated Sporting and Dramatic Review*, 20 Jan. 1938.
168 See, for example, *New Zealand Graphic*, 2 July 1904, p.64; 21 Dec. 1907, p.33; *Press*, 8 May 1909, p.7.
169 *Truth*, 6 Dec. 1919, p.8.
170 *Truth*, 19 Dec. 1934, p.8; 6 July 1938, p.26.
171 *Truth*, 4 June 1931, p.5; 6 Aug. 1931, p.5. See also the case of 'Jeannette', *Truth*, 11 Jan. 1939, p.7.
172 This act, and its impact on local bodies, is discussed in Ch. 7.

THREE **BEAUTIFUL BODIES**

1 An earlier version of parts of this Ch. was first presented at the Women and Modernity Conference, University of Melbourne, 2000. I am grateful to conference participants for their comments and questions. See also Caroline Daley, 'The Body Builder and Beauty Contests', *Journal of Australian Studies*, 71, 2001, pp.55-66, 158-60.
2 *Evening Post*, 13 Dec. 1902, Supplement p.2.
3 *Truth*, 26 Jan. 1907, p.1.
4 *Truth*, 16 Feb. 1907, p.1, hinted at pregnancies as a result of the visit. The 'dusky Don Juan' comment and assertion that '13 young half-caste Fijians' had recently been born was made in an editorial in *Truth*, 4 April 1908, p.4.
5 *Sandow's Magazine*, 27 July 1905, p.94.
6 *Sandow's Magazine*, Jan. 1900, pp.38-42.
7 *Sandow's Magazine*, June 1902, pp.424-5.
8 *Sandow's Magazine*, Dec. 1900, p.404; June 1902, p.421. As Lois Banner has noted, 'Praise for [the Venus de Milo's] appearance runs like a leitmotif throughout the beauty literature of the nineteenth century.' Lois W. Banner, *American Beauty*, New York, 1983, p.110.
9 See, for example, *Sandow's Magazine*, Feb. 1903, pp.83-9.
10 Banner, *American Beauty*, pp.110-11.
11 *Sandow's Magazine*, Dec. 1900, p.404. He repeated this message in the Mar. 1903 issue, p.164.
12 *Sandow's Magazine*, Aug. 1904, p.85.
13 The classic article on the male gaze is Laura Mulvey, 'Visual Pleasure and Narrative Cinema', *Screen*, 16, 3, 1975, pp.6-18.
14 These ideas have been explored in pre-First World War Germany. See Christopher Kenway, 'Nudism, Health and Modernity:

The Natural Cure as Proposed by the German Physical Culture Movement 1900-1914', *Nineteenth-Century Prose*, 25, 1, 1998, p.109.
15 On pornographic postcards see Lisa Z. Sigel, 'Filth in the Wrong People's Hands: Postcards and the Expansion of Pornography in Britain and the Atlantic World, 1880-1914', *Journal of Social History*, 33, 4, 2000, pp.859-85.
16 Sandra Chesterman discusses the difficulties New Zealand art students and artists had in securing nude female models in *FigureWork: The Nude and Life Modelling in New Zealand Art*, Dunedin, 2002, esp. Ch. 1.
17 *Truth*, 13 Oct. 1906, p.4.
18 *Truth*, 13 Oct. 1906, p.3. Emphasis in original.
19 *Truth*, 22 Nov. 1906, p.1.
20 Caroline Daley, 'A Gendered Domain: Leisure in Auckland, 1890-1940', in Caroline Daley and Deborah Montgomerie (eds), *The Gendered Kiwi*, Auckland, 1999, pp.87-8.
21 In 1878 Theophilus Heale donated 22 statues and 11 busts to the Auckland Institute. Included in the donation were statues of the Venus Pudica and Venus de Medici. Chesterman, *FigureWork*, pp.4, 6.
22 James Belich, *Paradise Reforged: A History of New Zealanders From the 1880s to the Year 2000*, Auckland, 2001, esp. Ch. 5.
23 See, for example, the case against Mr Wilkinson, for selling a postcard of 'Adam and Eve'. Wilkinson was fined £5 and costs. *Truth*, 18 Aug. 1906, p.1. See also: *Truth*, 30 Dec. 1916, p.6; *Auckland Truth*, 23 June 1917, p.5; 22 Mar. 1919, p.2.
24 Banner, *American Beauty*, p.110.
25 *Truth*, 13 June 1908, p.5. The tailor in question had been displaying pictures in his shop window for fifteen years.
26 *Truth*, 13 Oct. 1906, p.3.
27 *Auckland Weekly News*, 30 Jan. 1908, p.30; *Truth*, 1 Feb. 1908, p.6.
28 On Deamer's short story success, with a sexually explicit tale called 'As It Was In the Beginning', see *Truth*, 18 Jan. 1908, p.4. She soon left Featherston for a career on stage, married and settled in Sydney where she became a public advocate of nudism and a novelist. See *Truth*, 23 May 1908, p.1; 5 Sept.1908, p.1; 15 Jan. 1910, p.1; *Smith's Weekly*, 19 Mar. 1938, p.6.
29 For a less than flattering assessment on the *Lone Hand* see *Truth*, 25 May 1907, p.7. The *Bulletin* and the *Lone Hand* were, of course, competitors for *Truth* in Australia and New Zealand. Both Australian publications were widely available in New Zealand.
30 *Lone Hand*, 2 Mar. 1908, p.465. The arguments of nudists are explored in Ch. 5.

31 Posing as 'The Wrestlers', they illustrated the cover of *Sandow's Magazine*, 20 Dec. 1906. A photograph of them as 'Samson and Delilah' was used to illustrate an article on living statues in the issue of 16 May 1907, p.625. The pose seems to have been inspired by Andrea Mantegna's 'Samson and Delilah', purchased by London's National Gallery in 1883. See also the article by P. A. Lette on the Seldoms, *Sandow's Magazine*, 3 Jan. 1907, pp.1-2. For historical accounts of the craze for living statues see Maurizia Boscagli, *Eye On The Flesh: Fashions of Masculinity in the Early Twentieth Century*, Boulder CO, 1996, pp.109-10; Michael Anton Budd, *The Sculpture Machine: Physical Culture and Body Politics in the Age of Empire*, New York, 1997, pp.36, 41-2.

32 *Sandow's Magazine*, 16 May 1907, p.624.

33 *Sandow's Magazine*, 31 May 1906. See also the article on her, 3 May 1906, pp.560-63.

34 In the 1940s Freda Stark (b. 1910), became infamous in Auckland for dancing in a near-nude state before servicemen. Under the lights, her paint-covered body appeared gold. See Dianne Haworth and Diane Miller, *Freda Stark: Her Extraordinary Life*, Auckland, 2000.

35 See, for example, *AS*, 30 Sept.1905, p.8. The message was repeated in the interview Montague gave in London, after her initial success at the London Pavilion. *Sandow's Magazine*, 3 May 1906, p.560.

36 Local physical culturists attended her performance on 16 Nov., for example. *Press*, 16 Nov. 1905, p.1.

37 *Press*, 11 Nov. 1905, p.1.

38 *Lone Hand*, 1 Mar. 1917, p.176.

39 *AS*, 7 Oct. 1905, p.8.

40 *AS*, 5 Oct. 1905, p.8.

41 *AS*, 10 Oct. 1905, p.8.

42 For example, in 1907 Miss Ruby White posed on stage. *New Zealand Graphic*, 4 May 1907, p.21. The following year 'Ziska' did the same. *AS*, 3 Feb. 1908, p.6.

43 See, for example, *New Zealand Graphic*, 18 Aug. 1906, p.40; 22 June 1907, p.47; *AS*, 1 Aug. 1908, p.12; 19 Sept.1908, p.12; *Truth*, 15 May 1909, p.1; 17 Feb. 1912, p.8; *Auckland Truth*, 1 Nov. 1913, p.3.

44 *Truth*, 6 July 1907, p.7.

45 *Truth*, 12 Oct. 1907, p.6; 18 Jan. 1908, p.6.

46 See, for example, *Truth*, 18 Aug. 1906, pp.1, 5.

47 *Auckland Truth*, 1 Nov. 1913, p.3.

48 *Sandow's Magazine*, Jan. 1903, p.80.

49 On 'The Great Competition' see *Sandow's Magazine*, July 1898, pp.79-80; Dec. 1898, pp.453-55; Nov. 1899, p.475; Jan. 1900, pp.88-93; Oct. 1901, pp.286-91.

50 For the rules of his first 'Best Developed Baby' contest see *Sandow's Magazine*, Oct. 1901, p.310. For competitions of children aged between three and eight, and between eight and twelve, the instructions were that the child should be 'photographed nude to the waist'. *Sandow's Magazine*, Jan. 1902, p.68; June 1902, p.464.

51 *Sandow's Magazine*, April 1903, p.296.

52 *Ibid*.

53 *Sandow's Magazine*, May 1903, p.347.

54 *Sandow's Magazine*, June 1903, p.417.

55 *Sandow's Magazine*, July 1903, p.39.

56 *Ibid*., p.108.

57 *Ibid*., p.39.

58 *Sandow's Magazine*, Oct. 1903, p.331; Dec. 1903, p.408; Feb. 1904, p.143. Contestants in these competitions tended to wear either a full body tight, or a modified swimsuit, revealing their bare arms, and their bare legs from mid-thigh down. See illustrations of the Leeds contest in the French physical culture magazine *L'Education Physique*, 31 Oct. 1904, pp.418-21. I am grateful to David Chapman for sending me a copy of this article.

59 *Sandow's Magazine*, April 1904, pp.247-8. See also April 1904, p.303.

60 Macfadden was an American physical culturist and entrepreneur very like Sandow. On his role in beauty contests see Jan Todd, 'Bernarr Macfadden: Reformer of Feminine Form', *Journal of Sport History*, 14, 1, 1987, pp.61-75.

61 See, for example, *New Zealand Graphic*, 30 Jan. 1904, p.65; 20 Aug. 1904, p.61; 18 Feb. 1905, p.61.

62 See, for example, *AS*, 5 Sept.1903, Supplement p.2; 5 Dec. 1903, Supplement p.2.

63 *New Zealand Graphic*, 30 May 1903, p.1543. On the early history of beauty contests see Candace Savage, *Beauty Queens: A Playful History*, New York, 1998, esp. pp.11-15.

64 A recent history of the Exhibition is available, but it neglects to mention the proposed beauty contest. See John Mansfield Thomson, ed., *Farewell Colonialism: The New Zealand International Exhibition, Christchurch, 1906-07*, Palmerston North, 1998.

65 *Lyttelton Times*, 12 Mar. 1907, p.1.

66 *Ibid*., p.8.

67 *Lyttelton Times*, 19 Mar. 1907, p.4.

68 *Lyttelton Times*, 14 Mar. 1907, p.9. See also *New Zealand Graphic*, 23 Mar. 1907, p.18.

69 *Lyttelton Times*, 14 Mar. 1907, p.9. See also the letter to the editor from H. W. Hofmeister, *Lyttelton Times*, 16 Mar. 1907, p.7; telegram from Mr Ell to Minister in charge of the Exhibition, *Lyttelton Times*, 19 Mar. 1907, p.4; letter to the editor from 'Decency', *Lyttelton Times*, 19 Mar. 1907, p.8.

70 *Star* [Christchurch], 15 Mar. 1907, p.2. See also *Lyttelton Times*, 15 Mar. 1907, p.6.

71 *Lyttelton Times*, 15 Mar. 1907, p.8.

72 *Lyttelton Times*, 16 Mar. 1907, p.7.

73 For a report on the first contest, won by Kathleen, see *Health and Efficiency*, July 1953, p.5. For a report on the 'Miss Venus of the Nudists' contests held in England, see *Australian Sunbather*, Nov. 1952, p.34.

74 *Canterbury Times*, 10 Nov. 1909, p.43.

75 *Lyttelton Times*, 21 Mar. 1907, p.7; *Star*, 22 Mar. 1907, p.3; *Lyttelton Times*, 22 Mar. 1907, p.8.

76 *Lyttelton Times*, 21 Mar. 1907, p.1.

77 *Lyttelton Times*, 23 Mar. 1907, p.10. See also *Star*, 23 Mar. 1907, p.4.

78 For the cartoon, see *Exhibition Sketcher*, 23 Mar. 1907, p.7. For the men's contest, see *Exhibition Sketcher*, 30 Mar. 1907, p.6.

79 *Lone Hand*, 1 Nov. 1907, p.12.

80 This was a condition in the American contest, so was replicated in Australasia.

81 *Lone Hand*, 2 Dec. 1907, p.xxiv. The identity of the judges was not revealed until after the competition had closed.

82 *Lone Hand*, 2 Dec. 1907, pp.144-7. Eight photographs were reproduced.

83 *Lone Hand*, 2 Dec. 1907, p.147.

84 *Lone Hand*, 1 Feb. 1908, p.364.

85 For the picture of McCarthy see *Lone Hand*, 1 April 1908, p.611; for Hayes see 1 April 1908, p.612; for Yates see 1 May 1908, p.49.

86 *Lone Hand*, 1 Oct. 1908, pp.629-34; 1 Feb. 1909, pp.410-13.

87 *Lone Hand*, 1 Feb. 1909, p.412.

88 *Lone Hand*, 1 Oct. 1908, p.632.

89 For example, Christchurch's Theatre Royal held a contest from 1 to 8 May 1909. This was followed, in early June, by a similar contest at the Royal Albert Hall in Auckland. Contests were well advertised in the local press, and covered with other entertainment news in the city's newspapers.

90 It was around this time that permanent picture theatres emerged, as opposed to theatres showing movies some of the time, or as part of vaudeville shows. For the early history of movie going in New Zealand, see Geoffrey B. Churman (ed.), *Celluloid Dreams: A Century of Film in New Zealand*, Wellington, 1997; Nerida Elliott, 'Anzac, Hollywood and Home: Cinemas and Filmgoing in Auckland, 1909–1939', MA Thesis, University of Auckland, 1989.

91 These were some of the short films showing at the time of the Christchurch contest. *Press*, 1 May 1909, p.1.

92 *NZH*, 18 May 1909, p.1.

93 *NZH*, 7 June 1909, p.3.

94 *Press*, 5 May 1909, p.1.

95 *Press*, 8 May 1909, p.1.

96 *Press*, 10 May 1909, p.1.

97 *Ibid.*, p.7.

98 *Lyttelton Times*, 2 Sept.1910, p.8.

99 *NZH*, 14 June 1909, p.3. Her identity was revealed only after the final decision was announced.

100 *Lone Hand*, 1 May 1911, pp.lxi, 79.

101 *Ibid.*, p.lxi.

102 *Lone Hand*, 1 July 1912, p.xxxiii.

103 *Lone Hand*, 2 Dec. 1912, n.p.

104 *Lone Hand*, 1 July 1916, p.66.

105 *Lone Hand*, 1 Aug. 1916, p.126.

106 *Lone Hand*, 2 Oct. 1916, n.p.; 1 Feb. 1917, p.132.

107 *Lone Hand*, 1 Feb. 1918, p.132.

108 *Lone Hand*, 1 April 1918, p.225; 1 May 1918, p.270; 1 June 1918, p.299.

109 *Pictorial News*, 6 May 1924, p.8; 14 May 1924, p.8. The *Pictorial News* was a mass market illustrated paper. At 3d an issue, it was cheaper than many other weekly publications.

110 On the New Lynn Queen Carnival, held in 1921, see Series 275, Box 37, Item 21/217, Auckland City Council Archives, Auckland (ACCA). On the Ohaupo School Queen Carnival contest, which raised £273, and was won by Miss Cora Teddy, the Sports Queen, see *Pictorial News*, 15 Nov. 1924, p.5.

111 The Strand contest was announced on 21 Mar. 1925. *AS*, 21 Mar. 1925, p.20.

112 *AS*, 27 Mar. 1925, p.10.

113 *AS*, 1 April 1925, pp.8, 9; 3 April 1925, p.9; 4 April 1925, p.7; 6 April 1925, p.8; 7 April 1925, p.15; 11 April 1925, pp.14, 22.

114 *AS*, 2 April 1925, p.20.

115 On the rise of bathing suit contests, see Savage, *Beauty Queens*, esp. pp.47-57.

116 *AS*, 16 Mar. 1923, p.7; 19 Mar. 1923, p.4; 20 Mar. 1923, p.7.

117 *AS*, 14 Feb. 1925, p.16.

118 *AS*, 16 Feb. 1925, p.14.

119 *AS*, 17 Feb. 1925, p.16.

120 *AS*, 18 April 1925, p.23. The contest ran for a month and was won by Miss Rua of Milford. *AS*, 24 Feb. 1925, p.16; 5 Mar. 1925, p.20; 16 Mar. 1925, p.16.

121 *Truth*, 7 Nov. 1925, pp.5, 17.

122 *Evening Post*, 26 Dec. 1925, p.6; 28 Dec. 1925, p.8.

123 *Evening Post*, 8 Jan. 1926, p.2.

124 In 1926, 72 per cent of certified female school teachers earned less than £250 per annum. Less than 10 per cent earned over £300 a year. *AJHR*, 1927, E-1, p.15.

125 *AS*, 30 Aug. 1926, p.10.

126 *AS*, 6 Sept.1926, p.10.

127 The comment was made by Miss World New Zealand 1989, Helen Rowney. Quoted in Stephen Morris, '"I Want to be a Model": Changing Attitudes of New Zealand Women to the Miss New Zealand Pageant 1960–1999', MA Thesis, University of Auckland, 2002, p.87.

128 *AS*, 31 Aug. 1926, p.8.

129 *AS*, 9 Sept.1926, p.9.

130 *AS*, 25 Oct. 1926, p.9. Contestants of all ages were permitted to enter, some in their early teens doing so. From the photographs, it does not appear that many women past their early 20s entered the contest. *AS*, 10 Sept.1926, p.9.

131 *AS*, 30 Aug. 1926, p.10.

132 See, for example, *AS*, 13 Sept.1926, p.8; 20 Sept.1926, p.8; 1 Oct. 1926, p.8.

133 *Press*, 27 Nov. 1926, p.16.

134 See, for example, comments by the Salvation Army, *Press*, 5 Oct. 1926, p.5; Auckland Congregationalists, *AS*, 8 Nov. 1926, p.9 and *Press*, 9 Nov. 1926, p.5; North Canterbury Methodists, *Press*, 18 Nov. 1926, p.3.

135 *AS*, 3 Dec. 1926, p.10.

136 *AS*, 28 Aug. 1926, p.10.

137 *AS*, 30 Aug. 1926, p.10.

138 See, for example, *AS*, 11 Sept.1926, p.10; 13 Sept.1926, p.8; 14 Sept.1926, p.10; 27 Sept.1926, p.8. On the first two Miss Australia contests, see Judith Smart, 'Feminists, Flappers and Miss Australia', *Journal of Australian Studies*, 71, 2001, pp.1-15, 149-51.

139 Most of the scholarly writing on beauty contests is concerned with the recent past and with the idea of women's bodies representing their nations in international contests. See, for example, Sarah Banet-Weiser, *The Most Beautiful Girl in the World: Beauty Pageants and National Identity*, Berkley CA, 1999; Natasha B. Barnes, 'Face of the Nation: Race, Nationalism and Identities in Jamaican Beauty Pageants', *Massachusetts Review*, 35, 3-4, 1994, pp.471-92; Colleen Ballerino Cohen, Richard Wilk and Beverly Stoeltje (eds), *Beauty Queens on the Global Stage: Gender, Contests, and Power*, New York, 1996.

140 *Pictorial News*, 18 June 1924, p.20.

141 *AS*, 16 Nov. 1926, p.8.

142 *AS*, 24 Nov. 1926, p.10.

143 *AS*, 6 Sept.1926, p.10.

144 *AS*, 18 Oct. 1926, p.11.

145 *AS*, 20 Oct. 1926, p.11.

146 Banner, *American Beauty*, p.203.

147 *AS*, 3 Nov. 1926, p.10.

148 *AS*, 18 Nov. 1926, p.10.

149 *AS*, 18 May 1979, p.2.

150 *AS*, 23 Nov. 1926, p.9. She continued to play tennis into her 70s, and was also a keen golfer later in life.

151 *AS*, 10 Sept.1926, p.9.

152 *Ibid.*

153 *AS*, 27 Sept.1926, p.8.

154 *AS*, 10 Sept.1926, p.10.

155 *Truth*, 23 Sept.1926, p.6.; 11 Nov. 1926, p.1; 18 Nov. 1926, p.7; 25 Nov. 1926, p.7; 2 Dec. 1926, p.7; 19 May 1927, p.5. *Truth*'s antagonism seems to have been generated largely by concerns over newspaper circulation figures. It was anxious to retain its position as the most popular paper in the country. During the contest, readers filled out a coupon in the *Star* to vote for their favourite contestant. *Truth* feared that this increased the sales, but not the actual readership of papers like the *Star*, but that this distinction would not figure in audited circulation figures.

156 *AS*, 1 Nov. 1926, p.9.

157 *AS*, 3 Nov. 1926, p.10.

158 *AS*, 9 Nov. 1926, p.8.

159 *AS*, 13 Nov. 1926, p.13.

160 *AS*, 18 May 1979, p.2.

161 *AS*, 20 Nov. 1926, p.19.

162 *AS*, 7 Sept.1926, p.19.

163 *AS*, 11 Oct. 1926, p.10.

164 For the letter by 'Mere Man', see *AS*, 4 Sept.1926, p.11. The Venus de Milo's measurements were given in the *AS* on 30 Aug. 1926, p.10; Thelma McMillan's measurements appeared in the issue of 20 Oct. 1926, p.11.

165 A brief history of the 1927 pageant is given in Sandra Coney, *Standing in the Sunshine: A History of New Zealand Women Since They Won the Vote*, Auckland, 1993, pp.162-3.

166 On the post-1960 pageants, see Lynne McMorran, 'A Body of Perfection: The Increasing Standardisation of the Female Body in Televised Miss New Zealand Beauty Pageants 1964–1992', MA Thesis, Massey University, 1996; Morris, '"I Want to be a Model"'.

167 *Health and Sunshine*, 16 Nov. 1936, p.6.

168 *New Zealand Health News*, Sept.1938, p.4.

169 Dr Sheldon's advertisement was headed 'What Women Want'. Its text read: 'Health means beauty. Beauty brings power. Power achieves happiness.' The campaign ran through the 1920s. For an instance of it, see *Truth*, 9 Dec. 1922, p.7.

FOUR IN THE SWIM

1 Yvonne Christian to Town Clerk, 3 Dec. 1956. Parnell Baths, Series 275, Box 423, Item 56/39, Auckland City Council Archives, Auckland (ACCA).

2 Lucy McClement to Town Clerk, 4 Dec. 1956. Series 275, Box 423, Item 56/39, ACCA.

3 City Engineer to Mayor and Council of the

City of Auckland, 10 Feb. 1908, p.8. Hobson Street Baths, Series 275, Box 1, Item 13/23, Part 1, ACCA.

4 Parnell Baths, Series 275, Box 6, Item 14/36c, ACCA.

5 Assistant City Engineer to Town Clerk, 2 Sept.1919. Parnell Baths, Series 275, Box 29, Item 19/53, ACCA.

6 Town Clerk to Mr E H Cornes, 31 Oct. 1919. Series 275, Box 29, Item 19/53, ACCA.

7 Baths – General, Series 275, Box 165, Item 31/118, Parts 1 and 2, ACCA.

8 *ODT*, 15 Dec. 1884, p.3.

9 City Engineer's Three Reports on Baths, 8 Nov. 1906. Series 275, Box 1, Item 13/23, Part 1, ACCA.

10 *Ibid.*, p.5.

11 *Canterbury Times*, 20 May 1908, p.53.

12 See Douglas Booth, *Australian Beach Cultures: The History of Sun, Sand and Surf*, London, 2001, p.33.

13 Catherine Horwood, '"Girls Who Arouse Dangerous Passions": women and bathing, 1900–39', *Women's History Review*, 9, 4, 2000, p.656.

14 Richard Rutt defines swimming as 'self-propulsion through water without touching the bottom or bank' and notes that bathing 'may include some swimming' but 'means entering water for hygiene, therapy or pleasure'. Richard Rutt, 'The Englishman's Swimwear', *Costume*, 24, 1990, p.69.

15 *Sandow's Magazine*, Aug. 1898, pp.137-9.

16 W. A. Chapple, *Physical Education in our State Schools*, Wellington, 1894, p.8. This is a published version of a paper he read before the Citizens' Institute, Wellington, in Jan. 1894.

17 *Sandow's Magazine*, Mar. 1902, p.192.

18 *Sandow's Magazine*, 24 Aug. 1905, pp.197-8; 29 Nov. 1906, p.673. The first article in support of swimming appeared in the issue of Aug. 1898, pp.137-9.

19 *Canterbury Times*, 10 June 1908, p.54.

20 *AJHR*, 1901, E-1, p.xvi.

21 *New Zealand Graphic*, 8 Nov. 1902, p.1156.

22 *New Zealand Graphic*, 4 Jan. 1908, p.5.

23 In 1910, for example, it had about 100 women under instruction in Auckland alone. Minute Book, 15 Dec. 1910, ACC 101, Item 19, ACCA.

24 See the advertisement for water wings, *New Zealand Graphic*, 27 Oct. 1906, p.27.

25 *Star* [Christchurch], 22 Jan. 1913, p.4.

26 *Truth*, 16 April 1910, p.4.

27 *City of Auckland Bye-Laws*, Auckland, 1882, pp.41-2. These bathing regulations were effective from 3 July 1871.

28 Quoted in Stephen Barnett and Richard Wolfe, *At The Beach: The Great New Zealand Holiday*, Auckland, 1993, p.17. The precise reference is not given.

29 See Barnett and Wolfe, *At The Beach*, pp.20-1.

30 Booth claims that there were no surf life-saving clubs in New Zealand before 1910, and that in July 1910 a club was formed at New Brighton, soon to be followed by clubs at Lyall Bay, Worser Bay, Dunedin, Wanganui and other Christchurch and Wellington beaches: Douglas Booth, 'Healthy, Economic, Disciplined Bodies: Surfbathing and Surf Lifesaving in Australia and New Zealand, 1890–1950', *New Zealand Journal of History*, 32, 1, 1998, p.51. However, in 1947 the Honorary Secretary of the Royal Life Saving Society of New Zealand, Mr J. Breward, claimed that the first life-saving club in New Zealand was formed in 1909, in Wanganui, and was followed in 1910 by clubs in Auckland and other centres around New Zealand: Letter from J. Breward, Hon. Secretary, Royal Life Saving Society, New Zealand Council, to Assistant Under-Secretary, Department of Internal Affairs, 11 Aug. 1947. History of Sport in New Zealand – General File re. Internal Affairs (IA), Series 1, 139/234, Archives New Zealand, Wellington (ANZ).

31 Town Clerk to Mr D. B. Anderson, 25 Jan. 1915. Hobson Street Baths, Series 275, Box 8, Item 15/36, Part 1, ACCA; *Truth*, 2 June 1954, p.3.

32 *New Zealand Listener*, 15 Dec. 1939, p.38.

33 M. E. Champion to Town Clerk, 10 Oct. 1920. Hobson Street Baths, Series 275, Box 32, Item 20/43, ACCA.

34 Mr P. L. B. Janis to Town Clerk, 14 July 1922; Town Clerk to Mr P. L. B. Janis, 3 Aug. 1922. Hobson Street Baths, Series 275, Box 45, Item 22/43, ACCA.

35 McGregor & Lowrie, Barristers & Solicitors, to Town Clerk, 13 Sept.1915. Hobson Street Baths, Series 275, Box 8, Item 15/36, Part 2, ACCA.

36 Copy of Report on Hobson Street Baths to Town Clerk, 8 April 1924. Parks Committee Minutes, Series 107, Item 1, ACCA.

37 See, for example, the advertisement for 'Champion's Boys' and rolled oats, Waitemata Amateur Swimming Club Third Carnival Season 1920–21 Official Programme Tepid Baths, Auckland, 8 p.m. Tuesday, Jan. 25th. Sport – Swimming Folder 1920–29, Ephemera Collection, Special Collections, Auckland City Libraries.

38 *Truth*, 7 Aug. 1930, p.7; Dismissal of M. E. Champion from Position of Bathskeeper, Series 275, Box 235, Item 38/489, ACCA.

39 *Bye-Laws of the Council of the City of Auckland,* Auckland, 1890, p.154; *Auckland City Council By-Laws 1-25 and Standing Orders,* Auckland, 1913, p.73; *Auckland City Council By Laws 1-5 Milk Regulations,* Auckland, 1917, p.161; *Auckland City By-Laws, Nos. 1-14 1925–1934,* Auckland, 1934, p.198.

40 Auckland pools, for example, closed at 10 a.m. on Sundays until the 1920s, when the hours were extended until midday at the Teps. The caretakers at the Shelly Beach and Parnell pools allowed swimming from 2 to 4 p.m. on Sundays, although this breached the regulated opening hours. See *Bye-Laws of the Council of the City of Auckland,* 1890, p.153; Parks Committee Minutes, 14 Feb. 1922. Series 107, Item 1, ACCA; Town Clerk to City Engineer, 24 Feb. 1922. Closing of Shelly Beach & Hobson Street Baths on Sunday. Series 275, Box 48, Item 22/222, ACCA; Parks Committee Minutes, 24 Sept.1928. Series 107, Item 2, ACCA. For Toye's complaint, see Arthur E. Toye to Mayor and Members of the City Council, 20 Jan. 1922. Series 275, Box 48, Item 22/222, ACCA.

41 *Bye-Laws of the Council of the City of Auckland,* 1890, p.153; *Auckland City Council By-Laws 1-25 and Standing Orders,* 1913, p.72.

42 *New Zealand Graphic,* 26 Sept.1903, p.929.

43 See, for example, *Sandow's Magazine,* July 1899, pp.49-55; Mar. 1902, p.188; April 1904, p.282.

44 Kellermann's surname was (and is) often spelt Kellerman. For the sake of consistency, I have chosen to spell her name Kellermann, as this was the spelling used for her 1918 book.

45 *AS,* 8 Aug. 1903, Supplement p.2. For the 'Australian Mermaid' label see *Sandow's Magazine,* 21 Dec. 1905, pp.698-701.

46 As with the Modern Milo, New Zealanders could follow Kellermann's career through the press, and buy tickets to her performances on her visits to the country. See, for example, *New Zealand Graphic,* 1 Dec. 1906, p.37, and 26 Oct. 1907, p.30; *Lyttelton Times,* 4 Feb. 1911, p.8; *Truth,* 20 July 1912, p.8; *Press,* 14 Nov. 1921, p.11; *Auckland Truth,* 17 Dec. 1921, p.2; *Truth,* 18 Feb. 1922, p.2, and 12 April 1939, p.19. In the 1920s her film 'Venus of the South Seas' was shot in Nelson and Takaka (*Pictorial News,* 6 May 1924, p.15).

47 *Truth,* 20 July 1912, p.8.

48 Annette Kellermann, *Physical Beauty: How To Keep It,* London, 1918, pp.83-5.

49 Booth, *Australian Beach Cultures,* p.27.

50 Miss E. M. Swallow to Town Clerk, 11 Mar. 1914; Town Clerk to Miss E. M. Swallow, 13 Mar. 1914; Miss E. M Swallow to Town Clerk, 19 Mar. 1914; City Engineer to Town Clerk,

24 Mar. 1914; Town Clerk to Bathskeeper, Parnell Baths, 7 April 1914. Series 275, Box 6, Item 14/36c, ACCA.

51 *Truth,* 18 Jan. 1910, p.4; 29 Jan. 1910, p.1.

52 *Auckland City Council By-Laws 1-25 and Standing Orders,* 1913, p.161. Nudists are discussed in the next Ch..

53 *Lyttelton Times,* 10 Dec. 1912, p.5.

54 Mr C. H. Wood to Town Clerk, 22 May 1916. Shelly Beach Baths, Series 275, Box 11, Item 16/36, ACCA.

55 See, for example, the report of the 'discovery' of Lyall Bay in Wellington as a seaside resort, thanks to a new tram line to the beach. *Dominion,* 8 Jan. 1910, p.14. On Boxing Day 1909 10,000 people were said to have visited Lyall Bay.

56 *New Zealand Graphic,* 14 Nov. 1903, p.16.

57 By 1914, for example, it was claimed that 'thousands' swam every day at New Brighton in Christchurch. *Lyttelton Times,* 14 Jan. 1914, p.10.

58 From the 1880s through to the 1930s, for example, a by-law was in place to restrict swimmers to a half-hour session in all Auckland City Council pools. On Sunday swimming at St Clair in Dunedin, see *Truth,* 14 Jan. 1911, p.1. At Caroline Bay in Timaru, though, the authorities prohibited Sunday sea bathing until the 1920s. *Truth,* 22 Dec. 1927, p.1.

59 *Star,* 22 Jan. 1913, p.4.

60 *NZH,* 21 April 1913, p.4. On Australian references see Booth, *Australian Beach Cultures,* p.42.

61 *Daily Telegraph,* 24 Jan. 1911.

62 *Lyttelton Times,* 1 Mar. 1910, p.7.

63 *Truth,* 12 Mar. 1910, p.1.

64 *Lyttelton Times,* 1 Mar. 1910, p.7. See also, *Lyttelton Times,* 3 Mar. 1910, pp.7-8.

65 *Auckland City Council By-Laws 1-25 and Standing Orders,* 1913, p.162. This was reiterated in a 1917 by-law. See *Auckland City Council By Laws 1-5 Milk Regulations,* 1917, p.163.

66 Leone Huntsman, *Sand in Our Souls: The Beach in Australian History,* Carlton South, 2001, p.60.

67 Sunbathing enclosures were also built at Manly Beach in Sydney. Huntsman, *Sand in Our Souls,* p.60.

68 *Lyttelton Times,* 11 Jan. 1913, p.13.

69 *Truth,* 30 Dec. 1922, p.4. The report centred on Caroline Bay in Timaru. In Auckland, a by-law that came into effect in 1925 repeated the direction that swimmers were not allowed to loiter on the beach. *Auckland City By-Laws, Nos. 1-14 1925–1934,* 1934, p.199.

70 *Truth,* 16 Jan. 1930, p.17.

71   City Engineer to Town Clerk, 27 Aug. 1934. Series 275, Box 165, Item 31/118, Part 1, ACCA.

72   Health Committee to Town Clerk, 28 Jan. 1948. Baths – General, Series 275, Box 319, Item 48/118, ACCA. See the report and photograph of the new sundeck, *NZH*, 22 Nov. 1954, p.8.

73   *Truth*, 16 Jan. 1930, p.17.

74   *Dominion*, 19 May 1931, p.8.

75   *Press*, 30 Oct. 1922, p.4. See also *HPC*, 1 Mar. 1931, pp.14-16; 1 Oct. 1931, pp.12-13, 37.

76   *AS*, 1 Oct. 1926, p.9.

77   On 2 April 1934 he gave a radio talk on station 3YA as part of a series of lectures organised by the Sunlight League of New Zealand. Sunlight Society, Christchurch 1931–36. Health (H), Series 1, 35/95, ANZ.

78   *Pictorial News*, 31 Jan. 1925, p.2.

79   For American Indians (the term used at the time), see *New Zealand New Health Journal*, Nov. 1926, p.5. For Maori, see *Press*, 15 May 1931, p.13.

80   *New Zealand Graphic*, 2 Sept.1905, p.61.

81   *NZH*, 21 April 1913, p.4.

82   *Truth*, 27 Dec. 1928, p.15.

83   See, for example, *New Zealand New Health Journal*, Dec. 1928, pp.20-1, 23-5; Jan. 1929, pp.11-12.

84   *New Zealand New Health Journal*, Jan. 1929, pp.11-12; *NZH*, 17 Dec. 1930, p.7.

85   *New Zealand New Health Journal*, Oct. 1927, p.1.

86   *Evening Post*, 16 Jan. 1926, p.20.

87   *HPC*, 1 Mar. 1931, pp.14-16.

88   *Dominion*, 14 May 1931, p.8.

89   See, for example, *Press*, 30 Oct. 1922, p.4; *Evening Post*, 2 Jan. 1926, p.11 and 16 Jan. 1926, p.20; *New Zealand New Health Journal*, 20 Nov. 1926, pp.4-5; *HPC*, 1 Mar. 1931, pp.14-16; *Press*, 15 May 1931, p.13; Seabathing and Sunlight are Nature's Greatest Cures. Cora Wilding Papers, 1.18. Macmillan Brown Library, University of Canterbury; *New Zealand National Review*, 15 Feb. 1946, pp.89, 91, 93.

90   On the ways Australians made a scientific case for sunbathing, see Booth, *Australian Beach Cultures*, p.43.

91   *AS*, 1 Oct. 1926, p.9.

92   *Truth*, 21 Nov. 1929, p.19; 28 Nov. 1929, p.19.

93   *New Zealand New Health Journal*, Sept.1927, p.13.

94   *Press*, 15 May 1931, p.13.

95   Press clipping, 9 May 1931. H, Series 1, 35/95, ANZ.

96   *Press*, 15 May 1931, p.13.

97   *Press*, 11 April 1931, p.17.

98   *Press*, 12 May 1934, p.11.

99   *Sunlight League of New Zealand*, Christchurch, 1934. H, Series 1, 35/95, ANZ.

100   For example, in Milner's 1931 address he held up the German youth movement as something for New Zealand to aspire to. *Dominion*, 14 May 1931, p.8.

101   *Press*, 12 May 1934, p.11.

102   *Sunlight League of New Zealand*, Christchurch, 1934, pp.2-3.

103   Sunlight Society, Christchurch 1937–44. H, Series 1, 35/27/1, ANZ. This 'mission statement' dates from 1944 to 1945.

104   For a discussion of very similar ideas in the Australian context see Grant Rodwell, '"The Sense of Victorious Struggle": The Eugenic Dynamic in Australian Popular Surf-Culture, 1900–50', *Journal of Australian Studies*, 62, 1999, pp.56-63.

105   James Walvin, *Beside the Seaside: A Social History of the Popular Seaside Holiday*, London, 1978, p.121; Rutt, 'The Englishman's Swimwear', p.75.

106   This was the topic of a talk given by Mrs Gillespie, the matron of the Karitane Hospital, in Nov. 1931. Radio-Talks From 3 Z.C. Christchurch. H, Series 1, 35/95, ANZ.

107   Sunlight League of New Zealand, Third Annual Report for Year Ending 9th May, 1934. H, Series 1, 35/95, ANZ.

108   *New Zealand Graphic*, 22 Feb. 1908, p.9.

109   See, for example, *Press*, 30 Oct. 1922, p.4; *Evening Post*, 2 Jan. 1926, p.11; *New Zealand New Health Journal*, Nov. 1926, p.5; *Truth*, 19 Dec. 1929, p.22; *Truth*, 16 Jan. 1930, p.17; *HPC*, 1 Oct. 1931, pp.12-13, 37; Alfred J. Briton, *The Book of Life: A Work for Everyman, His Wife and His Family*, Sydney, 1933, pp.322-4.

110   *Truth*, 16 Jan. 1930, p.17; 4 Mar. 1936, p.22. Briton also advocated rose water: Briton, *The Book of Life*, p.323.

111   *Press*, 21 Jan. 1929, p.8; *Dominion*, 19 May 1931, p.8.

112   Sunlight League of New Zealand, Annual Report and Balance Sheet for Year Ending May 9, 1932. H, Series 1, 35/95, ANZ.

113   Printed note on file, c. 1933. H, Series 1, 35/95, ANZ. Emphasis in original.

114   For example, in Oct. 1931 Dr Hazel Allison spoke on 3ZC about sunbathing for children. Note on file 'Radio-Talks From 3.Z.C. Christchurch'; Dr Gordon Rich talked about safe sunbathing on 3YA in Dec. 1933. H, Series 1, 35/95, ANZ. Dr P. Allison gave a radio lecture on 'How to Sunbathe' in 1935. Sunlight League Annual Report For the Year Ending May 9th, 1936. H, Series 1, 35/27/1, ANZ.

115   Sunlight League Annual Report For the Year

Ending May 9th, 1935. H, Series 1, 35/95, ANZ.

116 Sunlight League Annual Report For the Year Ending May 9th, 1936. H, Series 1, 35/27/1, ANZ.

117 Briton, *The Book of Life*, p.323; *NZH*, 4 July 1936, Supplement p.3.

118 Sunlight League Annual Report For the Year Ending May 9th, 1937; Sunlight League Annual Report For the Year Ending May 9th, 1939. H, Series 1, 35/27/1, ANZ.

119 *AS*, 20 May 1922, p.5; *Truth*, 20 May 1922, p.6.

120 Michel Rainis, 'French Beach Sports Culture in the Twentieth Century', *International Journal of the History of Sport*, 17, 1, 2000, pp.144-58; Marla Matzer Rose, *Muscle Beach*, New York, 2001.

121 *HPC*, 1 Oct. 1933, pp.42-3, 53.

122 *Truth*, 23 Nov. 1938, p.5; 5 Dec. 1934, p.39.

123 Printed note on file, c. 1933. H, Series 1, 35/95, ANZ.

124 *Truth*, 14 Jan. 1911, p.1.

125 *NZH*, 21 April 1913, p.4.

126 *Truth*, 30 Dec. 1922, p.4. See, for example, the advertisement for Spinet, 'The super cigarette', which is illustrated with a picture of a man lying on the beach, enjoying his cigarette, while a woman sits beside him. *Truth*, 27 Jan. 1923, p.11.

127 *Truth*, 7 Feb. 1920, p.5.

128 *Truth*, 12 Jan. 1924, p.1.

129 *Truth*, 13 Jan. 1923, p.2.

130 *Truth*, 2 Jan. 1930, p.2.

131 *Truth*, 3 Mar. 1937, p.28.

132 See, for example, the report on new season swimwear and women's desire for a 'briefer, snappier and more backless bathing suit'. *Truth*, 5 Feb. 1931, p.9.

133 *New Zealand Graphic*, 6 Aug. 1904, p.14.

134 Angela Latham has written about American women and bathing costumes as a performance. See Angela J. Latham, *Posing a Threat: Flappers, Chorus Girls, and Other Brazen Performers of the American 1920s*, Hanover, 2000, Ch. 3.

135 Rutt, 'The Englishman's Swimwear', pp.70-1.

136 See, for example, the 1871 regulations as to bathing, *City of Auckland Bye-Laws*, 1882, p.41.

137 *New Zealand Graphic*, 21 Nov. 1903, p.12.

138 *Truth*, 11 Aug. 1906, p.5; 11 Jan. 1908, p.1.

139 *NZH*, 21 April 1913, p.4.

140 Fiona McKergow, 'Bodies At The Beach: A History of Swimwear', *Bearings*, 3, 4, 1991, p.18. The outfit was recommended in the *New Zealand Graphic* in 1893.

141 See, for example, pictures of women's bathing attire: *New Zealand Graphic*, 29 Dec. 1900, p.1236; 7 Feb. 1903, p.410; 2 Jan. 1904, p.63;

30 Jan. 1904, p.67.

142 Waitemata Amateur Swimming Club Programme 5th Carnival Season 1909–10, 22 Mar. 1910. Sport – Swimming Folder 1900–1919, Ephemera Collection, Special Collections, Auckland City Libraries.

143 For a discussion of the same phenomenon in America, see Maxine James Johns and Jane Farrell-Beck, '"Cut Out the Sleeves": Nineteenth-Century U.S. Women Swimmers and Their Attire', *Dress*, 28, 2001, pp.53-63.

144 *Sandow's Magazine*, July 1899, pp.49-55; April 1904, pp.283-4.

145 For the English rules see Rutt, 'The Englishman's Swimwear', p.73. For the local application of the rules see *Auckland Weekly News*, 2 Feb. 1900, p.18; 2 Mar. 1900, p.21; 9 Mar. 1900, p.19. Swimming clubs suggested that their costume rules should also be enforced on beach goers. See Minute Book, 2 Dec. 1909. ACC 101, Item 18, ACCA.

146 *Bye-Laws of the Council of the City of Auckland*, 1890, p.153.

147 City Engineer to Sragood [*sic*] Son & Ewen, Ross & Glendenning, Arch. Clark & Sons, R. & W. Meek, A. W. Smith, and F. W. Gaze, 18 Nov. 1914. New Customs Street Baths, Series 219, Box 5, Item 12/420, ACCA.

148 See, for example, *Auckland City Council By-Laws 1-25 and Standing Orders*, 1913, p.143.

149 *Lyttelton Times*, 1 Mar. 1910, p.8.

150 *Daily Telegraph*, 31 Jan. 1911.

151 *Truth*, 2 Jan. 1909, p.6.

152 For New Brighton see *Truth*, 1 Oct. 1910, p.6. In Auckland, the council introduced the trunks requirement for foreshore swimming in 1917. See *Auckland City Council By Laws 1-5 Milk Regulations*, 1917, p.162.

153 *Lyttelton Times*, 7 Mar. 1910, p.8.

154 Booth, *Australian Beach Cultures*, pp.44-5. The quote is from p.45.

155 *Auckland Truth*, 1 Jan. 1916, p.3.

156 *Auckland City Council By-Laws 1-25 and Standing Orders*, 1913, p.143; *Auckland City Council By Laws 1-5 Milk Regulations*, 1917, p.162; *Auckland City By-Laws, Nos. 1-4 1925–1934*, 1934, p.199.

157 *Daily Telegraph*, 12 Feb. 1938, p.9.

158 *Press*, 17 May 1946, p.6.

159 *Truth*, 27 Nov. 1956, p.16.

160 *AS*, 29 Oct. 1926, p.14.

161 *Press*, 21 Jan. 1929, p.8.

162 *Truth*, 7 Feb. 1929, p.6.

163 *Truth*, 2 Jan. 1935, p.1.

164 New Zealand National Swimming Championships Season 1934–35 Controlled by the Auckland Centre, N.Z.A.S.A Tepid Baths, Auckland Feb. 16, 18, 20, 1935. Sport – Swimming Folder 1930–39, Ephemera

Collection, Special Collections, Auckland City Libraries.

165 *Truth*, 15 Sept.1923, p.14.

166 Rutt, 'The Englishman's Swimwear', p.74.

167 *Auckland Truth*, 11 Jan. 1919, p.2. On the importance of Hollywood to beach culture in the 1930s see Horwood, '"Girls Who Arouse Dangerous Passions"', p.663.

168 *Truth*, 13 Jan. 1927, p.3. That season popular colours were sea blue, sand yellow, emerald green and scarlet, and wraps were sleeveless.

169 *Truth*, 13 Jan. 1927, p.3.

170 *Press*, 5 Feb. 1929, p.15; 26 Mar. 1929, p.6; 27 Mar. 1929, p.16; *New Zealand New Health Journal*, Feb. 1929, p.1.

171 *AS*, 23 Jan. 1925, p.9.

172 *Truth*, 31 Oct. 1929, p.10.

173 *Truth*, 5 Feb. 1931, p.9.

174 *Truth*, 3 Dec. 1931, p.18.

175 *Truth*, 7 Nov. 1934, p.15.

176 *Truth*, 28 Nov. 1934, p.13.

177 On Jantzen's need to create a mass swimwear market see Lena Lencek and Gideon Bosker, *The Beach: The History of Paradise on Earth*, London, 1998, esp. p.188.

178 Joanna Bourke, 'The Great Male Renunciation: Men's Dress Reform in Inter-war Britain', *Journal of Design History*, 9, 1, 1996, pp.23-33.

179 *Press*, 15 May 1931, p.13. Reddell was the secretary of the Christchurch Dress Reform League. *New Zealand New Health Journal*, Feb. 1929, p.1.

180 *Truth*, 12 Dec. 1934, p.15. Trunks had become common on the Riviera in 1928 and in England by 1932. Rutt, 'The Englishman's Swimwear', p.76.

181 *Truth*, 2 Jan. 1935, p.1.

182 On the technology of swimwear see Lena Lencek and Gideon Bosker, *Making Waves: Swimsuits and the Undressing of America*, San Francisco, 1989, esp. pp.61-3.

183 *Truth*, 14 Oct. 1936, p.22.

184 *Truth*, 2 Jan. 1935, p.1.

185 *Daily Telegraph*, 31 Jan. 1911.

186 *Truth*, 25 Feb. 1922, p.2.

187 *Truth*, 16 Jan. 1930, p.17.

188 *Truth*, 16 Sept.1936, p.9.

189 *Press*, 13 Oct. 1945, p.6; *Truth*, 31 Oct. 1945, p.5; 5 Dec. 1945, p.7.

190 *Truth*, 14 Nov. 1945, p.5.

191 *Press*, 13 Oct. 1945, p.6.

192 *Press*, 7 Oct. 1946, p.3.

193 *Truth*, 17 Jan. 1951, p.22.

194 See, for example, *Truth*, 9 June 1954, p.33; 2 Oct. 1956, p.28; 16 April 1957, p.1; 14 May 1957, p.27; 5 Jan. 1960, p.1.

195 Booth notes a similar pattern in Australia. Certain beaches banned the wearing of

bikinis when they first appeared; by the 1950s they were 'flooding' local beaches. Booth, *Australian Beach Cultures*, pp.50-2.

196 *Press*, 24 Dec. 1946, p.8; 26 Dec. 1946, p.3.

197 *HPC*, 1 Mar. 1931, p.16.

198 See, for example, *HPC*, 1 June 1941, p.36; 1 May 1942, pp.32-3.

199 *New Zealand Illustrated Sporting and Dramatic Review*, 3 Feb. 1937, p.4.

200 *New Zealand New Health Journal*, Oct. 1928, pp.30-2.

201 For accounts of midnight skinny dipping see, for example, *Truth*, 17 Feb. 1927 p. 1; 16 Feb. 1928, p.7; 2 Jan. 1935, p.1; 24 April 1940, p.13. The 2 Jan. 1935 report made a reference to locals interested in gymnosophy.

FIVE INDECENT EXPOSURE?

1 An earlier version of this Ch. was presented at the New Zealand Historical Association Conference, Christchurch, Dec. 2001. I am grateful to those present at the session for their helpful questions, comments and suggestions. I would esp. like to acknowledge the contributions of Barbara Brookes and Charlotte Macdonald that day and in subsequent correspondence.

2 *Truth*, 29 Nov. 1933, p.9.

3 *Dominion*, 24 Nov. 1933, p.13. I am grateful to Peter Boston for pointing out this reference to me.

4 See, for example, *Truth*, 2 Jan. 1935, p.1; 15 Mar. 1939, p.1; 20 Dec. 1939, p.1; 21 Dec. 1955, p.1.

5 *Sandow's Magazine*, June 1899, pp.413-17.

6 *Sandow's Magazine*, May 1901, pp.371-2.

7 *Truth*, 5 Oct. 1907, p.1. On the Doukhobors see John McLaren, 'The Despicable Crime of Nudity: Law, the State, and Civil Protest Among the Sons of Freedom Sect of Doukhobors, 1899–1935', *Journal of the West*, 38, 3, 1999, pp.27-33.

8 *Truth* was fond of reporting cases of indecent pictures and postcards. See, for example, 18 Aug. 1906, p.1; 18 Aug. 1906, p.5; 13 Oct. 1906, pp.3, 4; 30 Jan. 1908, p.30; 1 Feb. 1908, p.6; 13 June 1908, p.5; 13 Aug. 1910, p.5.

9 *Truth*, 16 April 1910, p.6.

10 *Truth*, 26 Jan. 1924, p.11.

11 Percy W. Cousins, 'Nudism in New Zealand', *Solaire Universelle de Nudisme Magazine*, September–Oct. 1955, p.7.

12 *Truth*, 22 Oct. 1931, p.5.

13 Miriam Saphira, *A Man's Man: A Daughter's Story*, Auckland, 1997, esp. pp.87-93.

14 *HPC*, 1 Mar. 1933, pp.15, 46. The article was entitled 'We Dared to Go Nudist!'. On health camps see Margaret Tennant, *Children's Health, The Nation's Wealth: A History of*

Children's Health Camps, Wellington, 1994.

15 *HPC*, 1 June 1933, pp.49, 62. The article was entitled 'Our Annual Sun-Bake Camp: A Semi-Nude Holiday Camp'.

16 *Truth*, 15 Aug. 1934, p.16.

17 *Truth*, 19 Sept.1934, p.15 (a case in Constantinople); 16 June 1937, p.13 (a case in Melbourne).

18 *Truth*, 17 Oct. 1934, p.20 (nude sunbathing on a Spanish beach); 13 June 1934, p.15 and 20 Mar. 1935, p.11 (nudist club in New York); 6 Mar. 1935, p.10 (nudist club in Cape Town).

19 *Man*, Dec. 1936, p.94.

20 *Truth*, 31 July 1935, p.12.

21 *Truth*, 24 Jan. 1934, p.8.

22 *Truth*, 19 Sept.1934, p.8.

23 *Ibid.*

24 The Auckland Sun Group, the Wellington Sunshine Club, the Hawke's Bay Sun Club and the Gisborne club were all formed in early 1938. See *Daily Telegraph*, 8 Jan. 1938, p.8 (Auckland); 10 Jan. 1938, p.8 (Wellington); 21 Jan. 1938, p.10 (Napier); 27 Jan. 1938, p.9 (Gisborne).

25 *New Zealand Illustrated Sporting and Dramatic Review*, 24 Feb. 1938, p.2.

26 This report was reproduced in the Australian newspaper *Smith's Weekly*, 21 Aug. 1937, pp.1-2.

27 *Truth*, 23 Aug. 1939, p.17.

28 *Truth*, 24 Jan. 1934, p.8.

29 For a potted history of German nudism see Adam Clapham and Robin Constable, *As Nature Intended: A Pictorial History of The Nudists*, London, 1982, pp.6-30. The organised movement can be traced back to the late nineteenth century in Germany, with the first resort opening in 1903 (p.14). See also Christopher Kenway, 'Nudism, Health, and Modernity: The Natural Cure as Proposed by the German Physical Culture Movement 1900–1914', *Nineteenth-Century Prose*, 25, 1, 1998, pp.102-115; Karl Toepfer, *Empire of Ecstasy: Nudity and Movement in German Body Culture, 1910–1935*, Berkeley and London, 1997.

30 Clapham and Constable, *As Nature Intended*, p.37. Others claim 1924. See Arnd Krÿger, 'There Goes This Art of Manliness: Naturism and Racial Hygiene in Germany', *Journal of Sport History*, 18, 1, 1991, p.135.

31 Cec Cinder, *The Nudist Idea*, Riverside CA, 1998, p.507. See also Clapham and Constable, *As Nature Intended*, pp.66-81. Other sources suggest the first club was formed in 1931. See Anthony M. Turano, 'Nudism Denuded', *American Mercury*, 38, 150, June 1936, pp.161-6.

32 By 1935 there were at least three formal nudist clubs in Australia. See Magnus Clarke, *Nudism in Australia: A First Study*, Warun Ponds VIC, 1982, p.53.

33 Anthony Kay, 'The Nude Cults of Germany', *HPC*, 1 Sept.1929, pp.13-15.

34 Nudism was aired in 'The Charm of Concealment', *HPC*, 1 July 1931, pp.10-11, 18. By late 1931 articles on Australasia were appearing. For 1930s articles see 'The Inside Story of Sydney's Nude Cult', *HPC*, 1 Nov. 1931, pp.14-15, 43, 48; 'Sun-Cultures in Victoria', *HPC*, 1 Mar. 1932, p.42; 'Mixed Bathing – In the Nude?', *HPC*, 1 May 1932, pp.13, 48-9; 'The Psychology of Nudism', *HPC*, 1 July 1932, pp.17, 22; 'We Holidayed in the Nude', *HPC*, 1 July 1932, pp.30, 50; 'The Nude Cult Arrives', *HPC*, 1 Oct. 1932, pp.16-18; 'We Dared to Go Nudist', *HPC*, 1 Mar. 1933, pp.15, 46; 'Nudist or Not? Week Ending With the Sun Bake Cult Near Sydney', *HPC*, 1 May 1933, pp.40-1, 56; 'Our Annual Sun-Bake Camp', *HPC*, 1 June 1933, pp.49, 62; 'Is Nudism Neurotic?', *HPC*, 1 Aug. 1933, pp.30, 47, 50; 'He Shocked 'Em 30 Years Ago', *HPC*, 1 Sept.1933, pp.28, 48; 'How Nudism Saved My Life', *HPC*, 1 Sept.1933, pp.41, 52-53; 'What Is the Future of Nudism?', *HPC*, 1 Oct. 1933, pp.49, 58; 'The Editor Is Assailed By Angry Nudists', *HPC*, 1 Feb. 1935, pp.20-1, 59; 'Let's O.K. Sane But Semi-Nudism', *HPC*, 1 Mar. 1935, pp.44-5; 'My First Nudist Holiday', *HPC*, 1 July 1935, pp.30-1, 52; 'Why is Society Going Nude', *HPC*, 1 Aug. 1935, pp.22-3, 58; '50,000 Naked Britons', *HPC*, 1 Sept.1937, pp.17, 62; 'If You Must be a Nudist', *HPC*, 1 Oct. 1937, p.9; 'Getting Among the Nudists', *HPC*, 1 Dec. 1937, pp.28-9, 40; 'Sidelights on Certain Sunbathing Rackets Exposed', *HPC*, 1 May 1938, pp.48-9, 56; 'A Fortnight of Sunshine Makes an Ideal Holiday!', *HPC*, 1 June 1938, pp.26-7; 'Is This Nudism All A Sham?', *HPC*, 1 Feb. 1939, pp.32-3; 'A Naturist's Paradise for Hundreds in England', *HPC*, 1 May 1939, pp.30-1; 'Can This Naturism Be a Healthy Pastime', *HPC*, 1 May 1939, pp.55-6, 63; 'A Nudist Attacks Scoffers of the Cult', *HPC*, 1 July 1939, pp.20-1; 'Nudes Versus Prudes', *HPC*, 1 Oct. 1939, pp.18-19, 42; 'Away with Mock Modesty', *HPC*, 1 Nov. 1939, p.30. Letters to the editor on nudism were also published. See *HPC*, 1 Nov. 1932, p.49; 1 June 1933, p.46; 1 Sept.1933, p.42.

35 The title page of the book claimed that this was 'A comprehensible work of inestimable value to everyone having the welfare of their body at heart'. No author was given, but the book was published by Briton Publications.

Mixed Nudist Camps Throughout the World, Sydney, 1939.

36 The British movement preferred the term naturist to nudist. *Health and Efficiency* was clearly available in New Zealand at this time as it was cited in a case against the New Zealand magazine, *Health and Sunshine*. See *Truth*, 16 June 1937, p.17. For Deamer see *Smith's Weekly*, 19 Mar. 1938, p.6.

37 Trevor G. Bain, *Nudism – Is It Desirable?*, Auckland, 1937, pp.13-15, 47-8; letter from 'A Distant Reader' from Nelson, New Zealand, *HPC*, 1 Feb. 1939, p.3.

38 As well as publishing letters about nudism (*Health and Sunshine*, 16 Nov. 1936, pp.2, 10; April–May 1937, pp.4-5; July 1937, p.457), it contained articles about the German nudist movement (April–May 1937, p.4), instructions on how to form a nudist club (April–May 1937, p.5), an article on roof-top gardens for nudists (July 1937, p.456), and a piece of nudism and the classical games (July 1937, p.467).

39 *Health and Sunshine*, 16 Nov. 1936, pp.2, 10. This was the second issue of the magazine. The first issue is not available, but in the second issue one of the correspondents mentioned that in the first issue there had been an article by Bain called 'Nudism: Is It Desirable?' (p.2), the same title he used in issue two.

40 Bain, *Nudism*, p.9.

41 Bain, *Nudism*, p.23.

42 Bain, *Nudism*, pp. 50, 37.

43 Bain, *Nudism*, pp.47-8.

44 William Wellby, *Naked and Unashamed: Nudism from Six Points of View*, London, 1934, p.72.

45 Bain, *Nudism*, p.49.

46 Wellby, *Naked and Unashamed*, p.44.

47 Wellby, *Naked and Unashamed*, p.29; Bain, *Nudism*, pp.35-6.

48 *Daily Telegraph*, 21 Jan. 1938, p.10.

49 Wellby, *Naked and Unashamed*, p.36.

50 Wellby, *Naked and Unashamed*, p.54.

51 *HPC*, 1 May 1932, p.48.

52 *HPC*, 1 Nov. 1933, p.49.

53 *HPC*, 1 July 1938, p.33.

54 *HPC*, 1 Sept.1933, pp.41, 52-53.

55 Wellby, *Naked and Unashamed*, p.35; Bain, *Nudism*, p.54; *HPC*, 1 Nov. 1931, p.49; 1 Mar. 1932, p.42; 1 Sept.1937, p.17; 1 May 1938, p.48; 1 June 1938, pp.26-7; 1 Feb. 1939, p.33.

56 Bain, *Nudism*, p.10; *Daily Telegraph*, 11 Feb. 1938, p.8.

57 See, for example, Bain, *Nudism*, pp.11-12; E. de Villiers, 'Nudism and the Classic Games', *Health and Sunshine*, July 1937, p.467; Allen P. Gascoigne, *HPC*, 1 Feb. 1940, p.44; Wellby,

Naked and Unashamed, p.12. For a scholarly discussion of this phenomenon, see John Mouratidis, 'The Origin of Nudity in Greek Athletics', *Journal of Sport History*, 12, 3, 1985, pp.213-32.

58 Bain, *Nudism*, back page.

59 *Health and Sunshine*, July 1937, p.457.

60 See, for example, the spokesman for the proposed Wellington nudist club, *Daily Telegraph*, 10 Jan. 1938, p.8; 'Nudist' of Napier, *Daily Telegraph*, 31 Jan. 1938, p.8; the secretary of the Hawke's Bay Sun Club, *Daily Telegraph*, 24 Feb. 1938, p.8; 'A Gospel Minister', *HPC*, 1 Oct. 1939, pp.18-19.

61 Bain, *Nudism*, p.13. Bain is quoting Wellby.

62 *HPC*, 1 July 1938, p.32. Emphasis in original.

63 See, for example, Clapham and Constable, *As Nature Intended*, p.5.

64 Bain, *Nudism*, p.11.

65 Clapham and Constable, *As Nature Intended*, p.13. (Clapham wrote the text, and Constable took the photographs.)

66 See, for example, *HPC*, 1 July 1931, pp.10-11; 1 Nov. 1931, p.49; 1 May 1932, p.48; 1 Aug. 1933, p.50; 1 Oct. 1933, p.58; 1 Sept.1937, p.17; 1 June 1938, p.27; 1 Feb. 1939, p.32; 1 May 1939, p.56; 1 July 1939, pp.20-1.

67 See, for example, 'Lux Lucet In Tenebris', *Daily Telegraph*, 5 Feb. 1938, p.8; G. R. H., *Daily Telegraph*, 8 Feb. 1938, p.8; Bertram J. Spencer, *HPC*, 1 Feb. 1939, p.33. Spencer claimed that removing every stitch of clothing was 'ridiculous'.

68 See, for example, Hector Poole, *HPC*, 1 Mar. 1935, p.45; 'New Zealander', *Daily Telegraph*, 9 Feb. 1938, p.8; E.E.D., *HPC*, 1 Oct. 1939, p.19.

69 This claim was made long before the first nudist camp was established in New Zealand. See *Truth*, 30 Aug. 1913, p.4. See also Wellby, *Naked and Unashamed*, p.9; Bain, *Nudism*, p.25; *Truth*, 16 June 1937, p.17; *Truth*, 15 Mar. 1939, p.1, quoting Lillian Smith of Takapuna.

70 *HPC*, 1 July 1931, pp.10-11.

71 *HPC*, 1 June 1933, pp.49, 62.

72 Wellby, *Naked and Unashamed*, p.28.

73 Editorial, *Health and Sunshine*, July 1937, p.453.

74 For the 'disgusting' claim see Bain, *Nudism*, p.93. See also *HPC*, 1 Feb. 1938, pp.14-15, 55, 57; *Daily Telegraph*, 8 Mar. 1938, p.8.

75 Wellby, *Naked and Unashamed*, p.31.

76 *HPC*, 1 May 1939, p.57. See also *Health and Sunshine*, 16 Nov. 1936, p.2.

77 Bain, *Nudism*, p.75.

78 *Daily Telegraph*, 24 Feb. 1938, p.8.

79 *New Zealand Illustrated Sporting and Dramatic Review*, 24 Feb. 1938, p.3.

80 *HPC*, 1 June 1933, p.46.

81 See, for example, Alfred J. Briton's attack on mixed-sex nudism, *HPC*, 1 Oct. 1937, p.9. See also *HPC*, 1 May 1938, p.48; 1 Feb. 1939, p.33.

82 *Daily Telegraph*, 5 Mar. 1938, p.8. See also *HPC*, 1 July 1938, p.32.

83 Wellby, *Naked and Unashamed*, p.29.

84 Bain, *Nudism*, p.36.

85 *HPC*, 1 July 1935, p.31. They were only near-nude because it was the first day of their holiday. They soon discarded all clothes.

86 *HPC*, 1 May 1932, p.48.

87 *Man Junior*, Jan. 1938, pp.34-8. Quotes from pp.34, 35.

88 *Man Junior*, Jan. 1938, p.36.

89 Wellby, *Naked and Unashamed*, p.50.

90 *Here & Now*, Mar. 1957, p.26.

91 The paragraph was reprinted in the second issue of his magazine. *Health and Sunshine*, 16 Nov. 1936, p.2.

92 See *Daily Telegraph*, 21 Jan. 1938, p.10; Wellby, *Naked and Unashamed*, pp.62, 63.

93 *Health and Sunshine*, April–May 1937, p.5.

94 Little information is available on the nudist movement during the war years. It seems that many of the clubs formed in the 1930s disbanded during the 1940s. Wartime conditions meant people had neither the time nor the resources (esp. petrol for travel to secluded bush retreats) to continue nudist clubs.

95 On the transformative potential of leisure sites, see Rob Shields, *Places on the Margin: Alternative geographies of modernity*, London and New York, 1991.

96 *Truth*, 21 Dec. 1955, p.1.

97 *Daily Telegraph*, 21 Jan. 1938, p.10.

98 *Truth*, 25 Jan. 1956, p.15. See also a report of the expulsion of a man from a Lower Hutt nudist club for making indecent suggestions to a teenage girl, *Truth*, 3 Sept.1957, p.19.

99 *Health and Sunshine*, April–May 1937, p.5.

100 Wellby, *Naked and Unashamed*, p.29. See also Bain, *Nudism*, p.22.

101 For Germany see *Health and Sunshine*, April–May 1937, p.4; for the Dunedin Gymnosophy club see *HPC*, 1 Jan. 1935, p.47; for the West Auckland club, see *Australasian Sunbathing Quarterly Review*, Autumn 1948, p.16; for the Auckland Sunbathing Club, see *Australian Sunbather*, Sept.1948, p.30; for a report on the fourth annual national nudist rally, see *Truth*, 25 Jan. 1956, p.15; for a report on the Auckland Outdoor Health Club's first 40 years of existence, see *Bare In Mind: A Nudist News Service*, Nov. 1990, p.17.

102 Bain, *Nudism*, p.22; *Australasian Sunbathing Quarterly Review*, Summer 1949, p.19.

103 *Truth*, 21 Dec. 1955, p.1.

104 *Health and Sunshine*, April–May 1937, p.5.

105 See, for example, *Daily Telegraph*, 7 Feb. 1938, p.8; *Truth*, 12 Jan. 1955, p.5.

106 *Australasian Sunbathing Quarterly Review*, Summer 1949, p.9.

107 *Australian Sunbather*, July 1949, p.5.

108 *Australian Sunbather*, Sept.1950, p.16.

109 Writing about his experiences at the Cap d'Agde nudist resort, Paul Ableman noted that, during the entire week he was there, 'I never so much as brushed against another person'. For Ableman this was a most unnatural and unnerving experience. Paul Ableman, *The Banished Body*, London, 1984 (first published as *Anatomy of Nakedness*, 1982), p.103.

110 Even in the 1990s, 'older members' of the Auckland Outdoor Health Club argued that holding hands should not be allowed. *More Magazine*, Mar. 1996, pp.38, 39.

111 Bain, *Nudism*, p.62.

112 See, for example, Jonathon Harper's report on Auckland's nudist clubs, *Auckland Metro*, Mar. 1984, pp.103-12 and Cathrin Schaer's article on the 44th annual nudist rally, *More Magazine*, Mar. 1996, p.40.

113 Bain, *Nudism*, p.68.

114 In 1954 a commission on juvenile sexual immortality was held, following reports of teenagers engaging in after-school orgies. These activities, and the report of the commission, have generated a large body of historical literature. See, in particular, Susan Glazebrook, 'The Mazengarb Report, 1954: Impotent Victorianism', Research Essay, University of Auckland, 1978; Maureen Molloy, 'Science, Myth and the Adolescent Female: The Mazengarb Report, the Parker-Hulme Trial, and the Adoption Act of 1955', *Women's Studies Journal*, 9, 1, 1993, pp.1-25; Roy Shuker, Roger Openshaw and Janet Soler, *Youth, Media and Moral Panic in New Zealand*, Palmerston North, 1990; Janet Soler, 'Drifting Towards Moral Chaos: the 1954 Mazengarb Report', MPhil Thesis, Massey University, 1988; Redmer Yska, *All Shook Up: The Flash Bodgie and the Rise of the New Zealand Teenager in the Fifties*, Auckland, 1993.

115 Secretary for Justice to Minister of Justice, 29 June 1955. Nudist Literature. Justice (J), Series 1, W2304, 18/45/7, ANZ.

116 Secretary for Justice to Minister of Justice, 13 Nov. 1956. J, 1, W2304, 18/45/7, ANZ.

117 See the editorial in the New Zealand nudist quarterly, *National Review*, Autumn 1957, p.1. See also *Australian Sunbather*, April 1951, p.33. Some artists turned to nudist magazines to source pictures of the liberated

male body, a use of the photographs which the nudists did not anticipate. See David McCarthy, 'Social Nudism, Masculinity and the Male Nude in the Work of William Theo Brown and Wynn Chamberlain in the 1960s', *Archives of American Art Journal*, 38, 1-2, 1998, pp.28-38.

118 *Australian Sunbather*, Jan. 1952, p.24.

119 See, for example, *Truth*, 14 Sept.1955, p.25. See also a 1956 information brochure for the Wellington Sun and Health Society. J, 1, W2304, 18/45/7, ANZ. The claim was repeated in an article in praise of nudism which appeared in a New Zealand police training school magazine, and was reprinted in *Sun and Health* (International Edition), 29, 301, 1965, p.27. See also *New Zealand Naturist*, Winter 1967, p.25.

120 Secretary for Justice to Minister of Justice, 26 June 1956; Secretary for Justice to Minister of Justice, 13 Nov. 1956. J, 1, W2304, 18/45/7, ANZ; *Truth*, 15 Sept.1959, p.28.

121 *Health and Sunshine*, April–May 1937, p.5.

122 *Daily Telegraph*, 9 Mar. 1938, p.8.

123 *Man Junior*, Jan. 1938, p.38.

124 Ormond Wilson, *An Outsider Looks Back: Reflections on Experience*, Wellington, 1982, pp.36-7. Wilson was elected to parliament in 1935. Chris Maclean notes that Wilson introduced the concept of nude tramping to others, such as Bill Sutch. See Chris Maclean, *Tararua: the story of a mountain range*, Wellington, 1994, p.150.

125 *HPC*, 1 June 1933, pp.49, 62.

126 Bain, *Nudism*, p.65.

127 *Health and Efficiency*, Jan. 1945, p.8.

128 *Health and Efficiency*, Dec. 1946, p.278.

129 For the British movement and the idea of 'idyll-izing' the rural, see David Bell and Ruth Holliday, 'Naked as Nature Intended', *Body & Society*, 6, 3-4, 2000, pp.127-40. For examples of Australians arguing for the bush as their Eden, see *HPC*, 1 July 1935, pp.30-1, 52; *Man Junior*, Jan. 1938, pp.36-7.

130 *Man Junior*, Mar. 1939, p.107; June 1947, p.67.

131 *Man Junior*, Jan. 1946, p.33.

132 *Man Junior*, June 1947, p.67; Oct. 1959, p.10.

133 *Man Junior*, Dec. 1959, p.30.

134 *Truth*, 16 June 1937, p.17.

135 *Truth*, 30 June 1937, p.16; 7 July 1937, p.18.

136 *Truth*, 8 Nov. 1950, p.9.

137 *Auckland Star (AS)*, 5 Aug. 1975, p.23; 8 Aug. 1975, p.1; *NZH*, 9 Aug. 1975, p.3.

138 For discussion and advocacy of nudism on public beaches see, *Man*, Oct. 1939, p.75; *Truth*, 22 Sept.1959, p.14; 26 April 1960, p.3; 3 May 1960, p.13; *New Zealand Naturist*, Summer 1961, p.3; Summer 1963, p.10.

139 *Man*, Oct. 1939, p.75.

140 In 1961 Gerald Wakely suggested that the ultimate goal of the New Zealand nudist movement should be 'The abolition of nudist clubs *as nudist clubs* and the acceptance and tolerance of nudity on beaches'. His article first appeared in the Aug. 1961 issue of *New Zealand Naturist* and was reprinted in the Summer 1963 issue, p.10. Emphasis in original.

141 *AS*, 8 Aug. 1975, p.1.

142 *AS*, 8 Aug. 1975, p.1.

143 *AS*, 10 Sept.1976, p.8. See also *New Zealand Listener*, 16 Oct. 1976, p.113.

144 On police inaction see *AS*, 23 Sept.1975, p.3. For the poll of 2000 people, see *AS*, 5 Aug. 1975, p.23. The poll revealed that three-quarters of people under 40 (but only half of those other 40) supported 'open' beaches.

145 *New Zealand Woman's Weekly*, 3 April 1978, p.11.

146 *Star Weekender*, 10 Jan. 1981, p.1; *AS*, 25 Nov. 1983, Section B, p.1.

147 See, for example, *Auckland Metro*, Mar. 1984, pp.103-12; *Wellington Cosmo*, Feb. 1985, pp.79-83; *New Zealand Woman's Weekly*, 14 Sept.1987, pp.56-9; *Evening Post*, 15 Jan. 1996, p.9; *More Magazine*, Mar. 1996, pp.36-40, 42.

148 *New Zealand Listener*, 21 Feb. 1998, p.35.

SIX **SWINGS AND ROUNDABOUTS**

1 David Kirk, 'Gender Associations: Sport, State Schools and Australian Culture', *International Journal of the History of Sport*, 17, 2-3, 2000, p.55. See also Kirk's *Schooling Bodies: School Practice and Public Discourse 1880–1950*, London, 1998.

2 R. A. Stothart, *A Chronology of New Zealand Physical Education 1850–1990*, Wellington, 1991, p.2.

3 The Education Act, 1877, s. 85, *New Zealand Statutes, 1877*.

4 On school attendance in general see C. T. Paxton, 'Childhood in New Zealand, 1862–1921: Child Labour and the Gradual Popular Acceptance of Primary School Attendance', MA Thesis, University of Auckland, 1987. In 1883 physical education was made compulsory in Auckland primary schools. Stothart, *A Chronology*, p.4.

5 Judith Simon (ed.), *Nga Kura Maori: the Native Schools System 1867–1969*, Auckland, 1998, p.18.

6 W. A. Chapple, *Physical Education in our State Schools*, Wellington, 1894, p.4.

7 Chapple, *Physical Education*, pp.6-8.

8 Chapple, *Physical Education*, pp.11-12. Oscar David was expressing similar sentiments

around the same time. See Robert A. Stothart, *The Development of Physical Education in New Zealand*, Auckland, 1974, pp.4-6.

9   *White Ribbon*, Feb. 1896, pp.3-4. See also Stothart, *A Chronology*, p.5.

10   *Sandow's Magazine*, May 1900, p.442; Nov. 1901, p.394. In his 1897 book he advocated parents buying their babies 'light wooden dumb-bells as playthings'. Eugen Sandow, *Strength and How to Obtain It*, London, 1897, p.19.

11   *Sandow's Magazine*, Sept.1898, p.195.

12   See, for example, *Sandow's Magazine*, Nov. 1898, pp.375-83; July 1899, p.64; July 1900, p.75; Oct. 1900, p.287; Nov. 1900, p.387; Nov. 1901, pp.393-94; Jan. 1902, p.68.

13   *Sandow's Magazine*, Oct. 1901, p.310.

14   *Sandow's Magazine*, Jan. 1902, p.68.

15   *Sandow's Magazine*, June 1902, p.464.

16   *Sandow's Magazine*, June 1900, p.515.

17   Sandow, *Strength and How to Obtain It*, pp.19-22; Eugen Sandow, *Body-Building, or Man in the Making: How to Become Healthy & Strong*, London, 1904, esp. Ch. XV.

18   *Sandow's Magazine*, June 1900, p.515.

19   *Sandow's Magazine*, July 1900, p.76.

20   *Sandow's Magazine*, Sept.1900, p.163.

21   *New Zealand Parliamentary Debates* (*NZPD*), 116, 1901, p.300.

22   *AJHR*, 1902, E-1, p.xvii. There was no set syllabus in physical education for the teachers to follow.

23   John Welshman, 'Physical Culture and Sport in Schools in England and Wales, 1900–40', *International Journal of the History of Sport*, 15, 1, 1998, pp.54-75; Kirk, *Schooling Bodies*.

24   *New Zealand Graphic*, 27 Dec. 1902, p.1635.

25   *Wanganui Chronicle*, 28 Nov. 1902, p.2.

26   *AJHR*, 1902, E-12, p.10; 1903, E-12, p.15.

27   *Wanganui Chronicle*, 28 Nov. 1902, p.2.

28   *ODT*, 30 Dec. 1902, p.2.

29   See, for example, *Auckland Star* (*AS*), 7 Nov. 1903, p.5; *New Zealand Graphic*, 5 Dec. 1903, p.29; 28 Dec. 1903, p.33; 29 Oct. 1904, p.35; 19 Nov. 1904, p.30; *Lyttelton Times*, 31 Oct. 1906, p.6.

30   *New Zealand Graphic*, 24 Jan. 1903, p.237; 22 Aug. 1903, p.532.

31   *AJHR*, 1904, E-12, p.22.

32   *New Zealand Graphic*, 2 Jan. 1904, p.28.

33   *Canterbury Times*, 9 Mar. 1904, p.24.

34   *AJHR*, 1903, E-12, p.31. In 1903 the school had an average attendance of 120 pupils, 65 of whom attended Tankard's gym. *AJHR*, 1904, E-12, p.6.

35   In 1903, 100,280 children received instruction (*AJHR*, 1903, E-1, p.xvii). This increased to 109,648 in 1904 (*AJHR*, 1904, E-1, p.xvi) and 119,624 by 1905 (*AJHR*, 1905, E-1, p.xv).

In 1909 143,580 or 94 per cent of pupils at primary schools were being instructed in physical drill (*AJHR*, 1909, E-1, p.14).

36   Regarding Wanganui, see *AJHR*, 1905, E-1, p.75; for a complaint of lack of instruction see *NZPD*, 129, 1904, p.699; for reports of mass displays see *New Zealand Graphic*, 26 Mar. 1904, pp.22-3; *Press*, 27 Nov. 1905, p.7.

37   *Canterbury Times*, 11 Nov. 1908, p.32.

38   *AJHR*, 1910, E-3, p.5. See also Judith Simon and Linda Tuhiwai Smith (eds), *A Civilising Mission? Perceptions and Representations of the New Zealand Native Schools System*, Auckland, 2001, p.232.

39   *AJHR*, 1911, E-2, Appendix C, p.ix.

40   Letter from G. M. Burlinson, Manager, Industrial School, Caversham, to Secretary for Education, 24 June 1904. Caverhsam – Physical Training. Child Welfare (CW), W1043, 40/19/9, ANZ.

41   Memorandum to Secretary for Education, 13 Sept.1910. Boys' Training Farm – Weraroa – Instruction of Inmates – Physical Instruction. CW, W1043, 40/19/5, ANZ.

42   See, for example, the positive reports regarding instruction in the Wellington area (*AJHR*, 1909, E-2, Appendix C, p.103), South Canterbury (*AJHR*, 1911, E-2, Appendix A, p.xix) and Otago (*AJHR*, 1911, E-2, Appendix A, p.xxi). For reports on physical instruction within training colleges see *AJHR*, 1910, E-2, Appendix D, p.154; E-2, 1912, Appendix D, p.ix.

43   *Sandow's Magazine*, 10 Jan. 1907, p.57. This article was a comment on Gorst's recent book, *The Children of the Nation*.

44   *Canterbury Times*, 25 Nov. 1908, p.32.

45   *NZPD*, 129, 1904, p.699.

46   As a young man, Thomas Boothroyd Garlick, known as Royd, was a Brisbane bank clerk with a heart condition. He moved to New Zealand, took up physical culture and became a living specimen of the benefits of systematic exercise. R. A. Stothart, *A "Who's Who" of New Zealand Physical Education and Recreation*, Wellington, c. 1973, p.17.

47   Stothart, *A Chronology*, p.8. Stothart spells his name as Dovey while Bedggood writes Davey. See L. R. Bedggood, *Health and Physical Education in New Zealand*, Hamilton, 1954, p.17.

48   Diana McCurdy, 'Feminine Identity in New Zealand: The Girl Peace Scout Movement 1908–1925', MA thesis, University of Canterbury, 2000, p.126.

49   Resolutions Passed by the Advisory Committee in Regard to the Minister's Minute of Reference, 18 Sept.1912. Physical Education – Report of Advisory Committee

and Cabinet Approval of New Scheme. E-W, W1012, 36/1A, Box 42, ANZ.

50 Memorandum for Minister of Education, 1 Nov. 1912. E-W, W1012, 36/1A, Box 42, ANZ.

51 *NZPD*, 162, 1913, pp.301, 312, 328; *NZPD*, 166, 1913, pp.237, 277; *Auckland Truth*, 19 July 1913, p.7.

52 Welshman, 'Physical Culture and Sport in Schools in England and Wales, 1900–40', p.56; David Kirk and Karen Twigg, 'Regulating Australian Bodies: Eugenics, Anthropometrics and School Medical Inspections in Victoria, 1900-1940', *History of Education Review*, 23, 1, 1994, p.21.

53 Medical inspection of school children was inaugurated in 1912 with a staff of four doctors. On measuring and weighing school children see Memorandum from R. Crowe, Education Board, Auckland, to Inspector-General of Schools, Wellington, 17 Oct. 1912. Scheme of Medical Inspection and Physical Instruction – General. Education (E), Series 2, 1922/2b, E36/1/2, ANZ. Owing to funding, not all children were examined, but children in schools of over 120 pupils could expect to be examined when they were in Standard II and, if funding allowed, in Standard V. Teachers could also ask the school doctors to examine pupils identified as having a physical defect.

54 James C. Scott, *Seeing Like a State: How Certain Schemes to Improve the Human Condition Have Failed*, New Haven and London, 1998, p.92.

55 *AJHR*, 1913, E-1, p.10.

56 Bedggood, *Health and Physical Education in New Zealand*, p.19.

57 *New Zealand Gazette*, Volume II, 1913, p.3267. The government bought 3000 copies of the exercise book to assist teachers with this. *NZPD*, 163, 1913, p.197.

58 *AJHR*, 1913, E-1, p.10.

59 On Milnes see J. A. Mangan and Colm Hickey, 'A Pioneer of the Proletariat: Herbert Milnes and the Games Cult in New Zealand', *International Journal of the History of Sport*, 17, 2-3, 2000, pp.31-48.

60 *AJHR*, 1915, E-1, p.18.

61 See, for example, the criticism of the scheme in the Otago Education Board's annual report, *AJHR*, 1913, E-2, Appendix A, p.xxvi. See also T. B. Strong, Acting Senior Inspector, Education Board of the District of Wanganui, to Director of Education, Wellington, 8 Jan. 1916. Physical Instruction and Medical Inspection. E, W773, 36/1/3, ANZ.

62 *Lyttelton Times*, 7 April 1916, p.11.

63 Memorandum for Physical Instructors from Physical Education Branch, 7 Dec. 1915.

Physical Education – General – Special Classes for Physically Defective Children. E2, 1947/34a, E36/1/6, ANZ.

64 *AJHR*, 1917, E-1, p.22.

65 *AJHR*, 1917, E-11, p.1.

66 *AJHR*, 1917, E-11, p.8.

67 Memorandum for All Head Teachers of Public Schools, 31 July 1920. Physical Education – General – Table of Physical Exercises For Corrective Treatment. E, W773, 36/1/18, ANZ.

68 Education Department, *Syllabus of Physical Training For Schools*, Wellington, 1920, p.176. The syllabus was adapted, with permission, from the London Board of Education's system.

69 Education Department, *Syllabus of Physical Training For Schools*, p.1.

70 *AJHR*, 1923, E-1, p.12.

71 This is not to say that the state was not using education in general to reinforce gendered ideologies. For a discussion of this see Caroline Daley, *Girls & Women, Men & Boys: Gender in Taradale 1886–1930*, Auckland, 1999, pp.1-3, 48, 93, 115-16.

72 Education Department, *Syllabus of Physical Training For Schools*, p.2.

73 Mount Cook School Leaving Letter, MS-Papers-5564, ATL.

74 *AJHR*, 1927, E-1, p.12.

75 An editorial in the *New Zealand New Health Journal* condemned the 'lamentable laxity of parents and guardians with regard to the need of physical exercise of the right kind and quality' for youth. *New Zealand New Health Journal*, 19 April 1927, p.1.

76 Memorandum from A. P. Roydhouse, Physical Instructor, Education Department, Dunedin to Chief Physical Instructor, Education Department, Wellington, 14 April 1928. Special & Industrial Schools – Instruction of Inmates – Special School for Boys' – Otekaike – Physical Instruction. CW, W1043, 40/19/45, ANZ.

77 Forms – Physical Education, Area Organization. E, W773, 38/9/1, ANZ.

78 Inspection Report on the Physical Training of The Otago Boys' High School, 12 Nov. 1929. Physical Education Inspection of School Work. E, W773, 36/1/1, ANZ. Northey was a gold medal pupil, who had moved to Dunedin in 1907 and established his own physical culture studio. He was appointed to OBHS in 1920. Stothart, *A "Who's Who"*, p.46.

79 Maori and Pakeha, A Study in Comparative Health (Report by Dr Turbott, Medical Officer of Health and School Medical Officer, Gisborne, 1929). Physical Education

– General – Physique of School Children. E, W773, 36/1/26, ANZ.

80 Extract from report by Dr. Gurr [*sic*] School Medical Officer for the month ending 20th July 1928 on 'Sunlight Treatment'. Medical Inspection of Schools – Sunlight Treatment for School Children. Health (H), Series 1, 35/86, ANZ.

81 *ODT*, 6 July 1928, p.10.

82 See, for example, *ODT*, 7 July 1928, p.10; Memorandum to the Director, Education Department, 19 July 1928. E, W773, 36/1/26, ANZ.

83 *ODT*, 11 Aug. 1928, p.20.

84 *AS*, 6 July 1929, p.12.

85 P. A. Smithells, 'James Renfrew White: A Tribute', *New Zealand Journal of Physical Education*, 26, April 1962, p.48; Stothart, *The Development of Physical Education*, p.22.

86 *National Education*, 1 July 1939, p.223.

87 J. Renfrew White, *The Growing Body: Its Nature, Needs and Training*, Dunedin, 1932. It remained the core text from 1932 to 1937.

88 J. Renfrew White, *Your Children's Health and Physique: A Book for Parents*, Dunedin, 1932.

89 See, for example, White, *The Growing Body*, p.370.

90 *Ibid.*, p.363.

91 *New Zealand Education Gazette*, XI, 2, 1 Feb. 1932, pp.1, 12, 30; *New Zealand Herald (NZH)*, 8 Feb. 1932, p.11.

92 On the importance of posture in British schools at this time see Richenda Power, 'Healthy Motion: Images of "Natural" and "Cultured" Movement in Early Twentieth-Century Britain', *Women's Studies International Forum*, 19, 5, 1996, p.553.

93 *AS*, 2 Oct. 1929, p.9.

94 *NZH*, 31 July 1929, p.16.

95 *Truth*, 30 Dec. 1922, p.4.

96 *HPC*, 1 June 1930, p.5; 1 Dec. 1934, p.18.

97 White, *Your Children's Health and Physique*, pp.126-30.

98 *AS*, 2 Mar. 1927, p.11; *Dominion*, 1 Dec. 1928, p.8; *AS*, 6 July 1929, p.12; *Truth*, 12 Feb. 1931, p.16; *Wanganui Herald*, 20 April 1931, p.4; *Press*, 5 Dec. 1931, p.15.

99 Edith M. Hart, 'The Organised Activities of Christchurch Children Outside the School', MA Thesis, Canterbury University College, 1934, pp.15-16, 31-2. Hay was the national president of the YMCA at this time.

100 *NZH*, 18 April 1931, p.8.

101 *HPC*, 1 June 1930, p.41; 1 July 1936, p.56.

102 *Evening Post*, 1 May 1930, p.18. See also *Evening Post*, 14 July 1930, p.8; *Wanganui Herald*, 20 April 1931, p.4.

103 *HPC*, 1 Aug. 1938, pp.14-15.

104 Director to Minister of Education, 1 June

1935. Physical Education – Scheme & General. E, W773, 36/1/27, ANZ.

105 Children's Playgrounds, c. Jan. 1940. Children's Playgrounds – Layout of etc. – General File. Internal Affairs (IA), Series 1, 139/45/2, ANZ.

106 Dr J. W. Barrett, 'Garden Cities, Town-Planning, and Public Recreation Centres', in Australasian Medical Congress, *Transactions of the Tenth Session, Held in Auckland, New Zealand, Feb., 1914*, Wellington, 1916, pp.96-104. See also Dominick Cavallo, *Muscles and Morals: Organized Playgrounds and Urban Reform, 1880–1920*, Philadelphia, 1981.

107 See, for example, Charles Zueblin, 'Municipal Playgrounds in Chicago', *American Journal of Sociology*, 4, 2, Sept.1898, pp.145-58; Sadie American, 'The Movement for Small Playgrounds', *American Journal of Sociology*, 4, 2, Sept.1898, pp.159-70; Henry S. Curtis, 'The Playground Survey', *American Journal of Sociology*, 19, 6, May 1914, pp.792-812.

108 *Sandow's Magazine*, 15 June 1905, pp.607-09. Quote from p.609. For more on Chicago's playgrounds see *Sandow's Magazine*, 14 Mar. 1907, pp.322-3; 28 Mar. 1907, pp.409-10.

109 *Sandow's Magazine*, 24 Jan. 1907, p.113.

110 *Canterbury Times*, 29 July 1908, p.74.

111 *Auckland Truth*, 4 Oct. 1913, p.4.

112 Town Clerk to City Engineer, 13 Nov. 1916, and City Engineer to Town Clerk, 21 Nov. 1916. Myers Park (General). Series 275, Box 15, Item 17/129, ACCA.

113 For a copy of the league's 'Open Letter to the Acting-Premier and the Hon. Minister of Education' see The Rights of Childhood League. Series 275, Box 29, Item 19/215, ACCA. The league was led by unionist and poet 'Billy Banjo' (Edward Hunter). See Len Richardson, '"Billy Banjo": Coalminer, Socialist, Poet and Novelist', in Pat Moloney and Kerry Taylor (eds), *On the Left: Essays on Socialism in New Zealand*, Dunedin, 2002, pp.73-86.

114 Margaret Wood, 'A Daughter of John Court Remembers', *Auckland-Waikato Historical Journal*, 41, Sept.1982, p.15. I am grateful to Helen Laurenson for this reference.

115 *AS*, 11 Feb. 1925, p.7.

116 *AS*, 3 Sept.1926, p.9.

117 W. S. Moxson, Secretary, Auckland LRC, NZ Labour Party, to Councillor E. Phelan, 2 Sept.1926. Parks and Reserves – General. Series 275, Box 113, Item 26/334, Part 1, ACCA.

118 Parks Committee Minutes, 28 Aug. 1923. Series 107, Item 1, ACCA.

119 *AS*, 15 Dec. 1926, p.6.

120 Nellie E. Ferner, Hon. Superintendent,

Auckland Civic League, to the Mayor, 7 Feb. 1921. Children's Games in Parks. Series 275, Box 50, Item 22/304, ACCA.

121 *AS*, 1 Dec. 1926, p.11. The article noted that, during the previous Christmas holidays, the Play Association had also provided some supervision. During the summer of 1926–27 they provided supervision at Grey Lynn Park between 11 a.m. and 5 p.m. each day. Parks Committee Minutes, 14 Dec. 1926. Series 107, Item 1, ACCA.

122 *AS*, 2 Dec. 1926, p.8; 1 Dec. 1926, p.11.

123 See Myers Park, Resignation of W. Smith as Caretaker. Series 275, Box 41, Item 21/654, ACCA; Parks Committee Minutes, 10 May 1921 and 22 Nov. 1921. Series 107, Item 1, ACCA.

124 See Lady Supervisor of Children's Games: Reports and General. Series 275, Box 78, Item 32/299, ACCA. On Moore Park see *HPC*, 1 Mar. 1937, p.59. See also Minutes of Play Area Committee Meeting, 18 Mar. 1932, Wellington Boys' and Girls' Institute Records, 90-048, ATL.

125 Memorandum from Stipendiary Magistrate in charge of Children's Court, Auckland, to Town Clerk, 1 Aug. 1932. Series 275, Box 78, Item 32/299, ACCA.

126 Minutes of the Deputations to the Parks Committee, 2 Aug. 1932. Series 275, Box 78, Item 32/299, ACCA.

127 Letter from Superintendent of Parks to Town Clerk, 15 Aug. 1932. Series 275, Box 78, Item 32/299, ACCA.

128 Open Letter to the Acting-Premier and the Hon. Minister of Education. Series 275, Box 29, Item 19/215, ACCA.

129 Copy of Report Received From the Supervisor of Children's Games, Dated 19th July 1937. Series 275, Box 78, Item 32/299, ACCA.

130 Parks Committee Minutes, 8 Sept. 1925 and 23 Feb. 1926. Series 107, Item 2, ACCA.

131 Copy of Report Received From the Supervisor of Children's Games, Dated 16th July 1934. Series 275, Box 78, Item 32/299, ACCA.

132 See, for example, George D. Butler (ed.), *Playgrounds: Their Administration and Operation*, New York, 1936, pp.53-4.

133 Copy of Report Received From the Supervisor of Children's Games, Dated 30th Jan. 1933. Series 275, Box 78, Item 32/299, ACCA.

134 Copy of Report Received From the Supervisor of Children's Games, Dated 30th Jan. 1935. Series 275, Box 78, Item 32/299, ACCA.

135 Copy of Report Received From the Supervisor of Children's Games, Dated 31st Jan. 1938. Series 275, Box 78, Item 32/299, ACCA.

136 Copy of Report Received From the Supervisor of Children's Games, Dated 19th May 1936. Series 275, Box 78, Item 32/299, ACCA. See also Copy of Report Received From the Supervisor of Children's Games, Dated 8th Feb. 1937; Copy of Report Received From the Supervisor of Children's Games, Dated 19th July 1937. Series 275, Box 78, Item 32/299, ACCA.

137 Copy of Report Received From the Supervisor of Children's Games, Dated 7th Sept.1936; Copy of Report Received From the Supervisor of Children's Games, Dated 8th Feb. 1937. Series 275, Box 78, Item 32/299, ACCA.

138 In 1935 the council voted ten to nine that play equipment no longer be locked up on Sundays. *Truth*, 13 Feb. 1935, p.22.

139 *Truth*, 10 June 1922, p.2.

140 Parks Committee Minutes, 6 May 1924. Series 107, Item 1, ACCA.

141 Copy of Report Received From the Supervisor of Children's Games, Dated 26th July, 1932; 5th September, 1932; 15th May 1933; 5th June 1933; 30th Oct. 1933; Dated 12th Dec. 1933; Dated 4th April 1934. Series 275, Box 78, Item 32/299, ACCA.

142 Copy of Report Received From the Supervisor of Children's Games, Dated 26th July, 1932. Series 275, Box 78, Item 32/299, ACCA.

143 See, for example, *Auckland Truth*, 20 Jan. 1917, p.2 and 24 Jan. 1920, p.6; M. Beaumont, Dis. Secy Auckland Mothers Union, 7 Sept.1926, and Sister Esther, Hon. Sec. Auckland Social Workers' Assn, to Town Clerk, 12 Dec. 1929. Series 275, Box 113, Item 26/334, Part 1, ACCA; *Truth*, 5 June 1930, p.7.

144 On the men's toilets see Vernon Drew, Gen. Sec., Auckland YMCA, to Town Clerk, 6 Dec. 1926, and T. E. Pearson, Superintendent of Parks, to Town Clerk, 11 Dec. 1926. Myers Park – General. Series 275, Box 72, Item 24/325, ACCA. On the women's toilets see Mrs Jolly to City Council, c. 25 Aug. 1940, and Superintendent of Parks to Town Clerk, 29 Aug. 1940. Series 275, Box 72, Item 24/325, ACCA.

145 Copy of Report Received From the Supervisor of Children's Games, Dated 25th Nov. 1935. Series 275, Box 78, Item 32/299, ACCA.

146 Copy of Report Received From the Supervisor of Children's Games, Dated 17th Oct. 1932. Series 275, Box 78, Item 32/299, ACCA.

147 Copy of Report Received From the Supervisor of Children's Games, Dated 9th Jan. 1933; 16th July 1934; 25th Nov. 1935; 25th Feb. 1936; 5th April 1937; 23rd May 1938. Series 275, Box 78, Item 32/299, ACCA.

148 Education Department, *Syllabus of Physical Training For Schools*, p.175.

149 Memorandum for Principals of Training
     Colleges, 29 April 1930. E, W773, 36/1/27,
     ANZ.

SEVEN STATE EXPERIMENTS

1 *Truth*, 25 Nov. 1936, p.5.
2 The full title of the legislation was 'An Act
   to provide for the Development of Facilities
   for, and the Encouragement of, Physical
   Training, Exercise, Sport, and Recreation, and
   to facilitate the Establishment of Centres for
   Social Activities related thereto'. It was passed
   in Nov. 1937.
3 *Truth*, 25 Nov. 1936, p.5.
4 Auckland Police Athletic Carnival 24–25
   Nov. 1919, Programme, back cover. Sport
   – Athletics Folder, Ephemera Collection,
   Special Collections, Auckland City Libraries.
5 *Truth*, 2 Aug. 1924, p.4.
6 *AJHR*, 1937, H-22, p.2; *Truth*, 10 Mar. 1937,
   p.11.
7 *AJHR*, 1938, H-22, p.3.
8 *NZPD*, 249, 1937, p.415.
9 See, in particular, the speech of Colonel
   Hargest, the Opposition Member for Awarua,
   who was the most vocal critic of the bill.
   NZPD, 249, 1937, pp.421-3.
10 *Press*, 16 Nov. 1937, p.10.
11 *NZPD*, 249, 1937, p.530.
12 *Ibid*., pp.531-3. As Mariel Grant has pointed
    out, Neville Chamberlain made a speech in
    Oct. 1936, suggesting government plans to
    conduct a campaign to support the nation's
    physical fitness. It is unclear whether Parry
    was familiar with this speech. Mariel Grant,
    'The National Health Campaigns of 1937–
    1938', in Derek Fraser (ed.), *Cities, Class and
    Communication: Essays in Honour of Asa Briggs*,
    London, 1990, p.217.
13 *NZPD*, 249, 1937, pp.531-3. Germany was
    also mentioned by Mr McKeen (Wellington
    South), p.518, Mr Fagan, the Leader of the
    Legislative Council, p.610, and Mr Ward,
    p.613.
14 *NZPD*, 249, 1937, p.518.
15 For example, when the National Fitness
    Council was established in England,
    opponents claimed it was 'a portent of
    militarism'. Jeffrey Hill, *Sport, Leisure
    and Culture In Twentieth-Century Britain*,
    Basingstoke, 2002, p.152.
16 Janet Alexander, 'Recreation: An
    Inappropriate Concept for Legislation? An
    examination of two attempts at legislating
    for recreation in New Zealand: The Physical
    Welfare and Recreation Act 1937; and The
    Recreation and Sports Act 1973', Research
    Essay, Victoria University of Wellington,
    1981, p.50, note 10.

17 J. W. Heenan, Under-Secretary, to Dr Hercus,
    Medical School, University of Otago, 16
    Nov. 1937. Sport – Physical Education
    – Regulations for course – Otago University.
    Internal Affairs (IA), Series 1, 139/9, ANZ;
    Dominion, 16 Nov. 1937, p.8.
18 See, for example, the parliamentary debate
    on the bill's second reading, *NZPD*, 249,
    1937, pp.421-3; *Press*, 16 Nov. 1937, p.10;
    Dominion, 20 Nov. 1937, p.13.
19 For example, the act is not mentioned in
    Bruce Brown, *The Rise of New Zealand Labour:
    A history of the New Zealand Labour Party from
    1916 to 1940*, Wellington, 1962 or in the
    biographies of John A. Lee (Erik Olssen, *John
    A. Lee*, Dunedin, 1977) or Michael Savage
    (Barry Gustafson, *From The Cradle To The
    Grave: A biography of Michael Joseph Savage*,
    Auckland, 1988).
20 It does not, for example, rate a mention in
    Geoffrey W. Rice (ed.), *The Oxford History
    of New Zealand*, 2nd edn, Auckland, 1992
    or Keith Sinclair (ed.), *The Oxford Illustrated
    History of New Zealand*, Auckland, 1990.
    Although there is a brief reference to Parry's
    efforts in *Paradise Reforged*, the details are
    inaccurate (James Belich, *Paradise Reforged: A
    History of the New Zealanders, From the 1880s
    to the Year 2000*, Auckland, 2001, p.529).
    The exceptions to this claim are Michael
    Bassett's history of the Department of Internal
    Affairs (Michael Bassett, *The Mother of All
    Departments: The History of the Department of
    Internal Affairs*, Auckland, 1997) and those
    studies only concerned with recreation. For
    example, the act has been studied by a couple
    of thesis students: Alexander, 'Recreation:
    An Inappropriate Concept for Legislation?';
    Hugh D. Buchanan, 'A Critical Analysis of the
    1937 Physical Welfare and Recreation Act and
    of Government Involvement in Recreation
    and Sport, 1937–1957', MA (Applied) Thesis,
    Victoria University of Wellington, 1978.
21 Mr Holland, the member for Christchurch
    North, raised the spectre of C3 nationhood
    in his speech on the bill's second reading,
    NZPD, 249, 1937, p.520. Parry made
    extensive comments about the advancements
    in science and engineering and their
    consequences for physical fitness in a speech
    to the New Zealand Institute of Public
    Administrators a year after the legislation
    was passed. William Edward Parry, 'The Old
    and New Order of Things', 17 Nov. 1938,
    qMS-1629, ATL. For an example of another
    government being motivated by similar
    concerns, see Grant, 'The National Health
    Campaigns of 1937–1938', esp. pp.217-18.
22 *Truth*, 18 Aug. 1927, p.6.

23 For example, the Shops and Offices Amendment Act, 1936, introduced a 44-hour week, while the Factories Amendment Act, 1936 and the Industrial, Conciliation and Arbitration Amendment Act, 1936, worked on a 40-hour week.

24 *New Zealand Medical Journal*, XXXV, June 1936, p.144.

25 The eugenic C3 and A1 rankings appeared in numerous articles at this time. For example, see *Health and Sunshine*, 16 Nov. 1936, p.2; *New Zealand Illustrated Sporting and Dramatic Review*, 21 April 1938, p.32; *Truth*, 6 Sept.1939, p.17.

26 Hindman was writing for one of Trevor Bain's magazines, *Human Touch*, July–Aug. 1936, p.28. For articles expressing similar sentiments see *New Zealand Illustrated Sporting and Dramatic Review*, 10 Feb. 1937, p.19; *Truth*, 13 Oct. 1937, p.34; *New Zealand Illustrated Sporting and Dramatic Review*, 18 Nov. 1937, p.10.

27 *HPC*, 1 Oct. 1937, pp.27-9.

28 *HPC*, 1 Sept.1937, pp.26-7. See also *HPC*, 1 April 1937, pp.24-5, 51; 1 July 1942, pp.36-7, 47.

29 For details on the council and the general workings of the act, see Buchanan, 'A Critical Analysis of the 1937 Physical Welfare and Recreation Act', esp. pp.34-46.

30 Physical Fitness Campaign, Feb. 1939. Suggested Skeleton Programme for Guidance of Local Authorities' Physical Welfare Committee. Joseph William Allan Heenan Papers. Folder 283, MS-Papers-1132, ATL.

31 Patrick Day, *The Radio Years: A History of Broadcasting in New Zealand*, Volume One, Auckland, 1994, pp.213-14.

32 Letter from J. W. Heenan to Messrs. Carlton-Cruthers Ltd., 6 Feb. 1939. Physical Fitness Week – Radio Broadcasts. IA, Series 1, 139/32/1, ANZ.

33 Speech Notes for Minister of Internal Affairs, Opening Ceremony of Fitness Week, 18 Feb. 1939 [broadcast on 2YA national hook-up]. IA, Series 1, 139/32/1, ANZ.

34 Speech Notes for Governor-General's Address to 'Fitness Week' [2YA national hook-up on Sunday 19 Feb. 1939]. IA, Series 1, 139/32/1, ANZ.

35 *AS*, 18 Feb. 1939, p.17; 25 Feb. 1939, p.12.

36 The Saturday shows were broadcast later in the morning. *New Zealand Illustrated Sporting and Dramatic Review*, 2 June 1938, p.10; 1 Sept.1938, p.10.

37 In 1937 the Australian government began to use the 'A' class radio stations to disseminate health knowledge. *HPC*, 1 July 1937, p.7. Tom Langridge, a well-known Sydney

physical culturist, was unhappy with the rote exercises and cheery music format, and began his own show on 2KY. *HPC*, 1 Jan. 1941, pp.38, 41. On the situation in Britain and Europe see Grant, 'The National Health Campaigns of 1937–1938', pp.227-8.

38 See, for example, the editorials in the *AS* at the beginning and end of the week: *AS*, 18 Feb. 1939, p.8; 25 Feb. 1939, p.8.

39 The term 'spectatoritis' was used in an article 'Youth Faces the Problem of Leisure', *HPC*, 1 April 1937, p.51. Many commentators noted the general problem of people being spectators rather than participants. See, for example, Talk Over 2YA [7 Aug. 1939, Miss Black]; Talk Over 3YA – Aug. 28th 1939 by Miss Black. Propaganda and Publicity – Radio Talks – Preparation Of For Daily Newspapers. IA, Series 1, 139/43/2, ANZ; *NZH*, 30 Sept.1939, p.14 and 2 Oct. 1939, p.6; *New Zealand Listener*, 12 July 1940, p.22.

40 *NZH*, 20 Feb. 1939, p.11.

41 *AS*, 18 Feb. 1939, p.24.

42 *NZH*, 18 Feb. 1939, p.24.

43 See reports in the daily press 18–27 Feb. 1939.

44 *AS*, 20 Feb. 1939, p.11.

45 *AS*, 22 Feb. 1939, p.14.

46 *NZH*, 27 Feb. 1939, p.11.

47 The Physical Welfare & Recreation Branch. Report Dealing With Activities of Branch Since Last Meeting of Council in Mar., 1939. Sport – Circulars Issued by Physical Welfare and Recreation Branch. IA, Series 1, 139/85, ANZ.

48 Memorandum for Minister of Internal Affairs, 28 Mar. 1939. Sport – Publication – Booklet or folder of exercises – Printing of – General File. IA, Series 1, 139/59, ANZ.

49 Memorandum from the Acting Minister in Charge of Broadcasting to the Minister of Internal Affairs, 30 May 1939; Memorandum from Minister of Internal Affairs to Acting Minister in Charge of Broadcasting, 8 June 1939. Physical Fitness and Recreation – Newspaper and Radio Propaganda and Publicity – General File. IA, Series 1, 139/43, ANZ.

50 Sport – Publication – Booklet or folder of exercises – Printing of – General File. IA, Series 1, 139/59, ANZ.

51 Buchanan, 'A Critical Analysis of the 1937 Physical Welfare and Recreation Act', esp. pp.20-2.

52 Letter from Miss Emmie Cannell, Ngunguru School (via Whangarei) to Miss Kennedy, 7 Oct. 1939. Scheme for Maori Recreation – General File. IA, Series 1, 139/2/3, ANZ.

53 Memorandum from Assistant Secretary

of Department of Labour (Employment Division) to Under-Secretary of Department of Internal Affairs, 14 July 1939. Investigation of Boys' and Girls' Leisure Time Activities – General File. IA, Series 1, 139/30, ANZ. The file also contains a copy of the Government Youth Survey of Juvenile Leisure-Time Activities, conducted between 1 Nov. 1938 – 31 Jan. 1939. The survey asked 1157 young people in Auckland, Wellington, Christchurch and Dunedin about their indoor and outdoor activities.

54 Neighbourhood Playgrounds [talk on 2YA, 30 May 1939, C. R. Bach]. IA, Series 1, 139/43/2, ANZ.

55 For statements along these lines, see, for example: Play-Ground Theatres. Sunbeams for Footlights. Propaganda and Publicity – Radio Talks – Preparation Of For Daily Newspapers. IA, Series 1, 139/43/1, ANZ; Lecture 2. Leisure Time Activities in the Community, as Applied to Children, Adolescents and Adults. Children [undated and unsourced 8 p. transcript]. IA, Series 1, 139/30, ANZ; Talk Over 2YA [7 Aug. 1939, Miss Black]. IA, Series 1, 139/43/2, ANZ.

56 In Auckland, young women volunteers from local secondary schools and groups like the Girls' Life Brigade were very important in the success of the playground scheme. These young women underwent a leadership training course with branch officers, before working in the parks. Note on file from G. M. Gebbie, 27 Nov. 1940; Note on file from G. M. Gebbie, 9 Dec. 1940. Auckland Area Instructors – Women Leader's Class. IA, Series 1, 139/104, ANZ; Holiday Recreation – Playground Scheme [c. 1944]. Auckland Area Instructors – Children's Playgrounds – Supervision and General File re. IA, Series 1, 139/104/6, ANZ.

57 Note on File, Pt. Chevalier, 23 Oct. 1940, written by Gladys M. Gebbie, Recreation Officer, Auckland. Auckland Area Instructors – Women's Swimming Club. IA, Series 1, 139/104/5, ANZ.

58 Memorandum for Under-Secretary, 12 Feb. 1940. Sport – Physical Education in Australia – Visit of Miss Black – Report re. IA, Series 1, 139/107, ANZ.

59 Children's Playground – Victoria Park. Report for the Period 19th Dec., 1941 to 31st Jan., 1942 (School Holiday Period). IA, Series 1, 139/104/6, ANZ.

60 Lecture 2. Leisure Time Activities in the Community, as Applied to Children, Adolescents and Adults. Children [undated and unsourced eight-page transcript]. IA, Series 1, 139/30, ANZ.

61 See, for example, the hopeful claim of the Auckland officer in Report on Victoria Park Playground for three months ended 30th April, 1942. IA, Series 1, 139/104/6, ANZ.

62 HPC, 1 July 1936, p.56.

63 New Zealand Illustrated Sporting and Dramatic Review, 21 Oct. 1937, p.3.

64 Letter from Charlie Dawson, Auckland to Bill [W. E. Parry], 18 Aug. 1939. District Committee – Auckland City. IA, Series 1, 139/21/12, ANZ.

65 Address Given by Mr C. R. Bach, BSc, 21 Feb. 1939. IA, Series 1, 139/32/1, ANZ.

66 Letter of Introduction for Noel Gibson from Herr E. Ramm, Consul General of Germany, Wellington, 1 Mar. 1939. Sport – Visit of Mr. Noel Gibson to European Counties – Report of. IA, Series 1, 139/48, ANZ.

67 Memorandum from Auckland Area Physical Welfare Officer to Under-Secretary, Department of Internal Affairs, 14 Feb. 1941. Scheme for the Enrolment in Physical Welfare and Recreation Activities of Children Leaving School. IA, Series 1, 139/89, ANZ.

68 See the file Scheme for the Enrolment in Physical Welfare and Recreation Activities of Children Leaving School. IA, Series 1, 139/89, ANZ.

69 Memorandum from Under-Secretary of Department of Internal Affairs to All Physical Welfare Officers, 1 June 1943. IA, Series 1, 139/30, ANZ.

70 HPC, 1 July 1935, pp.56-7.

71 See, for example, HPC, 1 July 1938, p.7; 1 Feb. 1939, p.24. Around the time that Parry's legislation was being introduced into parliament, Truth began a weekly 'Why Grow Old?' column for women. Written by 'Hygeia', the first column (6 Oct. 1937, p.25) dealt with exercise in general. The next (13 Oct. 1937, p.25) provided instruction on limbering up for swimming. Later columns dealt with exercises and picnics (10 Nov. 1937, p.27) and how to improve your silhouette for summer (24 Nov. 1937, p.31).

72 New Zealand Illustrated Sporting and Dramatic Review, 17 Mar. 1938, p.11.

73 The film screened in New Zealand around the same time as Parry's legislation was passed. For one of many reports on it, see Hawke's Bay Herald, 5 Jan. 1938, p.10.

74 Notes for the Hon. Minister's Private Secretary on Certain Phases of Physical Fitness Campaign. Propaganda and Publicity - Speeches and Addresses – Preparation of. IA, Series 1, 139/43/3, ANZ.

75 Circular for Members of the Short Training Course Held May 15th–19th [1939]. Teachers of Physical Recreation in Girls' Clubs

– Proposal to Hold Course in Wellington, 1939. IA, Series 1, 139/56, ANZ.

76 Arrangements with Various Women's Organisations – General file re. IA, Series 1, 139/65, ANZ.

77 Talk Over 3YA – Aug. 28th 1939 by Miss Black. IA, Series 1, 139/43/2, ANZ.

78 Physical Welfare and Recreation – A Modern Crusade [c. 16 April 1940]. IA, Series 1, 139/43/1, ANZ.

79 Memorandum from Physical Welfare Officer, Auckland, to Under-Secretary, Department of Internal Affairs, 19 June 1942. Recreation – Arrangements for American Forces – General File. IA, Series 1, 139/164, ANZ.

80 Letter from Physical Welfare Officer, Gisborne, to Under-Secretary of Department of Internal Affairs, 2 Sept.1941. IA, Series 1, 139/2/3, ANZ.

81 Memorandum from Chief Physical Welfare Officer to Under-Secretary, Department of Internal Affairs, 11 Nov. 1941. IA, Series 1, 139/2/3, ANZ. While the answer was 'yes', no such person was appointed.

82 Press Release from Parry, 27 June 1941. IA, Series 1, 139/43/1, ANZ.

83 Fitness for Service [c. 6 Nov. 1941]. IA, Series 1, 139/43/2, ANZ.

84 *Physical Welfare Bulletin*, Vol. V, Aug. 1941, pp.27-8.

85 See file Auckland Area Instructors – Women's Swimming Club. IA, Series 1, 139/104/5, ANZ; *AJHR*, 1944, H-22B, pp.2-3.

86 Material for B.B.C. Middle East Broadcast Recording [c. 24 Oct. 1941]. IA, Series 1, 139/43/2, ANZ.

87 *AJHR*, 1941, H-22, p.8; 1942, H-22, p.3.

88 *Physical Welfare Bulletin*, Vol. VII, Oct. 1941, p.36.

89 E. Jenkins to Secretary, National Council of Physical Welfare and Recreation, 6 May 1938. Sport – Proposed Establishment of Physical Culture Classes for Public Service. IA, W2578, 139/33, ANZ.

90 Business Arising from the Third Meeting of the National Council of Physical Welfare and Recreation, Wednesday, 14th September, 1938; Memorandum for Minister of Internal Affairs from J. W. Heenan, Under-Secretary, 27 Feb. 1939. IA, W2578, 139/33, ANZ.

91 Chair and Honorary Secretary, Public Service Sports Society, To Under-Secretary, Department of Internal Affairs, 26 Oct. 1939. IA, W2578, 139/33, ANZ.

92 Memorandum for Under-Secretary, Department of Internal Affairs, from C. R. Bach, Physical Welfare Officer, 31 Jan. 1940. IA, W2578, 139/33, ANZ; Memorandum for Commissioner of Police, 19 Aug. 1941.

Sport – Physical Training scheme – Adoption by Police Department – Co-operation re – General File. IA, Series 1, 139/145, ANZ; Memorandum from W. E. Parry to Under-Secretary, Department of Internal Affairs, 4 Sept.1943. Recreation – Girls Employed in Refreshment Rooms – Mercer. IA, Series 1, 139/104/25, ANZ.

93 Memorandum for Under-Secretary, Department of Internal Affairs, from C. R. Bach, Physical Welfare Officer, 31 Jan. 1940. IA, W2578, 139/33, ANZ.

94 Letter from Auckland Area Physical Welfare Officer to Secretary, Employers' Association, Auckland, 12 Feb. 1941. Auckland Area Instructors – Lunch Hour Recreation – Factory Workers etc. IA, Series 1, 139/104/7, ANZ.

95 Factory Recreation in Wellington. Sport – Factory Recreation – General file re. IA, Series 1, 139/155, ANZ.

96 On interwar programmes in department stores see Evan Roberts, 'From Mail Order to Female Order? The Work Culture of Department Store Employees in New Zealand, 1890–1960', Research Essay, Victoria University of Wellington, 1999, pp.65-70, 84-6.

97 Note on File, 27 June 1940, written by Gladys M. Gebbie, Recreation Officer, Auckland. Auckland Area Instructors – Women's Activities – General File. IA, Series 1, 139/104/2, ANZ.

98 Note on File, 13 June 1940, written by Gladys M. Gebbie, Recreation Officer, Auckland. IA, Series 1, 139/104/2, ANZ.

99 *Truth*, 23 Aug. 1944, p.16; 24 Jan. 1945, p.17.

100 Extract for memorandum from the Under-Secretary to the Hon. Minister of Internal Affairs, dated 19th April, 1939. Sport – Weekend Recreation Camps – Establishment of – Suggestion re. IA, W2578, 139/82/1, ANZ.

101 On the failed attempted at RÿGen see Peter Monteath, 'Swastikas By The Seaside', *History Today*, 50, 5, 2000, pp.31-5. Building began in 1936 but was never completed.

102 Letter from Mrs E. J. C. Bennet, Christchurch, to W. E. Parry, Minister of Internal Affairs, 12 Sept.1939. Weekend Recreation Camps – Establishment of – For Assistance re – Labour Representation Committee – Christchurch. IA, Series 1, 139/82, ANZ; Memorandum from W. E. Parry to Under-Secretary of Internal Affairs, 18 July 1944. Holiday Camps for Workers – General File. IA, Series 1, 139/104/28, ANZ; Letter from General Secretary of the Northern Industrial District Amalgamated Engineering, Coachbuilding & Related Trades

Industrial Union of Workers, to W. E. Parry, 9 Aug. 1944. IA, Series 1, 139/104/28, ANZ.

103 Letter from W. E. Parry, Minister of Internal Affairs, to Mrs E. J. C. Bennet, Christchurch, 10 Oct. 1939. IA, Series 1, 139/82, ANZ; *Public Service Journal*, Feb. 1942, p.91, in Joseph William Allan Heenan Papers, Folder 283, MS-Papers-1132, ATL; Memorandum from W. E. Parry to Under-Secretary of Internal Affairs, 18 July 1944; Letter from W. E. Parry to General Secretary of the Northern Industrial District Amalgamated Engineering, Coachbuilding & Related Trades Industrial Union of Workers, 18 Aug. 1944. IA, Series 1, 139/104/28, ANZ.

104 *Public Service Journal*, Feb. 1942, p.91, in Joseph William Allan Heenan Papers, Folder 283, MS-Papers-1132, ATL.

105 Letter from W. E. Parry to A. G. Osborne, MP, 20 Sept.1944. IA, Series 1, 139/104/28, ANZ.

106 Letter from Ruby Keedwell, Masterton, to W. E. Parry, Minister of Internal Affairs, 14 Jan. 1946. Family Health Camps – General file re. IA, Series 1, 139/192, ANZ. Skegness, the first of Butlin's holiday camps, opened in 1936.

107 Post War Recreation: Family Health Camps. Written by L. Anderson, Physical Welfare Officer, Wellington [undated 2 p. typescript, c. 19 July 1945]. IA, Series 1, 139/192, ANZ.

108 See, for example, the memorandum from Lance Cross (Memorandum from Lance Cross, Physical Welfare Officer (On Leave with H.M.F.) to Under-Secretary, Department of Internal Affairs, 15 Feb. 1945. IA, Series 1, 139/192, ANZ); the request from A. F. Long (A. F. Long to Mr McLagan, Minister of Labour, 15 April 1947, and W. E. Parry to A. F. Long, 30 June 1947. Sport – Industrial Recreation – General file re. IA, Series 1, 139/111/2, ANZ); and Letter from K. Baxter, Secretary, New Zealand Federation of Labour, to Minister in Charge of Tourist and Health Resorts (Hon. W. E. Parry), 17 May 1948. IA, Series 1, 139/104/28, ANZ.

109 *Daily Telegraph* [Sydney], 19 June 1948, p.9.

110 Memorandum from A. G. Harper, Assistant Under-Secretary to Physical Welfare Officer, Auckland, 21 Oct. 1947. Information re – Playgrounds. IA, W2578, 139/238/3, ANZ.

111 *AJHR*, 1950, H-22, pp.10-11.

112 On working with women's groups see, for example, Memorandum from Rona Bailey, Senior Physical Welfare Officer, to Secretary for Internal Affairs, 8 Aug. 1951. Arrangements with Various Women's Organisations – General file re. IA, Series 1, 139/65, ANZ. On radio see, for example, the file Women's Radio Session – General File re. IA, Series 1, 139/43/11, ANZ and

Memorandum from Canterbury Physical Welfare Officer to Secretary, Department of Internal Affairs, 25 June 1952. IA, Series 1, 139/43, ANZ.

113 For the 'fresh effort' reference see Recreation for Industrial Workers [c. 15 April 1946]. IA, Series 1, 139/43/1, ANZ. One of these efforts was at the Otahuhu railway workshop (Letter from R. Macdonald, Branch Secretary, Amalgamated Society of Railway Servants of New Zealand, Otahuhu Branch, to W. E. Parry, Minister of Internal Affairs, 26 June 1946. Trade Union Movement – Appointment of fulltime Physical Welfare Officer for. IA, Series 1, 139/47/9, ANZ), another was at the Dominion Manufacturing Company in Dunedin (Memorandum for Under-Secretary, 22 July 1946. IA, Series 1, 139/111/2, ANZ).

114 *Truth*, 21 Aug. 1946, p.24.

115 For the southern camps see Memorandum for Under-Secretary, 22 July 1946. IA, Series 1, 139/111/2, ANZ; *AJHR*, 1949, H-22, p.16; *AJHR*, 1950, H-22, p.13. On Gebbie's efforts see 'Industrial Recreation – Auckland', written by Gladys M. Gebbie, Physical Welfare Officer, 26 Aug. 1946. IA, Series 1, 139/111/2, ANZ.

116 *AJHR*, 1952, H-22, p.8. See also Memorandum for Under-Secretary, Internal Affairs, 17 June 1948. Sport – Physical Welfare – Assistance for Government Assisted Immigrants. IA, Series 1, 139/44/15, ANZ; Bassett, *The Mother of All Departments*, p.151.

117 R. Sheffield, Physical Welfare Officer, Gisborne, Urewera Country Survey, Feb. 15th/18th, 1949. IA, Series 1, 139/2/3, ANZ. See also R. Sheffield, Physical Welfare Officer, Gisborne, to Under-Secretary, Department of Internal Affairs, 23 Feb. 1949. IA, Series 1, 139/111/2, ANZ; *AJHR*, 1949, H-22, p.18.

118 Memorandum for W. H. Allan, Physical Welfare Officer, Palmerston North, 23 June 1949. Sport – Palmerston North Area Officer – Recreation facilities – Ratana Pa. IA, Series 1, 139/129/13, ANZ; Memorandum from K. G. Blair, District Supervisor, Physical Welfare Branch, Auckland, to Secretary for Internal Affairs, 1 Nov. 1951. IA, Series 1, 139/2/3, ANZ.

119 Letter from Physical Welfare Officer to Chief Inspector of Prisons, 8 Jan. 1951; Letter from A. G. Harper, Secretary for Internal Affairs, to Miss J. Robertson, Social Sciences Department, Victoria University College, 20 Sept.1951. Physical Recreational Training etc. – Arohata Women's Borstal – General File re. IA, Series 1, 139/274, ANZ.

120 Buchanan argues that this was a major

failing of the act and was instrumental in the
ultimate failure of the legislation. Buchanan,
'A Critical Analysis of the 1937 Physical
Welfare and Recreation Act', esp. pp.20-2.
121 Buchanan, 'A Critical Analysis of the 1937
Physical Welfare and Recreation Act', pp.117-
24; Memorandum for Minister of Internal
Affairs/Minister of Education, 23 Feb. 1950.
Sport – Physical Welfare Branch – Future
Activities of – Policy re. IA, Series 1, 139/251,
ANZ.
122 On the demise of the branch see Bassett,
The Mother of All Departments, pp.160-1;
Buchanan, 'A Critical Analysis of the 1937
Physical Welfare and Recreation Act',
pp.135-46; *Truth*, 12 Aug. 1953, p.17; the
file Sport – Physical Welfare Branch – Future
Activities of – Policy re. IA, Series 1, 139/
251, ANZ; and the annual reports of the
Department of Internal Affairs, *AJHR*, H-22.
By 1952 the report noted that vacancies had
not been filled (*AJHR*, 1952, H-22, p.6).
In 1953 it lamented that, owing to lack of
resources, it had been unable to 'provide
for the community the full service that it
anticipated' (*AJHR*, 1953, H-22, p.9). By
1955 the sub-section dealing with the branch
was moved to the end of the department's
report and became even briefer (see, for
example, *AJHR*, 1955, H-22, p.39; 1957,
p.50; 1959, p.65).
123 Roderick J. Simmons, 'Joe Walding and
Labour's Physical Welfare Ideal: The
Establishment of the Ministry of Recreation
and Sport 1972-5', MA Thesis, Massey
University, 1998; Bassett, *The Mother of All
Departments*, p.205.
124 Bob Gidlow, Grant Cushman and Harvey
Perkins, 'Whatever happened to "recreation"?
Changes in New Zealand state leisure policy',
in Grant Cushman, Clare Simpson and Linda
Trenberth (eds), *ANZALS: Leisure Research
Series*, 2, 1995, pp.76-93.

CONCLUSION

1 Frank Sargeson, *Memoirs of a Peon*, Auckland,
1994, p.161. The novel was first published in
1965. I am grateful to Kim Phillips for alerting
me to this reference.
2 Lloyd Jones, *The Book of Fame: A Novel*,
Auckland, 2000, p.153. Although the book
is a novel, Jones conducted a lot of primary
research on the 1905 tour. Sandow met
the All Blacks during their tour and 'visited
[them] at their baths' after a game. He 'really
amazed to see what magnificently developed
men they are' and took much of the credit for
their splendid physiques, claiming that they
followed his exercise programme. *Sandow's
Magazine*, 16 Nov. 1905, p.544.
3 Eugen Sandow, *Body-Building, or Man in the
Making: How to Become Healthy & Strong*,
London, 1904, p.115. Emphasis in the
original.
4 On Macfadden see Robert Ernst, *Weakness Is
a Crime: The Life of Bernarr Macfadden*, New
York, 1990. Much of the work on Desbonnet
is in French, but for a discussion of his
influence see David L. Chapman, *Sandow the
Magnificent: Eugen Sandow and the Beginnings
of Bodybuilding*, Urbana and Chicago, 1994.
5 *Lyttelton Times*, 1 July 1911, p.11.
6 In 1911 the vote for national prohibition was
55.83 per cent. Sixty per cent was required
to carry the vote, so New Zealand remained
wet. A. R. Grigg, 'Prohibition and Women:
The Preservation of an Ideal and a Myth', *New
Zealand Journal of History*, 17, 2, 1983, p.158.
7 For a copy of his letterhead see W. Norman
Kerr to The Mayor, 16 Dec. 1914. Hobson
Street Baths, Series 275, Box 8, Item 15/36,
Part 1, Auckland City Council Archives,
Auckland.
8 *Manawatu Evening Standard*, 27 Nov. 1902,
p.2.
9 *Canterbury Times*, 10 June 1908, p.54.
10 *Health and Physical Culture*, 1 April 1937, p.51.

Bibliography

PRIMARY

ALEXANDER TURNBULL LIBRARY, WELLINGTON
Fisher, F. M. B., Physical Needs of The Empire, MS 0772.
Heenan, Joseph William Allan, Papers, MS-Papers-1132.
Hornibrook, Frederick A., Scrapbook, 1907–1963, MSZ 0594.
Mount Cook School Leaving Letter, MS-Papers-5564.
Parker, Robert, Papers, MS-Papers-5303-1.
Parry, William Edward, 'The Old and New Order of Things', 17 November 1938, qMS-1629.
Sceats, Geoffrey James, Some Fundamentals In Education Through the Physical, MS-1854.
Seddon Family Papers, MS-Papers-1619-195.
Taylor, Lucy, Papers, 90-262.
Wellington Boys' and Girls' Institute Records, 90-048.
Wellington Civil Service Amateur Sports Club Papers, MS Papers 2064.
Western, Marie Jane, Human Analysis, qMS-2183.
YMCA Records, MS 95-017-02/02.

ARCHIVES NEW ZEALAND, AUCKLAND
J. Herdman, Notes of Evidence, Civil Criminal and Circuit, 1924, Volume 3, BBAE A304 412.
New Zealand Police Gazette 1924, BBAN 5803 48a.

ARCHIVES NEW ZEALAND/TE WHARE TOHU TUHITUHINGA
O AOTEAROA, WELLINGTON
CHILD WELFARE
Boys' Training Farm – Weraroa – Instruction of Inmates – Physical Instruction. CW, W1043, 40/19/5.
Caversham – Physical Training. CW, W1043, 40/19/9.
Special & Industrial Schools – Instruction of Inmates – Special School for Boys' – Otekaike – Physical Instruction. CW, W1043, 40/19/45.

EDUCATION
Forms – Physical Education, Area Organization. E, W773, 38/9/1.
Physical Education – General – Physique of School Children. E, W773, 36/1/26.
Physical Education – General – Special Classes for Physically Defective Children. E2, 1947/34a, E36/1/6.
Physical Education – General – Table of Physical Exercises For Corrective Treatment. E, W773, 36/1/18.
Physical Education Inspection of School Work. E, W773, 36/1/1.
Physical Education – Report of Advisory Committee and Cabinet Approval of New Scheme. E-W, W1012, 36/1A, Box 42.
Physical Education – Scheme & General. E, W773, 36/1/27.
Physical Instruction and Medical Inspection. E, W773, 36/1/3.
Scheme of Medical Inspection and Physical Instruction – General. E, Series 2, 1922/2b, E36/1/2.

HEALTH
Medical Inspection of Schools – Sunlight Treatment for School Children. H, Series 1, 35/86.

Sunlight Society, Christchurch 1931–36. H, Series 1, 35/95.
Sunlight Society, Christchurch 1937–44. H, Series 1, 35/27/1.

INTERNAL AFFAIRS

Arrangements with Various Women's Organisations – General file re. IA, Series 1, 139/65.
Auckland Area Instructors – Children's Playgrounds – Supervision and General File re. IA, Series 1, 139/104/6.
Auckland Area Instructors – Lunch Hour Recreation – Factory Workers etc. IA, Series 1, 139/104/7.
Auckland Area Instructors – Women Leader's Class. IA, Series 1, 139/104.
Auckland Area Instructors – Women's Activities – General File. IA, Series 1, 139/104/2.
Auckland Area Instructors – Women's Swimming Club. IA, Series 1, 139/104/5.
Auckland Area Instructors – Women's War Auxiliary. IA, Series 1, 139/104/3.
Children's Playgrounds – Layout of etc. – General File. IA, Series 1, 139/45/2.
District Committee – Auckland City. IA, Series 1, 139/21/12.
Family Health Camps – General file re. IA, Series 1, 139/192.
History of Sport in New Zealand – General File re. IA, Series 1, 139/234.
Holiday Camps for Workers – General File. IA, Series 1, 139/104/28.
Information re – Playgrounds. IA, W2578, 139/238/3.
Investigation of Boys' and Girls' Leisure Time Activities – General File. IA, Series 1, 139/30.
Physical Fitness and Recreation – Newspaper and Radio Propaganda and Publicity – General File. IA, Series 1, 139/43.
Physical Fitness Week – Auckland. IA, Series 1, 139/32/6.
Physical Fitness Week – Radio Broadcasts. IA, Series 1, 139/32/1.
Physical Recreational Training etc. – Arohata Women's Borstal – General File re. IA, Series 1, 139/274.
Playgrounds – Work and Activities etc. – General File. IA, Series 1, 139/45/3.
Propaganda and Publicity – Radio Talks – Preparation Of For Daily Newspapers. IA, Series 1, 139/43/1.
Propaganda and Publicity – Radio Talks – Preparation Of For Daily Newspapers. IA, Series 1, 139/43/2.
Propaganda and Publicity – Speeches and Addresses – Preparation of. IA, Series 1, 139/43/3.
Recreation – Arrangements for American Forces – General File. IA, Series 1, 139/164.
Recreation – Girls Employed in Refreshment Rooms – Mercer. IA, Series 1, 139/104/25.
Scheme for Maori Recreation – General File. IA, Series 1, 139/2/3.
Scheme for the Enrolment in Physical Welfare and Recreation Activities of Children Leaving School. IA, Series 1, 139/89.
Sport – Circulars Issued by Physical Welfare and Recreation Branch. IA, Series 1, 139/85.
Sport – Factory Recreation – General file re. IA, Series 1, 139/155.
Sport – Industrial Recreation – General file re. IA, Series 1, 139/111/2.
Sport – Palmerston North Area Officer – Recreation facilities – Ratana Pa. IA, Series 1, 139/129/13.
Sport – Physical Education in Australia – Visit of Miss Black – Report re. IA, Series 1, 139/107.
Sport – Physical Education – Regulations for course – Otago University. IA, Series 1, 139/9.
Sport – Physical Training scheme – Adoption by Police Department – Co-operation re – General File. IA, Series 1, 139/145.
Sport – Physical Welfare – Assistance for Government Assisted Immigrants. IA, Series 1, 139/44/15.
Sport – Physical Welfare Branch – Future Activities of – Policy re. IA, Series 1, 139/251.
Sport – Proposed Establishment of Physical Culture Classes for Public Service. IA, W2578, 139/33.
Sport – Publication –Booklet or folder of exercises – Printing of – General File. IA, Series 1, 139/59.
Sport – Visit of Mr. Noel Gibson to European Counties – Report of. IA, Series 1, 139/48.
Sport – Weekend Recreation Camps – Establishment of – Suggestion re. IA, W2578, 139/82/1.
Teachers of Physical Recreation in Girls' Clubs – Proposal to Hold Course in Wellington, 1939. IA, Series 1, 139/56.
Trade Union Movement – Appointment of fulltime Physical Welfare Officer for. IA, Series 1, 139/47/9.
Weekend Recreation Camps – Establishment of – For Assistance re – Labour Representation Committee – Christchurch. IA, Series 1, 139/82.
Women's National Organisations – War 1939 – Women's Land Army – Suggested Formation of National Service Corp. IA, Series 1, 139/95.
Women's Radio Session – General File re. IA, Series 1, 139/43/11.

JUSTICE

Nudist Literature. J, Series 1, W2304, 18/45/7.

AUCKLAND CITY COUNCIL ARCHIVES
COUNCIL MINUTES, SERIES 101
Minute Book, Item 18.
Minute Book, Item 19.

PARKS COMMITTEE MINUTES, SERIES 107
Minute Book, Item 1.
Minute Book, Item 2.

TOWN CLERK/SECRETARIAL DEPARTMENT CLASSIFIED SUBJECT FILES, SERIES 275
Baths – General, Box 165, Item 31/118, Parts 1 and 2.
Baths – General, Box 319, Item 48/118.
Children's Games in Parks, Box 50, Item 22/304.
Closing of Shelly Beach & Hobson Street Baths on Sunday, Box 48, Item 22/222.
Dismissal of M. E. Champion from Position of Bathskeeper, Box 235, Item 38/489.
Hobson Street Baths, Box 1, Item 13/23, Part 1.
Hobson Street Baths, Box 8, Item 15/36, Parts 1 and 2.
Hobson Street Baths, Box 32, Item 20/43.
Hobson Street Baths, Box 45, Item 22/43.
Lady Supervisor of Children's Games: Reports and General, Box 78, Item 32/299.
Myers Park (General), Box 15, Item 17/129.
Myers Park – General, Box 72, Item 24/325.
Myers Park, Resignation of W. Smith as Caretaker, Box 41, Item 21/654.
Parks and Reserves – General, Box 113, Item 26/334, Part 1.
Parnell Baths, Box 6, Item 14/36c.
Parnell Baths, Box 29, Item 19/53.
Parnell Baths, Box 423, Item 56/39.
Shelly Beach Baths, Box 11, Item 16/36.
The Rights of Childhood League, Box 29, Item 19/215.

WORKS DEPARTMENT CLASSIFIED FILES, SERIES 219
New Customs Street Baths, Box 5, Item 12/420.

AUCKLAND CITY LIBRARIES, SPECIAL COLLECTIONS
Sport – Athletics Folder, Ephemera Collection.
Sport – Swimming Folders, Ephemera Collection.

AUCKLAND WAR MEMORIAL MUSEUM LIBRARY
George Henry Dixon, 1905 All Black Tour, Tour Diary 1905–1906, Folder 1, MS 748 (1).

CANTERBURY MUSEUM, CHRISTCHURCH
Brundall, Monica, Diary 1926–30, Folder 1529, ARC 1998.113.
Wilding Family Papers, ARC 1989.124.

CONTEMPORARY PUBLICATIONS
Auckland City By-Laws, Nos. 1-14 1925-1934, Auckland, 1934.
Auckland City Council By Laws 1-5 Milk Regulations, Auckland, 1917.
Auckland City Council By-Laws 1-25 and Standing Orders, Auckland, 1913.
Australian Sunbather Annual 1947.
Australian Sunbather Annual 1948.
Australian Sunbather Annual 1949.
Australian Sunbather Annual 1950.
Bye-Laws of the Council of the City of Auckland, Auckland, 1890.
City of Auckland Bye-Laws, Auckland, 1882.
Cyclopedia of New Zealand, Volume 1, Wellington Provincial District, Cyclopedia Co., Ltd, Wellington, 1897.
Cyclopedia of New Zealand, Volume 3, Canterbury Provincial District, Cyclopedia Co., Ltd, Christchurch,
    1903.

Cyclopedia of New Zealand, Volume 4, Otago and Southland Provincial Districts, Cyclopedia Co., Ltd, Christchurch, 1905.

Cyclopedia of New Zealand, Volume 6, Taranaki, Hawke's Bay, and Wellington Provincial Districts, Cyclopedia Co., Ltd, Christchurch, 1908.

The Gospel of Strength According to Sandow: A Series of Talks on the Sandow System of Physical Culture, by its Founder, T. Shaw Fitchett, Melbourne, 1902.

Mixed Nudist Camps Throughout the World, Health and Physical Culture Publishing Co. Ltd, Sydney, 1939.

'Sandow: the Strongest Man on Earth', *Theatre Quarterly*, X, 39, 1981, pp.59–61 [reprint from *The Playgoer*, December 1901].

Secrets of the Toilet: How to Become & Remain Beautiful, Health Culture Association, Melbourne, 1916.

Withrow's Physical Culture Annual 1921.

Withrow's Physical Culture Annual 1926

American, Sadie, 'The Movement for Small Playgrounds', *American Journal of Sociology*, 4, 2, September 1898, pp.159–70.

Bain, Trevor G., *Nudism — Is It Desirable?* Auckland, 1937.

Barrett, Dr J. W., 'Garden Cities, Town-Planning, and Public Recreation Centres', in Australasian Medical Congress, *Transactions of the Tenth Session, Held in Auckland, New Zealand, February, 1914*, Wellington, 1916, pp.96–104.

Briton, Alfred J., *The Book of Life: A Work for Everyman, His Wife and His Family. A comprehensive work for all interested in the art of right living, including chapters on some of the more vital social problems, eugenics and health, together with information and counsel for young people, those about to marry, and the married*. Health & Physical Culture Publishing Co. Ltd, Sydney, 1933.

Briton, Alfred J., *The Book of Life: A comprehensive work for all interested in the art of right living, including chapters on some of the more vital social problems, eugenics and health, together with information and counsel for young people, those about to marry, and the married*, Health & Physical Culture Publishing Co. Ltd, Sydney, 1940.

Butler, George D.(ed.), *Playgrounds: Their Administration and Operation*, A. S. Barnes & Company Incorporated, New York, 1936.

Chapple, W. A., *The Fertility of the Unfit*, Melbourne, 1903.

Chapple, W. A., *Physical Education in our State Schools*, Wellington, 1894.

Curtis, Henry S., 'The Playground Survey', *American Journal of Sociology*, 19, 6, May 1914, pp.792–812.

du Faur, Freda, *The Conquest of Mount Cook, and Other Climbs: An Account of Four Seasons' Mountaineering on the Southern Alps of New Zealand*, Allen & Unwin, London, 1915.

Education Department, *Syllabus of Physical Training For Schools*, Wellington, 1920.

Gore, Jacqueline, *Good Looks and Long Life: A Guide to Beauty and Health in Australasia*, T. Shaw Fitchett, Melbourne, 1913.

Hornibrook, F. A., *The Culture of the Abdomen: The Cure of Obesity and Constipation*, 12th edn, William Heinemann (Medical Books) Ltd, London, 1938.

Hornibrook, F. A., *Without Reserve*, William Heinemann, London, 1935.

Kellermann, Annette, *Physical Beauty: How To Keep It*, William Heinemann, London, 1918.

Rout, Ettie A., *Sex and Exercise: A Study of the Sex Function in Women and Its Relation to Exercise*, William Heinemann (Medical Books) Ltd, London, 1925.

Sandow, Eugen, *Body-Building, or Man in the Making: How to Become Healthy & Strong*, Gale and Polden, Ltd, London, 1904.

Sandow, Eugen, 'My Reminiscences', *Strand Magazine*, March 1910, pp.144–52.

Sandow, Eugen, *Strength and How to Obtain It*, Gale and Polden, Ltd, London, 1897.

Scholefield, Guy H. and E. Schwabe (eds), *Who's Who in New Zealand and the Western Pacific, 1908*, Gordon & Gotch, Wellington, 1908.

Turano, Anthony M., 'Nudism Denuded', *American Mercury*, 38, 150, June 1936, pp.161–6.

Ward, Charles J., *The Sandow System of Physical Culture in New Zealand by Charles J. Ward*, n.p., n.d. [c.1899–1900].

Wellby, William, *Naked and Unashamed: Nudism from Six Points of View*, Thorsons, London, 1934.

White, J. Renfrew, *The Growing Body: Its Nature, Needs and Training*, Coulls Somerville Wilkie, Dunedin, 1932.

White, J. Renfrew, *Your Children's Health and Physique: A Book for Parents*, Coulls Somerville Wilkie, Dunedin, 1932.

Zueblin, Charles, 'Municipal Playgrounds in Chicago', *American Journal of Sociology*, 4, 2, September 1898, pp.145–58.

MACMILLAN BROWN LIBRARY, UNIVERSITY OF CANTERBURY
CORA WILDING PAPERS, MB183.

NEWSPAPERS AND PERIODICALS

Adelaide Advertiser
Adelaide Register
Auckland Metro
Auckland Star
Auckland Truth
Auckland Weekly News
Australasian Sunbathing Quarterly Review (Sydney)
Australian Sunbather (Sydney)
Bare In Mind: A Nudist News Service
Budget and Taranaki Weekly Herald
Canterbury Times
Daily Telegraph (Napier)
Daily Telegraph (Sydney)
Evening Post
Evening Star (Dunedin)
Exhibition Sketcher (Christchurch)
Gisborne Times
Hawke's Bay Herald
Health and Efficiency
Health and Physical Culture (Sydney)
Health and Sunshine (Auckland)
Here & Now
Human Touch (Auckland)
Journal of Physical Culture
Journal of Physical Culture & Health (Sydney)
Kennaway's Fun (Christchurch)
L'Education Physique
Lone Hand (Sydney)
Lyttelton Times
Man (Sydney)
Man Junior (Sydney)
Manawatu Daily Times
Manawatu Evening Standard
More Magazine
National Education
National Review
Naturism Illustrated (Sydney)
New Zealand Education Gazette

New Zealand Graphic
New Zealand Health First Journal
New Zealand Health News
New Zealand Herald
New Zealand Illustrated Sporting and Dramatic
    Review
New Zealand Journal of Physical Education
New Zealand Listener
New Zealand Mail
New Zealand Medical Journal
New Zealand National Review
New Zealand Naturist
New Zealand New Health Journal
New Zealand Woman's Weekly
Oamaru Mail
Otago Daily Times
Otago Witness
Physical Welfare Bulletin
Pictorial News
Press (Christchurch)
Sandow's Magazine
Smith's Weekly (Sydney)
Solaire Universelle de Nudisme Magazine
Southland Daily News
Southland Times
Star (Christchurch)
Star Weekender (Auckland)
Sun and Health (International Edition)
Timaru Herald
Truth
Wairarapa Daily Times
Wanganui Chronicle
Wanganui Herald
Weekly Press (Christchurch)
Wellington Cosmo
White Ribbon
Yeoman
Young Man's Magazine

OFFICIAL PUBLICATIONS

Appendices to the Journals of the House of Representatives
New Zealand Gazette
New Zealand Parliamentary Debates
New Zealand Statutes

SECONDARY

PUBLISHED

Ableman, Paul, The Banished Body, Sphere Books Limited, London, 1984 (first published as Anatomy of
    Nakedness, Orbis Publishing Ltd, London, 1982).
Armstrong, Tim (ed.), American Bodies: Cultural Histories of the Physique, Sheffield Academic Press,
    Sheffield, 1996.

Bailey, Peter, 'The Politics and Poetics of Modern British Leisure: A late twentieth-century review', *Rethinking History*, 3, 2, 1999, pp.131–75.

Baker, Paul, *King and Country Call: New Zealanders, Conscription and the Great War*, Auckland University Press, Auckland, 1988.

Banet-Weiser, Sarah, *The Most Beautiful Girl in the World: Beauty Pageants and National Identity*, University of California Press, Berkeley, 1999.

Banner, Lois W., *American Beauty*, Alfred A. Knopf, New York, 1983.

Barnes, Natasha B., 'Face of the Nation: Race, Nationalisms and Identities in Jamaican Beauty Pageants', *Massachusetts Review*, 35, 3–4, 1994, pp.471–92.

Barnett, Stephen and Richard Wolfe, *At The Beach: The Great New Zealand Holiday*, Hodder & Stoughton, Auckland, 1993.

Bassett, Michael, *The Mother of All Departments: The History of the Department of Internal Affairs*, Auckland University Press, Auckland, 1997.

Bedggood, L. R., *Health and Physical Education in New Zealand*, Hamilton, 1954.

Belich, James, *Paradise Reforged: A History of the New Zealanders From the 1880s to the Year 2000*, Allen Lane, Penguin Press, Auckland, 2001.

Bell, David and Ruth Holliday, 'Naked as Nature Intended', *Body & Society*, 6, 3-4, 2000, pp.127–40.

Binney, Judith, Gillian Chaplin and Craig Wallace, *Mihaia: The Prophet Rua Kenana and His Community at Maungapohatu*, Oxford University Press, Auckland, 1979.

Booth, Douglas, *Australian Beach Cultures: The History of Sun, Sand and Surf*, Frank Cass, London, 2001.

Booth, Douglas, 'Healthy, Economic, Disciplined Bodies: Surfbathing and Surf Lifesaving in Australia and New Zealand, 1890–1950', *New Zealand Journal of History*, 32, 1, 1998, pp.43–58.

Boscagli, Maurizia, *Eye On The Flesh: Fashions of Masculinity in the Early Twentieth Century*, Westview Press, Boulder CO, 1996.

Bourke, Joanna, 'The Great Male Renunciation: Men's Dress Reform in Inter-war Britain', *Journal of Design History*, 9, 1, 1996, pp.23–33.

Brookes, Barbara, 'Reproductive Rights: The Debate over Abortion and Birth Control in the 1930s', in Barbara Brookes, Charlotte Macdonald and Margaret Tennant (eds), *Women in History: Essays on European Women in New Zealand*, Allen and Unwin/Port Nicholson Press, Wellington, 1986, pp.119–36.

Brown, Bruce, *The Rise of New Zealand Labour: A history of the New Zealand Labour Party from 1916 to 1940*, Price Milburn, Wellington, 1962.

Budd, Michael Anton, *The Sculpture Machine: Physical Culture and Body Politics in the Age of Empire*, New York University Press, New York, 1997.

Cavallo, Dominick, *Muscles and Morals: Organized Playgrounds and Urban Reform, 1880–1920*, University of Pennsylvania Press, Philadelphia, 1981.

Chapman, David L., *Sandow the Magnificent: Eugen Sandow and the Beginnings of Bodybuilding*, University of Illinois Press, Urbana and Chicago, 1994.

Chesterman, Sandra, *FigureWork: The Nude and Life Modelling in New Zealand Art*, University of Otago Press, Dunedin, 2002.

Churman, Geoffrey B. (ed.), *Celluloid Dreams: A Century of Film in New Zealand*, IPL Books, Wellington, 1997.

Cinder, Cec, *The Nudist Idea*, Ultraviolet Press, Riverside CA, 1998.

Clapham, Adam and Robin Constable, *As Nature Intended: A Pictorial History of The Nudists*, Heinemann/Quixote Press, London, 1982.

Clarke, Magnus, *Nudism in Australia: A First Study*, Deakin University Press, Warun Ponds VIC, 1982.

Cohen, Colleen Ballerino, Richard Wilk and Beverly Stoeltje (eds), *Beauty Queens on the Global Stage: Gender, Contests, and Power*, Routledge, New York, 1996.

Coney, Sandra, *Every Girl: A Social History of Women and the YWCA in Auckland, 1885–1985*, Auckland YWCA, Auckland, 1986.

Coney, Sandra, *Standing in the Sunshine: A History of New Zealand Women Since They Won the Vote*, Viking, Auckland, 1993.

Daley, Caroline, 'The Body Builder and Beauty Contests', *Journal of Australian Studies*, 71, 2001, pp.55–66, 158–60.

Daley, Caroline, 'A Gendered Domain: Leisure in Auckland, 1890-1940', in Caroline Daley and Deborah Montgomerie (eds), *The Gendered Kiwi*, Auckland University Press, Auckland, 1999, pp.87–111.

Daley, Caroline, *Girls & Women, Men & Boys: Gender in Taradale 1886-1930*, Auckland University Press, Auckland, 1999.

Daley, Caroline, 'Selling Sandow: Modernity and Leisure in Early Twentieth-Century New Zealand', *New*

Zealand Journal of History, 34, 2, 2000, pp.241–61.

Daley, Caroline, 'The Strongman of Eugenics, Eugen Sandow', *Australian Historical Studies*, 33, 120, 2002, pp.233–48.

Daley, Caroline, 'Taradale Meets The Ideal Society and its Enemies', *New Zealand Journal of History*, 25, 2, 1991, pp.129–46.

Dalley, Bronwyn, *Family Matters: Child Welfare in Twentieth-Century New Zealand*, Auckland University Press, Auckland, 1998.

Dalley, Bronwyn, *Living in the 20th Century: New Zealand History in Photographs 1900-1980*, Bridget Williams Books, Craig Potton Publishing, in association with the Ministry for Culture and Heritage, Wellington, 2000.

Dalley, Bronwyn, 'Lolly Shops "of the red-light kind" and "soldiers of the King": Suppressing One-Woman Brothels in New Zealand, 1908–1916', *New Zealand Journal of History*, 30, 1, 1996, pp.3–23.

Day, Patrick, *The Radio Years: A History of Broadcasting in New Zealand*, Volume One, Auckland University Press in association with the Broadcasting History Trust, Auckland, 1994.

Dutton, Kenneth R., *The Perfectible Body: The Western Ideal of Physical Development*, Cassell, London, 1995.

Dutton, Kenneth R. and Ronald S. Laura, 'Towards a History of Bodybuilding', *Sporting Traditions*, 6, 1, 1989, pp.25–41.

Eldred-Grigg, Stevan, *Pleasures of the Flesh: Sex and Drugs in Colonial New Zealand 1840–1915*, Reed, Wellington, 1984.

Ernst, Robert, *Weakness Is a Crime: The Life of Bernarr Macfadden*, Syracuse University Press, New York, 1990.

Fairburn, Miles, *The Ideal Society and its Enemies: The Foundation of Modern New Zealand Society, 1850-1900*, Auckland University Press, Auckland, 1989.

Fleming, P., 'Fighting the "Red Plague": Observations on the Response to Venereal Disease in New Zealand 1910–45', *New Zealand Journal of History*, 22, 1, 1988, pp.56–64.

Foucault, Michel, *Discipline and Punish: The Birth of the Prison*, translated from the French by Alan Sheridan, Pantheon Books, New York, 1977.

Fougere, Geoff, 'Sport, Culture and Identity: The Case of Rugby Football', in David Novitz and Bill Willmott (eds), *Culture and Identity in New Zealand*, GP Books, Wellington, 1989, pp.110–22.

Foulkes, Julia L., *Modern Bodies: Dance and American Modernism from Martha Graham to Alvin Ailey*, University of North Carolina Press, Chapel Hill and London, 2002.

Fry, Ruth, '"Don't let down the side": Physical Education for New Zealand Schoolgirls, 1900-1945', in Barbara Brookes, Charlotte Macdonald and Margaret Tennant (eds), *Women in History: Essays on European Women in New Zealand*, Allen and Unwin/Port Nicholson Press, Wellington, 1986, pp.101–17.

Garb, Tamar, *Bodies of Modernity: Figure and Flesh in Fin-de-Siecle France*, Thames and Hudson Ltd, London, 1998.

Gidlow, Bob, Grant Cushman and Harvey Perkins, 'Whatever happened to "recreation"? Changes in New Zealand state leisure policy', in Grant Cushman, Clare Simpson and Linda Trenberth (eds), *ANZALS: Leisure Research Series*, 2, 1995, pp.76–93.

Gibbons, Peter, 'The Far Side of the Search for Identity: Reconsidering New Zealand History', *New Zealand Journal of History*, 37, 1, 2003, pp.38–49.

Grant, Mariel, 'The National Health Campaigns of 1937–1938', in Derek Fraser (ed.), *Cities, Class and Communication: Essays in Honour of Asa Briggs*, Harvester Wheatsheaf, London, 1990, pp.216–33.

Grigg, A. R., 'Prohibition, the Church and Labour: a Programme for Social Reform, 1890–1914', *New Zealand Journal of History*, 15, 2, 1981, pp.135–56.

Grigg, A. R., 'Prohibition and Women: The Preservation of an Ideal and a Myth', *New Zealand Journal of History*, 17, 2, 1983, pp.144–65.

Gustafson, Barry, *From The Cradle To The Grave: A biography of Michael Joseph Savage*, Penguin, Auckland, 1988.

Haworth, Dianne and Diane Miller, *Freda Stark: Her Extraordinary Life*, HarperCollins, Auckland, 2000.

Hill, Jeffrey, *Sport, Leisure and Culture In Twentieth-Century Britain*, Palgrave, Basingstoke, 2002.

Horwood, Catherine, '"Girls Who Arouse Dangerous Passions": women and bathing, 1900–39', *Women's History Review*, 9, 4, 2000, pp.653–73.

Huggins, Mike J., 'More Sinful Pleasures? Leisure, Respectability and the Male Middle Classes in Victorian England', *Journal of Social History*, 33, 3, 2000, pp.585–600.

Huntsman, Leone, *Sand in Our Souls: The Beach in Australian History*, Melbourne University Press, Carlton South, 2001.

Irwin, Sally, *Between Heaven and Earth: the life of a mountaineer, Freda Du Faur 1882-1935*, White Crane

Press, Melbourne, 2000.

Johns, Maxine James and Jane Farrell-Beck, '"Cut Out the Sleeves": Nineteenth-Century U.S. Women Swimmers and Their Attire', *Dress*, 28, 2001, pp.53–63.

Jones, Lloyd, *The Book of Fame: A Novel*, Penguin Books, Auckland, 2000.

Kasson, John F., *Houdini, Tarzan and The Perfect Man: The White Male Body and The Challenge of Modernity in America*, Hill & Wang, New York, 2001.

Kenway, Christopher, 'Nudism, Health, and Modernity: The Natural Cure as Proposed by the German Physical Culture Movement 1900–1914', *Nineteenth-Century Prose*, 25, 1, 1998, pp.102–15.

Kirk, David, 'Gender Associations: Sport, State Schools and Australian Culture', *International Journal of the History of Sport*, 17, 2–3, 2000, pp.49–64.

Kirk, David, *Schooling Bodies: School Practice and Public Discourse 1880–1950*, Leicester University Press, London, 1998.

Kirk, David and Karen Twigg, 'Regulating Australian Bodies: Eugenics, Anthropometrics and School Medical Inspections in Victoria, 1900–1940', *History of Education Review*, 23, 1, 1994, pp.19–37.

Krüger, Arnd, 'There Goes This Art of Manliness: Naturism and Racial Hygiene in Germany', *Journal of Sport History*, 18, 1, 1991, pp.135–58.

Latham, Angela J., *Posing a Threat: Flappers, Chorus Girls, and Other Brazen Performers of the American 1920s*, Wesleyan University Press/University Press of New England, Hanover, 2000.

Lencek, Lena and Gideon Bosker, *The Beach: The History of Paradise on Earth*, Secker & Warburg, London, 1998.

Lencek, Lena and Gideon Bosker, *Making Waves: Swimsuits and the Undressing of America*, Chronicle Books, San Francisco, 1989.

McCarthy, David, 'Social Nudism, Masculinity and the Male Nude in the Work of William Theo Brown and Wynn Chamberlain in the 1960s', *Archives of American Art Journal*, 38, 1–2, 1998, pp.28–38.

Macdonald, Charlotte, 'The "Social Evil": Prostitution and the Passage of the Contagious Diseases Act', in Barbara Brookes, Charlotte Macdonald and Margaret Tennant (eds), *Women in History: Essays on European Women in New Zealand*, Allen and Unwin/Port Nicholson Press, Wellington, 1986, pp.13–34.

Macdonald Charlotte, 'The Unbalanced Parallel', in Anne Else (ed.), *Women Together: A History of Women's Organisations in New Zealand/Nga Ropu Wahine o te Motu*, Daphne Brasell Associates Press and Historical Branch, Department of Internal Affairs, Wellington, 1993, pp.403–44.

McKergow, Fiona, 'Bodies At The Beach: A History of Swimwear', *Bearings*, 3, 4, 1991, pp.16–22.

McLaren, John, 'The Despicable Crime of Nudity: Law, the State, and Civil Protest Among the Sons of Freedom Sect of Doukhobors, 1899–1935', *Journal of the West*, 38, 3, 1999, pp.27–33.

Maclean, Chris, *Tararua: the story of a mountain range*, Whitcombe Press, Wellington, 1994.

Maier, Charles S., *In Search of Stability: Explorations in Historical Political Economy*, Cambridge University Press, Cambridge MA., 1987.

Mangan, J. A. and Colm Hickey, 'A Pioneer of the Proletariat: Herbert Milnes and the Games Cult in New Zealand', *International Journal of the History of Sport*, 17, 2–3, 2000, pp.31–48.

Mein Smith, Philippa, 'Truby King in Australia: A Revisionist View of Reduced Infant Mortality', *New Zealand Journal of History*, 22, 1, 1988, pp.23–43.

Molloy, Maureen, 'Science, Myth and the Adolescent Female: The Mazengarb Report, the Parker-Hulme Trial, and the Adoption Act of 1955', *Women's Studies Journal*, 9, 1, 1993, pp.1–25.

Monteath, Peter, 'Swastikas By The Seaside', *History Today*, 50, 5, 2000, pp.31–5.

Mouratidis, John, 'The Origin of Nudity in Greek Athletics', *Journal of Sport History*, 12, 3, 1985, pp.213–32.

Mulvey, Laura, 'Visual Pleasure and Narrative Cinema', *Screen*, 16, 3, 1975, pp.6–18.

Nicholson, Heather, *The Loving Stitch: A history of knitting and spinning in New Zealand*, Auckland University Press, Auckland, 1998.

Olssen, Erik, *John A. Lee*, University of Otago Press, Dunedin, 1977.

Olssen, Erik 'Towards a New Society', in Geoffrey W. Rice (ed.), *The Oxford History of New Zealand*, 2nd edn, Oxford University Press, Auckland, 1992, pp.254–84.

Olssen, Erik, 'Truby King and the Plunket Society: An Analysis of a Prescriptive Ideology', *New Zealand Journal of History*, 15, 1, 1981, pp.3–23.

Phillips, Jock, *A Man's Country? The Image of the Pakeha Male – A History*, revised edn, Penguin, Auckland, 1996.

Power, Richenda, 'Healthy Motion: Images of "Natural" and "Cultured" Movement in Early Twentieth-Century Britain', *Women's Studies International Forum*, 19, 5, 1996, pp.551–65.

Rabinbach, Anson, *The Human Motor: Energy, Fatigue, and the Origins of Modernity*, BasicBooks, New York,

1990.

Rainis, Michel, 'French Beach Sports Culture in the Twentieth Century', *International Journal of the History of Sport*, 17, 1, 2000, pp.144–58.

Rice, Geoffrey W. (ed.), *The Oxford History of New Zealand*, 2nd edn, Oxford University Press, Auckland, 1992.

Richardson, Len, '"Billy Banjo": Coalminer, Socialist, Poet and Novelist', in Pat Moloney and Kerry Taylor (eds), *On the Left: Essays on Socialism in New Zealand*, Dunedin, 2002, pp.73–86.

Rodwell, Grant, '"The Sense of Victorious Struggle": The Eugenic Dynamic in Australian Popular Surf-Culture, 1900–50', *Journal of Australian Studies*, 62, 1999, pp.56–63.

Rose, Marla Matzer, *Muscle Beach*, LA Weekly Book for St Martin's Griffin, New York, 2001.

Ross, Kirstie, '"Schooled by Nature": Pakeha Tramping Between the Wars', *New Zealand Journal of History*, 36, 1, 2002, pp.51–65.

Rutt, Richard, 'The Englishman's Swimwear', *Costume*, 24, 1990, pp.69–84.

Ryan, Greg, 'Rural Myth and Urban Actuality: The Anatomy of All Black and New Zealand Rugby 1884–1938', *New Zealand Journal of History*, 35, 1, 2001, pp.45–69.

Saphira, Miriam, *A Man's Man: A Daughter's Story*, Papers Inc., Auckland, 1997.

Sargeson, Frank, *Memoirs of a Peon*, Godwit, Auckland, 1994.

Savage, Candace, *Beauty Queens: A Playful History*, Abbeville Press, New York, London, Paris, 1998.

Scott, James C., *Seeing Like a State: How Certain Schemes to Improve the Human Condition Have Failed*, Yale University Press, New Haven and London, 1998.

Segel, Harold B., *Body Ascendant: Modernism and the Physical Imperative*, Johns Hopkins University Press, Baltimore and London, 1998.

Shields, Rob, *Places on the Margin: Alternative geographies of modernity*, Routledge, London and New York, 1991.

Shuker, Roy, Roger Openshaw and Janet Soler, *Youth, Media and Moral Panic in New Zealand*, Department of Education, Massey University, Palmerston North, 1990.

Sigel, Lisa Z., 'Filth in the Wrong People's Hands: Postcards and the Expansion of Pornography in Britain and the Atlantic World, 1880–1914', *Journal of Social History*, 33, 4, 2000, pp.859–85.

Simon, Judith (ed.), *Nga Kura Maori: the Native Schools System 1867–1969*, Auckland University Press, Auckland, 1998.

Simon, Judith and Linda Tuhiwai Smith (eds), *A Civilising Mission? Perceptions and Representations of the New Zealand Native Schools System*, Auckland University Press, Auckland, 2001.

Sinclair, Keith, *A Destiny Apart: New Zealand's Search for National Identity*, Allen and Unwin/Port Nicholson Press, Wellington, 1986.

Sinclair, Keith (ed.), *The Oxford Illustrated History of New Zealand*, Oxford University Press, Auckland, 1990.

Smart, Judith, 'Feminists, Flappers and Miss Australia', *Journal of Australian Studies*, 71, 2001, pp.1–15, 149–51.

Smithells, P. A., 'James Renfrew White: A Tribute', *New Zealand Journal of Physical Education*, 26, April 1962, pp.48–51.

Stearns, Peter N., *Fat History: Bodies and Beauty in the Modern West*, New York University Press, New York and London, 1997.

Stewart, Mary Lynn, *For Health and Beauty: Physical Culture for Frenchwomen, 1880s–1930s*, Johns Hopkins University Press, Baltimore and London, 2001.

Stothart, Robert A., *The Development of Physical Education in New Zealand*, Heinemann Educational Books, Auckland, 1974.

Stothart, R. A., *A Chronology of New Zealand Physical Education 1850–1990*, Physical Education New Zealand Inc., Wellington, 1991.

Stothart, R. A., *A "Who's Who" of New Zealand Physical Education and Recreation*, New Zealand Association of Health, Physical Education & Recreation, Wellington, c.1973.

Tennant, Margaret, *Children's Health, The Nation's Wealth: A History of Children's Health Camps*, Bridget Williams Books and Historical Branch, Department of Internal Affairs, Wellington, 1994.

Tennant, Margaret, *Paupers and Providers: Charitable Aid in New Zealand*, Allen and Unwin/Historical Branch, Wellington, 1989.

Thomson, John Mansfield (ed.), *Farewell Colonialism: The New Zealand International Exhibition, Christchurch, 1906-07*, Dunmore Press, Palmerston North, 1998.

Todd, Jan, 'Bernarr Macfadden: Reformer of Feminine Form', *Journal of Sport History*, 14, 1, 1987, pp.61–75.

Toepfer, Karl, *Empire of Ecstasy: Nudity and Movement in German Body Culture, 1910–1935*, University of

California Press, Berkeley and London, 1997.

Tolerton, Jane, *Ettie: A Life of Ettie Rout*, Penguin Books, Auckland, 1992.

Toon, Elizabeth and Janet Golden, 'Rethinking Charles Atlas', *Rethinking History*, 4, 1, 2000, pp.80–4.

Walvin, James, *Beside the Seaside: A Social History of the Popular Seaside Holiday*, Allen Lane, London, 1978.

Welshman, John, 'Physical Culture and Sport in Schools in England and Wales, 1900–40', *International Journal of the History of Sport*, 15, 1, 1998, pp.54–75.

Wilson, Ormond, *An Outsider Looks Back: Reflections on Experience*, Port Nicholson Press, Wellington, 1982.

Wood, Margaret, 'A Daughter of John Court Remembers', *Auckland-Waikato Historical Journal*, 41, September 1982, pp.14–16.

Yska, Redmer, *All Shook Up: The Flash Bodgie and the Rise of the New Zealand Teenager in the Fifties*, Auckland, 1993.

UNPUBLISHED

Alexander, Janet, 'Recreation: An Inappropriate Concept for Legislation? An examination of two attempts at legislating for recreation in New Zealand: The Physical Welfare and Recreation Act 1937; and The Recreation and Sports Act 1973', Research Essay, Victoria University of Wellington, 1981.

Buchanan, Hugh D., 'A Critical Analysis of the 1937 Physical Welfare and Recreation Act and of Government Involvement in Recreation and Sport, 1937–1957', MA (Applied) Thesis, Victoria University of Wellington, 1978.

Elliott, Nerida, 'Anzac, Hollywood and Home: Cinemas and Filmgoing in Auckland, 1909–1939', MA Thesis, University of Auckland, 1989.

Fleming, Philip J., 'Eugenics in New Zealand 1900–1940', MA Thesis, Massey University, 1981.

Glazebrook, Susan, 'The Mazengarb Report: 1954 Impotent Victorianism', Research Essay, University of Auckland, 1978.

Gregory, Penelope Ann, 'Saving the Children in New Zealand: A Study of Social Attitudes Towards Larrikinism in the Later Nineteenth Century', BA (Hons) Thesis, Massey University, 1975.

Hammer, Margaret A. E., '"Something Else in the World to Live For": Sport and the Physical Emancipation of Women and Girls in Auckland 1880–1920', MA Thesis, University of Auckland, 1990.

Hart, Edith M., 'The Organised Activities of Christchurch Children Outside the School', MA Thesis, Canterbury University College, 1934.

Langton, Graham, 'A History of Mountain Climbing in New Zealand to 1953', PhD Thesis, University of Canterbury, 1996.

McCurdy, Diana, 'Feminine Identity in New Zealand: The Girl Peace Scout Movement 1908–1925', MA Thesis, University of Canterbury, 2000.

McKimmey, Paul, 'The Temperance Movement in New Zealand, 1853–1894', MA Thesis, University of Auckland, 1968.

McMorran, Lynne, 'A Body of Perfection: The Increasing Standardisation of the Female Body in Televised Miss New Zealand Beauty Pageants 1964–1992', MA Thesis, Massey University, 1996.

Morris, Stephen, '"I Want to be a Model": Changing Attitudes of New Zealand Women to the Miss New Zealand Pageant 1960–1999', MA Thesis, University of Auckland, 2002.

Parcell, K. V., 'The 1922 Committee of Inquiry into Venereal Disease in New Zealand', Research Essay, University of Auckland, 1970.

Paxton, C. T., 'Childhood in New Zealand, 1862–1921: Child Labour and the Gradual Popular Acceptance of Primary School Attendance', MA Thesis, University of Auckland, 1987.

Roberts, Evan, 'From Mail Order to Female Order? The Work Culture of Department Store Employees in New Zealand, 1890–1960', Research Essay, Victoria University of Wellington, 1999.

Ross, Kirstie, 'Signs of Landing: Pakeha Outdoor Recreation and the Cultural Colonisation of New Zealand', MA Thesis, University of Auckland, 1999.

Simmons, Roderick J., 'Joe Walding and Labour's Physical Welfare Ideal: The Establishment of the Ministry of Recreation and Sport 1972–5', MA Thesis, Massey University, 1998.

Soler, Janet, 'Drifting Towards Moral Chaos: the 1954 Mazengarb Report', MPhil Thesis, Massey University, 1988.

Turney, Craig, 'The New Zealand Alliance and Auckland, 1905–1920', MA Thesis, University of Auckland, 1996.

Index